US Presidential Elections
and Foreign Policy

US PRESIDENTIAL ELECTIONS AND FOREIGN POLICY

CANDIDATES, CAMPAIGNS, AND GLOBAL POLITICS FROM FDR TO BILL CLINTON

Edited by
ANDREW JOHNSTONE
and
ANDREW PRIEST

UNIVERSITY PRESS OF KENTUCKY

Copyright © 2017 by The University Press of Kentucky

Scholarly publisher for the Commonwealth,
serving Bellarmine University, Berea College, Centre College of Kentucky, Eastern
Kentucky University, The Filson Historical Society, Georgetown College,
Kentucky Historical Society, Kentucky State University, Morehead State
University, Murray State University, Northern Kentucky University, Transylvania
University, University of Kentucky, University of Louisville, and Western
Kentucky University.

Editorial and Sales Offices: The University Press of Kentucky
663 South Limestone Street, Lexington, Kentucky 40508-4008
www.kentuckypress.com

Cataloging-in-Publication data available from the Library of Congress

978-0-8131-6905-7 (hardcover : alk. paper)
978-0-8131-6906-4 (epub)
978-0-8131-6907-1 (pdf)

This book is printed on acid-free paper meeting the requirements of the American
National Standard for Permanence in Paper for Printed Library Materials.

Manufactured in the United States of America.

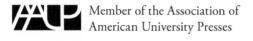 Member of the Association of
American University Presses

Contents

Introduction

Andrew Johnstone and Andrew Priest

During the 1992 presidential election, the Democratic strategist James Carville famously coined the campaign slogan "The economy, stupid."[1] More than just a politically savvy catchphrase, Carville's words echoed the conventional wisdom that domestic issues rule when it comes to Americans choosing their presidents. Yet, while matters domestic certainly loom large for voters, they are far from the whole story. For example, an analysis of historic polling data released by the Pew Research Center in 2004 suggested that, from 1948 through 1972, voters saw foreign and security issues to be more significant national problems than the economy.[2]

Claims that foreign policy is important in elections may appear to be self-evident. In recent years, televised presidential debates have included entire sessions dedicated to foreign policy, providing moments of opportunity as well as potential pitfalls for candidates in the public eye. American media increasingly portray a lack of experience in foreign affairs as a handicap for presidential candidates. The events of September 11, 2001, George W. Bush's declaration of a "war on terror," and the subsequent invasions of Afghanistan and Iraq have all demonstrated the intimate links between American policies at home and abroad. The apparent need for would-be presidents to appear statesmanlike has even seen overseas campaign stops in recent elections, most notably Barack Obama's trip to Europe in 2008 and Mitt Romney's 2012 visit to the United Kingdom, Poland, and Israel. This phenomenon is not new; rather, it has a long list of antecedents, and the connections between the foreign, the domestic, and the democratic process have always been present in American politics.

Nonetheless, the persistent lack of attention to the relationship between foreign policy and American presidential elections is striking in both popular attitudes and scholarly studies. In the academic literature, and among historians in particular, this relationship is underdeveloped as part of a broader neglect of the influence of domestic politics and public opinion on foreign policy. Therefore, this collection examines this often-neglected relationship. Moving through each consecutive presidential election from 1940 to 1992, it seeks to understand the relative importance of US foreign policy to domestic elections, campaign strategies, electoral positions and election outcomes—and, conversely, the impact of electoral issues on the formation of foreign policy. These questions hold special significance during an era of heightened international tension for the United States, when, as John F. Kennedy noted, "domestic policy can only defeat us; foreign policy can kill us."[3]

Curiously, scholars of American foreign relations have paid little attention to the influence of foreign policy on elections, and there are almost no books on the topic. The notable exception to this is Robert Divine's two-volume *Foreign Policy and US Presidential Elections*, published in 1974. Yet this work covers the years 1940–1960 only and so is obviously limited in its scope. In addition, Divine (deliberately) makes no significant attempt to draw broader conclusions from the separate elections he studies, except to say he believes "that American presidential candidates have often behaved irresponsibly in dealing with diplomatic issues." He suggests that, because these candidates feared the public would not understand what he calls "the subtle intricacies of international affairs," they "often reduced complex issues to banal slogans, thereby preventing a rational debate over American foreign policy."[4]

Two recent additions to the literature suggest an acknowledgment that the relationship between foreign policy and elections has been ignored for far too long. Michael Armacost's *Ballots, Bullets, and Bargains* adopts a thematic structure to examine different parts of the election campaign, from the nomination through the campaign and the transition era to the start of a new term, illustrated by examples since 1948. A similar approach, backed by an even broader range of examples going back to 1900 and including congressional midterm elections, is used in Andrew Preston's essay "Beyond the Water's Edge." Like Armacost, Preston argues that the long and complicated relationship between foreign policy and elections is both important and underexamined.[5]

This lack of academic attention in part derives from the president's dominance of the foreign-policy-making process, which, if anything, expanded over the course of the twentieth century despite some attempts to curtail it. As a result, scholars have largely regarded presidents as essentially having a free hand when it comes to foreign affairs. This tendency may also have been exacerbated by the strength of realism as a school of thought in scholarship on American international relations and diplomatic history. Both classical and neorealists have traditionally seen the making of foreign policy as an elite activity in which public opinion does not, and usually should not, have a great deal of influence.[6]

Some recent scholarship on the history of American foreign relations has, however, begun to reexamine the vital nexus between foreign policy and domestic policy to show the domestic sources of foreign relations and the impact of international affairs on politics at home.[7] A 2005 article by Robert McMahon noted the lack of interaction between scholars of domestic policy and scholars of diplomatic history, who, he suggested, "have far more in common than most of them recognize." In his 2008 presidential address to the Society for Historians of American Foreign Relations, Thomas Alan Schwartz argued: "Explaining the history of American foreign relations without carefully examining public opinion and domestic politics was a bit like explaining the functioning of a car without discussing the internal combustion engine." Similarly, in a 2009 roundtable in the *Journal of American History,* Fredrik Logevall noted "how often studies altogether omit domestic politics, treating professional politicians involved in foreign relations as though they were not politicians at all." And, in his 2010 *Vietnam's Second Front,* the historian Andrew Johns argued: "The role of domestic political considerations remains conspicuously absent in the history of US foreign relations, limiting our understanding of how and why the United States acts internationally."[8] Yet, although there are a few books that deal directly with the historical relationship between the US public and foreign policy, connections between foreign policy and elections have been largely overlooked.[9] This collection aims to address this neglect to situate elections and domestic politics in a more central position in the study of US foreign relations.

All the authors included in this collection agree that foreign policy concerns have been central to American national life since 1940 and have affected electoral politics in various and complex ways. The rise of the United States to superpower status, the impact of World War II, and the onset of the Cold War raised questions about national security, defense, and America's overseas role, forcing politicians and the public to consider foreign affairs alongside traditional domestic concerns as they made decisions about the future of the nation. After 1945, the development of nuclear weapons further increased Americans' concerns that politicians—and particularly presidential candidates—had to be responsible and sensible enough to avoid confrontation with the Soviet Union. These factors inevitably affected electoral campaigns because, while voters were not necessarily concerned with the intricate details of foreign affairs, they were aware that such issues could have a major—and potentially devastating—impact on their lives.[10] These issues were often important in presidential campaigns and elections even when major events such as wars were not imminent or ongoing. Despite the Cold War consensus that apparently existed for more than two decades after 1945, and despite the popular aphorism, politics rarely stopped at the water's edge.

Candidates' positions on foreign policy and national defense could serve different ends. They could help establish (or undermine) their credentials and ultimately their potential or actual presidential authority. They could also help draw distinctions between their abilities and those of other candidates. This was often more important for the perceptions those positions fostered about the candidates than what they said about their attitudes on a particular issue. This may be one of the reasons why researchers have found so little evidence of the direct impact of a candidate's views of foreign affairs on voter choices, with voters tending to derive general ideas about a candidate's competence for office from those specific views.[11] This might also explain why, during the Cold War especially, presidential candidates spent so much time discussing foreign issues when there appeared to be so few demonstrable electoral benefits to doing so. Presidents and presidential candidates may have been wary of the damage that foreign policy could do to their political standing because poor performance could undermine public perceptions of their strength and authority even while intelligent use of foreign policy issues could bolster them.[12]

Of course, as Douglas Foyle has suggested in his study of the role of public opinion in foreign policy making, the extent to which presidents (or presidential candidates) considered the populace in the formation of their foreign affairs agenda was conditioned by their preexisting ideas about the role of public opinion in such matters as well as by the context in which the agenda was formed.[13] Yet, in a democracy like the United States, no one who aspired to gain, or retain, the office of the presidency could ignore the electorate when making foreign policy decisions. To a greater or lesser extent, high office seekers have tailored their foreign policy positions according to perceived impacts on electoral politics. Even if a sitting president was unconcerned with reelection himself, his decisions might rebound on his party and other domestic allies.[14] Taking the nation to war in particular involved potentially wide-ranging and damaging costs that could then affect the president as office holder or candidate and his party's electoral chances in any upcoming race.[15]

Contingency also plays its part in determining the role of foreign policy in election campaigns, particularly in considering who gains the nomination in the first instance. While parties pick their candidates based on any number of factors, the need for presidents to have authority is especially important, and foreign policy experience can provide this. As the chapters in this volume reveal, some candidates play to their foreign policy strengths. Wendell Willkie secured the 1940 Republican nomination in large part owing to his internationalist stance on aiding Britain. In 1952, Dwight D. Eisenhower's credentials made him a more viable candidate for the nomination of the Republican Party than the early frontrunner, Robert Taft, whom many leading Republicans saw as parochial and out of touch, while Eisenhower's decision to run was based on Taft's refusal to endorse American involvement in the defense of Europe. In 1976, Ronald Reagan came close to toppling President Ford's quest for nomination as the Republican Party candidate in his own right by conducting a right-wing attack on Ford and foreign affairs. In 1988, had the Democratic contender Gary Hart not been undone by a sex scandal, he might have achieved the nomination and made defense and foreign policy—areas in which he had considerable experience—important features of the campaign in the subsequent election.

Foreign policy issues clearly defined some presidential election campaigns. Among those examined here, the elections of 1940, 1944, 1952, and 1968 are perhaps the most obvious cases because they all took place when the United States either faced the prospect of war or was already mired in conflict. The 1940 election was dominated by a war in Europe that threatened to drag in the United States. In chapter 1, Andrew Johnstone examines the debate between President Franklin D. Roosevelt and his Republican rival, Wendell Willkie, in 1940 to suggest that foreign affairs was a more important dividing issue between the two candidates than has generally been understood, one made all the more significant because Willkie was not a self-declared isolationist. Willkie therefore had to tread a fine line between support for national preparedness and criticism of FDR's policies toward Britain because he needed to appeal to the right wing of the Republican Party to gain the nomination and pick up votes. Roosevelt also had to strike a balance between preparedness and aiding Britain while avoiding charges of warmongering. Four years later, the election of November 1944 occurred when the United States was fully involved in a global war, although one that was by then already manifestly nearing its end. As J. Simon Rofe argues in chapter 2, foreign policy was important not just because the United States was engaged in a struggle for national survival but also because of the blurring of the lines between domestic and foreign concerns that would come to define the postwar national security agenda and be a central theme of elections in the decades that followed.

When voters felt the effects of foreign policy issues at home, they could respond strongly. Post–World War II conflicts—especially Korea and Vietnam, which were long, domestically controversial, and militarily indecisive—had important effects on voters. Opinion polls demonstrated that the public was disillusioned with these wars as polling day approached, and it is significant that both the 1952 and the 1968 elections led to changes in the party in power; although no candidate in either election was an incumbent, both wars had a direct impact on the respective presidents, Harry Truman and Lyndon Johnson, choosing not to run. In 1952, Chinese intervention in Korea showed Americans that the Cold War had entered a dangerous new phase, and the candidates had to respond. In chapter 4, Steven Casey shows that the Republican nominee Dwight D. Eisenhower, desperate to win the White House for his party for the first time since 1928, left it until late in the campaign to attack the Democrats about their policies in Korea and never questioned the need to be involved in the first place. The deteriorating military and diplomatic situation in East Asia played into Eisenhower's hands, as Casey puts it, and allowed Ike to make his famous proclamation that he would "go to Korea." This brought the Korean issue center stage and thus changed the nature of the campaign.[16]

Yet, in foreign policy terms, the election of 1968 perhaps trumps them all because of the tumultuous and divisive nature of the Vietnam War and, crucially, its impact on American domestic politics. Scholars usually see 1968 as marking the end of the Cold War consensus, and it certainly seems that voters became much more engaged in foreign policy matters because of the ongoing war. Yet the impact on domestic politics also meant that the specifics of foreign policy and what the newly elected president would actually do about the situation in Vietnam were often less important than people's concerns about the apparent consequences of the war at home; including racial tensions, urban unrest, and antiwar activism. During the campaign, the Republican candidate, Richard Nixon, was successful in drawing on the foreign policy credentials he had established as vice president in the 1950s. As Sandra Scanlon shows in chapter 8, Nixon also subtly drew a connection between the incumbent administration's failures to achieve peace or victory in Vietnam and the correlated upsurge in domestic discontent in the United States to tarnish Vice President Hubert Humphrey's bid. She then demonstrates how the successes of Nixon's first term—and especially his development of a rhetorical strategy that culminated in his famous "silent majority" speech of November 1969—were laid during the 1968 campaign.[17]

These four elections were unusual in that foreign affairs dominated the agenda. More often, candidates had some latitude in emphasizing or playing down foreign policy concerns according to their own strengths and interests as well as the importance they believed particular issues might have among the electorate. Perhaps understandably, most presidential candidates tended to refrain from engaging in risky discussions or behaviors about global affairs during campaigns. Whether they were aspirants or office holders, they usually said that they wanted peace and would resist pressures to send American troops overseas, even if they broke this promise after they were elected. This can be seen in this collection in the struggles between Franklin Roosevelt and Wendell Willkie in 1940 and Lyndon Johnson and Barry Goldwater in 1964. Both of the incumbent presidents were successful at least in part because they claimed that they would not send troops abroad to fight in foreign wars.[18] Both also broke their promises, although for very different reasons.

In chapter 7, Thomas Tunstall Allcock points out that even the election of 1964, which many consider to be a testament to the Democrat

Lyndon Johnson's ability to position himself as a moderate liberal on social policy in contrast to the right-wing Republican firebrand Barry Goldwater, was influenced by foreign policy matters. The role of nuclear weapons in American global policy and the smoldering issue of the war in Vietnam were important influences on voters. Johnson's crushing electoral victory is often remembered as the high point of American postwar liberalism, with the president successfully building a coalition to marshal legislation on civil rights and antipoverty programs through the Congress in search of the "Great Society." Yet people remember the campaign more for the infamous "daisy girl" commercial, which hinted that Goldwater might start a nuclear war if he was given access to the button.[19] Indeed, it was a great irony that Johnson's presidential term following his landslide electoral victory became so negatively dominated by foreign affairs when Johnson had used and manipulated the issue with such skill during the campaign itself. It was, above all, a testament to his ability to highlight the issue that Johnson wanted voters to consider, nuclear weapons, while downplaying the one that he did not, the Vietnam War.

The 1964 election may also demonstrate the fact that voters' interest in foreign policy tended to be fairly superficial outside a group that (in a study of post-Vietnam foreign policy) Richard Melanson has called the "attentive public."[20] While voters had a broad interest in whether they believed one candidate would place them and their families in greater danger than another, they often lacked detailed knowledge of foreign policy issues. This was certainly the case in 1964, when, as Tunstall Allcock shows, few Americans took any great interest in the situation in Vietnam. In effect, this meant that Johnson was able to keep the issue off the agenda, but his success was also facilitated by his opponent's refusal or inability to make it into a campaign issue—an irony when it was one of the few weaknesses of Johnson's campaign. It thus gave Johnson an advantage that he ruthlessly exploited.

Indeed, it is striking that several of the elections under consideration in this volume took place at pivotal points in the development of the Cold War yet featured little discussion of foreign affairs. As Michael F. Hopkins shows in chapter 3, although in 1948 voters made their decisions against the backdrop of growing Cold War tensions in Europe and East Asia, these events appear to have had little impact. This had as much to do with the way in which the candidates conducted themselves as it did with the foreign issues themselves. President Harry Truman had carved out a set of policies to deal with the Soviet threat that his Republican rival, Thomas Dewey, broadly agreed with and refused to attack. Meanwhile, the third-party candidate, Henry Wallace, whose position set him squarely against Truman, could not craft a successful strategy. Not only was this because Wallace was unable to win the support of the liberal wing of the Democratic Party, which tended to regard him as a naive and misguided idealist about the Soviet Union, but it was also due to his weaknesses as a campaigner. The result was that foreign affairs were effectively removed from the agenda.

Similarly, in 1956 President Eisenhower was largely successful in excluding external influences from his reelection campaign, despite ongoing international crises involving key American allies attempting to retake control of the Suez Canal from Egypt and a Soviet crackdown in Eastern Europe. Only late in the day was Eisenhower forced to confront these matters head on, and his skill in campaigning meant that he could present them as nonparty issues. This gave his opponent, Adlai Stevenson, little ammunition for an attack, despite the possibility, however remote, that the United States would be dragged into a military confrontation. In the particular case of the Suez crisis, Eisenhower was clear that his actions toward the protagonists were driven entirely by policy and not by political considerations. He thus convincingly argued that he would follow the correct course for the United States and the world, rather than one that was electorally expedient. Yet his position may have been unusual. He had a healthy lead in the polls and knew that his authority in foreign affairs was already well established, a position that allowed him to take a relatively relaxed view of the potential electoral repercussions even if he was disturbed by the diplomatic ones. He was also able to act relatively independently of public opinion because of the Democrats' weak response.

Yet, while momentous foreign events that took place during a presidential campaign rarely, if ever, significantly affected the outcome of an election, longer-term developments were often important in establishing or undermining the authority of candidates. This could give sitting presidents distinct advantages, as with President Richard Nixon's carefully timed visit to China in early 1972 just a few months before his successful reelection. Nixon was lagging behind in the polls before he announced in July 1971 that he would make his trip the following year. While the visit itself was therefore momentous in geopolitical terms, its political and electoral significance at home was not lost on the president, who benefited from a significant bounce in the polls on the back of it. Thomas Alan Schwartz discusses this in chapter 9, as he does Nixon's desire for a peace agreement in Vietnam in the fall of 1972 to increase his momentum in the final weeks of the campaign and to demonstrate that he had fulfilled the 1968 campaign pledge of "peace with honor." In the end, all he could do in 1972 was proclaim through his national security adviser, Henry Kissinger, that peace was "at hand," which turned out to be a bold and brilliant political move, although it was no doubt helped by the fact that Nixon already had by that stage an almost unassailable lead in the polls.[21]

Conversely, both President Gerald Ford in 1976 and President Jimmy Carter in 1980 suffered from the perception that they lacked presidential authority, the direct result of foreign policy mistakes. In the former case, it was because of something the president said rather than something he did. As Andrew Priest acknowledges in chapter 10, Ford was far behind his Democratic rival, Jimmy Carter, in the polls for most of the campaign. Yet his momentum in the final weeks as he attempted to take advantage of the authority in foreign affairs afforded him by incumbency was undermined by a gaffe on the status of Eastern Europe in a televised presidential debate with his opponent. This may not have prevented him from retaining the presidency, but it undermined his claims of competence and stalled his resurgence in the polls. In the latter case, rather than a campaigning gaffe, Carter was effectively hamstrung by the turn of international events, especially the Iranian hostage crisis, which was ongoing throughout the campaign, and the Soviet invasion of Afghanistan. His inability to deal effectively with the hostage situation severely undermined his authority and turned voters against him. Although economic concerns were vital in both 1976 and 1980, foreign policy mistakes did not help either incumbent with their campaigns.

Ford's poorly timed comment in the television debate illustrates another theme that becomes increasingly salient over the course of this collection: the growing role of the media in campaigning. Although the extent to which television has proved decisive in campaigns remains contested, the much-celebrated era of television debates has led to suggestions that they can make or break a candidacy. Yet, in this study, only the first set of debates—held in 1960—seems to have significantly changed the electoral landscape.[22] His success in the 1960 debates was not just because John F. Kennedy looked younger and more energetic than his opponent, Richard Nixon; he was also able to attack Nixon's record in government. As Sylvia Ellis demonstrates in chapter 6, foreign policy played an important part in the 1960 election and arguably negatively affected the Kennedy campaign. In particular, his refusal to confirm that he would be willing to defend the islands of Quemoy-Matsu just off the coast of Communist China but occupied by the Nationalists hurt Kennedy in the second and third debates because Nixon was able to make political capital by suggesting that Kennedy was weak on communism. This saw Nixon narrow the gap with Kennedy in the final weeks of the campaign. In such instances, the complexities of foreign affairs could often be difficult to explain to voters, and candidates' attempts at nuance could backfire. Kennedy's sophistication on Quemoy-Matsu led to his slipping in the polls, perhaps in an oddly similar way to the desire to show that he understood the subtleties of Eastern European politics that led Ford to misspeak in 1976. Ellis shows that foreign policy appears to have resulted in a tighter result than might otherwise have been expected in 1960 because of the Quemoy-Matsu issues and because Kennedy failed to exploit the relatively weak position of the Republicans on national security issues in the wake of the Soviet launch of the Sputnik satellite and the supposed missile gap.

While foreign policy has often been central to election campaigns, the election process can also have an important impact internationally. In both 1956 and 1972, for example, presidential elections influenced the ways in which enemies and allies crafted their own foreign policies. As Scott Lucas points out in chapter 5, Britain and France proceeded with their plans for the invasion of the Sinai Peninsula in an attempt to regain control of the Suez Canal at least in part because they believed that Eisenhower would be unable to respond owing to electoral considerations. Lucas shows that this judgment was ill founded. In 1972, North Vietnam launched its April "Easter Offensive" similarly convinced that public opinion in the United States would constrain President Nixon's response in an election year (much as Johnson had been affected four years earlier). This was the wrong conclusion to draw and severely underestimated Nixon and Kissinger's fears that a South Vietnamese collapse would rebound negatively on Nixon's chances of being returned to power. This meant that Nixon was willing to inflict significant damage on Northern forces to ensure that the regime in Saigon survived beyond November. Nixon's success in the polls in the months that followed at the expense of his liberal Democratic rival, George McGovern, also led Hanoi to change the terms of its demands to allow South Vietnamese president Nguyen Van Thieu to remain in power as part of a peace agreement because they knew this was a red line for Nixon. This had no effect on President Thieu himself, who rejected key parts of the deal. It also delayed the collapse of South Vietnam for only another two years.

Following the end of war in 1975, the legacies of Vietnam cast long shadows over many subsequent elections, especially as policymakers believed that public opinion was more of a constraint than before.[23] Vietnam appeared to contribute to the slow erosion of American power—or at least to the realization of its limits—that has been another theme of elections since at least the 1960s. To be sure, the oil crisis of the 1970s—which exposed to many Americans in stark terms the extent to which they were dependent on foreign oil and how this dependence could affect the traditional areas of domestic concern in elections, for example, the economy, unemployment, wages, and inflation—also played its part. Added to this, the 1980 election was played out in the denouement of the Iranian hostage crisis, which exemplified to many voters not only Jimmy Carter's incompetence in the realm of foreign affairs but also America's impotence in the face of a challenge from a set of fanatical extremists.

Yet the post-Vietnam era also saw a distinct shift in voter preferences. As Robert Mason notes in chapter 11, the election of Ronald Reagan in 1980 represented more of an ongoing conservative turn in attitudes toward foreign policy amid concerns about the declining status of the United States than it did a growing conservatism in the domestic political realm. As Mason argues, the decline of détente in the 1970s not only undid the Ford and Carter administrations but also galvanized the New Right and neoconservatives in the Republican Party and gave them life in the Reagan era and beyond. Underlining changes in voters' perceptions—and the state of the world—from sixteen years before, in 1980 Carter was unable to portray Reagan as a trigger-happy warmonger just as Lyndon Johnson had done with such devastating success against Barry Goldwater in 1964. Yet this went only so far. Significantly, as David Ryan shows in chapter 12, Reagan was forced to moderate his aggressive rhetoric in the 1984 campaign because of his vulnerability on policies in Lebanon and

Central America as well as concerns about a possible escalation of tensions with the Soviets. Even though the economy was the pivotal concern of the campaign, Reagan knew that he was vulnerable, particularly on his Central American policies.

More recently, the end of the Cold War seemed to signal a shift away from issues of national security and toward homegrown concerns. These could certainly have a foreign dimension, such as the threat that American jobs were moving to developing countries or that American communities were being affected by illegally imported drugs, but candidates in the 1988 and 1992 elections, the final two examined in this collection, increasingly focused on what they saw as traditional domestic issues, such as the economy and family values. Policy differences between the main political candidates appeared to be vanishingly small, partly because of the end of the ideological battles of the Cold War, and partly because of the constraints of growing government budget deficits. This applied particularly to foreign policy, where, as Robert A. Strong suggests in chapter 13, the narrow gap between the candidates in the 1988 elections and the lack of informed discussion of issues may have been because there were few important differences between them, differences that could have affected voter choices. Yet the 1988 election took place at a momentous time in the history of global politics; the United States and the Soviet Union had reached pivotal agreements on nuclear weapons, and the Cold War was nearing its denouement. Despite this, as Strong shows, the candidates engaged in often highly personalized attacks on each other's domestic records and little else. This was especially the case for the eventual winner, George H. W. Bush, despite his pedigree and knowledge of foreign affairs. As Strong suggests, the "foreign policy dog did not bark."

Yet, just because foreign policy did not feature in a presidential campaign did not mean that it would not be a feature of that presidential term. Despite the paucity of foreign policy discussion in 1988, dramatic events, including the end of the Cold War, the collapse of the Soviet Union, and war in the Middle East, would go on to dominate George H. W. Bush's single term in office. Much like that of 1964, the 1988 election told voters little about what was to follow.

It is therefore particularly notable that discussions that took place during the final election campaign covered in this study were even less concerned with international matters than were those in elections that had preceded it. In 1992, George Bush was unable to take advantage of his foreign policy credentials and the stunning success he had seen in expelling Saddam Hussein's forces from Kuwait by assembling a wide-ranging international coalition in early 1991. As John Dumbrell states in chapter 14, domestic matters dominated in 1992, and foreign affairs intruded only in areas such as the international economy, particularly trade. By the 1990s, concerns about national security, which had so dominated elections during World War II and the Cold War period, appeared to be receding as Americans focused more on domestic affairs.

While the end of the Cold War might have led some to believe in the end of history and thus to question the need for an active foreign policy, the 9/11 attacks of 2001 ensured that future historians will need to examine elections beyond 1992. Of course, the picture will still be a complex one. There is some evidence to suggest that even the events of 9/11, the War on Terror, and the wars in Afghanistan and Iraq gave way to a renewed focus on the home front as Americans struggled with the economic downturn following 2008. The main areas of bipartisan consensus since then have been about the need to deal with internal problems, even if there is little agreement on how to do so.[24] Indeed, Daniel Drezner has contended that voters' lack of concern with global affairs has given presidents even more maneuverability in their foreign policies once they are in office.[25] However, the continued need for a foreign policy debate in election campaigns reveals at the very least that the perception that foreign policy is important remains and in more general terms that the nation is a long way from any kind of retreat into isolation, however *isolation* might be defined.

Perhaps the era covered in this volume may have been unusual in that the position of the United States as a global superpower and especially its involvement in hot and cold wars forced voters to contend with international matters to an unprecedented degree. Even so, this collection shows that the relationship between foreign policy and electoral politics could remain important even when international affairs were not overt campaign issues. As Miroslav Nincic has put it recently: "American foreign policy reflects domestic politics, elections in particular. Except when external threats are stark and immediate (a rare occurrence), much about how the United States deals with the international community flows from partisan politics and electoral calculations."[26] Thus, the following chapters suggest that scholars of American foreign relations need to consider the influence of elections more seriously in their work.

Notes

1. Bill Clinton, *My Life* (New York: Knopf, 2004), 425.

2. "Foreign Policy Attitudes Now Driven by 9/11 and Iraq," Pew Research Center for the People and the Press, August 18, 2004, http://www.people-press .org/2004/08/18/foreign-policy-attitudes-now-driven-by-911-and-iraq.

3. Kennedy quoted in Arthur M. Schlesinger Jr., *The Imperial Presidency* (Boston: Houghton Mifflin, 1973), 401.

4. Robert A. Divine, *Foreign Policy and U.S. Presidential Elections, 1952–1960* (New York: New Viewpoints, 1974), ix. See also Robert A. Divine, *Foreign Policy and U.S. Presidential Elections, 1940–1948* (New York: New Viewpoints, 1974).

5. Michael H. Armacost, *Ballots, Bullets, and Bargains: American Foreign Policy and Presidential Elections* (New York: Columbia University Press, 2015); Andrew Preston, "Beyond the Water's Edge: Foreign Policy and Electoral Politics," in *America at the Ballot Box: Elections and Political History*, ed. Gareth Davies and Julian E. Zelizer (Philadelphia: University of Pennsylvania Press, 2015), 219–37.

6. For a discussion, see Ole Holsti, *Public Opinion and Foreign Policy* (Ann Arbor: University of Michigan Press, 2009), 3–14. As Holsti puts it: "Realists usually describe public opinion as a barrier to any thoughtful and coherent policy, hindering efforts to promote national interests that may transcend the moods and passions of the moment." Ibid., 6.

7. For a summary of this literature, see Andrew Johnstone, "Before the Water's Edge: Domestic Politics and U.S. Foreign Relations," *Passport: The Society for Historians of American Foreign Relations Review* 45, no. 3 (2015): 25–29.

8. Robert J. McMahon, "Diplomatic History and Policy History: Finding Common Ground," *Journal of Policy History* 17, no. 1 (2005): 93–109, 106; Thomas Alan Schwartz, "'Henry, . . . Winning an Election Is Terribly Important': Partisan Politics in the History of U.S. Foreign Relations," *Diplomatic History* 33, no. 2 (2009): 173–90, 177; Fredrik Logevall, "Politics and Foreign Relations," *Journal of American History* 95, no. 4 (2009): 1074–78, 1076–77; Andrew L. Johns, *Vietnam's Second Front: Domestic Politics, the Republican Party, and the War* (Lexington: University Press of Kentucky, 2010), 6.

9. Recent books that deal with domestic politics and foreign policy include Andrew Johnstone and Helen Laville, eds., *The US Public and American Foreign Policy* (London: Routledge, 2010); Melvin Small, *Democracy and Diplomacy* (Baltimore: Johns Hopkins University Press, 1996); and Ralph Levering, *The Public and American Foreign Policy, 1918–1978* (New York: Morrow, 1978). Other recent works that have emphasized the importance of domestic politics in its broadest sense include Julian E. Zelizer, *Arsenal of Democracy: The Politics of National Secu-*

rity—from World War II to the War on Terrorism (New York: Basic, 2010); Kenneth Osgood and Andrew K. Frank, eds., *Selling War in a Media Age: The Presidency and Public Opinion in the American Century* (Gainesville: University Press of Florida, 2010); and Campbell Craig and Fredrik Logevall, *America's Cold War: The Politics of Insecurity* (Cambridge, MA: Belknap Press of Harvard University Press, 2009).

10. This view is supported by some of the political science literature that focuses on voter behavior and foreign policy matters. See, e.g., John H. Aldrich, John L. Sullivan, and Eugene Borgida, "Foreign Affairs and Issue Voting: Do Presidential Candidates 'Waltz Before a Blind Audience?'" *American Political Science Review* 83, no. 1 (1989): 123–41, esp. 126–27; and Miroslav Nincic and Barbara Hinckley, "Foreign Policy and the Evaluation of Presidential Candidates," *Journal of Conflict Resolution* 35, no. 2 (1991): 333–55. Adam Berinsky has suggested that, even during times of war, political elites are able to shape opinion within the domestic arena so that the public's view of the war in question generally reflects influences at home more than it does the impact of the events themselves. See Adam J. Berinsky, *In Time of War: Understanding American Public Opinion from World War II to Iraq* (Chicago: University of Chicago Press, 2009).

11. Nincic and Hinckley, "Foreign Policy," 334–35.

12. On this point, see John H. Aldrich, Christopher Gelpi, Peter Feaver, Jason Reifler, and Kristin Thompson Sharp, "Foreign Policy and the Electoral Connection," *Annual Review of Political Science* 9 (2006): 477–502, esp. 494.

13. Douglas C. Foyle, *Counting the Public In: Presidents, Public Opinion, and Foreign Policy* (New York: Columbia University Press, 1999). In chapter 5 of this collection, Scott Lucas critiques Foyle's model by applying it to the 1956 election.

14. In all but one of the elections under consideration in this collection, every contest contained either an incumbent president or a vice president as a candidate (the exception was 1952, when President Harry Truman and Vice President Alben Barkley did not run and the Democratic candidate, Illinois governor Adlai Stevenson, was defeated by NATO's supreme allied commander, Dwight D. Eisenhower, representing the Republican Party).

15. Of course, foreign policy positions promoted during election campaigns can also affect the formation of foreign policies once a candidate wins the presidency. However, the impact of campaigning positions on any given candidate's ultimate foreign policy record is beyond the scope of this particular volume.

16. Dwight D. Eisenhower, Text of Address Delivered at Detroit, MI, October 24, 1952, Dwight D. Eisenhower Library, http://www.eisenhower.archives.gov/research/online_documents/korean_war/I_Shall_Go_To_Korea_1952_10_24.pdf.

17. Richard Nixon, Address to the Nation on the War in Vietnam, November 3, 1969, *The American Presidency Project,* http://www.presidency.ucsb.edu/ws/?pid=2303.

18. See Franklin D. Roosevelt, Campaign Address at Boston, MA, October 30, 1940, *American Presidency Project,* http://www.presidency.ucsb.edu/ws/index.php?pid=15887&st=&st1=; and Lyndon B. Johnson, Remarks in Memorial Hall,

Akron University, October 21, 1964, *American Presidency Project,* http://www .presidency.ucsb.edu/ws/index.php?pid=26635&st=&st1=.

19. "1964 Presidential Campaign Spot," Lyndon Baines Johnson Library, http:// www.lbjlib.utexas.edu/johnson/media/daisyspot.

20. Richard A. Melanson, *American Foreign Policy since the Vietnam War: The Search for Consensus from Richard Nixon to George W. Bush* (2000), 4th ed. (Armonk, NY: M. E. Sharpe, 2005), 36.

21. Bernard Gwertzman, "Kissinger Asserts That 'Peace Is at Hand'; Saigon Says It Will Agree to a Cease-Fire," *New York Times,* October 27, 1972, 1.

22. Lydia Saad, "Presidential Debates Rarely Game-Changers," Gallup, September 25, 2008, www.gallup.com/poll/110674/presidential-debates-rarely-gamechangers .aspx.

23. Richard Sobel, *The Impact of Public Opinion on U.S. Foreign Policy since Vietnam: Constraining the Colossus* (New York: Oxford University Press, 2001). As William Lunch and Peter Sperlich note, however: "No matter what the actual pre-disposition of public opinion about foreign policy, elites may constrain themselves if they believe a negative public reaction would be registered at the next election." William L. Lunch and Peter W. Sperlich, "American Public Opinion and the Viet-nam War," *Western Political Quarterly* 32, no. 1 (1979): 21–44, 32. See also Trevor McCrisken, *American Exceptionalism and the Legacy of Vietnam: US Foreign Policy since 1974* (London: Palgrave, 2003); Marvin Kalb and Deborah Kalb, *Haunting Legacy: Vietnam and the American Presidency from Ford to Obama* (Washington, DC: Brookings Institution, 2011).

24. See, e.g., Stuart Stevens, "American Voters Don't Get Foreign Policy," *Daily Beast,* July 31, 2014, http://www.thedailybeast.com/articles/2014/07/31/american-voters-don-t-get-foreign-policy.html.

25. Daniel W. Drezner, "Why Presidents Love Foreign Affairs," *New York Times,* September 20, 2012, http://campaignstops.blogs.nytimes.com/2012/09/20/ why-presidents-love-foreign-affairs/?_r=0.

26. Miroslav Nincic, "External Affairs and the Electoral Connection," in *Domestic Sources of American Foreign Policy: Insights and Evidence* (1988; 6th ed.), ed. James M. McCormick (Lanham, MD: Rowman & Littlefield, 2012), 139–55, 153.

1

"A Godsend to the Country"?

Roosevelt, Willkie, and the Election of 1940

Andrew Johnstone

In his famous *Roosevelt and Hopkins,* Robert Sherwood wrote that Franklin Roosevelt considered Wendell Willkie's June 1940 nomination as the Republican candidate for the presidency to be a "Godsend to the country." This was because it supposedly removed the "isolationist-interventionist" issue from the campaign. Given the dramatic events in Europe of the preceding two months, Roosevelt was relieved that there would be continuity in US foreign policy regardless of the election's outcome. The frightening prospect of Roosevelt campaigning against an old-school noninterventionist such as Robert Taft or Thomas Dewey had been removed. As Sherwood wrote: "The importance of this consideration could hardly be overestimated."[1]

Yet this chapter argues that Sherwood did in fact overestimate the danger of such a development, a fact that has led to a misunderstanding of the nature of the 1940 election. While a straight and potentially bitter contest between isolationist and interventionist candidates was avoided and the continuity of the policy of aid to Britain was ensured, foreign policy was not neutralized as an election issue, and it remained a key theme for both candidates throughout the campaign. Roosevelt continued to be extremely cautious regarding foreign issues throughout the following four months. This was in part because he recognized that Willkie did not wholly reflect the Republican Party on foreign policy matters and that congressional noninterventionism was extremely strong. However,

Willkie was also more critical of Roosevelt on foreign policy issues than has generally been accepted. This was largely a result of straightforward party politics: Willkie had an election to win. While the situation could perhaps have been worse, the selection of Willkie as the Republican candidate certainly did not mean that foreign policy issues were off the table. Even if FDR could afford to be less cautious regarding foreign policy issues, there is little evidence to suggest that he was.

Sherwood's "Godsend" line has made it into much of the literature on the 1940 election. It appears in Steve Neal's biography of Willkie supporting the idea that the country would be spared an isolationist-interventionist fight and that continuity of policy would be ensured.[2] It also features in Susan Dunn's *1940* for the same reasons and in *Roosevelt's Second Act,* with Richard Moe highlighting the quote while conceding that it was not entirely accurate.[3] Yet it is not alone in perpetuating the idea that the choice of Willkie neutralized foreign policy as an issue, as other scholars have also expressed variants of the same argument. In *Freedom from Fear,* David Kennedy argued: "Willkie shared enough of Roosevelt's own internationalist convictions that his candidacy, along with the [Frank] Knox and [Henry] Stimson appointments, helped to neutralize foreign policy as an issue for much of the campaign." Only in the final days of the campaign did this change, he suggests, as "Willkie's mounting political desperation and the abrasive nagging of isolationist Republicans like Vandenberg temporarily eclipsed the candidate's internationalist convictions."[4] Again, however, this chapter argues that foreign policy clearly remained a critical issue for both candidates throughout the campaign and not just in the final days. With little to choose between the two men on domestic issues either, the war in Europe ensured that foreign policy would in fact be at the top of the campaign agenda in the election of 1940.

Similarly, from a political science perspective, Adam Berinsky noted in his recent *In Time of War:* "For most of the fall of 1940, a single message emanated from both campaigns regarding the wisdom of involvement in the Second World War."[5] Yet, even if we accept that a single message existed for *some* of the fall, it was clear that there was a great deal of political maneuvering and concern behind the scenes. In his volume on foreign policy and elections, Robert Divine is one of the few historians to acknowledge that "foreign policy played a crucial role in Willkie's calculations," in that Willkie hoped to steal undecided voters who supported aid to Britain as well as Democrats who opposed Roosevelt's breaking of the third-term tradition. But Willkie was also far more open in his criticisms of Roosevelt's policies. For his part, Roosevelt—or, more accurately, members of his administration—took the risk of loosely equating Willkie with pro-Hitler sentiment, conceding that not all Republicans were pro-Hitler but that all isolationists were likely to vote Republican.[6]

The Candidates

Examining the candidates in 1940, it is clear that the election affected the choice of even those who ran. Given his personal history as a registered Democrat until 1939, it was by no means certain that the Indiana lawyer Wendell Willkie would have been the Republican choice without the war in Europe. The rapid rise in Willkie's popularity between April and June 1940 happened at the same time as the Nazi blitzkrieg of Western Europe, and this was no coincidence. Given the popularity of the idea of supporting the Allies in Europe in their fight against fascist aggression, Willkie's internationalist message of aid to Britain and France was more popular with many Republicans than the old-fashioned isolationism of Thomas Dewey or Robert Taft. Foreign policy was not Willkie's top priority before the convention; his focus was, rather, on criticizing Roosevelt for being antibusiness at home. However, while he certainly did not sell himself as interventionist, Willkie made reference to the need to "sell whatever we want to those defending themselves from aggression." By the time of the Republican convention, with France having fallen just two days before the GOP met in Philadelphia, Willkie's stock had risen to the point where he was the Republican front-runner despite his trailing a distant second behind Dewey just a month earlier.[7]

In fact, opinion polls at this point suggested that a contest between a Democrat and a noninterventionist such as Dewey would have been no more challenging and could in fact have been less challenging than one between a Democrat and the more internationally minded Willkie. This is not simply because polls in early May—taken before the Nazi blitzkrieg—had not only Roosevelt but also *Cordell Hull* ahead of Dewey in what would have appeared to be a straight fight between the forces of internationalism and those of isolationism. The blitzkrieg only strengthened American support for Willkie's message of aid to Europe and weakened the noninterventionist argument, suggesting that, while a battle against Dewey might have been bitterer, it might also have been easier. Instead, Willkie was ultimately chosen despite the Republicans' struggle to reconcile their desire to support victims of fascist aggression with their desire to stay out of war, a struggle reflected in the party platform, which called for aid to all those fighting for liberty as long as that aid was not "in violation of international law or inconsistent with the requirements of our own national defense."[8]

While there is still some debate on the issue, it seems clear that Roosevelt made his final decision to run again only in early July, following the Republican choice of Willkie. Of course, he had been considering running again prior to that because of the nature of world events, but he had the potential unpopularity of an unprecedented third term to think about. Even if the third-term issue threatened to hurt him, however, he was still the most attractive Democratic candidate, and his final decision was made in large part because he believed that he was the only Democrat who could beat Willkie, as Donahoe has previously argued. Polls revealed that FDR was far more popular than any other figure from his party, with 92 percent of support among Democrats. And, despite Cordell Hull's foreign policy expertise, a clear majority of Democrats thought that the sitting president would handle the country's foreign affairs best. This proved crucial in the summer of 1940.[9]

The Summer of 1940: Destroyer-Bases and Selective Service

Willkie secured the Republican nomination in the early hours of June 28, 1940, with Roosevelt securing the Democratic nomination on July 17. Yet the campaign trail did not begin in earnest until September, when Willkie began his trip around the nation. Willkie did surprisingly little in the interim aside from making his acceptance speech in Elwood, Indiana, on August 17, while Roosevelt actively avoided the campaign and focused on looking presidential. In this gap, the foreign policy focus switched to two contentious issues: the destroyer-bases exchange and the Selective Training and Service Act. Despite the fact that both candidates supported both measures, these issues generated heated domestic political debate and became part of the election campaign.

After the fall of France, Britain stood alone in Western Europe. To help secure itself from German invasion, and to ensure the Atlantic life-line to the United States, British prime minister Winston Churchill asked Roosevelt on June 15 for American destroyers. Over one hundred of these ships dating from the Great War had been recently refurbished; how-ever, they had been refurbished for the defense of the United States, not the United Kingdom. Roosevelt initially saw no way to get the ships to Britain without opening himself up to sharp domestic criticism. With the United States undergoing its own preparedness campaign, giving the ships to Britain was a potential betrayal of national defense, and the pos-sibility of the ships ending up in German hands could not be ruled out in July 1940.[10]

However, by the end of July, with the Battle of Britain under way, a further plea from Churchill for "50 or 60 of your oldest destroyers" met with greater support. As it became clear that Britain was not going to fall, Roosevelt was increasingly persuaded by the need to get more destroyers to Britain. With an upcoming election campaign looming, the question was how it could be done. With congressional authority deemed unlikely, it appeared that the best way to proceed was through executive action. Yet, while it was clear that Roosevelt wanted to facilitate a transfer of destroyers to Britain, he clearly wanted to do it on his own terms and—given the election—in as politically secure a manner as possible.[11]

On the issue, Roosevelt had the support of a number of influential private citizens from two recently formed nonpartisan organizations: the Committee to Defend America by Aiding the Allies and the Century Group. The former was been set up in May to publicly urge greater aid to democratic nations in Western Europe in the face of the Nazi blitzkrieg; the latter was more private and evolved through June and July, working behind the scenes to influence the Roosevelt administration. At a July 25 meeting of the Century Group, it was suggested that the recently recon-ditioned destroyers be handed over to Britain. The group also argued that the ships be given in exchange for "naval and air concessions in British possessions in the Western hemisphere." On August 1, three members of both organizations—Herbert Agar, Ward Cheney, and Clark Eichel-berger—visited Roosevelt and put the suggestion of an exchange to him.[12]

The following day, Roosevelt's cabinet meeting focused on ensuring the sale of fifty or sixty destroyers to Britain. The consensus at the meeting was that congressional legislation was required for any such arrangement.

This meant that caution was required, and it was agreed that the president would contact William Allen White, the chairman of the Committee to Defend America by Aiding the Allies, who had recently spoken to Willkie on the subject. After speaking with Roosevelt, White was to get Willkie's approval to speak to and secure support from House minority leader Joe Martin and Senate minority leader and vice presidential candidate Charles McNary. Later that evening, White assured Roosevelt that Willkie's view was the same as the president's. Roosevelt countered that this was insufficient, noting: "Willkie's attitude was not what counted. . . . Republican policy in Congress was the one essential." The incident suggested that the president was less interested in the implications for the election than he was in securing the necessary legislation, but the fact that he used White to go through Willkie revealed a desire to keep Willkie close.[13]

White remained the main intermediary between Roosevelt and Willkie, even visiting the Republican in Colorado in an attempt to secure his support for the president. However, he was unsuccessful in his efforts to convince Willkie to publically support any destroyer sale or exchange. Willkie privately approved of the action, but he was unwilling to alienate more reluctant Republicans in Congress. He also preferred to wait until specific legislation was forthcoming, refusing to comment on proposals. White subsequently informed the president that he could not "guarantee either of you to the other" but that "there is not two bits difference between you on the issues pending." The closest the president would get to an endorsement came on August 17, when Willkie stated in his acceptance speech that the loss of the British fleet would "greatly weaken" American defenses and German domination of the Atlantic would "be a calamity for us."[14]

However, by that point, Roosevelt was already negotiating with the British over the details of an exchange. As it became clear that the chances of congressional agreement on a destroyer sale were limited, he looked to find ways around Congress. Increasingly swayed by legal arguments that claimed he already had the authority to act, he moved to make the transfer work on his own, informing Churchill of his plans on August 13. The decision to circumvent Congress showed his determination to act, but it also meant that Roosevelt became even more concerned with the domestic political implications. He had faced the criticism of being a "dictator" through much of his second term, notably with his plan to enlarge the Supreme Court in 1937 and his attempts to influence the midterm Democratic primaries in 1938. The suggestion arose again in 1940 with his break from the two-term tradition, and any attempt to avoid Congress was likely to arouse further criticism.[15]

In order to defend himself, Roosevelt emphasized the benefits for America's own national defense. In a press conference on August 16, he claimed that ongoing discussions with the British were solely regarding the acquisition of naval and air bases for the defense of the American hemisphere, with special reference to the Panama Canal. He largely evaded suggestions from reporters of a quid pro quo for destroyers, albeit clumsily. On September 3, the destroyer-bases exchange was announced to the public. The United States acquired the right to lease eight naval and air bases in the Western Hemisphere from Newfoundland to British Guiana. Newfoundland and Bermuda were gifts from Great Britain, while the other six were in exchange for fifty naval destroyers. Roosevelt justified the exchange on the grounds that it would improve the nation's security "beyond calculation."[16]

As expected, Willkie suggested that the country would support the deal, but he deemed the fact that the president had not taken the issue before Congress "regrettable." He highlighted that the democratic processes should not be ignored in the fight between totalitarianism and democracy, but the measured nature of his response revealed his largely supportive attitude. That attitude was not shared by everyone in his party. Republican senator Gerald Nye called it a "dictatorial step," while Republican representative Hamilton Fish argued: "It usurps the power of Congress, and violates international laws, the law of the United States and the Constitution. It is virtually an act of war." Building on that congressional criticism, and belatedly recognizing that he was running for president, Willkie quickly allowed his own criticism of the deal to become more forceful. From his initial mild denouncement of the way in which the deal was conducted, he quickly took a harder line. Within three days, he called the trade "the most arbitrary and dictatorial action ever taken by any President in the history of the United States."[17]

In the end, Roosevelt was convinced that he could act without an agreement and at the risk of subsequent criticism from Willkie. Yet, even if Willkie was not opposed to the idea of the destroyer-bases exchange, many Republicans in Congress were, and there were still political risks to the exchange that Roosevelt sought to limit by selling it as being in the nation's interest and to its benefit. And, even though Willkie supported the idea of the exchange, his subsequent delayed criticism of the way in which it was carried out was a clear attempt to score political points in the campaign. His decision to criticize Roosevelt marked a point of departure, and, for the final two months of the campaign, he took an increasingly hard line against the president.

Running alongside destroyer-bases was the issue of selective service and the congressional debate over the Burke-Wadsworth bill. Just as there was general agreement between Roosevelt and Willkie over the need to aid Britain, there was agreement over the need to build up the nation's defenses. There was also a consensus within the nation as a whole. Polls in May 1940 suggested that 90 percent of Americans believed that the nation should increase the size of its armed forces and that 86 percent approved of additional spending by Congress on the armed forces. However, those polled split equally on the suggestion that the nation's young people should be required to serve a year in the armed forces, though the number in support of universal military training was up to 64 percent in June and 67 percent by July, no doubt as a result of events in Europe. When a poll was taken in mid-August, 71 percent favored increasing the nation's armed forces through a draft. However, that consensus did not remove the issue from the domestic political arena or the election campaign.[18]

Despite this seemingly overwhelming support, Roosevelt was reluctant to speak out strongly for the Burke-Wadsworth bill as it worked its way through Congress in June and July. While he had been criticized for allowing the national defense to lapse to a point of inadequacy, he was even more wary of being criticized as a warmonger who wanted to send American boys to fight in Europe. He was also cautious about pushing the bill too hard for fear of the dictator charge resurfacing. Finally, he had no firm idea of how Willkie would respond. Once again, he let private citizens take the initiative, led by the lawyer Grenville Clark. Clark had been part of the Plattsburg Movement in support of military training in 1915, prior to American entry into the previous war, and, in May 1940, he began a second push for military training. Given the political implications and the polling results from May, Roosevelt's support for the bill was initially restricted to encouragement from behind the scenes.[19]

Yet, despite increasingly encouraging polling numbers, the bill made slow progress through the summer, and Roosevelt found himself under increasing pressure to speak out, not just from Grenville Clark but also from members of his own administration. Notable here were the two Republicans added to the cabinet in June: Henry Stimson as secretary of war and Frank Knox as secretary of the navy. A friend of Clark's, Stimson was particularly forceful in supporting selective service, and he pushed the president to be more public in his support. That support finally arrived at an August 2 press conference, when Roosevelt announced that it was "perfectly clear" that he was "in favor of a selective training bill," considering it to be "essential to adequate national defense."[20]

The question was how Willkie would respond. Roosevelt was clearly suspicious of Willkie's motives and remained so in the two weeks between his press conference and Willkie's Elwood speech. When Representative Edward Taylor suggested that the president invite Willkie to a conference so that a bipartisan program on military training could be agreed on, Roosevelt responded that Willkie had "no desire to cooperate and is merely playing politics." The president had taken a calculated risk, a fact he conceded to a Democrat who feared for the impact of selective service on votes in the election, in that it "may very easily defeat the Democratic National ticket." However, Roosevelt urged that the issues be thought through "in terms of national safety and not just in terms of votes." Appealing to the notion that some issues were above party politics, he claimed: "There are some occasions in the national history where leaders have to move for the preservation of American liberties and not just drift with what may or may not be a political doubt of the moment."[21]

Yet the doubt remained even after Willkie spoke on August 17. Willkie stated: "I cannot ask the American people to put their faith in me, without recording my conviction that some form of selective service is the only democratic way in which to secure the trained and competent manpower we need for national defense." He prefaced this relatively unambiguous sounding statement by refusing to specifically examine the Burke-Wadsworth bill or the intentions of the administration toward it. Instead, he agreed with some in his party "that these intentions must be closely watched." For some supporters of the plan, such as Grenville Clark, this was far too ambiguous a statement; for noninterventionists, it suggested that there was little to choose between the two candidates. Yet, while the speech was largely seen as amounting to an endorsement, it was hardly an unqualified one, and, as will be seen, selective service was not finished as a campaign issue.[22]

As with the destroyer-bases exchange, the treatment of the selective service bill revealed tension between the two candidates on foreign policy matters. On the one hand, Willkie's general sympathy with both the need to aid Britain and the need to build up national defense meant that neither issue was to be a significant point of policy disagreement in the campaign. Yet, at the same time, neither Roosevelt nor Willkie was relaxed about foreign policy issues, and neither was willing to remove them from the campaign entirely—especially Willkie. Recognizing that he needed to find a way to defeat Roosevelt (but also appeal to noninterventionist Republicans), Willkie kept open the option to criticize Roosevelt on specific details and methods of implementation, even on issues where they were largely in agreement. As the campaign began in earnest, he looked to criticize the president even more. Despite his best efforts to remain above the campaign, the president was ultimately compelled to respond.

The Campaign

Willkie began his campaign with the Ellwood speech, in which he came out in agreement with the need for both aid to Britain and some form of selective service. It is the relatively even tone of this speech that has done the most to portray him as a candidate who wanted to avoid making foreign policy an issue and who put national security above party politics. However, often overlooked is the fact that, in that speech, Willkie also attacked the president's conduct of foreign policy, stating that he could not "follow the President in his conduct of foreign affairs in this critical time."[23]

Suggesting that "many of us have wondered if he is deliberately inciting us to war," Willkie appealed to the noninterventionist voices within his own party and moved to position himself as the peace candidate. He accused the president of engaging in "inflammatory statements and manufactured panics" that represented "useless and dangerous" attacks on foreign powers that the country was in no position to support. In contrast to his aggressive rhetoric abroad, Roosevelt was accused of being economical with the truth at home. Slow to explain matters to the American people, the president had, Willkie claimed, "hesitated to report facts, to explain situations, or to define realistic objectives." In contrast to Roosevelt's lack of transparency, he promised to "consider our diplomacy as part of the people's business."[24]

This set the tone for the campaign that followed, with Willkie agreeing with Roosevelt on broader principles, but disagreeing wherever possible on specifics, and occasionally going even further in portraying the president as a warmonger. This critical approach was seen following the conclusion of the destroyer-bases exchange and was even more prevalent once Willkie's railroad tour of the nation began in September. However, the attacks were not one-way. Unsurprisingly, the administration sought to criticize and discredit Willkie. However, this was done not through the president himself but rather through other members of his administration. Roosevelt believed that the best way to win was to take full advantage of his current position by simply acting presidentially. Most of his appearances in the summer of 1940 were in his role as commander in chief—announcing increases in defense spending or inspecting military facilities—not as a presidential candidate. Republican congressman Dewey Short (R-MO) noted that, in doing so, Roosevelt was running not against Wendell Willkie but against Adolf Hitler.[25]

Of course, Roosevelt was running against Willkie, but the attacks on Willkie came from the president's allies, such as Secretary of the Interior Harold Ickes, Secretary of State Cordell Hull, New York governor Herbert Lehman, and the Democratic vice presidential candidate, Henry Wallace. Ickes responded specifically to Willkie's Ellwood speech by highlighting the contrast in credibility between the incumbent and the challenger. He described Willkie's suggestion that Roosevelt was dragging the nation to war as "contemptible," adding: "This sort of demagoguery cuts to the heart of Mr. Willkie's assumptions of statesmanship." Ickes also took the opportunity to highlight Roosevelt's own experience. Responding to the idea that there should be a series of debates, he countered: "The President cannot adjourn the Battle of Britain in order to ride the circuit with Mr. Willkie."[26]

Wallace followed with an attack on Willkie in his own acceptance speech at the end of August. Noting that the dictators would welcome the election campaign, he described Roosevelt as the worldwide symbol of democracy. Stating that he "did not wish to imply that the Republican leaders are willfully or consciously giving aid and comfort to Hitler," he claimed that defeat for Roosevelt, "even if it were by the most patriotic leadership that could be found, would cause Hitler to rejoice." The *New York Times* was highly critical of Wallace's rhetoric, summarizing that a vote for Willkie was "a vote for Hitler." Yet Roosevelt did nothing to stop him, and Wallace led the campaigning in September, hammering away at the appeasement line. As the president himself admitted: "You can't say everyone who is opposed to Roosevelt is pro-Nazi, but you can say with truth that everyone who is pro-Hitler in this country is also pro-Willkie." Roosevelt clearly felt that the war was a campaign issue on which he held the upper hand and one on which he could press home his advantage as much as possible.[27]

The attacks from Roosevelt's allies continued. At the end of September, New York governor Herbert Lehman gave a very similar message, implying that a win for Willkie would be a win for the dictators. He stated: "Nothing that could happen in the United States could give Hitler, Mussolini, Stalin, and the government of Japan more satisfaction than the defeat of the man who typifies to the whole world the kind of free, humane government which dictators despise—Franklin Roosevelt." Willkie responded by calling the comments "false, malicious and subversive," but Lehman defended them, arguing that, if he became president, Willkie would have to deal with a "miscellaneous assortment of appeasers and extreme isolationists in his own party."[28]

The speeches by Wallace, Ickes, and Lehman reflected a common line of attack from Roosevelt's supporters: while Willkie himself was not necessarily an appeaser, he represented the party of appeasement. The fact that Willkie was struggling to reconcile his own broader internationalist views on aid to Britain with the more noninterventionist attitudes of many in his own party provided an opportunity for Democrats to attack. And, in suggesting that a defeat for Roosevelt would be a win for Hitler, a subtle, if unstated, link was made between Willkie and the dictators. Of course, there were staunch noninterventionists in the Democratic Party, such as Montana senator Burton Wheeler, but Roosevelt's foreign policy priorities appeared relatively clear compared to Willkie's.

The president's one appearance on the campaign trail in September took place before the International Teamsters Union. In a speech that otherwise focused largely on labor issues, Roosevelt concluded with comments that appeared to speak directly to Willkie's suggestion that he, Roosevelt, was taking the nation to war. Echoing remarks made on the campaign trail four years previously, he stated: "I hate war now more than ever. I have one supreme determination—to do all that I can to keep war away from these shores for all time." He then repeated the Democratic Party platform plank that he would not send armed forces overseas except in the event of attack. While it was clear he wanted to provide more aid to Britain, he also wanted to reassure his audience that a vote for him was not a vote for war.[29]

Willkie on the Attack

Willkie had to respond. The main problem he faced was deciding how to discredit Roosevelt without betraying his own convictions about the need to aid Britain and build up the nation's defenses. So, while still calling for support for Britain, he went on the attack from a number of different angles as he crossed the country from mid-September. His scattershot approach revealed both the incoherence and the opportunism of his foreign policy strategy. However, at the heart of his campaign for the final eight weeks was the idea that he was the candidate of peace and that Roosevelt was in fact the candidate of war.

Willkie began his campaign in Chicago on September 13 by stating that he would "not send one American boy into the shambles of a European war." This noninterventionist passage of his speech echoed Roosevelt's comments and received the greatest applause. It was a message Willkie repeated over the following days in places such as Pittsburg, Kansas, where he again raised the "shambles of European trenches" as something to be avoided—"except for the protection of this beloved land of ours." Newspaper editorials noted that Willkie was clearly moving to portray himself as the peace candidate.[30]

Having established his own noninterventionist credibility, Willkie sought to undermine that of the president. In a number of speeches over the following days, including those at Pittsburg and Stockton, California, he reminded listeners of Roosevelt's Teamsters speech in which he promised to uphold the party platform and keep the nation out of war. He then recounted how eight years previously Roosevelt had made a commitment to support the 1932 Democratic Party platform, which had pledged to reduce the cost of the federal government by 25 percent. Given how New

Deal spending meant that that promise was never kept, he hoped that Roosevelt "remembers his pledge of 1940 better than he did his pledge of 1932." In Corona, California, Willkie provocatively added that, if Roosevelt kept his promise as well this time around, "you'd better begin to get on the transports pretty fast."[31]

However, Willkie's other main line of attack as his tour of the nation began was to turn the appeasement line back against the president and blame Roosevelt for the ongoing European conflict. On September 14, in both Peoria and Joliet, Illinois, Willkie confronted foreign matters head on, claiming that he was reluctantly drawn into commenting on foreign policy by the recent comments of Henry Wallace. However, he then boldly attacked eight years of Roosevelt's foreign policy, stating: "Roosevelt has been one of the principal contributors to the breakdown in Europe." Going all the way back to 1933, he assailed Roosevelt for torpedoing the London Economic Conference and limiting recovery. However, in an even bolder statement with regard to the Munich agreement, he claimed that it was Roosevelt who was the appeaser, "telephoning Hitler and Mussolini and Chamberlain, urging them to Munich, where they sacrificed Czecho-Slovakia," which, he claimed, had been sold "down the river."[32]

While Roosevelt attempted to remain above the fray, Cordell Hull provided the strongest response from the administration to Willkie's attack. He denied Willkie's specific allegation with relation to Munich, countering that the president had never spoken to Hitler or Mussolini by telephone while at the same time ignoring the wider suggestion that Roosevelt had supported the Munich agreement. This caused Willkie to step back from his remarks, and he subsequently corrected his statement to say simply that Roosevelt had urged a settlement. In a major speech in Coffeyville on September 16, he further modified his attack, though not considerably, referring to Roosevelt as "the godfather of that unhappy conference at Munich."[33]

Willkie's approach left him criticizing Roosevelt for creating a terrible, threatening war while simultaneously arguing that the war was not so threatening that the nation should join it. The lack of a clear approach was not helped by that fact that, after less than a week of campaigning, Willkie was forced to change his foreign policy adviser. He had begun his whistle-stop tour with the assistance of the Foreign Policy Association's Raymond Leslie Buell, but Buell fell ill in Kansas City and was replaced by Brooks Emeny of the Cleveland Council on World Affairs. However, it made little difference to the campaign's overall strategy as Willkie continued to attack the president on foreign policy wherever possible. In fact, his plan was to take an even broader line of attack on foreign policy, as his adviser Russell Davenport was searching for ways to support the argument that Roosevelt missed legitimate opportunities over the previous eight years to support democracies.[34]

After a few days during which his focus switched largely, if not solely, to domestic affairs, Willkie came back with a major foreign policy speech at San Francisco. In it, he reiterated many of the main lines of attack from his first week of campaigning. He claimed that he was reluctant to "play politics with your safety and perhaps your lives" but that, as Wallace had brought foreign policy into the campaign by connecting the Republican Party to appeasement, he had no choice but to respond. Once again, the president came under strong attack for his decisions at the London Economic Conference, which Willkie claimed weakened the chances of international recovery and therefore peace. The extended attack here reflected Davenport's desire to highlight missed opportunities. The reference to Munich was merely a passing one compared to previous speeches, but Roosevelt was still charged with "a direct share of the responsibility for the present war."[35]

Willkie concluded by emphasizing aid to Britain, an issue that had been largely missing from his first run of campaign speeches. He claimed that, if Britain were to fall, then the United States would be alone and that that loneliness was "a direct result of the foreign policies of the last eight years." As a result, the nation needed to keep sending aid to Britain, "our first line of defense and our only remaining friend." Yet he also made reference to another friend, China, and said that economic aid was needed to ensure that that country remained "free, strong and democratically progressive." The emphasis on aid marked a slight shift, one that reflected the ongoing Battle of Britain. As popular support fell behind the stubborn British resistance, Willkie found himself struggling to follow the administration's policy of support while trying to criticize it at the same time.[36]

The Final Month

September 27 saw the announcement of the Tripartite Pact between Germany, Italy, and Japan, which promised that the three nations would

come to the aid of each other if one was attacked by a nation not currently at war. It was clearly aimed at the United States. In the context of
the campaign, Willkie responded first in Cleveland on October 2, arguing that the three dictatorships clearly had war with the United States
in mind. Unfortunately, the United States was, thanks to the Roosevelt
administration, unprepared, not just because its foreign policies had failed
but also because it had "played politics with preparedness" and national
defense. Willkie was clearly willing to do so in a different way, in order to
try and win the election.[37]

Roosevelt's response came in a Columbus Day address in Dayton,
Ohio, on October 12. The speech on hemispheric defense made no reference to Willkie or the election. Nor did it explicitly refer to the Tripartite
Pact. Instead, the president simply argued that "no combination of dictator countries of Europe and Asia will stop the help we are giving to almost
the last free people now fighting to hold them at bay." Openly rejecting the doctrine of appeasement, and supporting the "heroic defense"
of the British, Roosevelt reiterated his existing policies while seemingly
remaining above the partisan concerns of the election. The speech was
well received, and it was clear that the president was succeeding in looking presidential.[38]

Willkie clearly needed a stronger line of attack, and, moving through
October, he reverted more firmly than before to the line that Roosevelt
was leading the nation to war. This shift was not as dramatic as has
been previously suggested, and many of Willkie's comments during this
period had already been made on the campaign trail. The challenger also
continued to call for aid to Britain and build on the suggestion made
in Cleveland that Democrats had not done enough in terms of national
defense. However, his focus on Roosevelt as warmonger dominated the
final month of his campaign. This firmer antiwar stance had the benefit of putting more distance between himself and the president while
also appealing to the base of the Republican Party. It may not have been
Willkie's preferred approach on principle, but the stance paid off in terms
of polling numbers as he closed in on Roosevelt in the final weeks of the
campaign.

In St. Louis on October 18, Willkie made one of his more dramatic
speeches, asking whether Roosevelt had "entered into any secret pact or
agreement with any foreign power which may involve us in war." He also

suggested that, while he would not send American boys to war overseas, "if you re-elect the third-term candidate, I believe they will be sent." In Chicago a week later, he reiterated his earlier campaign argument that, if Roosevelt's promise to keep out of foreign wars was as good as his promise to balance the budget, then the troops were "almost on the transports." The attacks seemed to be working as Roosevelt's lead in the polls dropped from 12 percent at the beginning of October to 9 percent in mid-October to 4 percent in the last week of October.[39]

At this point, those around Roosevelt were concerned as they recognized that the portrayal of the president as a warmonger appeared to be working. The administration had been keeping a close eye on Willkie's foreign policy attacks, with Cordell Hull and the speechwriter Samuel Rosenman collecting excerpts from the Republican's speeches. The prospect of postponing the draft lottery until after the election was briefly considered but rejected as being against national defense and too obviously political. However, it was decided that the president finally needed to join the campaign trail for five speeches, beginning on October 23 in Philadelphia. In this first speech, Roosevelt confronted Willkie's misstatements or "deliberate falsifications," including the charges that the president had sold Czechoslovakia down the river and entered into secret treaties. On October 28 in New York, he responded to more of Willkie's attacks, challenging the critics of his record on national defense by highlighting Republican opposition to efforts to expand the armed forces; before turning to counter the charge of warmongering by taking credit for the Neutrality Acts he had worked against in 1935 and 1937.[40]

Two days later in Boston, Roosevelt gave his most famous speech of the campaign. He notably stated: "I have said this before, but I shall say it again and again: your boys are not going to be sent into any foreign wars." He omitted the phrase "except in case of attack" that he had used in previous speeches as he felt it to be obvious that, if the United States was attacked, the war was no longer a foreign one. Willkie is noted to have responded with: "That hypocritical son of a bitch. This is going to beat me." Roosevelt reiterated the same message informally in Buffalo on November 2, stating: "Your president says this country is not going to war." Later that day, in his final campaign address, he noted: "The first purpose of our foreign policy is to keep our country out of war."[41]

Conclusion

Did the war issue make a difference in the overall election? Of course, it is very difficult to come to firm conclusions, but there is little doubt that the election would have been closer without the issue of war. In fact, chances are that Willkie would have won (though, of course, without the war issue, it is not certain that Willkie would have been the Republican candidate in the first place). A poll in mid-August asked whom Americans wanted as president in the event that the United States was required to fight Germany, and 58 percent of those who expressed an opinion replied Roosevelt. In a Gallup poll taken in the final week of October, 61 percent of Americans believed that Roosevelt would do a better job of strengthening American national defense, and 60 percent would rather have Roosevelt as president should the United States get involved in the war. This compared to a general poll on the election from the same week that had Roosevelt up only 52 to 48. However, a poll in mid-August asked Americans whom they would vote for if there were no war in Europe. Here, Willkie was ahead, with Roosevelt at just 47 percent and Willkie at 53 percent.[42]

The choice of Willkie as the Republican candidate may have avoided a straight fight between an internationalist and a noninterventionist. Yet even if the choice of Willkie meant that foreign policy was not at the forefront of voters' minds in the ballot booth—which is by no means certain—there was no question that foreign policy issues were prominent, if not dominant, during the 1940 campaign. True, this was by no means a single-issue campaign, as presidential elections never are, but the looming threat of war meant that foreign policy certainly overshadowed not only the third-term question but also many domestic issues.

The domestic political climate affected the way Roosevelt acted in the 1940 campaign. It was seen in the caution with which he dealt with both selective service and the destroyer-bases exchange and the way he sold both as matters of national defense first and foremost. It was also seen in the way he attacked Willkie through political surrogates like Ickes and Wallace, only belatedly going after Willkie himself. The domestic political climate also affected Willkie's campaign, though clearly for the worse in that it became tangled up in an effort to straddle the entrenched non-interventionism of the Republican Party and Willkie's own desire to aid

Britain. This arguably helped doom Willkie, although a poor strategy, amateurish campaign management, and a failure to differentiate himself on many domestic issues also did not help.

But did those campaign issues and the election ultimately affect foreign policy? The answer is also yes, though to a lesser extent. By playing to the noninterventionist crowd for reelection in 1940, FDR committed himself to a more limited "aid-short-of-war" approach, from which it was hard to return. True, he would likely have gone ahead with the destroyer-bases exchange even if Dewey had been his challenger as popular support for aid to Britain would likely have seen him through. And he still had the freedom to go ahead with Lend-Lease in the aftermath of the election. But, beyond that, he narrowed his options for the future. His ability to promote greater involvement in a war that he genuinely believed affected America's political, economic, and national security interests was constrained in 1941. The result would be a year in which a growing economy with the truth would be ended only with the Japanese attack on Pearl Harbor.

Notes

1. Robert E. Sherwood, *Roosevelt and Hopkins: An Intimate History* (New York: Harper & Bros., 1948), 174.

2. Steve Neal, *Dark Horse: A Biography of Wendell Willkie* (Garden City, NY: Doubleday, 1984), 122.

3. Susan Dunn, *1940: FDR, Willkie, Lindbergh, Hitler—the Election amid the Storm* (New Haven, CT: Yale University Press, 2013), 119; Richard Moe, *Roosevelt's Second Act: The Election of 1940 and the Politics of War* (Oxford: Oxford University Press, 2013), 171.

4. David M. Kennedy, *Freedom from Fear: The American People in Depression and War* (Oxford: Oxford University Press, 1999), 459, 462.

5. Adam Berinsky, *In Time of War: Understanding American Public Opinion from World War II to Iraq* (Chicago: University of Chicago Press, 2009), 99.

6. Robert A. Divine, *Foreign Policy and U.S. Presidential Elections, 1940–1948* (New York: New Viewpoints, 1974), 42.

7. Wendell Willkie, "We, the People: A Foundation for a Political Platform for Recovery," reprinted from *Fortune* magazine, April 1940, Folder: Willkie, Wendell, box 299, Alexander Sachs Papers, Franklin D. Roosevelt Library, Hyde Park, NY (hereafter FDRL); George H. Gallup, *The Gallup Poll, 1935–1971* (New York: Random House, 1972), 228, 231.

8. Gallup, *The Gallup Poll*, 222–23; Republican Platform 1940, 5, Folder: Campaign 1940 Republican Platform 1940, box 159, Wendell Willkie Papers, Lilly Library, Indiana University.

9. On Roosevelt's decision to run again, see Moe, *Roosevelt's Second Act,* 170–97. See also Bernard F. Donahoe, *Private Plans and Public Dangers: The Story of FDR's Third Nomination* (Notre Dame, IN: University of Notre Dame Press, 1965), 195; and Gallup, *The Gallup Poll*, 230, 225.

10. Churchill to Roosevelt, June 15, 1940, in *Roosevelt and Churchill: The Complete Correspondence* (3 vols.), ed. Warren Kimball (Princeton, NJ: Princeton University Press, 1984), 1:49–51.

11. Ibid., 56–57.

12. Memorandum of Meeting, July 25, 1940, folder 22, box 50, Fight for Freedom Papers, Seeley G. Mudd Library, Princeton University; William L. Langer and S. Everett Gleason, *The Challenge to Isolation, 1937–1940* (New York: Harper & Bros., 1952), 749.

13. Memorandum, August 2, 1940, Folder: Navy, Destroyers and Naval Bases, 1940 Part 1, PSF box 62, FDRL.

14. Walter Johnson, *The Challenge against Isolation* (Chicago: University of Chicago Press, 1944), 128; Acceptance Speech, August 17 1940, Folder: Speeches, WLW Acceptance Speech, Etc., box 159, Willkie Papers.

15. Roosevelt to Churchill, August 13, 1940, in Kimball, ed., *Roosevelt and Churchill*, 1:58–59.

16. Press Conference no. 671, August 16 1940, http://www.fdrlibrary.marist.edu/_resources/images/pc/pc0106.pdf; Franklin D. Roosevelt, *The Public Papers and Addresses of Franklin D. Roosevelt,* 13 vols. (vols. 1–5, New York: Random House, 1938; vols. 6–9, New York: Macmillan, 1941; vols. 10–13, New York: Harper & Bros., 1950), 9:391–407.

17. Press Release, September 3, 1940, Folder: Statements by Willkie, 1940, September 1–November 11 and Undated, box 100, Willkie Papers; *New York Times,* September 4, 1940, 16; *New York Times,* September 7, 1940, 8.

18. Gallup, *The Gallup Poll*, 225, 226, 229, 234, 238.

19. On the selective service debate, see J. Garry Clifford and Samuel R. Spencer Jr., *The First Peacetime Draft* (Lawrence: University Press of Kansas, 1986).

20. Henry L. Stimson and McGeorge Bundy, *On Active Service in Peace and War* (New York: Harper & Bros., 1948), 345–47; Roosevelt, *Public Papers and Addresses,* 9:321.

21. Roosevelt to Edward Taylor, August 12, 1940, and Roosevelt to L. B. Sheley, August 26, 1940, in *F.D.R.: His Personal Letters, 1928–1945,* ed. Elliot Roosevelt (New York: Duell, Sloan & Pearce, 1950), 1055, 1058–59.

22. Wendell Willkie, Acceptance Speech, August 17, 1940, Folder: Speeches, WLW Acceptance Speech, Etc., box 159, Willkie Papers; Clifford and Spencer, *The First Peacetime Draft,* 194–96.

23. Willkie, Acceptance Speech, August 17, 1940.

24. Ibid.

25. Neal, *Dark Horse*, 150.

26. *New York Times*, August 20, 1940, 1.

27. *New York Times*, August 30, 1940, 15; Divine, *Foreign Policy and U.S. Presidential Elections*, 49–50, 59.

28. Press Release, October 2, 1940, Folder: Statements by Willkie, 1940, September 1–November 11 and Undated, box 100, Willkie Papers; *New York Times*, October 3, 1940, 19.

29. *New York Times*, September 12, 1940, 14.

30. *New York Times*, September 14, 1940, 1, 10; Pittsburg, Kansas, Press Release, September 16, 1940, Folder: 1940 September 16 Campaign Speeches Kansas, Pittsburg, Coffeyville, box 105, Willkie Papers. For a selection of editorials, see Folder: September 15 1940 Willkie Campaign, box 120, Willkie Papers.

31. Pittsburg, Kansas, Press Release, September 16, 1940, Folder: 1940 Sept 16 Campaign Speeches Kansas, Pittsburg, Coffeyville, box 105, Stockton, California Press Release, September 20, 1940, Folder: 1940 Sept 20 Campaign Speeches California, box 105, and Corona, California Press Release, September 18, 1940, Folder: 1940 Sept 18 Campaign Speeches Arizona, California, box 105, all Willkie Papers.

32. *New York Times*, September 15, 1940, 2.

33. *New York Times*, September 17, 1940, 12, 10.

34. *New York Times*, September 17, 1940, 1, 10; Russell Davenport Memorandum, September 16, 1940, Folder: Willkie, Wendell Campaign, box 89, Sachs Papers.

35. San Francisco, California Press Release, September 21, 1940, Folder: 1940 September 21 Campaign Speeches California, box 105, Willkie Papers.

36. Ibid.

37. *New York Times*, October 3, 1940, 18.

38. Roosevelt, *Public Papers and Addresses*, 9:466–67.

39. *New York Times*, October 18, 1940, 1; *New York Times*, October 23, 1940, 16; Gallup, *The Gallup Poll*, 244–45, 248, 249.

40. For collections of Willkie speeches, see Folder: Hull, Cordell, October 1939–1940, PSF box 74, FDRL; Folder: Willkie Statements, 1940 Campaign, box 6, Samuel I. Rosenman Papers, FDRL; James Rowe to Roosevelt, Folder: War 1940 Draft, PSF box 81, FDRL; and Roosevelt, *Public Papers and Addresses*, 9:485–95, 499–510.

41. Robert Dallek, *Franklin D. Roosevelt and American Foreign Policy, 1932–1945* (New York: Oxford University Press, 1995), 250; Roosevelt, *Public Papers and Addresses*, 9:517, 543, 546; Samuel I. Rosenman, *Working with Roosevelt* (New York: Harper & Bros., 1952), 242; Moe, *Roosevelt's Second Act*, 301.

42. Gallup, *The Gallup Poll*, 239–40, 250, 249, 247.

2

FDR's Closest Contender

Thomas E. Dewey and the 1944 Election

J. Simon Rofe

The 1944 presidential election stands alone as the only election fought since 1940 while the United States was an active belligerent in a war of national survival: the Second World War. In that light, the reelection of the thirty-second president of the United States, Franklin Roosevelt, in November 1944 while millions of Americans were active combatants would seem to have been a foregone conclusion. This is the starting point for David M. Jordan's 2011 *FDR, Dewey, and the Election of 1944*.[1] Yet the vigorous contest between the forty-two-year-old New York governor Thomas E. Dewey and Roosevelt was the closest the incumbent fought as president. Dewey polled almost 46 percent of the popular vote to Roosevelt's 53 percent.[2] While Jordan asserts that the "biggest issue in the campaign was who was better suited to bring the war to a conclusion and handle the issues of peace thereafter," at the time Roosevelt's leading speech writer, Samuel Rosenman, thought differently.[3] He wrote that, outwardly at least, "there seemed to be very little difference between the parties on foreign policy."[4]

In light of this difference of opinion, this chapter will explore the influence of foreign policy on the 1944 presidential election. It will begin by explaining how Dewey's background came to influence his political outlook and therefore his presidential campaign in 1944. It will then identify twin foreign policy influences on the 1944 election. The first and most straightforward was that the United States was a nation, like many others, at war, and this had a huge impact on the campaign. The influence of the war—the main if not sole focus of the Roosevelt administration's foreign policy—was felt by those at home as well as by those in uniform overseas. The second influence was the decision by Dewey not to campaign on the extent of the administration's prior knowledge of the Japanese attack on Pearl Harbor. While the precise level of explicit knowledge was the subject of postwar Senate hearings (and numerous postwar conspiracy theories), Dewey's begrudging discretion, strongly encouraged by US Army chief of staff General George C. Marshall, limited the scope of his ability to critique the administration and its prosecution of the war. Marshall counseled that campaigning on Pearl Harbor would alert the Japanese to US success in decrypting the Japanese "Purple" code at time when Japan was far from defeated. The extent to which such a critique would have landed a mortal blow to Roosevelt's reelection in 1944 can only be a matter of conjecture. What cannot be doubted is that Dewey's decision to heed Marshall's concern removed from the Republican's arsenal a weapon to damage Roosevelt. Dewey's discretion helps illustrate, in the words of the historian Gaddis Smith, "a man of integrity, almost compulsive competence, and considerable insight into himself and others." Smith concludes: "He would have been a good President."[5] Given the twin influences outlined above and discussed in depth in the pages that follow, the chapter draws the conclusion that foreign policy inescapably contributed to the 1944 presidential campaign and its outcome. Importantly, too, the 1944 election, exemplified by the Marshall correspondence, hints at broader discussions of the US role in the world and the fusing of what were once considered "foreign" and "domestic" matters in the concept of "national security." This phenomenon would come to define to a greater extent the influence of foreign policy in the elections after 1944.

Thomas E. Dewey's Political Education

That Thomas Dewey contested the 1944 presidential election against Roosevelt was itself a remarkable achievement. Dewey—the first candidate born in the twentieth century—had emerged from a politicized contest in the Republican Party to win the nomination on the first ballot at the convention in Chicago in late June.

Dewey's triumph in Chicago reflected a hard-nosed dedication to the task at hand. He was known as a fighter from his days as New York City's special prosecutor for organized crime (1936–1938), his success as an Eastern equivalent of Chicago's Elliot Ness (he secured seventy-two of seventy-three prosecutions) having given him a national profile "second only to Lindbergh" by the time he was in his mid-thirties.[6] His repeated critique of domestic New Deal legislation and opposition to US involvement in international affairs meant that he was an early contender for the 1940 Republican nomination, with *United States News* predicting in April of that year that he was "the probable nominee."[7] However, his youth and the increasing prospect of US involvement in the war in some capacity diminished his chances.[8] Importantly for the 1944 election, Dewey successfully managed to drop "at least to all outward appearances . . . any semblance of isolationism." As will be seen, this would have implications for a campaign in which the slogan "politics should stop at the 'water's edge'" was often deployed.[9] Before then, Dewey recovered from the adversity of missing out on the 1940 nomination, as he would after his devastating 1948 defeat, to orchestrate his own reelection in New York and Eisenhower's victory in the 1952 presidential contest. He had won the 1942 New York State governorship handsomely, having lost narrowly to the popular incumbent, Herbert Lehman, in 1938, and would be reelected by record margins in 1946 and 1950 on a platform of fiscal conservatism and the first state civil rights laws in the country. His resilience was to the fore as he arrived in Chicago in June 1944 to accept the Republican nomination. While tame by comparison with contemporary primary contests, the 1944 Republican primaries (March 14–May 19) received greater attention because General Douglas MacArthur was considered a candidate. Although the general did not make any contribution to the primaries (he was then allied commander in the Pacific), his supporters added his name to the ballot, and this served to split the conservative vote.[10]

So what of Roosevelt's attitude to Dewey? While Dewey was a moderate Republican in many regards, FDR was not predisposed to him. A letter to John J. Bennett Jr., the Democratic candidate for the 1942 New York Governorship (a post FDR himself had held between 1928 and 1932), endorsed Bennett over Dewey. FDR wrote: "As a citizen and voter of New York, I express the sincere hope that you and not Mr Dewey will be our next Governor." Revealing his concerns about Dewey, Roosevelt went on to say: "Under you there will be no danger that the long series of enactments of liberal legislation for the benefit of the average citizen during the past three Governorships will be repealed or emasculated."[11] The previous three governors of New York were Roosevelt himself, his longtime friend Herbert Lehman (1933–1942), and Charles Poletti (1942), the latter being the shortest-serving governor in New York State history— just twenty-nine days.[12] That the administration did not hold a very high opinion of Dewey is seen in a memorandum of September 1943 that, in commenting on Republican maneuverings, said the then governor was "a backward child" and that some of the "best political psychologists that Wall Street can pay for, are rapidly educating Dewey politically in manner and substance."[13] Yet, for all these slights, the Roosevelt administration recognized that Dewey would mount a considerable challenge: he was "smart" and an "active, spirited and able campaigner."[14] And so it would prove when it came to the November 1944 contest.

Fighting a War and a Presidential Election

Illinois congressman Everett M. Dirksen described November 1944 as "truly an epic month" with the centerpiece being "a war-time election to test our interest in the process of self-government."[15] Dirksen's remarks reveal a faith in the republic that was shared by vast swathes of the American population, a faith that had been reinforced by the improving fortunes of the UN alliance during the course of 1943 and into 1944. US military victories at Midway, the Coral Sea, and Guadalcanal had accompanied Allied success in Italy, Soviet triumphs at Stalingrad and Kursk, and then the arrival of Allied troops in continental Europe in June 1944.

By the fall of 1944, the people of the United States had largely accepted wartime responsibilities according to British diarist Alistair Cooke.[16] With considerable material costs beyond the emotional burdens of fathers, sons, and brothers as combatants, and without the immediate danger of those in places such as the United Kingdom, the American people were geared toward the ultimate victory of the UN alliance. The 11,623,468 individuals who served in the US military during the course of the Second World War constituted almost 10 percent of the population of 132,165,129, according to the 1940 census.[17] As the majority of these people were drafted, the influence of the federal government had been brought home to every corner of the United States. Indeed, the Selective Training and Service Act, enacted in September 1940, was by 1944 part of the fabric of the nation at war. Equally evident to Americans was the involvement of the federal government in two regards: the first was the collection of federal income taxes, which had become near universal, and the second was the rationing that became part of their lives from 1942.[18] The latter applied to all manner of household goods but perhaps most notably to gasoline. Restricted to four gallons a week in order to preserve the rubber needed for tires as much as the oil needed for fuel, Americans were consistently reminded by the likes of the War Production Board and the Office of Price Administration that they were contributing to the war effort.

While there are numerous examples of local projects to assist the war effort, from Wisconsin dairy farmers to Detroit autoworkers, the reconfiguration of the workforce to include women, younger people, and African Americans was to have profound influences on society that would shape the domestic milieu from which US foreign policy would be made in the years after victory. As such, one can see in the increased levels of federal involvement in the lives of its citizens a precursor to the national security state that, although contested, became part of people's lives in the second half of the twentieth century.

Before then, the 1944 presidential campaign came to life in late September. Since accepting the Democratic nomination on July 20, 1944, Roosevelt had kept to his word to concentrate on fighting the war and not his opponent. He had stated: "I shall not campaign. . . . In these days of tragic sorrow, I do not consider it fitting."[19] Being the political animal that he was, his move was a means of taking advantage of his incumbency while not distracting from the immediate task of leading a nation at war. Nevertheless, it gave Dewey a window to "swing his bat" at the incumbent president as he traveled the nation and made headway in the polls. He questioned Roosevelt's fitness to govern by attacking "the 'tired old men'" who were running the government and "the frequent bickering among members of the Administration" as well as continuing with his well-established critique of the New Deal. "He argued that the 'time for change' had come," Rosenman noted, and, in pointing to his own youth, that "the affairs of government should be turned over to fresh younger and more enthusiastic hands."[20] These attacks were a concern to the administration.

Rosenman recorded that, in the late summer of 1944, Roosevelt "looked more disabled" and that a radio address delivered from the Puget Sound Navy Yard in early August had prompted many "comments" about his delivery "in Washington, New York, and all over—at dinners, at cocktail parties and official conferences."[21]

It was against this backdrop that Roosevelt entered the campaign on September 23 with a skillful address to the Teamsters Union annual dinner in Washington, DC. Rosenman described it as "the greatest political speech of his career—in his most vigorous and effective form."[22] The address would become known as the "Fala" speech, in reference to the President's staunch defense of his dog, Fala. The Republicans had sought to illustrate the government's excesses by accusing FDR of having sent a US naval ship to pick up Fala during the president's later summer tour of the Pacific. FDR skillfully used the case of the Republicans' attack on my "little dog, Fala," to illustrate their preparedness to create falsehoods in the campaign. "Oh, just forget what we used to say, we have changed our minds now," he stated. "We have been reading the public opinion polls about these things and now we know what the American people want."[23] The reception was raucous. A further excerpt addressing foreign policy serves to illustrate why Rosenman was able to describe the speech in the following terms: "The speech was spiced with biting sarcasm, pleasant ridicule, bitter denunciation; but it expressed his deep conviction of the soundness of American democracy, and a fixed determination to keep peace in the world."[24] Roosevelt directly addressed Republican attacks: "Don't leave the task of making the peace to those old men who first urged it and who have already laid the foundations for it, and who have had to fight all of us inch by inch during the last five years to do it. Why, just turn it all over to us. We'll do it so skillfully that we won't lose a single isolationist vote or a single isolationist campaign contribution."[25] The mention of isolationism to his audience was in part tub thumping on Roosevelt's part, but it equally revealed a link to the debate about foreign policy for Americans in understanding their place in the world.

The enthusiastic reaction in the room was replicated in the Democratic Party nationwide: "The Democratic forces were electrified." However, there is some debate as to the galvanizing effect of the speech as the key catalyst to Roosevelt's victory in early November. Richard Norton Smith's sympathetic account in *Thomas E. Dewey and His Times* suggests that the speech animated Dewey to deliver his "most effective address of his campaign," described as "an all-out partisan assault on Democratic pretensions to indispensability," and that this stimulated larger crowds.[26]

The speech was accusatory in content and tone and showed Dewey to be the able campaigner the administration suspected he would be. Dewey began by pointing to Roosevelt's length of service: "Last Saturday night the man who wants to be President for sixteen years made his first speech of this campaign." He then referred back to Roosevelt's own words in accepting his party's nomination: "Forgotten were these days of tragic sorrow. It was a speech of mud-slinging, ridicule and wise-cracks." He continued: "My opponent, however, has chosen to wage his campaign on the record of the past and has indulged in charges of fraud and falsehood. I am compelled, therefore, to divert, this evening, long enough to keep the record straight. He has made the charges. He has asked for it. Here it is."[27] However, Dewey's own reserve intervened—he described it later as "the worst damned speech I ever made in my life"—and he drew back from his animated performance (a reserve that would count against him again in 1948). In contrast, Rosenman's contemporaneous account points to the impact on Dewey, noting that he was "fighting mad, and showed it in his next few speeches by swinging wildly in a way that damaged himself rather than the champ." Rosenman's counsel to Dewey was "that it was the kind of political speech which was so hard to answer that he should simply have ignored it."[28]

Explicit discussions of foreign policy issues were relatively few. Both parties had pledged that politics would stop at the water's edge and largely kept to that pledge. Dewey's individual adherence to that undertaking in relation to Pearl Harbor is discussed in the next section. In light of the pledge, Roosevelt and Dewey each avoided foreign policy during the course of the campaign, bar one exchange on the subject in mid-October. Dewey's reference to foreign policy came in St. Louis, Missouri, on October 18 and was prefaced by his typical stump speech interrogating the New Deal and the effectiveness of the administration given that it was full of "constant bickering, quarreling and backbiting." Dewey asked the voters: "Can an administration which is so disunited and unsuccessful at home be any better abroad? Can an administration which is filled with quarreling and backbiting where we can see it be any better abroad where we cannot see it?" *Time* commented that this was "the kind of talk any voter could understand."[29] And, according to Rosenman, this provided the administration with an opportunity. Believing that Dewey was "hoping to catch what remained of the isolationist vote in the country," the administration decided "to take full advantage . . . in the foreign policy speech."[30]

Importantly, in the campaign of 1944, Roosevelt's speech to the Foreign Policy Association in New York on October 21 was preceded by an act of political acumen that addressed the issue of his health in running for a fourth term and served to illustrate that foreign policy was a consideration in the electoral politics of 1944.[31] Roosevelt delivered his address having spent the day touring New York, campaigning "in the usual partisan sense" with his July pledge not to campaign having expired. In pouring rain, and with the car roof down so that he was visible to all, he visited the Brooklyn army and navy bases to crowds of forty and seventy thousand workers, respectively. He spoke at Ebbets Field in support of the New Deal supporter New York senator Bob Wagner and then embarked on a fifty-mile route through New York traveling at twenty-five miles per hour. Despite the inclement weather, the police believed that over 1.5 million people turned out. While sodden, Roosevelt was in good spirits throughout and, buoyed by "old fire-horse enthusiasm," arranged for repeat performances in Philadelphia and Chicago. *Time* reported: "Two days later, Presidential Secretary Steve Early announced that the President 'did not have even a sniffle.'" The extent to which this tour addressed the concerns about the president's health is perhaps moot, but it was a notable precursor to the Foreign Policy Association speech that evening.[32]

The speech at the Waldorf Astoria saw Roosevelt in fine form.[33] Recounting the entirety of the foreign policy achievements of his administration, he slighted Dewey's "practice of twisting words out of context" and warned of the danger of Republican victories in the Senate that would see the likes of Senator Gerald P. Nye and Senator Hiram Johnson—the latter described as "an old friend"—assume positions such as the chair of the Senate Foreign Relations Committee.[34] "The internationalist-minded audience heartily booed the isolationist names," according to *Time* magazine.[35]

In making a foreign policy contribution to the 1944 campaign, Roosevelt spoke of his hopes for the United Nations. He called on the new organization to be empowered with "authority to act" by the American people: "So to my simple mind, it is clear that, if the world organization is to have any reality at all, our American representative must be endowed in advance by the people themselves, by constitutional means through their representatives in Congress, with authority to act."[36] He then "used a homely illustration" to make his point akin to the "firehose" remarks of December 1940 that had been a precursor to the Lend-Lease agreement of March 1941.[37] According to *Time* magazine: "He did not think, he said, that a policeman would be very effective if, on seeing a housebreaker, he would first have to call a meeting of the town council to get a warrant."[38] The president's conviction was clear: "We are seeking to avert and avoid war." And he was equally adept at speaking as plainly as Dewey had in Oklahoma. "Put this proposition any way you want, it is bound to come out the same way," he commented. "We either work with the other Great Nations, or we might some day have to fight them. And I am against that." He ended his remarks by appealing to the German American vote. He confirmed: "We bring no charge against the German race." Yet he added: "There is going to be a stern punishment for all those in Germany directly responsible for this agony of mankind."[39] Such thinking reflected broader discussions about the postwar world that were still being considered in Washington and among the UN allies more broadly. What it serves to illustrate is that the fate of the US role in the postwar world would be contingent on the outcome of the 1944 election.

Discretion and National Security: The Nonissue of Pearl Harbor

At the time of the 1944 presidential election, Pearl Harbor was not central to the campaign. Importantly for the analysis here, it might have been but for the discretion of Dewey. Its absence from widespread discussion is the focus of this section. The main reason for the nonexistent debate about Pearl Harbor in the 1944 national campaign is the intervention of US Army chief of staff General George C. Marshall and Dewey's reluctant decision to heed the general's counsel not to raise the subject directly.

Ever since the Pearl Harbor attacks, there has been considerable debate about events and interpretations of that infamous day. A revisionist school of historians began work almost immediately on the circumstances leading to the day of "infamy," with Charles A. Beard its most famous exponent.[40] While historians have debated the matter ever since, the subsequent influence of Pearl Harbor on the postwar United States is indisputable. It was, by early 1947, "already a chapter in history," according to George Morgenstern, whose book was the first of a number directly questioning the extent of the Roosevelt administration's knowledge of an attack.[41] Equally, the attack itself played an important scene-setting role in the formation of the national security state that emerged at the outset of the Cold War and in more recent debates about the place of the United States in the world.[42] While the impact of the attacks was mitigated by the immediacy of the ongoing war, the wound of Pearl Harbor would not heal well and scarred the American psyche into the postwar period.

During the course of the war, Pearl Harbor was omnipresent, sporadically grasping the attention of the American people as the matter was aired in Washington. The year 1944 saw a number of such instances, to the extent that *Time* by October referred to the case against the administration as an "oft-made charge."[43] Before then, in the spring, the Republican representative Dewey Jackson Short had called for "immediate justice" to be brought by court-martialing his namesake, General Walter C. Short, the area commander who was criticized along with Rear Admiral Husband E. Kimmel by the Roberts Commission, which examined the circumstances of the attack on Pearl Harbor prior to the November election, or the impeachment of members of the administration.[44] The representative, known to be a strong opponent of Roosevelt and the New Deal and described by *Time* as "obstreperous," argued that the trials should determine "whether any blame for the success of the Japanese attacks could be attached to the secretaries of State, War and Navy, or the President himself."[45] Importantly, given the concern Marshall faced in September 1944, Representative Short claimed: "The courts martial could be held without aiding the Japanese no matter what facts were brought out."[46] Observing Short was Congressman Everett Dirksen. In considering what he termed the "ghost of Pearl Harbor," Dirksen recorded that everyone agreed that General Short and Admiral Kimmel "should have their day in court" but that "a political factor intruded." The matter hinged, according to Dirksen, on whether the case should "come before or after November": "The date was the controversial factor." A measure of resolution was found between the House and the Senate in mid-June, and the date for the courts-martial was set for December 7, 1944. Dirksen pointedly recorded: "*For the moment,* the ghost of Pearl Harbor had been laid." The ghost would not lie down permanently, however. Kimmel's counsel would later suggest that the administration's "inconsistent and dilatory" influence procedure "is a specious pretext to keep the truth of Pearl Harbor hidden from Dec. 7, 1941 to Nov. 7, 1944."[47]

As the congressional session headed toward its end in the fall, there were a number of speeches in Congress on the subject of Pearl Harbor.[48] An address by the Republican Forrest A. Harness on September 11 in particular became the rationale for General Marshall to intervene with Dewey.[49] In criticizing the Roosevelt administration on a broad front, Harness alluded to information he had seen that he claimed exonerated Short and Kimmel.[50] A member of the Military Affairs Committee, and stating his sources "to be thoroughly reliable and trustworthy," Harness may well have had access to restricted information.[51] While he did not disclose sensitive information directly, the inferences to be made from his remarks were clear. For example, he stated: "The Government had learned very confidentially that instructions were sent out from the Japanese Government to all Japanese emissaries in this hemisphere to destroy the codes."[52] Marshall's concern was that Harness's remarks "would clearly suggest to the Japanese that we have been reading their codes."[53] Harness asked pointedly of the administration who in Washington was responsible for the failings in the Pacific: "On whom rests the responsibility for Pearl Harbor if it is not the Commander in Chief? Can the President as Commander in Chief claim credit for all victories and escape responsibility for our defeats?"[54]

Harness's address prompted further discussion among his congressional colleagues on September 21. John McCormack, the Democratic majority leader in the House, denounced Harness for spreading "a vicious and false rumor" and appealed for "nonpartisanship and national unity" in seeking to move beyond the issue. However, Republicans in the House were not satisfied.[55] Ralph Church (R-IL) retorted, quoting from an affidavit stating that the Australian minister to Washington, Sir Owen Dixon, had told members of a dinner party on December 7, 1943, that the Australians had relayed information to Washington about a Japanese task force at sea.[56] Harness's speech and his subtle allusions were instrumental, alongside the subsequent back and forth in Congress and Marshall's approach to Dewey on September 25, 1944.

Prior to Marshall's intervention, and on the eve of launching his election campaign in his September 23 speech, Roosevelt addressed the matter of Pearl Harbor directly, stating: "There would be lots of things like that—referring to charges that information about the Jap naval activity had been submitted to this government in advance of the attack—circulating day and night from now until Nov.7 [Election Day]."[57] Roosevelt's supposition turned out to be largely inaccurate, but, in his public remarks preceding the opening to his campaign, one can see the president steeling himself on the issue, and there is some foundation to Dewey's subsequent skepticism that Marshall's approach was apolitical.[58] Congressmen Dirksen noted at this stage—some six weeks shy of Election Day—that "the ghost of Pearl Harbor rides again."[59]

On September 25, 1944, Marshall approached Dewey by sending a secret letter disclosing information pertaining to Pearl Harbor. The general's care in crafting the approach and the form of his communication illustrate the sensitivity of addressing the issue during the election campaign and while the nation was still at war. Marshall said that he took this unprecedented step of writing to a presidential candidate as he felt that "the military hazards involved are so serious."[60]

Illustrating the gravity of the situation, Marshall consulted with only one other individual as he contemplated his approach to Dewey. That was Admiral Ernest J. King, Marshall's naval counterpart as commander in chief US Fleet. In writing to King, Marshall explained: "The whole thing is loaded with dynamite but I very much feel that something has to be done or the fat will be in the fire to our great loss in the Pacific, and possibly also in Europe."[61] The admiral, who was notorious for giving short shrift to the press and a focus on the Pacific theater, concurred with Marshall's approach.

Marshall then wrote directly to Dewey on September 25. The letter was hand delivered to the governor in a private audience in Tulsa, Oklahoma, by the officer in charge of cryptographic intelligence, Brigadier General Carter W. Clarke. It began with additional conditions indicating the gravity of the matter at hand: "What I have to tell you below is of such a highly secret nature that I feel compelled to ask you either to accept it on the basis of *your not communicating* its contents *to any other person* and returning this letter or not reading any further and returning the letter to the bearer."[62] Dewey was immediately skeptical, refusing to read on, and, according to Clarke, stating: "I am confident that Franklin Roosevelt is behind this whole thing." Dewey's skepticism was reinforced by his observation: "If this letter merely tells me that we were reading certain Japanese codes before Pearl Harbor and that at least two of them are still in current use, there is no point in my reading the letter because I already know that." Dewey's own views were clear; he believed that Roosevelt knew "all about it": "He knew what was happening before Pearl Harbor and instead of being reelected he ought to be impeached." He was on familiar ground in criticizing Roosevelt, having titled a chapter of his 1940 book *The Case against the New Deal* "The Insufficiency of the Navy Is the Insufficiency of Franklin Roosevelt."[63] In 1944, the governor sent Clarke on his way referring to "the whole Pearl Harbor mess."[64]

Compelled by the gravity of the situation, Marshall would not let the matter rest. Having received Clarke on the morning of the September 27, he redrafted his letter for the governor, asking Clarke to travel to meet Dewey again (then back in Albany, New York). The redraft began by addressing directly Dewey's concerns that he was being requested to keep a secret before turning to the question of the president's involvement. "I am trying my best to make plain to you that this letter is being addressed to you solely on my initiative," Marshall wrote, continuing: "I am persisting in the matter because the military hazards involved are so serious that I feel some action is necessary to protect the interests of our armed forces." The forceful, even plaintive tone of Marshall's words were followed by an acknowledgment that there was no opportunity for them to meet in person without being "subject to press and radio reactions as to why the Chief of Staff of the Army would be seeking an interview with you at this particular moment."[65]

Having framed his letter in such a fashion, Marshall termed the substance "the military dilemma." He recounted the endeavors of the military's code breakers, who since 1940 had been using the Japanese codes to learn not only about Japanese operations but also about events in Europe through Baron Ōshima, the Japanese ambassador to Berlin.[66] Marshall stated: "Our main basis of information regarding Hitler's intentions in Europe is obtained from Baron Oshima's messages from Berlin reporting his interviews with Hitler and other officials to the Japanese Government." In recounting the use of the information gleaned from the Japanese in the Pacific theater—by William Donovan's Office of Strategic Services, by General Eisenhower in Europe, and in conjunction with the British in the Atlantic—Marshall sought to illustrate the importance of these intercepts. "You will understand from the foregoing the utterly tragic consequences if the present political debates regarding Pearl Harbor disclose to the enemy, German or Jap, any suspicion of the vital sources of information we possess." He ended: "I am presenting this matter to you in the hope that you will see your way clear to avoid the tragic results with which we are now threatened in the present political campaign."[67]

Dewey remained unconvinced. "Why in hell haven't they [the Japanese] changed them [the codes]," he rhetorically questioned, "especially after what happened at Midway and the Coral Sea?" He gave Clarke equally short shrift. When he received Clarke, he stated that he was not prepared to continue reading the letter without consulting his trusty speechwriter, Elliott V. Bell. This necessitated a telephone call to Marshall, and, although it is clear that Dewey and Marshall spoke, there is no record of the precise nature of their words, beyond Marshall acceding to Dewey's request. Having read the letter, with Bell, he stated: "Well, Colonel, I do not believe that there are any questions I want to ask you nor do I care to have any discussion about the contents of the letter." According to Clarke, Dewey had "no message he wished to give to Marshall."[68] With this succinct statement, the direct correspondence between the Republican candidate and the most senior soldier in the US Army ended. Pearl Harbor was not an issue in the 1944 election. Dewey did adhere to Marshall's counsel. The general later noted: "There was no further mention of Pearl Harbor, as I recall, during the campaign."[69] His recollection was not wholly correct, given the remarks of Republican representative Melvin J. Maas of Minnesota in a speech in St. Paul in late October, but Marshall was accurate insofar as the issue drew no mention from the candidates.[70] It is worth considering that Dewey's decision not to press the matter also reflected his understanding that the American people who were potentially fatigued by the four official investigations into Pearl Harbor prior to Election Day in 1944.

As a postscript, it is worth considering the care that Marshall gave to explaining his correspondence with Dewey to then President Truman in the fall of 1945. Rumors emerged in September 1945 of Marshall's communications with Dewey, and the general, who was still chief of staff, wrote to Truman explaining that there was "a very heavy pressure from

the press and others for the release of the letter or some statement by me."
Marshall was keen to avoid this scenario, citing the fact that the letter referenced Admiral King and Great Britain. There was disagreement on how
to proceed. Truman, who would later make Marshall first his secretary of
state and then his secretary of defense, suggested to him that he disclose
the letters "to the press for tomorrow," adding: "It will stop all the dema-
gogues." Marshall failed to heed the advice and, rather than putting the
letters in the public domain, instead sent the correspondence to Admirals
Stark and Leahy (chief of staff to the commander in chief, 1942–1949).[71]

Marshall's reluctance to make this correspondence public came to
an end six weeks later. Army chief of staff Marshall was called to appear
in front of the Joint Committee on the Investigation of the Pearl Harbor
Attack. For three days (December 6–8, 1945), over the four-year anniversary of Pearl Harbor, Marshall was quizzed on his responsibilities in the
events leading up to the December 7 attacks. Preceding the public hearings of December 7, 1945, the committee held an executive meeting on
Marshall's letters to Dewey. Over his objections, Marshall was requested
to commit the correspondence to the record after a "minority argued vigorously for complete release and the committee ultimately agreed."[72] Marshall duly obeyed, and the letters were subsequently published widely in
the press. In December 1945, perhaps justifying Dewey's judgment that
the American people did not have a great appetite to reexamine Pearl Harbor at the time, the response to the committee, including the disclosure of
the letters, was a notable indifference.[73]

Conclusion

"Suppose the warning had been received and heeded? Suppose Pearl Harbor had not occurred? There might have been no declaration of war. What
would have been the course of our destiny? Futile speculations of course
but interesting."[74] These "futile speculations" posited in a congressman's
diary remained just that, but the what-if consequences of these speculations would have made for a very different election in 1944—an alternate
landscape for Philip Roth's *The Plot against America*.[75]

The outcome of the election of 1944 could indeed have been different;
and as such this chapter concludes that foreign policy was an inescapable
factor in the 1944 campaign and its outcome. The significance emerges

in two contrasting ways: one self-evident, the other a matter of discretion. First, the United States was at war, millions of Americans were in the armed forces, and millions more were undertaking roles to supply the Allies with war materiel to overcome the Axis threat. Foreign policy issues that would become ensconced in national security policy by the time of the next presidential election were increasingly important parts of the American people's thinking. The onset of the Cold War and the arrival, albeit unexpectedly, of a bipartisan consensus on foreign policy meant that the 1944 election was the last in which the issue of national security was absent. In its place was a contested understanding of "national interest." Roosevelt's conviction, bordering on arrogance, that as president he was its guardian meant that he did not campaign for reelection. In retrospect, we can see that that conviction denied Dewey the opportunity for a prolonged campaign in which the contender might have landed a greater number of blows, blows that the president may have found hard to rebuff. In the era before the "perpetual campaign," however, the incumbent president held perhaps an even greater advantage by setting the parameters of the campaign, and Roosevelt knew well how to exploit political advantage.

Of course, national security might have been a factor in the 1944 election as the second and unheralded influence of foreign policy had there been discussion of the Roosevelt administration's knowledge of Pearl Harbor. Dewey's decision to heed Marshall's counsel in the national interest meant that disclosure of the administration's prior knowledge did not emerge until the hearings of 1945–1946 and was therefore not a factor in November 1944. While the 1944 election was the closest contest Franklin Roosevelt fought, the potential impact on the overall result is a matter of speculation. Nonetheless, the postwar investigations illustrated that the military at Pearl Harbor was underprepared. and if this, and Roosevelt's duplicitous character, had become clearer at the time, the matter could well have undermined the thirty-second president. It is clear that, in 1944, "the full history of Pearl Harbor had yet to be written."[76]

Thomas Dewey has been described as "the century's closest might-have-been President."[77] It is perhaps, then, with no little irony that the serving president who attended his funeral in March 1971 was Richard Nixon, another politician who arguably failed to realize his full potential despite, in his case, attaining the highest office. Nixon, who had called on Dewey's advice for over twenty years on Capitol Hill and in the White

House and was due to meet him on the day he died, described Dewey as "a great patriot, a distinguished statesman, and a fine human being."[78] As such, Dewey's influence on the American presidency and the foreign policy that followed did not end with his failure to dislodge Franklin Roosevelt in November 1944 or, as the next chapter will explore, with his more celebrated failure to overcome Harry S. Truman in 1948.

Notes

1. David M. Jordan, *FDR, Dewey, and the Election of 1944* (Bloomington: Indiana University Press, 2011).
2. While the Electoral College vote was 432–99 in Roosevelt's favor, perhaps more revealing was the popular vote in New York State, from which both candidates hailed. It was a fiercely partisan campaign in which Dewey and the Republicans gained more votes than Roosevelt and the Democratic Party (2,987,647–2,478,598), but votes for the American Liberal Party and the American Labor Party were counted as being for Roosevelt, which gave him a 52.31 to 47.30 percent victory (3,304.238–2,987,647). Notably, Dewey won in Roosevelt's home county, Dutchess County, and the home town of the new vice president, Harry S. Truman, Independence, Missouri.
3. Jordan, *FDR, Dewey, and the Election of 1944*, x.
4. Samuel Rosenman, *Working with Roosevelt* (New York: Harper & Bros., 1952), 481.
5. Gaddis Smith, review of *Thomas E. Dewey and His Times* by Richard Norton Smith, *Foreign Affairs* 61, no. 2 (1982/83): 469.
6. Dewey recounts his battles with organized crime in Thomas E. Dewey, *Twenty against the Underworld* (New York: Doubleday, 1974).
7. Quoted in Justus Doenecke, *Storm on the Horizon: The Challenge to American Intervention, 1939–1941* (Lanham, MD: Rowman & Littlefield, 2000), 158.
8. Dewey's anti-interventionist supporters in 1940 included Progressive elements such as Colonel Theodore Roosevelt Jr. and Californian senator Hiram Johnson. See ibid., 417.
9. Rosenman, *Working with Roosevelt*, 481.
10. That MacArthur was being discussed in relation to the 1944 election can be seen in a September 1943 memo for the president reporting that "Dewey and MacArthur were names most favorably mentioned" and that Dewey would "by kind words for MacArthur" offer him "Secretary of War or Vice President in charge of war." Unsigned Memorandum, September 7, 1943, PSF Thomas E. Dewey, Franklin Roosevelt Presidential Library, Hyde Park, New York.
11. "To suggest that my support of you is formal and lukewarm is an untruth. I want to make perfectly clear that I meant what I said—that you are without any question the best qualified of all the candidates for the Governorship." Franklin D.

Roosevelt to John J. Bennett Jr., October 23, 1942, *The American Presidency Project,* http://www.presidency.ucsb.edu/ws/?pid=16182.

12. Lehman resigned to take up the post of director of foreign relief and rehabilitation operations for the State Department, before becoming director-general of the UN Relief and Rehabilitation Administration in early 1943. Poletti would go on to be a special assistant to Secretary of War Henry L. Stimson addressing racial integration in the armed forces while being integral to the reconstruction of postwar Italy. See Andrew J. Williams, "'Reconstruction' Before the Marshall Plan," *Review of International Studies* 31, no. 3 (2005): 541–58.

13. Unsigned Memorandum, September 7, 1943, PSF Thomas E. Dewey, Franklin Roosevelt Presidential Library.

14. Rosenman, *Working with Roosevelt,* 471.

15. Everett McKinley Dirksen, "Epic November," *The Congressional Front,* October 28, 1944, Dirksen Center, http://www.everettdirksen.name/guides_emd/Dirksen_Newsletters/Congressional%20Front%2010.28.44.pdf. Dirksen captured the faith that many of his countrymen had in the United States after almost four years of war: "Self-government is the art and the right of selecting those who shall make, enforce and interpret the laws under which we live. Those laws are the rules of the game we call 'living.' Its development took thousands of years. Its vitality depends on the intelligent use of the ballot. Let us use it."

16. Alistair Cooke, *The American Home Front, 1941–42* (London: Penguin, 2006).

17. "By the Numbers: The US Military," National World War II Museum, New Orleans, LA, http://www.nationalww2museum.org/learn/education/for-students/ww2-history/ww2-by-the-numbers/us-military.html.

18. Geoffrey Perrett, *Days of Sadness, Years of Triumph: The American People, 1939–1945* (Madison: University of Wisconsin Press, 1985).

19. Franklin D. Roosevelt, Address to the Democratic National Convention in Chicago, July 20, 1944, *American Presidency Project,* http://www.presidency.ucsb.edu/ws/?pid=16537.

20. Rosenman, *Working with Roosevelt,* 471. When confronted in 1940, when he was thirty-seven, by the issue of his youthfulness, Dewey responded: "Well greybeard though we be, we must insist that a man of 37 is not a child. Alexander Hamilton became Secretary of the Treasury at 32; Napoleon was crowned Emperor at 35; William Pitt the Younger 24 when became Prime Minister." Thomas E. Dewey, *Why Dewey Wins: The Career of Thomas E. Dewey as Seen by the American Press* (N.p.: Thomas E. Dewey Committee, 1940).

21. Rosenman, *Working with Roosevelt,* 462.

22. Ibid.

23. Franklin D. Roosevelt, Address at a Union Dinner, Washington, DC, September 23, 1944, *American Presidency Project,* http://www.presidency.ucsb.edu/ws/?pid=16563.

24. Rosenman, *Working with Roosevelt,* 471.

25. Roosevelt, Address at a Union Dinner.

26. Geoffrey C. Ward, review of Richard Norton Smith, *Thomas E. Dewey and His Times* (New York: Simon & Schuster, 1982), *New York Times Book Review,* August 22, 1982, 1.

27. Thomas E. Dewey, "We Must Have Integrity in Our Government," Acceptance Speech Delivered in Oklahoma City, OK, September 25, 1944, http://www.ibiblio.org/pha/policy/1944/1944-09-25a.html.

28. Rosenman, *Working with Roosevelt,* 478.

29. "Is It Honest?" *Time,* October 23, 1944, 23.

30. Rosenman, *Working with Roosevelt,* 482.

31. The issue of FDR's health and its influence as a campaign issue in 1944 is discussed in Frank Costigliola, *Roosevelt's Lost Alliances: How Personal Politics Helped Start the Cold War* (Princeton, NJ: Princeton University Press, 2012). See also Jordan, *FDR, Dewey, and the Election of 1944.*

32. "Ovation in the Rain," *Time,* October 30, 1944, 13.

33. Franklin D. Roosevelt, Radio Address at a Dinner of the Foreign Policy Association, New York, NY, October 21, 1944, *American Presidency Project,* http://www.presidency.ucsb.edu/ws/?pid=16456.

34. Rosenman, *Working with Roosevelt,* 495.

35. "U.S. at War: Dinner at the Waldorf," *Time,* October 30, 1944, 14.

36. Roosevelt, Radio Address at a Dinner of the Foreign Policy Association.

37. Franklin D. Roosevelt, Press Conference, December 17, 1940, *American Presidency Project,* http://www.presidency.ucsb.edu/ws/?pid=15913.

38. "Dinner at the Waldorf," 14.

39. Roosevelt, Radio Address at a Dinner of the Foreign Policy Association.

40. The work of Charles A. Beard is well-known in this regard. His *American Foreign Policy in the Making, 1932–1940: A Study in Responsibilities* (New Haven, CT: Yale University Press, 1946) and *President Roosevelt and the Coming of the War, 1941: A Study in Appearances and Realities* (New Haven, CT: Yale University Press, 1948) meticulously curate the evidence in support of the case that Roosevelt orchestrated US involvement in the Second World War. James P. Philbin's account of Beard's career captures well Beard's revisionism. See James P. Philbin, "Liberal Foe of American Nationalism," *Humanitas* 13, no. 2 (2000): 90–107. Others in the postwar era would follow Beard's lead. See, e.g., Charles C. Tansill, *Back Door to War: The Roosevelt Foreign Policy, 1933–1941* (Chicago: Henry Regnery, 1952).

41. George Morgenstern, *Pearl Harbor: The Story of the Secret War* (New York: Devin-Adair, 1947), vii–xi.

42. For consideration of the impact of Pearl Harbor on twenty-first-century conceptions of US national security, see John Lewis Gaddis, *Surprise, Security, and the American Experience* (Cambridge, MA: Harvard University Press, 2004).

43. "U.S. at War: Dec. 7 to Nov. 7," *Time,* October 30, 1944, 18.

44. The Roberts Commission, the first of eight official hearings into Pearl Harbor, reporting on January 23, 1942, predominately blamed the local area commanders, Admiral Kimmel and General Short, who were both relieved of their duties. The

National Security Agency account of Pearl Harbor can be found on its official Web page:https://www.nsa.gov/about/cryptologic-heritage/center-cryptologic-history/pearl-harbor-review/investigations.shtml. It inaccurately dates the Roberts Commission as concluding on December 23, 1942.

45. "U.S. at War: Why?" *Time*, June 19, 1944, 23.

46. Tom Reedy, "New Move to Courtmartial Kimmel, Short Impeachment Threat to Cabinet Heats Implied in House," *The Bee* (Danville, VA), May 12, 1944, 2.

47. "Dec. 7 to Nov. 7," 18 (emphasis added).

48. Dirksen recorded one speech by Representative Hugh D. Scott (R-PA). See Everett M. Dirksen, "Ghost of Pearl Harbor," *The Congressional Front,* September 23, 1944, Dirksen Center, http://www.everettdirksen.name/guides_emd/Dirksen_Newsletters/Congressional%20Front%2009.23.44.pdf.

49. In his September 27 letter, Marshall would write: "A recent speech in Congress by Representative Harness would clearly suggest to the Japanese that we have been reading their codes." Larry I. Bland and Sharon Ritenour Stevens, eds., *"Aggressive and Determined Leadership," June 1, 1943–December 31, 1944,* vol. 4 of *The Papers of George Catlett Marshall* (Lexington, VA: George C. Marshall Foundation, 1996), doc. 4-530, http://marshallfoundation.org/library/collection/marshall-papers/volume4-aggressive-and-determined-leadership/#!/collection=332.

50. In 1944, *Time* stated: "One thing was now certain: the famed Roberts report on Pearl Harbor issued in January 1942 did not tell the whole truth." "Dec. 7 to Nov. 7," 18.

51. Harness, *Congressional Record,* September 11, 1944, quoted in Beard, *President Roosevelt and the Coming of the War,* 279.

52. *Congressional Record,* 78th Cong., 2nd sess. (1944), 90:7649.

53. Bland and Stevens, eds., *"Aggressive and Determined Leadership,"* doc. 4-530.

54. Harness, *Congressional Record,* September 11, 1944, quoted in Beard, *President Roosevelt and the Coming of the War,* 279.

55. Beard, *President Roosevelt and the Coming of the War,* 283.

56. Dirksen, "Ghost of Pearl Harbor."

57. Beard, *President Roosevelt and the Coming of the War,* 288.

58. Republican representative Melvin J. Maas of Minnesota repeated the charge of presidential and administration culpability in late October, claiming "that they had six hours' notice of the time & place for the attack, but did not warn the Army & Navy in Hawaii." "Dec. 7 to Nov. 7," 18.

59. Dirksen, "Ghost of Pearl Harbor."

60. Bland and Stevens, eds., *"Aggressive and Determined Leadership,"* doc. 4-530.

61. Ibid., doc. 4-525.

62. Ibid., doc. 4-526.

63. The thrust of the book—whose chapter titles included "Roosevelt Must Go"—was clearly to support Dewey's presidential aspirations. See Thomas E. Dewey, *The Case against the New Deal* (New York: Harper & Bros., 1940).

64. Bland and Stevens, eds., *"Aggressive and Determined Leadership,"* doc. 4-526.

65. Ibid. The extent of Marshall's conviction is evinced in the redrafted letter of September 27 by the insertion of a number of adjectives. For example, instead of "I should have preferred," the September 27 version read "I should have much preferred."

66. See Carl Boyd, *Hitler's Japanese Confidant: General Ōshima Hiroshi and MAGIC Intelligence, 1941–1945* (Lawrence: University Press of Kansas, 1993).

67. Bland and Stevens, eds., *"Aggressive and Determined Leadership,"* doc. 4-530.

68. Statement for the Record of Participation of Brig. Gen. Carter W. Clarke, GSC in the Transmittal of Letters from Gen. George C. Marshall to Gov. Thomas E. Dewey the Latter Part of September 1944, Record Group 457, Studies on Cryptology, SRH-043, National Archives, College Park, MD.

69. Bland and Stevens, eds., *"Aggressive and Determined Leadership,"* doc. 4-530.

70. "Dec. 7 to Nov. 7," 18.

71. Larry I. Bland and Sharon Ritenour Stevens, eds., *The Finest Soldier, January 1, 1945–January 7, 1947,* vol. 5 of *The Papers of George Catlett Marshall* (Lexington, VA: George C. Marshall Foundation, 1996), doc. 5-235, http://marshallfoundation.org/library/collection/marshall-papers/volume5-the-finest-soldier/#!/collection=333.

72. Ibid., doc. 5-290.

73. The US Senate record notes: "The Pearl Harbor investigation never piqued the public interest like other notable Senate inquiries." US Senate, Joint Committee on the Investigation of the Pearl Harbor Attack, http://www.senate.gov/artandhistory/history/common/investigations/PearlHarbor.htm.

74. Dirksen, "Ghost of Pearl Harbor."

75. The novel plots an alternate outcome to the 1940 election, with FDR losing to Charles Lindbergh. See Philip Roth, *The Plot against America* (Boston: Houghton Mifflin, 2004).

76. "Dec. 7 to Nov. 7," 18.

77. Smith, review of *Thomas E. Dewey and His Times,* 469.

78. Richard Nixon: Statement on the Death of Thomas E. Dewey, March 16, 1971, *American Presidency Project,* http://www.presidency.ucsb.edu/ws/?pid=2939.

3

Containing Challenges

The Triumphs of Harry Truman in the Presidential Election of 1948

Michael F. Hopkins

The presidential election of 1948 is famous for being a great upset, epitomized by the headline of the early edition of the *Chicago Daily Tribune* on November 3: "Dewey Defeats Truman." Harry Truman, of course, won the election; and he joyfully posed with this edition of the newspaper as he celebrated his victory. The editorial was not as inept as it now seems. Polls favored Truman's Republican opponent, Thomas Dewey. Many Democrats did not expect Truman's victory—the Harvard historian Arthur Schlesinger described himself as "somewhat stunned" by the outcome.[1] A printers' strike made the task of producing a paper after the polls closed a major headache.[2]

The substantial literature on 1948 is characterized by a focus on the surprising outcome and has frequently placed an emphasis on the plucky performance by the president. Most studies have concentrated on the various domestic components in the result. This pattern was set when, soon after the election, journalists tried to account for the failure to predict Truman's victory. The *New Republic* attributed the result to the continued support of the Democratic candidate by the coalition of groups built up by Roosevelt: "Harry Truman won because Franklin Roosevelt had worked so well."[3] Samuel Lubell in the *Saturday Evening Post* narrowed this down to one particular part of this coalition. He declared: "[Given] the closeness of the 1948 election, the German-American swing can definitely be credited with giving Truman his margin of victory."[4] Journalists wrote the first book-length studies: Jules Abels in 1959 and Irwin Ross in 1968. Their titles convey an emphasis on the significant contribution of Truman.[5] A substantial article by Richard S. Kirkendall in a major edited study followed these.[6] The first major academic studies appeared in the 1990s—the volumes by Harold I. Gullan and Gary A. Donaldson. These were followed by the works of Zachary Karabell and David Pietrusza. Andrew E. Busch's study was published in 2012, and Thomas W. Devine's assessment of Wallace's role in the election appeared in 2013.[7] The main themes of these studies were the unexpected victory, Truman's role, and the various domestic ingredients in his success.

Foreign policy did not feature very prominently in any of these studies—even though the campaign played out in a year that was highly significant for America's role in the world. Cold War divisions began to solidify as the year witnessed the Communist coup in Czechoslovakia, the passage of the Marshall Aid Program, the onset of the Berlin blockade, and the opening of talks on a North Atlantic pact. It also saw the emergence and American recognition of the state of Israel and the continuing collapse of Kuomintang (Nationalist) forces in China despite substantial sums of US aid. In 1974, Robert Divine corrected this omission with his adept two-volume study of presidential elections and foreign policy from 1940 to 1960. He identified the limited focus on foreign affairs of Truman and Dewey during their campaigns and argued that Truman's victory institutionalized a Cold War policy that endured for the next two decades.[8] In the more than forty years since these volumes were published, new sources have become available, and we are able to see the issues and the individuals in a different light. But there has been no new study of the role foreign affairs played in the election campaign and the impact of Truman's victory on American foreign policy.

This chapter reexamines the connections between the presidential election and American foreign policy in 1948. First, it profiles the four candidates: Harry Truman, the Democratic Party incumbent; Thomas Dewey, the Republican Party challenger; Henry Wallace, the former vice president and commerce secretary and founder of the Progressive Party; and Strom Thurmond, the southern Democrat advocate of states' rights.

Second, it sets these candidates in the context of American foreign policy and how it impinged on ordinary Americans. Third, it considers the place of foreign affairs in the campaign strategies and actual campaigning activities of the four contenders and the significance of foreign policy in determining the election result. Finally, it analyses the consequences of Truman's triumph. Did it make a substantial impact on US foreign policy?

The Candidates

President Harry Truman sought election in 1948 in especially unusual and overlapping international and domestic circumstances. Although he was the incumbent, he had not been elected. Above all, he had to act in the shadow of Franklin Roosevelt, who had been elected four times, initiated the New Deal, led the country in war, and sought to establish the foundations for postwar peace and prosperity, only to die on the eve of military victory in April 1945. Truman lacked the physical appearance of Roosevelt, who looked like a president. While FDR displayed elegance in speech, Truman had a plain-speaking style and delivered his remarks with the cadences and accent of a Missourian.

When he assumed the presidency, Truman was largely unknown nationally, having served as vice president for only three months at the time of Roosevelt's death. But he had a stronger and more determined character than seemed apparent to observers in the early months of his administration. The writer John Gunther met Truman at a dinner party organized by the foreign affairs editor of the *Washington Post*. Gunther produced a memorable thumbnail sketch of his encounter: "He circulated around in as comfortable, unpretentious and agreeable a manner as could be." He added: "He was lively and animated. . . . I had the impression of bright grayness. . . . His conversational manner is alert and poised. He talks swiftly, yet with concision."[9] Those who worked with him knew that he had a keen sense of duty and was energetic, tenacious in his focus on issues, and decisive. His approval ratings reached 87 percent in June 1945 in the aftermath of the end of the war with Germany but sank by November 1946 to 34 percent. They rose again in May 1947 to 65 percent but were low once more in April 1948 at 36 percent.[10] These poor figures and other doubts about Truman's leadership and electability led to a movement to find someone else to be the Democratic Party's candidate. In March 1948, President Franklin D. Roosevelt's two sons, Elliott and Franklin Jr., proposed Dwight D. Eisenhower, who had been supreme commander of the Allied invasion of France in 1944, but Eisenhower resisted efforts to enlist him. Supreme Court justice William O. Douglas also rebuffed efforts to make him the nominee. When the Democratic national convention met in July, there was no realistic alternative to Truman. His riveting acceptance speech of July 15, 1948, removed any doubts among delegates as he laid out a positive vision while launching a partisan attack on the Republicans. It was an early intimation of the bravura style he would deploy as he campaigned.[11]

The 1948 acceptance speech revealed that Truman had a clear political outlook. He embraced government activism in pursuit of many New Deal ideals and spelled out the efforts he would make in a second term to tackle the need for better health care, educational provision, and housing. On July 26—eleven days after the speech and following Congress's blocking of attempts at a legislative solution—he issued Executive Order 9981, instructing the military authorities to desegregate the armed services.[12] But he could be tough on labor unions—he threatened to seize control of the railways when their union voted to strike in 1946. Moreover, fewer liberals formed part of his cabinet. Truman's inclination to take a clear and robust line was most evident in foreign affairs, where he developed a tough policy toward the Soviet Union. This outlook proved popular but alienated many who had worked closely with Roosevelt.

The chief challenger to Truman and the Republican candidate for president was Thomas Dewey, whose narrow loss to Roosevelt in 1944, the slimmest since 1916, had gained him credit for running a well-organized campaign. Dewey, who was eighteen years younger than Truman, possessed a rich voice that served him well in court but was a cautious, rather cold individual whose legendary self-control seemed mechanical. He never succeeded in winning the affection of the members of the press who followed his campaign—unlike the more engaging Truman.[13] One scholar has noted three weaknesses evident in Dewey's career up to 1947. He appeared to lack "the imaginative creativeness—almost the reckless optimism—requisite to inspire confidence." In addition, he seemed incapable of thinking or acting in ways much beyond what he interpreted as current public opinion. Finally, and possibly his greatest handicap was his "inability to project his concern for people as individuals."[14] Eben Ayers, Truman's assistant press secretary, was not an objective observer, but two days before the polls he tried to reflect honestly in his diary. He concluded: "The Dewey personality and campaign has not been one to attract voters. He is not liked—there is universal agreement on that. I have repeatedly asked individuals, newspapermen and others, if they could name one person who ever said he liked Dewey, and I have not found one to say 'yes.'"[15]

Dewey faced competition for the nomination at the Republican national convention in June 1948 from Senator Robert Taft and Harold Stassen, the former governor of Minnesota. As the son of President William Howard Taft and a politician known as "Mr. Republican" for his staunch commitment in the 1930s to the party causes of isolationism and opposition to the New Deal, Taft was the more serious challenger. Dewey won on the third ballot, even though he showed himself more liberal than many in his party: he refused to adopt the virulent anticommunism of many Republicans and even rejected the suggestion that the American Communist Party should be banned. In debating the issue with Stassen, he declared: "I am unalterably, wholeheartedly, and unswervingly against any scheme to write laws outlawing people because of their religion, political, social or economic ideas. . . . [I]t is immoral and nothing but totalitarianism itself." He achieved the nomination partly because he projected the most impressive national profile of the candidates, appearing to be a better vote getter than Taft, whose foreign policy views were not shared by Stassen or Senator Arthur Vandenberg, the leading Republican advocate of a bipartisan foreign policy. Dewey's success was also partly because his campaign team was far better organized than those of his competitors.[16]

Two further candidates stood for president. The first was motivated by the desire to pursue a different foreign policy; the second was principally driven by domestic concerns but used anti-Communist rhetoric, showing that even such long-standing constitutional issues as states' rights were entangled with Cold War considerations.

The former Democrat and third-party candidate was Henry A. Wallace, a serious-minded plant geneticist, author, lecturer, social thinker, firm advocate of civil rights, and Russian speaker who turned sixty in October 1948. He was a popular figure who was sometimes accused of being a dreamer. Wallace was the last of FDR's New Deal politicians still in Truman's cabinet. According to John Morton Blum, Truman kept him so as "to appease the restless liberal intellectuals and labor leaders." Wallace slowly learned that "he was just a symbol," for Truman did not intend to heed his counsel.[17] Blum sums him up: "Never gregarious, he was uncomfortable alike in smoke-filled rooms and noisy halls. Shy but candid and sometimes blunt, he lacked small talk. He detested both the manipulation of men and the prolonged conniving it demanded. He learned to campaign but his speeches, while often effective, made only clumsy concessions to the harmless blarney that ordinarily punctuated political oratory."[18]

Wallace's candidacy was rooted in his opposition to Truman's foreign policy. On September 6, 1946, Secretary of State James F. Byrnes gave a carefully publicized speech in Stuttgart committing the United States to helping to rebuild the western zones of Germany whether or not the Soviets agreed. He also said that American troops would remain in Germany beyond the eighteen months originally envisaged at Yalta/Potsdam. Byrnes ended this major speech by implicitly warning the Soviet Union: "We do not want Germany to become a satellite of any power. Therefore, as long as there is an occupation army in Germany, American armed forces will be part of that occupation."[19] Six days later, Secretary of Commerce Henry Wallace gave a speech in New York that was critical of the increasingly tough attitude toward the Soviet Union adopted by Byrnes. Truman had originally approved the speech without reading it carefully. But Byrnes was furious at its criticism of his policies and threatened to resign. Not wanting to lose his secretary of state, Truman decided instead to compel Wallace to resign on September 20.[20] Although the decision was partly political, it also reflected the shift from the cooperation with Moscow that Wallace advocated. Wallace decided to take his alternative vision of the US role in the world to the American electorate by declaring his candidacy for the presidency in December 1947. As a vehicle for his campaign, he created the New Party. At its convention on July 23, 1948, he secured the nomination of the party, which the delegates agreed to rename the Progressive Party.[21]

Liberal Democrats who backed Truman's tough policies toward the Soviets became concerned that Wallace might persuade other liberals in the party to turn against the president's stand. In January 1947, various liberals met at the Willard Hotel in Washington, DC, to found a new group, Americans for Democratic Action (ADA), that aimed to advance the liberal cause while freeing the democratic Left from Communist manipulation. Those attending included Eleanor Roosevelt and Franklin Roosevelt Jr., the theologian Reinhold Niebuhr, the politician Hubert Humphrey, the journalists Stewart Alsop and Elmer Davis, and the academics John Kenneth Galbraith and Arthur Schlesinger.[22]

The fourth candidate for president was J. Strom Thurmond, another rebellious Democrat who entered the race to defend the southern states against what he regarded as the depredations of the federal government. Aged forty-five in 1948, he was a vigorous attorney who had fought bravely in Normandy with the Eighty-Second Airborne Division, returning to be elected governor of South Carolina in 1946. A profile in the *Louisville Courier-Journal* described him as not being a typical race hater; rather, he was disturbed by social change. Thurmond castigated the Fair Employment Practices Committee (introduced by Roosevelt in June 1941 to ensure that there was no discrimination in the employment of workers in defense industries on the basis of race, creed, color, or national origins and retained in 1945 by Truman), regarding it as "communistic." He claimed that racial integration of the armed services was "un-American." He was a member of the southern Democrats, the "Dixiecrats," and he eventually joined the Republicans in 1964. He had originally backed Truman in 1947, but by March 1948 he led a delegation of southern governors to see Senator J. Howard McGrath, chairman of the Democratic National Committee, to object to the president's plans for civil rights laws. After Thurmond and his Dixiecrats had failed to prevent the convention from adopting a strong platform of civil rights measures, they met and formed the States' Rights Democratic Party. They chose Thurmond as their presidential nominee, yet it was never entirely clear whether they considered themselves a separate party or still a part of the Democratic Party.[23]

Foreign Policy in National Debates

By 1948, the dominant foreign policy concern was the growing tension in US-Soviet relations. The Truman Doctrine speech to Congress in March 1947 inaugurated the policy of *containment,* a term coined by the diplomat George Kennan in a July 1947 article.[24] The Marshall Plan aid program, designed to help Europeans rebuild their war-torn economies and thereby resist the rise of communism, passed into law in April 1948. In

February and March 1948, Communists seized control of the Czechoslovak government. The US ambassador to Czechoslovakia, Laurence Steinhardt, reported to Washington on February 26 how the Communists had "browbeaten and exercised a degree of duress on President Beneš strikingly similar to methods employed by Hitler in dealing with heads of state."[25] On March 10, the foreign minister, Jan Masaryk, was found dead below the window of his foreign ministry apartment. Truman told Congress that the Communist takeover symbolized the "increasing threat to governments who grant freedoms to their citizens." He requested the reintroduction of selective service and a program of universal military training lasting one year aimed at producing a sizable reserve. The Selective Service Act was signed into law on June 24, 1948.[26]

June 1948 also saw a major crisis over Berlin. In 1945, Germany had been divided into American, British, French, and Soviet zones of the occupation; and Berlin had been similarly divided into four occupation sectors. The progressive breakdown of cooperation between the four powers led to increasing economic collaboration between the three Western powers in Germany and, by 1948, to plans to build from their zones a separate West German state. When they decided to introduce a new currency into their zones and also into their sectors in Berlin, the Soviets imposed a blockade on all road, rail, and water routes out of Berlin. The Western powers agreed to remain united against this threat and responded with an airlift of supplies to Berlin.[27] The Berlin blockade only confirmed the fears of West Europeans and the Truman administration and, in July, hastened the beginning of projected talks on a North Atlantic security pact.

The Truman Doctrine, outrage at Communist action in Czechoslovakia, the Marshall Plan, a resolute commitment to the Berlin airlift, and even the unprecedented prospect of an entangling alliance with the West Europeans enjoyed the support of the Republicans, though some in the party had reservations. Taft, for example, questioned the scale of US assistance through the Marshall Plan.[28]

Democrats and Republicans also shared a concern about the threat of communism within the United States. Republicans had taken the lead in acting on their anxieties in this area. The House of Representatives' Un-American Activities Committee (HUAC), chaired by J. Parnell Thomas (R-NJ), became especially interested, after 1946, in investigating allegations of Communist influence in American society. Wallace on the left of politics and Dewey on the right showed a dislike for Red baiting. Yet the Truman administration also developed mechanisms for scrutiny that suggested a greater readiness to pursue Communists in the United States. In an executive order of March 22, 1947, Truman established loyalty boards in government agencies. This arose from the Temporary Commission on Employee Loyalty set up in 1946, and it followed the practices of the Attorney General's List of 1942 when FDR was president. In theory, it had legal safeguards against unfair process, but, in practice, the evidence was frequently withheld from the accused on grounds of secrecy. Truman introduced the boards to demonstrate his commitment to preventing Communist influence in government. By the end of his presidency, the government had dismissed some twelve hundred officials, and a further six thousand had resigned, yet not one spy or saboteur was uncovered. During the presidential campaign, Truman went even further: he authorized the prosecution of eleven leaders of the Communist Party whose convictions were later upheld by the Supreme Court. They were sentenced to five years in prison.[29]

Two other foreign policy issues featured in 1948. The first was the emergence of Israel as an independent state. In May 1948, the British surrendered their mandate over Palestine, accepting defeat in their attempts at finding a solution to the competing claims of Arabs and Jews for the future of the territory. Zionist Jews immediately declared the creation of the state of Israel. Over the course of the next sixteen months, there followed a war between the forces of Israel and the Arab armies of Jordan, Lebanon, Syria, and Egypt before a series of cease-fires that left most of the former Palestine as Israeli territory. Following the strong advice of his special counsel, Clark Clifford, but going against the position taken by Secretary of State George C. Marshall, Truman decided on May 15 to grant recognition to the new state of Israel, only hours after its creation.[30] Both Dewey and Wallace endorsed the president's decision, while Thurmond paid no significant attention to the matter.

There was no such harmony on the second foreign policy issue. A civil war had raged in China since 1945 between the Kuomintang government of Chiang Kai-shek and the Communists led by Mao Zedong. Truman tried to bring the two sides together, asking George Marshall, recently retired as army chief of staff, to undertake a mission to China to try and find a solution, but it proved a frustrating experience.[31] Marshall concluded that there was little point in further US aid, for the Nationalists were losing and were doing so because of poor performance.[32] This was not welcome to the so-called China lobby of mainly Republican supporters of Chiang. Truman commissioned a second mission, this time by General Albert C. Wedemeyer, army chief of plans and operations and former commander of US forces in China. Wedemeyer reported to the president on September 19, 1947, recommending significant American assistance to the Kuomintang. But Truman was unconvinced.[33] While Wallace accepted Truman's position and Thurmond paid little attention to the issue, Republicans disapproved, but the intensity of their disapproval was not great.

All these issues mattered to the American people. A Roper poll revealed that 49 percent of respondents regarded the foreign threat as their major worry and 30 percent identified domestic problems.[34] A poll in April 1948 asked about the most important issues facing the nation: 38 percent of those polled identified the need to prevent war, 27 percent stressed foreign policy, and 9 percent focused on domestic concerns. Another poll in July recorded 44 percent of respondents citing foreign policy as their most important concern while 23 percent identified the cost of living. In addition, 62 percent of those polled supported Truman's commitment to greater global engagement while 30 percent were opposed.[35] The domestic counterpart to the tensions with the Soviet Union—the fear of Communist infiltration—also preoccupied electors. A May 1948 poll saw 67 percent approval for banning Communists from holding civil service jobs.[36]

The Campaign

Such was the atmosphere, foreign and domestic, in which the presidential campaign took place. The campaign ran for a much shorter period than is usual today in the early twenty-first century. Indeed, Truman and Dewey embarked on serious politicking only in September. Truman's campaign was concentrated in the period between Labor Day in September and Election Day in November. The personalities and talents of the candidates were evident in the style and effectiveness of their campaigns and were important in shaping the result.

Truman largely followed the advice of a memorandum submitted to him by Clifford in November 1947. Although Clifford gave the memorandum to the president, it was actually written by James Rowe, a lawyer who had served as an administrative assistant to FDR.[37] It suggested that Truman should campaign around liberal measures. To win he needed to carry the West, and to do that he needed to embrace liberal policies. The memorandum identified the tensions with the Soviets as offering a political advantage because Americans tended to back the president in moments of crisis—and relations with Moscow would probably worsen in 1948. So the president should emphasize his resolute foreign policy but also demonstrate how the administration had kept the country on the road to peace, not war. Since the people associated Marshall rather than the president with foreign policy, Truman must do more to assert his leadership in this field in the eyes of the nation.[38] Rowe and Clifford also praised Truman for outflanking possible Republican criticism of the administration for being soft on domestic communism through its creation of the loyalty boards. This proved shrewd advice, which the president largely followed, to his advantage. In August 1948, Clifford sent Truman another memorandum on election strategy that repeated most of the recommendations of November 1947. It again stressed the need to pursue a liberal agenda in domestic affairs so as to rally the various elements of the New Deal coalition.[39]

As the campaign unfolded, Truman continued in the feisty vein of his July acceptance speech. In an address on March 17, he had declared: "I do not want and will not accept the political support of Henry Wallace and his Communists."[40] He emphasized his major asset—his role as a national leader in a time of crisis. In his campaign speeches in September—October, he never mentioned Wallace or Thurmond by name. He never criticized or ridiculed Dewey in a personal way.[41] He also embarked on the last real whistle-stop speaking tour of the country. In his memoirs, he claimed to have traveled thirty-one thousand miles and to have given 350 speeches.[42] In the speeches, he launched fierce attacks on the "do nothing" Republican-dominated Eightieth Congress, elected in 1946. He spoke sparingly about foreign affairs; and, when he did, he stressed the efforts of the administration toward keeping the world at peace. He praised Republicans for their bipartisan support for these policies but also referred to their high tariff policy and isolationism.[43]

Yet he worried about whether he was doing enough to persuade voters that he wanted to find a peaceful way forward over Berlin. So, when two of his speechwriters broached the possibility of a mission to Moscow by the chief justice of the Supreme Court, Fred Vinson, he welcomed the idea—at least for two days in October. Secretary of State Marshall was privately derisive and opposed the idea, and it seems that Truman also had second thoughts and decided against the scheme.[44] Although the visit to meet Stalin never materialized, the exploration of the idea is an interesting indication of how the president was thinking in the last weeks of the campaign.

Meanwhile, Dewey was crossing the country delivering speeches, buoyed by polls that gave him a healthy lead, and convinced that the momentum lay with the Republicans. Indeed, he succumbed to a dangerous overconfidence. Like Truman, he hardly mentioned his main opponent. In his campaign, he stressed national unity and sought to present a dignified presidential image. His restrained manner seemed partly to point up the contrast with Truman's demagoguery. Polls showed that Americans believed foreign policy to be the most important issue. Yet Dewey did not give that much attention to foreign affairs as he campaigned. This was partly because he supported Truman's basic strategy of containment, though he did criticize it for adopting policies that were too Eurocentric. When the Berlin crisis developed, he also backed the administration's response. Prominent Republicans such as Vandenberg and John Foster Dulles encouraged him in this approach. As his biographer observes: "Hemmed in by his own association with bipartisan foreign policy, and cautioned steadily by Dulles and others against saying anything that might undermine the confidence of America's allies in the forthcoming administration, [Dewey] held back from attacking policies which he, in any case, largely supported."[45]

Only on China did Dewey challenge Truman. On June 25, 1948, Dewey said that "one of the cardinal principles of his administration, if elected, would be to help China combat Communist influences within its borders." He accused the president of providing inadequate aid to Chiang's forces. He returned to the issue on September 30, when he spoke of the "tragic neglect of our ancient friend and ally China."[46] But China never became a central issue in his campaign.

Wallace's campaign could hardly have been more different. It began back in December 1947, long before Truman or Dewey started campaigning, and Wallace put foreign policy at the center of his appeal to the voters. His April 1948 *Toward World Peace* encapsulated his vision of international cooperation. He attacked the Truman Doctrine as "negative and militaristic." He also disagreed with Truman on the exclusion of Communists from American life. These views resonated with many liberals. But he did not handle his campaign in an effective way. J. Samuel Walker believes that it "highlighted the weaknesses rather than the strengths of his cold war critique": "His rhetoric was shrill and dogmatic, and his analysis of American diplomacy, particularly in the cases of the Czech coup and the Berlin crisis, demonstrated a lack of balance and careful reasoning." Wallace evinced too great a readiness to trust the Soviets while showing a stark skepticism about US intentions. His "strident and polemical tone" made him appear to have adopted "the temperament of a zealot." The Marshall Plan contained the very principles he favored, but he hesitated to endorse it, at first waffling about it, then denouncing it as a device of Wall Street financiers and referring to it as the "Martial Plan." His analysis of the situation was rooted in "a simplistic conspiracy theory rather than a thoughtful consideration of the ultimate implications of the growing collaboration between the armed services and big business for the American economy and foreign policy." His repeated focus on the need for a strong United Nations failed to recognize the weakness of the organization and the reticence of both the United States and the Soviet Union to place it at the center of efforts to settle major issues. Too much of his central foreign policy program depended on an institution that lacked the ability to accomplish his goals.[47]

Wallace's campaign provides another reason why foreign policy was not significant in shaping national debates and influencing the electorate. The one candidate who wished to place it at the heart of his appeal did such an unconvincing job of challenging the international policies of the Truman administration. The manifest limitations of Wallace as a campaigner made it difficult for his case to sway voters. But he also faced determined and well-organized opposition from a group made up of the very liberals he would have expected to support his cause. The anti-Communist ADA argued that containment was consistent with the ideals of Franklin Roosevelt and launched a major drive to promote this view. In December 1947, the ADA published a widely distributed pamphlet, *Toward Total Peace,* mainly written by Arthur Schlesinger, that called Wallace's proposed policy toward the Soviet Union an "irresponsible gamble" and depicted Wallace as a gullible idealist who had been fooled by the Communists. The ADA also produced a more populist pamphlet describing Wallace as a *Batboy for Reaction,* suggesting that votes for him and his party would divide the liberal vote and allow deeply conservative individuals to win election. These efforts proved very effective, leading many liberal Democrats who had been sympathetic to notions of the Popular Front to turn against Wallace and support the Marshall Plan and the increasingly anti-Soviet policies of the Truman administration—and to vote for him as president in November.[48]

Many scholars also emphasize the hostile circumstances that Wallace encountered. His biographer maintains: "Wallace fell victim to an atmosphere of rabid and frequently irrational fear of communism." The "country became increasingly unreceptive to his message of hope for a century of the common man and faith in the willingness of the Soviet Union to cooperate with the United States."[49] Certainly, the dramatic reemergence of the issue of the internal threat from communism hurt his campaign. Two former Communists testified before HUAC: on July 30, Elizabeth Bentley spoke about Communists serving in government positions; and, on August 3, Whittaker Chambers named the former State Department official Alger Hiss. They claimed that some had also spied for the Soviets, though they did not accuse Hiss of espionage at this point. In a press conference on August 5, Truman casually dismissed the claims by agreeing with a reporter that the spy scare was a "red herring."[50] Yet Truman had taken a leading role in encouraging a tough attitude on the issue of the loyalty of government officials. As Patterson explains: "If [J. Edgar] Hoover [of the FBI] and HUAC were the villains of the anti-Communist drama, Truman and his advisors clumsily—and sometimes recklessly—acted as spear carriers."[51]

The fourth and final candidate had an even less significant national impact. Indeed, he never managed to attract a genuinely national constituency: his appeal lay with southern voters sympathetic to states' rights. Thurmond's campaign was hectic and driven by a candidate who refused to listen to his advisers. His running mate was also a very reluctant campaigner, the campaign had limited funds, and it never developed a clear idea of its own identity. Moreover, there was a question of whether the States' Right Democratic Party was a separate party or part of the Democratic Party as it focused principally on resisting Truman's civil rights measures as an intrusion into the legal rights of the states.[52]

Foreign policy, consistently identified by voters as their most important concern, did not feature prominently in the campaign. Since Dewey agreed with most of Truman's Cold War initiatives, there was no serious discussion of America's place in the world and challenge to the outlook adopted by the president and his senior advisers. Wallace's dissent from this consensus never succeeded in attracting attention beyond a narrow constituency of liberals. So Truman gained in popularity as the leader facing Soviet threats to US policy. American policies seemed to be working, from Marshall Aid to the Berlin airlift.

Truman's Victory

Truman's victory was a great surprise because he mostly lagged in the polls. In January, he led Dewey 49 to 43.5 percent, but, by April, the margin was 42 to 50.5. Throughout the spring and summer, he remained at 41–42 percent, while Dewey polled 53–54 percent. Yet there was a late shift—an October 20 poll gave Truman 44 percent and Dewey 50. Most observers did not deem this single poll to be significant.[53] In the election on November 2, Truman polled 24.1 million votes, 49.5 percent of the votes, and took twenty-eight states, gaining 303 Electoral College votes. Dewey polled 21.9 million votes, 45.1 percent, and took sixteen states, gaining 189 Electoral College votes. Wallace and Thurmond were close on the popular vote—1.1157 million (winning no states) and 1.1175 million (winning four states—Alabama, Louisiana, Mississippi, and South Carolina), respectively. But the vagaries of the electoral system produced very different outcomes for the Electoral College. Thurmond secured 39 votes, while Wallace gained none at all. The turnout of 53 percent was the lowest since 1924 and the winning margin the narrowest since 1916. Truman's success spread to his party in the congressional elections. In the Senate, the Democrats won 54 seats to the Republicans' 42. In the House of Representatives, the Democrats won 263 seats to the Republicans' 171.[54]

The Impact of Victory

Victory boosted Truman's confidence. It emboldened him to try to enact his liberal agenda, which he now called the Fair Deal, but Congress again blocked any meaningful legislation. It did, however, endorse his foreign policy. Divine claims that the electoral result consolidated the Cold War as a central facet of America's place in the world: it "marked the institutionalization of the Cold War . . . [and] the end of meaningful dissent on foreign policy, as the two major parties imposed a Cold War consensus which was destined to prevail for nearly two decades." He adds: "Representatives of the same special interests he [Truman] denounced on domestic issues were the men in charge of his foreign policy. Wall Street bankers and corporation lawyers such as Robert Lovett, James Forrestal, Averell Harriman, and John Foster Dulles continued to manage the bipartisan policy." The presidential election of 1948 "failed to offer the American voter choices and alternatives in the crucial area of foreign policy; all he could do was ratify the policy of containment or throw away his vote on the eccentric and unstable Henry Wallace."[55] The latest study, by Andrew Busch, endorses this view: "The most significant long-term policy legacy of the 1948 election was the decisive ratification of containment."[56]

Certainly, the election campaign confirmed the support for containment and the limited appeal of Wallace's alternative vision of American foreign policy. Yet this was clear even before the campaigning was seriously under way. Republicans embraced the main lines of the Truman administration's Cold War policies, which was evident in Dewey's campaign. A Republican presidency would have continued to pursue containment. The electoral result was only part of the institutionalization of Cold War attitudes and policies. The more significant consequence of Truman's reelection was its impact on the Republican Party and its positions on foreign policy. The Republicans were critical of the China policy before November. Even Vandenberg, its chief advocate, had declared that bipartisanship did not apply to China. But Republican opposition intensified in 1949 and became positively hostile when Mao's Communists took control in October. Thereafter, Republicans constantly charged Truman with failing to do enough to support Chiang's forces, which had withdrawn to Taiwan. The new Republican position was partly the product of the collapse and defeat of Chiang's government. More important was its development as a political weapon by a party that felt wounded by its fifth successive defeat in a presidential election.[57]

Conclusion

Truman's success in 1948 was the second of three highpoints in his popularity as president. The first one was in 1945 as the United States emerged as a victor in the Second World War. The final one was at the beginning of the Korean War in June 1950. All three of these periods of public acclaim were linked to American global engagement. The 1948 campaign took place against the backdrop of major crises over Czechoslovakia and Berlin, the passage of Marshall Aid, the opening of talks on a North Atlantic security pact, American recognition of Israel, and the deteriorating position of the American-backed Nationalist government in China. The American people recognized the importance of these developments to their lives. Yet the Truman and Dewey campaigns downplayed foreign policy. Dewey did not question the essentials of Truman's foreign policy because he endorsed most of it. Only on China did he criticize official policies, and even here he was not very assertive. Foreign policy was a central feature of Wallace's campaign, but his message failed to attract voters. Indeed, it seemed simply to confirm the wisdom of the president's policy of firmness in face of Soviet provocations.

Given that the campaign contest featured limited disagreement between Dewey and Truman on foreign affairs, it might seem contradictory to claim that foreign policy was a vital component in Truman's victory. Yet it lay at the heart of his reelection. Voters backed their president as he confronted the crisis over Berlin. They endorsed both containment and the rugged investigations of allegations of domestic Communist activities. Their readiness to accept global engagement marked a major break for US foreign policy from before the Second World War. Since Truman, together with his secretaries of state, Marshall and Acheson, had cultivated this involvement in world affairs, it was natural that the American people should reward its architect. The president benefited from being the national leader at a time of crisis and the principal advocate of a widely supported response. Containing the Soviets proved central to Truman's success in containing the electoral challenge of the Republicans.

Each of these successes contained the seeds of future problems. Republicans accused Truman and Secretary of State Dean Acheson, after October 1949, of "losing" China. In 1950, Republican senator Joseph McCarthy charged the State Department with harboring Communists among its staff. These twin assaults barely halted for the remainder of Truman's presidency. The triumphs of 1948 gave way to an embattled administration and a president who decided not to stand in the 1952 election.

Notes

1. See Arthur Schlesinger Jr. to Averell Harriman, November 11, 1948, box 268, Folder: Schlesinger, Arthur, Jr. 1948–1950, Averell Harriman Papers, Library of Congress, Washington, DC.

2. The official archive of the newspaper has a different headline for that day's newspaper: "Early Dewey Lead Narrow, Douglas, Stevenson Win," *Chicago Daily Tribune,* November 3, 1948. For the circumstances at the newspaper, see Charles Storch, "Dewey Defeats Truman Was 'One for the Books,'" *Chicago Daily Tribune,* May 6, 1984.

3. "It Was Not Magic That Won," *New Republic,* November 15, 1948, 6.

4. Samuel Lubell, "Who *Really* Elected Truman?" *Saturday Evening Post,* January 22, 1949, 15–17, 54, 56, 58, 61, 64.

5. Jules Abels, *Out of the Jaws of Victory* (New York: Henry Holt, 1959); Irwin Ross, *The Loneliest Campaign: The Truman Victory of 1948* (New York: New American Library, 1968).

6. Richard S. Kirkendall, "Election of 1948," in *History of American Presidential Elections, 1789–1968* (4 vols.), ed. Arthur M. Schlesinger Jr. and Fred L. Israel (New York: Chelsea House, 1971), 8:3099–3145.

7. Harold I. Gullan, *The Upset That Wasn't: Harry S. Truman and the Crucial Election of 1948* (Chicago: Ivan R. Dee, 1998); Gary A. Donaldson, *Truman Defeats Dewey* (Lexington: University Press of Kentucky, 1999); Zachary Karabell, *The Last Campaign: How Harry Truman Won the 1948 Election* (New York: Knopf, 2000); David Pietrusza, *1948: Harry Truman's Improbable Victory and the Year That Transformed America* (New York: Union Square Press, 2011); Andrew E. Busch, *Truman Triumphs: The 1948 Election and the Making of Postwar America* (Lawrence: University Press of Kansas, 2012); Thomas W. Devine, *Henry Wallace's Presidential Campaign and the Future of Postwar Liberalism* (Chapel Hill: University of North Carolina Press, 2013).

8. Robert A. Divine, *Foreign Policy and U.S. Presidential Elections, 1940–1948* (New York: New Viewpoints, 1974), 167–276. See also Robert A. Divine, *Foreign Policy and U.S. Presidential Elections, 1952–1960* (New York: New Viewpoints, 1974).

9. Gunther quoted in David McCullough, *Truman* (New York: Simon & Schuster, 1992), 334.

10. Harry S. Truman Presidential Approval, Roper Center, https://presidential.roper.center.

11. On Truman, see Robert Ferrell, *Harry S. Truman: A Life* (Columbia: University of Missouri Press, 1994); McCullough, *Truman;* and Alonzo L. Hamby,

Man of the People: A Life of Harry S. Truman (New York: Oxford University Press, 1995).

12. President's Acceptance Speech, July 15, 1948, Harry S. Truman Papers, President's Secretary's Files, Harry S. Truman Library (hereafter HSTL), http://www.trumanlibrary.org/whistlestop/study_collections/1948campaign/large/docs/documents/pdfs/11-4.pdf#zoom=100; Executive Order 9981, July 26, 1948, http://www.trumanlibrary.org/executiveorders/index.php?pid=869&st=&st1=.

13. McCullough, *Truman,* 670–71.

14. Barry K. Beyer, *Thomas E. Dewey, 1937–1947: A Study in Political Leadership* (New York: Garland, 1979), 288–89, 290, 292–93.

15. Robert H. Ferrell, ed., *Truman in the White House: The Diary of Eben A. Ayers* (Columbia: University of Missouri Press, 1991), 280–81 (November 1, 1948).

16. James T. Patterson, *Grand Expectations: The United States, 1945–1974* (New York: Oxford University Press, 1996), 158; Kirkendall, "Election of 1948," 3115–16; Richard N. Smith, *Thomas E. Dewey and His Times* (New York: Simon & Schuster, 1984), 468–502 (quotation 493); James T. Patterson, *Mr. Republican: A Biography of Robert A. Taft* (Boston: Houghton Mifflin, 1972), 409–17.

17. John Morton Blum, ed., *The Price of Vision: The Diary of Henry A. Wallace* (Boston: Houghton Mifflin, 1973), 39.

18. Ibid., 9–10.

19. For the text of Byrnes's speech, see *Department of State Bulletin* 15, no. 376 (September 15, 1946): 496–501, 500.

20. For the text of Wallace's speech, see "The Way to Peace," in Blum, ed., *The Price of Vision,* 661–69. See also Donald Russell to Byrnes, September 20, 1946, box 13, Folder 8: Paris Peace Conference, James F. Byrnes Papers, Clemson University, Clemson, SC. Russell told Byrnes (who was away in Paris) that propagandists had manipulated Wallace. Harry S. Truman, *Year of Decisions* (New York: New American Library, 1965), 610–15.

21. Kirkendall, "Election of 1948," 3121; Busch, *Truman's Triumphs,* 118.

22. Andrew Schlesinger and Stephen Schlesinger, eds., *The Letters of Arthur Schlesinger Jr.* (New York: Random House, 2013), 17–18.

23. Patterson, *Grand Expectations,* 767; McCullough, *Truman,* 667; Busch, *Truman's Triumphs,* 42–43.

24. "X" [George Kennan], "The Sources of Soviet Conduct," *Foreign Affairs* 25, no. 4 (July 1947): 566–82.

25. US Department of State, *Foreign Relations of the United States* (hereafter *FRUS*) *1948,* vol. 4, *Eastern Europe; The Soviet Union* (Washington, DC: US Government Printing Office, 1974), 738–41.

26. Truman's Special Message to Congress, March 17, 1948, HSTL, http://trumanlibrary.org/publicpapers/index.php?pid=1417.

27. *FRUS 1948,* vol. 2, *Germany and Austria* (Washington, DC: US Government Printing Office, 1973), 908–9, 968–88, 989–93; Lucius D. Clay, *Decision in Germany* (London: Heinemann, 1950), 362–69.

80   MICHAEL F. HOPKINS

28. In a speech on February 12, 1948, Taft attacked the costly foreign schemes to combat communism. See George Eckel, "'Losing of Peace' Charged by Taft," *New York Times,* February 13, 1948, 4.

29. Patterson, *Grand Expectations,* 190–93; Robert J. Donovan, *Conflict and Crisis: The Presidency of Harry S. Truman, 1945–1948* (New York: Norton, 1977), 243, 292–98.

30. *FRUS 1948,* vol. 5, *South Asia and Africa* (Washington, DC: US Government Printing Office, 1978), 972–78; Clark Clifford, *Counsel to the President* (New York: Random House, 1991), 9–15; John Acacia, *Clark Clifford: The Wise Man of Washington* (Lexington: University Press of Kentucky, 2009), 104–9.

31. For a record of Marshall's mission, see State Department, *United States Relations with China with Special Reference to the Period 1944–1949* (Washington, DC: US Government Printing Office, 1949), 127–229, 605–95; and John Robinson Beal, *Marshall in China* (New York: Doubleday, 1970). The latter is a firsthand account by an American journalist sympathetic to the Chinese who was appointed to advise Chinese government officials on US government thinking and American public opinion.

32. Marshall Statement, January 7, 1947, *Department of State Bulletin* 16, no. 394 (January 19, 1947): 83–85.

33. *United States Relations with China,* 766–75. See also Albert C. Wedemeyer, *Wedemeyer Reports* (New York: Holt, 1958), a memoir criticizing Truman.

34. Smith, *Dewey,* 505; Busch, *Truman's Triumphs,* 121.

35. Mildred Strunk, ed., "The Quarter's Polls," *Public Opinion Quarterly* 12, no. 4 (Winter 1948): 754–84, 783.

36. Mildred Strunk, ed., "The Quarter's Polls," *Public Opinion Quarterly* 12, no. 3 (Fall 1948): 530–77, 557, 558, 537.

37. Clark Clifford to Harry S. Truman, Memorandum, November 19, 1947, Clark Clifford Papers, Political File, HSTL, http://www.trumanlibrary.org/whistlestop/study_collections/1948campaign/large/docs/documents/pdfs/1-1.pdf#zoom=100; Busch, *Truman's Triumphs,* 34–35. See also Clifford, *Counsel to the President,* 189–94; and Acacia, *Clifford,* 119–50. Acacia notes that Clifford was "an important member of the campaign team . . . [who] was constantly by Truman's side. . . . Along with George Elsey, he drafted Truman's off-the cuff speeches." Acacia also quotes Clifford's deputy, George Elsey: "The mastermind strategist behind the 1948 campaign was a guy named Harry S. Truman." Ibid., 150.

38. A poll in September 1948 asked who had done most to shape present foreign policy. Marshall gained 43.1 percent and Truman only 9.4 percent. Strunk, "Quarter's Polls" (Winter 1948), 758.

39. Clifford to Truman, Memorandum, August 17, 1948, Clifford Papers, http://www.trumanlibrary.org/whistlestop/study_collections/1948campaign/large/docs/documents/pdfs/1-2.pdf#zoom=100; Clifford, *Counsel to President,* 226.

40. Quoted in Randall B. Woods and Howard Jones, *Dawning of the Cold War: The United States' Quest for Order* (Athens: University of Georgia Press, 1991), 169.

41. McCullough, *Truman,* 667–68.

42. Harry S. Truman, *Years of Trial and Hope, 1946–1952* (New York: New American Library, 1965), 219. Kirkendall suggests 20,000 miles and 250 speeches. Kirkendall, "Election of 1948," 3126. Ross claims 21,928 miles and 275 speeches. Ross, *Loneliest Campaign*, 240.

43. List of Campaign Speeches, November 5, 1948, Charles S. Murphy Papers, box 81, Truman Administration File, HSTL, http://www.trumanlibrary.org/whistlestop/study_collections/1948campaign/large/docs/documents/pdfs/3-1.pdf#zoom=100.

44. Arthur H. Vandenberg Jr. and Joe Morris, eds., *The Private Papers of Arthur H. Vandenberg* (Boston: Houghton, Mifflin, 1952), 456–62; Ferrell, *Truman*, 262–63.

45. Smith, *Dewey*, 505. See also Busch, *Truman's Triumphs*, 128, 138.

46. Leo Egan, "Dewey Gives Plans," *New York Times*, June 26, 1948, and "Dewey Rules Out 'Munich' for Soviet as Way to Peace," *New York Times*, October 1, 1948, 1; "Text of Dewey's Salt Lake City Address," *New York Times*, October 1, 1948, 17; Divine, *Foreign Policy and U.S. Presidential Elections, 1940–1948*, 223, 245.

47. J. Samuel Walker, *Henry A. Wallace and American Foreign Policy* (Westport, CT: Greenwood, 1976), 198–99. See also Hamby, *Man of the People*, 401.

48. *Toward Total Peace: A Liberal Foreign Policy for the United States* (Washington, DC: Americans for Democratic Action, 1947), http://babel.hathitrust.org/cgi/pt?id=wu.89058480070#view=1up;seq=6; *Batboy for Reaction*, box 268, Schlesinger 1948–1950 Folder: Batboy for Reaction, Harriman Papers. See also Hamby, *Man of the People*, 501; and Mark L. Kleinman, *A World of Hope, a World of Fear: Henry A. Wallace, Reinhold Niebuhr and American Liberalism* (Columbus: Ohio State University, 2000), 340 n. 55.

49. Walker, *Wallace*, 201.

50. Hamby, *Man of the People*, 453; [Truman's] Press Conference, August 5, 1948, *The American Presidency Project*, http://www.presidency.ucsb.edu/ws/index.php?pid=13262&st=&st1=; Truman to Walter Hillman, August 13, 1948, cited in Divine, *Foreign Policy and U.S. Presidential Elections, 1940–1948*, 235–36.

51. Patterson, *Grand Expectations*, 190.

52. On Thurmond in 1948, see Joseph Crespino, *Strom Thurmond's America* (New York: Hill & Wang, 2012), 61–84; and Busch, *Truman's Triumphs*, 145–47.

53. Strunk, "Quarter's Polls" (Winter 1948), 767.

54. Patterson, *Grand Expectations*, 162; Busch, *Truman's Triumphs*, 229–30; C. P. Trussell, "Democrats Attain Senate Edge of 12," *New York Times*, November 4, 1948.

55. Divine, *Foreign Policy and U.S. Presidential Elections, 1940–1948*, 276.

56. Busch, *Truman's Triumphs*, ix.

57. On this shift, see David R. Kepley, *The Collapse of the Middle Way: Senate Republicans and the Bipartisan Foreign Policy, 1948–1952* (Westport, CT: Greenwood, 1988).

4

Confirming the Cold War Consensus

Eisenhower and the 1952 Election

Steven Casey

A simple counterfactual exercise provides the best way to draw out the significance of the 1952 election. Just imagine for a moment that the two candidates were not Adlai Stevenson and Dwight Eisenhower but Harry Truman and Robert Taft. In 1951, this scenario would have seemed perfectly plausible. Although Truman's approval ratings were in free fall, dragged downward by the ongoing stalemate in Korea and a series of corruption scandals, he was eligible to run again. The Twenty-Second Amendment, ratified in February 1951, specifically exempted Truman from its stipulations, and, with the vast patronage power of the presidency at his disposal, he might well have been able to manufacture his renomination at the Democratic national convention.[1] He had, after all, risen from political death four years before. And now, with no obvious heir, he initially refused to rule himself out of the running.

On the other side of the partisan divide, Taft seemed set to romp to the Republican nomination. Intensely ambitious to occupy the same position that his father had held between 1909 and 1913, he had been desperately seeking the top job for years. A nearly man at every Republican national convention since 1940, he had used his sweeping 1950 reelection triumph in the Ohio Senate race to jump-start his new presidential bid. Since then, he had done as much as possible to sew up the nomination, solidifying his close relationship with party bosses and securing the support of as many as four hundred delegates to the upcoming convention.[2]

As Truman and Taft surveyed their election prospects, both men reached a rare meeting of minds: they welcomed the chance to run against each other. In October 1951, the president told reporters that he hoped Taft would be the Republican nominee. A few days later, when Taft returned the compliment, his reasoning was revealing. "I don't want this to be a mutual admiration society," Taft explained in a press conference, "but I would like to see President Truman as candidate on the Democratic ticket. We then could go to the country on the real issues between the Republican Party and the Democratic Party."[3]

Put another way, both men reveled in the opportunity to turn the 1952 campaign into a final—and crucial—round of the so-called great debate that had been raging for much of 1951. This debate had been partly triggered by China's massive intervention in the Korean War during the winter of 1950–1951, which at first threatened to result in a major US military defeat and subsequently ensured that the fighting bogged down in a bloody stalemate. For both the Truman administration and its Republican opponents, China's intervention confirmed that the Cold War had now entered a much more dangerous phase, but there was little agreement on how the United States should react.

In the first place, while Truman decided to expedite the implementation of National Security Council Report 68 (NSC-68)—the program to mobilize American military power to deter future acts of Communist aggression—Taft and his conservative allies balked at the cost. They believed that the tens of billions of additional dollars the president proposed to spend on defense would result in an excessive tax burden. They also stressed the impact that NSC-68 would have on the whole American system of government, turning it into a centralized "garrison state" as Washington sent young men into uniform or imposed wage and price controls on workers and businesses. In the second place, while Truman decided that the United States needed to concentrate its power in the Cold War struggle in Europe, Taft and his allies believed that more had to be done to combat Communist China. On this question, Truman's most controversial decision had been to send four additional divisions to bolster the NATO at precisely the time that China was pushing American forces back down the Korean Peninsula. For many Republicans, Truman's decision not only raised a crucial policy question; in the third place, they also worried about the president's constitutional overreach. Truman had already decided to send American boys to fight in Korea in the summer of 1950 without asking for congressional authorization. In the early months of 1951, Senate Republicans challenged his power to send four divisions to Europe without their consent.[4]

Then, to cap it all, Truman decided to fire General Douglas MacArthur from his Korean War command in April 1951. As the charismatic general returned home to a tumultuous reception, Taft and his allies tried to use the opportunity to drive home their attack on Truman's foreign policy. Did the president have the authority to sack such an esteemed military figure, they asked? Certainly, they added, Truman should have heeded MacArthur's advice and sought victory against China in Korea, instead of getting sidetracked trying to bolster NATO. Perhaps, they concluded menacingly, Truman's obvious failings as a leader ought to result in his impeachment.[5]

Had President Truman become the Democratic candidate in 1952, Taft would have relished the opportunity to take these issues to the country. Unlike a contemporary focus-group-driven politician, he truly believed what he said—that the president's foreign policy was fundamentally misguided.[6] Truman's Korean War, Taft repeatedly charged, was little more than a "useless waste." NSC-68, he constantly declared, was corrupting the American polity. And the president's repeated efforts to bypass Congress, he loudly trumpeted, were dangerously skewing the constitutional framework in favor of the executive at the expense of legislative oversight. Even so, Taft was also convinced that strident attacks on the president's foreign policy made for good politics. As leader of the GOP's nationalist wing, he had long been convinced that the party's harrowing defeats in 1944 and 1948 were the fault of Dewey's meek "me-too-ism." The only way for Republicans to win back the White House now, he believed, would be to vehemently oppose the Democrats on every issue. "It is the right and the duty of the Republican Party," he declared, "to point out the mistakes and the unbelievably bad judgment of those who have conducted our foreign policy."[7]

Had Truman been the Democratic candidate in 1952, moreover, he would have doubtless relished the chance to respond in kind. Four years earlier, his stunning surprise victory had been based on a hard-hitting campaign, with numerous savage jibes against his partisan rivals. And now, in private strategy sessions, the White House once again planned to play hardball, jabbing straight back at any effort to exploit foreign policy for electoral gain. "Republican leaders," suggested one presidential aide, ought to be assailed whenever they threatened to fiddle "with our frustrations on Korea by using fake labels and giving us phony prescriptions." They ought to be lambasted whenever they suggested an easy way out of the Korean War in particular or the Cold War in general.[8]

In short, then, had Taft and Truman been candidates in 1952, the nation would have faced a real choice between two conflicting visions. More importantly, had Taft won—and 1952 seemed to be a Republican year, after five straight Democratic victories—then this election would have been "critical" to the future of the nation, rivaling the other great realigning elections of 1860, 1896, and 1932. As president, Taft would almost certainly have sought an immediate end to the Korean War, a massively pared-down, low-cost containment strategy, and a much more restrained presidential role in the making of foreign policy. America's response to the Soviet threat, which was only five years old and still lacked bipartisan support, would have taken a significantly different turn.[9]

Choosing the Candidates

But, of course, neither Truman nor Taft was a candidate, let alone a victor, in 1952. Instead, their place on the ballot was taken by two men who would turn the campaign and its aftermath into a confirming rather than a critical election—one that sought to build on or tinker with current American containment strategy rather than transform or overturn it completely.

Truman bowed out of the race gracefully in March, his popularity eroded by a steady flow of corruption stories, together with the ongoing stalemate of the war in Korea.[10] After a long and painful courtship, he finally threw his weight behind Adlai Stevenson at the Democratic national convention in July. Truman's backing was extremely important in swinging the nomination to the Illinois governor, but Stevenson was slow to show his gratitude. Fearing that too close an association with the unpopular president would be political suicide, he adopted a posture of symbolic aloofness. Rather than base his campaign headquarters in

Washington or New York, as was the custom, he set up shop in Spring-field, Illinois. He then angered Truman by his replacement of the Demo-cratic National Committee chair with his own man, by his reluctance to ask the president to campaign, and by his tepid endorsement of the administration's record.[11]

As a candidate, Stevenson could not have been more different from Truman. Whereas the president reveled in what one Stevenson aide described as "tart or acidulous comments," the governor was an elegant, cerebral figure who spent more time crafting language to sell a positive liberal program than he did getting into partisan scuffles with the oppo-sition. In recent years, he had "embraced a nonpartisan approach to state and local government."[12] Now he was convinced that candidates "for the presidency of the United States in this age and day, should not treat . . . [the electorate] as fourteen-year olds but as adults." Once on the stump, Stevenson therefore tried to turn the campaign into something more than a slinging match. He saw "a great opportunity to educate and elevate" while debating the fundamental issues of the day "sensibly and soberly."[13]

Taft's ejection from the race took longer but ultimately proved much more significant. Although the Ohioan believed that he could win the White House with a slashing partisan indictment of Truman's foreign policy, a group of East Coast moderates was not so sure. They worried that Taft lacked appeal among many swing voters. Even worse, they wor-ried about the consequences of a Taft presidency for America's position in the world. Taft was "backward-looking at home and utterly ignorant of the facts of life abroad," declared one highly influential Republican mod-erate. Yet among party regulars there was no obvious alternative. In the Senate, leading internationalists were all too young or too lacking in cha-risma, while Harold Stassen, the loudest voice outside Washington, was widely viewed as a craven opportunist. Only General Dwight D. Eisen-hower seemed to have a chance of stopping Taft. But Eisenhower had only recently gone to Europe as the first NATO commander. Would he leave his job in Europe? Would he be willing to campaign? Was he even a Republican?[14]

In trying to persuade Eisenhower to run, GOP moderates had a num-ber of advantages. They could rely on his intense ambition and desire for the top job. They could also garner support from a powerful network of political operatives and media luminaries, like Henry Luce, Paul Hoff-

man, and Lucius Clay, who had the know-how and wherewithal to generate grassroots support in the primary campaigns. And above all they
could play on the fact that the general shared their deep distrust of Taft
and the Right.[15]

In early 1951, Eisenhower had arranged a private meeting with Taft
to hear firsthand the senator's foreign policy vision. Before the meeting,
Eisenhower had told his advisers that he would "kill off any further speculation about me as a candidate for the presidency" if Taft agreed to support
America's broad involvement in European security arrangements. But the
talk did not go well. According to Ike, Taft seemed to be "playing politics" with foreign policy and was obsessed with "cutting the president, or
the presidency, down to size." Disturbed by these sentiments, Eisenhower
decided that he would have to run for the top job if this was the only way
to stop the GOP from turning to such an unreconstructed isolationist.[16]

By early 1952, Eisenhower had decided that he was the only person
who stood in Taft's path. From the very start, then, Ike's candidacy was
based not only on the normal hostility toward an opposition incumbent.
Crucially, it also revolved around opposition to the Republican Right and
its sharp attacks on current Cold War strategy.

Indicative of Eisenhower's basic position was his instinctive sympathy
with John Foster Dulles, the GOP's main bipartisan accommodator. In
April 1952, Dulles sent Eisenhower the advance text of an article that he
was about to publish in *Life*. With its attack on the excessive passivity of the
Democrats' containment policy and its call for the "liberation" of peoples
languishing under Communist rule, the article would shape an important
component of Republican rhetoric in the upcoming campaign. Yet, like
Eisenhower, Dulles had much more sympathy for Truman's foreign policy
than did anyone in the Taft wing of the party. Like Ike, he had even held a
formal position in the Truman administration, as a State Department official charged with negotiating the Japanese peace treaty. As such, his critique
was measured and limited. "The administration's policies are not without
good elements," Dulles insisted. "They have evoked a show of national vitality which, even if somewhat ill-directed, has in many ways heartened our
friends and caused the Soviet leaders some concern. In Korea—for all our
failure to deter attack—we did respond nobly when the attack came. President Truman's decision that the U.S. should go to the defense of the Korean
Republic was courageous, righteous, and in the national interest."[17]

Eisenhower on the Campaign Trail

Eisenhower's candidacy therefore derived from two basic principles: a desire to stop the right-wing assault on Truman's Cold War policy and the need to adopt a more moderate critique of the current containment strategy. These were the surface expressions of Ike's initial rhetoric, but beneath lay a sense—shared with Stevenson—that Taft-style isolationism was unrealistic in a modern, increasingly interdependent world. New means of communication like the airplane, radio, and even television meant, both candidates believed, that the United States could neither go it alone nor withdraw to the Western Hemisphere. It needed to project its power globally.

When it came to the mechanics of the presidential campaign, however, Eisenhower's team only partially bought into the notion that modern means of communication were crucial. After the convention, Republican Party staffers, determined to gain the White House for the first time in twenty-four years, decided to leave nothing to chance. This, as one of them boasted, was "the first time that a presidential campaign was planned and put on paper to the last detail."[18] One of their first decisions was how to reach out to the electorate. Some of Eisenhower's advisers believed that the whole nature of political campaigning was undergoing a fundamental shift. "Politics," they wistfully and provocatively argued, "is as subject to change as the times, the weather, or your wife's mind. The old-fashioned rallies are gone. Torchlight parades are a thing of the past. The electronic age has taken the old-time excitement out of politics. The campaign airplane is supplanting the campaign train. Television is supplanting the radio. Even the effectiveness of the campaign pamphlet is diminishing in these days of visual animation."[19]

As the campaign got under way, there was much to be said for this notion. The Republicans would give media consultants a prominent role in their campaign. They also relied quite heavily on polls, which had been made even more "scientific" after the fiasco of Dewey's predicted victory four years before. And, above all, the GOP would use television quite effectively, making sure that there were sufficient funds to produce pithy advertisements and informally staged speeches in a growing crescendo as polling day approached.[20]

All the same, Eisenhower's fall campaign would remain distinctly in the traditional mold. Television and the airplane might now be available, but Ike, like candidates of the recent past, still relied first and foremost on a series of whistle-stop trips across the nation that would take him to no fewer than thirty-seven states by polling day. A team dominated by Emmet Hughes and C. D. Jackson, who had both been borrowed from Henry Luce's empire for the duration, drafted the speeches that the candidate delivered on this journey. Working in New York's Commodore Hotel, these speechwriters faced such enormous pressures—both from the endless throng of well-wishers with their sage advice for winning the election and "the pitiless schedule" of churning out speech after speech—that they jokingly referred to themselves as "Clichés Incorporated." After drafting a new speech, they would pass it on to the so-called College of Cardinals, meaning the senior campaign staff, who read, edited, and sent their work to the campaign train, where it would often go through another round of redrafting and, in some instances, even shredding.

It was here, on the train, that Eisenhower's major campaign effort was undertaken. On board, Sherman Adams was in charge. As Eisenhower's personal campaign manager, Adams was often submerged beneath mountains of minutiae. But he was "a taciturn, hard-bitten professional," renowned for his efficiency, and did everything possible to cater to the working needs of the press: ensuring that texts of speeches were readily available, that the telegram machine worked properly, and that the candidate was available for informal chats. At smaller stops, Eisenhower would deliver his comments informally from the back of the train. In cities like Atlanta and Cincinnati, his cavalcade drove from the station to the auditorium, Ike appearing alongside senior local politicians, smiling and waving, while red fire torches were lit to mark his way. Wherever Ike went, the crowds were always impressive. In Atlanta, he received a ticker-tape welcome; in Cincinnati, an estimated 100,000 lined the roads.[21]

Before setting off on this arduous journey, Eisenhower made it his first order of business to make overtures to Taft, whose support would be vital in the crucial Midwest. On September 12, in Ike's home at Morningside Heights, New York, the two recent rivals reached an understanding. Taft agreed to campaign strongly for the Republican ticket; in return, Eisenhower pledged that, if he won, he would consider nationalist Republicans for official positions and would work hard to reduce taxes. The Democrats immediately dubbed these concessions the "surrender" at Morningside

Heights, but it would not be Ike's last effort to woo the Right. He had already chosen Richard M. Nixon as his running mate, a shrewd decision since Nixon was both an internationalist in foreign policy and a notorious diehard when it came to hunting internal subversives. At the end of September, in a campaign trip to Wisconsin, Eisenhower not only appeared with the much more notorious "red baiter," Senator Joseph McCarthy; he also agreed to delete a passage from his speech praising General George C. Marshall, which, given McCarthy's vicious attacks on Marshall, was widely seen as Eisenhower betraying his old mentor in a bid to buy support from the most extreme wing of the GOP.[22]

Eisenhower's visit to Wisconsin came during one of his whistle-stop tours. Although grueling, these helped the candidate refine his message. Recognizing that theirs was the minority party, GOP publicists had already drafted a plan aimed both at the party's twenty million or so core voters and at an estimated forty-five million "stay-at-homes" who bothered to go to the ballot box only "when discontent stirs them to vote against current conditions." Both groups, party bosses thought, could be won for Eisenhower if he savagely indicted Truman's record in three areas: corruption, communism, and Korea.[23]

Increasingly, Ike and his staff agreed with these conclusions. They thought it necessary to attack the administration on the corruption issue, which seemed likely to capitalize on the growing consensus that the Democrats had become stale and dishonest after twenty years in office. From the outset, they were also determined to indict certain elements of Truman's foreign policy. Eisenhower himself, although leery of making too much of the controversial notion of "liberation," was keen to batter the administration's expensive military mobilization program. In speech after speech, he insisted that the country needed a national security strategy that did not doom it to excessive taxation, cumbersome controls, and eventual economic collapse. Significantly, he also attacked Truman's style of making policy, which, he argued, was far too flaky and inconsistent. The country, he told an audience in Baltimore, had to end the current "stop-and-start planning," which emanated from the government's "swing[s] from optimism and panic." National security, he insisted, required "plan[ning] for the future on something more solid than yesterday's headlines."[24]

When it came to Korea, however, Ike and his advisers remained far more moderate, at least in the first phase of the campaign. True, during

September Eisenhower often spoke about the United States "stumbling" or "fumbling" its way into war. He also linked the conflict's causes to the famous litany of events: the "loss" of China and Secretary of State Dean Acheson's announcement in early 1950 that Korea was outside America's "defensive perimeter" in Asia. And he referred repeatedly to the 117,000 casualties the country had suffered before coming to the inevitable conclusion that it was time for a leadership change at the top.[25]

Yet Ike's rhetoric had another dimension, too. Apart from recommending that South Korea carry more of the burden, Eisenhower offered no panaceas for ending the war and was adamantly opposed to echoing MacArthur's calls for escalation. Despite suggestions from his speechwriters, he was reluctant to repeat the staple charge that the Democrats were the "war party" that had presided during America's past three conflicts. Above all, he was determined to stress the basic legitimacy of the conflict. "I proudly salute the gallant American fight in Korea," he declared in his major foreign policy address in September. "Moreover, I believe that the decision to fight to hold Korea . . . was an inescapable decision."[26]

The problem Eisenhower faced was that such statements hardly set the campaign on fire. In September, he even found himself in the uncomfortable position of receiving praise from his Democratic opponent, Stevenson declaring: "My distinguished opponent has already had occasion to disagree with conspicuous Republicans on foreign-policy issues. He has differed sharply with members of his party who have assailed the American action in Korea to stop and turn back aggression. He has gone further to set himself against the views of important members of his party who have called for enlarging the Korean War. I think he has done us all a service by saying these things."[27]

By this stage, polls revealed that Eisenhower still had a commanding nine-point lead over Stevenson. But senior Republicans, obsessed by Dewey's 1948 defeat, worried that Ike was repeating the familiar mistake of meek "me-tooism." Edgy and nervous, they also reacted to every subtle shift in the popular mood with exaggerated alarm. "There is a great amount of ferment and unrest," the campaign's pollsters recorded at the start of October, and "the trend is generally down. It must be stopped."[28] Agreeing with this gloomy assessment, Eisenhower and his advisers thought that the time was ripe to place the campaign "on another level."[29] Luckily for them, the Korean War provided a perfect opportunity to do so.

The Impact of the Korean War

In early October, the Korean War truce talks, which had dragged on for more than a year with no end in sight, went into indefinite recess. Later that same month, a series of high-profile propaganda tirades by the Soviet delegation at the UN General Assembly session confirmed that diplomacy was at an impasse.[30]

At the same time, the ground war, which had recently been relatively dormant, suddenly flared up. On October 6, the Chinese Communists launched an assault on White Horse Mountain, in the center of the allied line. For ten days, the enemy sent wave after wave against UN positions, failing to dislodge South Korean troops, but inflicting substantial losses. In response, US commanders initiated a series of counterattacks that "resulted in bitter and costly fighting for several inconsequential hills"— so costly in fact that they resulted in nine thousand casualties during the month.[31]

This bloody battle, as the radio broadcaster Albert Warner pointed out to his NBC listeners, "did not sound like an armistice negotiation, it did not look like a police action; it was war." On the Right, the Hearst and McCormick newspapers took the Communist assaults as irrefutable evidence that fifteen months of truce talks had "accomplished nothing except the buildup of the enemy's strength and the waste of American lives." The weekly magazines with a massive circulation agreed, with *Time* leading the way. "Bloodshed in the Hills" and "Then He Was Dead" boomed its headlines.[32] In a story published the day before the country went to the polls, the magazine described what was happening: "In Korea last week there was more dogged, costly, back & forth fighting for Triangle Hill, Sniper Ridge, Iron Horse Mountain. Temperatures dipped below freezing as another wretched winter approached, and this time, with no peace in sight, warm clothing and boots had been distributed early and efficiently. U.S. casualties were sharply up. Latest Defense Department figures listed 122,117 (an increase of 963 in one week). They include 21,377 battle deaths, 88,128 wounded, 10,793 missing, 1,819 known captured."[33]

As the election campaign entered its final phase, many Americans responded to these stories with frustration, dissatisfaction, and even disgust. Whereas in January 1952 only 33 percent had viewed Korea as one of the gravest issues facing the country, by October this figure had shot up to 52 percent. More significantly, as Election Day neared, one poll found that 56 percent of the population had reached the conclusion that "the war in Korea was *not* worth fighting"—a level of disillusionment not recorded since the period after China had first intervened in the war almost two years before.[34]

Informal interviews reinforced the impression that the public was turning decisively against both the war and the party that had led the nation into it. During the campaign, Samuel Lubell, the writer and noted political pollster, conducted numerous grassroots interviews with American voters, and he was in no doubt that Korea was playing a major role. Parents whose sons had been drafted, Lubell wrote, "were bitterly resentful of the [Truman] administration." Although Stevenson tried to change the basic narrative of the campaign by shifting the emphasis to the strength of the economy, even this initiative backfired. As Lubell put it: "Surprising numbers of voters came to resent the prevailing prosperity as being 'bought by the lives of boys in Korea.' The feeling was general that the Korean War was all that stood in the way of an economic recession. From accepting that belief, many persons moved on emotionally to where they felt something immoral and guilt-laden in the 'you've never had it better' argument of the Democrats."[35] Put another way, in 1952, the controversy over the current human cost of the war for once trumped the electorate's normal focus on bread-and-butter domestic issues.

As Election Day neared, the Democrats naturally tried hard to respond. Stevenson had started his campaign trying to emphasize the achievements of the past few years of Democratic rule: the Marshall Plan, NATO, and "building a strong system of military defense" in Europe. On the other side of the world, he had stressed the necessity of fighting in Korea. This, he had argued, had been the defensive dimension of America's task. Once it had been achieved, he had continued, a Stevenson presidency would focus on channeling Asian nationalism in a positive direction, especially by helping newly independent nations with their internal development. "The answer to communism," he had declared in September, "is, in the old-fashioned phrase, good works—good works inspired by love and dedicated to the whole man. The answer to the inhumanity of communism is humane respect for the individual. And the men and the women of Asia desire not only to rise from wretchedness of the body but from abasement of the spirit as well."[36]

Even Stevenson had conceded that this was pretty "visionary stuff," and, as Korea began to top the list of Americans' concerns, he began to replace it with a more impassioned effort to justify the stalemated war. "Every one of us knows in his heart why we have to stand up and fight in Korea," he told a television and radio audience in the last days of the campaign. "We all know that when the communists attacked across the thirty-eighth parallel that was the testing point for freedom throughout the world."[37]

As the campaign came to a climax, Truman also took to the stump in order to deliver a vigorous defense of his record. Meanwhile, back in Washington, the president's advisers undertook a desperate—and revealing—gambit to "do something about the huge casualties reported every week by the Department of Defense." As one reporter discovered, the White House was keen for the Pentagon "to get over to the public the point that the 122,000 casualties mentioned by Republican orators were not all dead; forever lost, and that the majority of the wounded had been returned to duty." On October 8, the military's public information office added a brief explanatory note to its regular casualty list, emphasizing that the overall total included wounded and missing, not just killed. A few days later, an official spokesman on a Pentagon-sponsored television show emphasized that "all casualties were not actually lost—that many returned to duty."[38]

Yet the diplomatic stalemate on Korea, together with the bloody battles on the ground, clearly played into Eisenhower's hands. Here, indeed, was Ike's chance to energize his candidacy and place his campaign "on another level." Eisenhower grasped the opportunity on October 24, in a nationally broadcast speech delivered in Detroit. "In this anxious autumn for America," he began, "one fact looms above all others in our people's minds. . . . One word shouts denial to those who foolishly pretend that ours is not a nation at war. This fact, this tragedy, this word is: Korea." The country, he continued, could not rely on the Truman administration "to repair what it failed to prevent." This task required new leadership. It also needed a "personal trip" by someone with impeccable credentials in war and peace. "I shall make that trip," Eisenhower concluded. "Only in that way . . . [can] I learn how best to serve the American people in the cause of peace. I shall go to Korea."[39]

By common media consent, this simple statement changed the whole dynamic of the campaign. "That does it—Ike is in," reporters immediately told Eisenhower's campaign chief. According to moderate newspapers like the *New York Herald Tribune,* in one sentence Eisenhower had "raised the spirits of men and cast a sudden ray of hope over a scene that has been obscured by uncertainty and doubt." He had tapped into the growing unpopularity of the war, coming up with a formula that, combined with his own enormous prestige, suggested to many voters that he was the one man who could end the bloodletting.[40]

Even at this point, however, Eisenhower did not challenge the basic legitimacy of the Korean conflict.[41] In fact, his pledge to go to Korea was essentially a moderate statement. "The origin of the speech was simple and inexorable in political logic," its author explained later. "It rose from the need to say something affirmative on the sharpest issue of the day—*without* engaging in frivolous assurances and *without* binding the future administration to policies or actions fashioned in mid-campaign by any distorting temptations of domestic politics." In other words, its goal was to place Korea at center stage in the campaign, but without embracing the simple panaceas of escalation so beloved of the Republican Right, and in such a way that a future Eisenhower administration would retain the freedom to maneuver.[42]

On Election Day, this restraint was to prove successful as well as statesmanlike. Across the nation, Eisenhower garnered an impressive 55.1 percent of the vote, compared to Stevenson's 44.4 percent, which translated into an Electoral College victory of 442–89. Vital in this big win was the support of moderates, both independents and registered Democrats. This became clear in the elections for the Eighty-Third Congress, where Eisenhower ran well ahead of the rest of the Republican ticket. Although his coattails were big enough to drag in a twelve-seat majority for the GOP in the House and a single-vote majority in the Senate, some of the most vocal critics of the war had not fared particularly well. Extremists like McCarthy had run far behind Eisenhower. And, significantly, a Truman Democrat, Henry "Scoop" Jackson, easily defeated Harry Cain of Washington State, who had been the most vocal critic of Korea on the floor of the Senate during 1951 and 1952.[43]

Of course, Korea had not been a vote winner for the Democrats. On the contrary, this increasingly unpopular war had helped end their twenty-year hold on the White House. Most close analyses of the result also concluded that the voters had expressed a clear desire for a swift exit from Korea. Nonetheless, Eisenhower's campaign statements had not committed him to a specific course of action. They had merely provided the president-elect with a degree of flexibility that he could use to find a way out of the Korean morass in the less frenzied postcampaign environment.

Eisenhower in Office

Eisenhower's actions during his first months in office demonstrated his desire to distance himself from Taft's conception of American foreign policy. His picks for key national security posts were a case in point. Although he selected a number of well-known businessmen for top positions—men such as Charles E. Wilson of General Motors, who became secretary of defense, and George M. Humphrey of the Mark A. Hanna Company, who became secretary of the treasury—his failure to consult with Taft beforehand created early resentments.[44]

Nor did Taft and his allies think much of Ike's other choices. Someone like C. D. Jackson, the Luce reporter whom Eisenhower appointed as his Cold War psychological warfare adviser, typified the type of East Coast internationalist that the new president preferred to have around. Because Jackson had a White House staff position, he escaped the rigors of a Senate hearing. But others were not so lucky. The main controversy in the early months of 1953 centered on Charles Bohlen's nomination as ambassador to the Soviet Union, a choice the Right hated because of the prominent positions Bohlen had occupied in the Roosevelt and Truman administrations. However, even less contentious appointments, like Dulles as secretary of state or Henry Cabot Lodge as ambassador to the United Nations, did not sit particularly well with nationalists. To compensate, Dulles picked his subordinates with care, bringing on board Scott McLeod, a former FBI agent, whose appointment to oversee internal security was widely seen as a nod to the McCarthyites, and Walter Robertson, whom the China-obsessed congressman Walter Judd had recommended for the position of assistant secretary of state.[45]

Eisenhower's inaugural address offered further evidence of his determination to position himself as an internationalist. Indeed, rather than marking a major break from past policy, the new president seemed more intent on highlighting his differences with the Taft wing of his own party.

True, his references to the vital importance of economic health implied that a cost-cutting reassessment of national security policy would soon be under way. But he also affirmed the importance of collective security, thereby repudiating the Taft wing's go-it-alone approach. And his firm rejection of appeasement suggested that any Korean truce would not be bought with major US concessions.[46]

During the campaign, Eisenhower had often aimed his attacks at the style, rather than the substance, of Truman's decision making. And it was here that he initiated some of the first major changes. The National Security Council (NSC), Eisenhower decreed, would play a much bigger role. Regular weekly NSC meetings would be attended by fully briefed senior advisers, supported by a planning board whose task was to look beyond messy compromises forged by warring departments, and chaired by a president who would take firm control over the decision-making apparatus.[47]

Yet, while Eisenhower's reforms of the NSC system promised a new era of thoroughly debated and well-informed policy choices, they also came with an obvious downside: it took time for these decisions to be reached. "I feel it a mistake for a new administration to be talking so soon after [the] inauguration," the new president recorded in his diary on February 2. "Basic principles, expounded in an inaugural talk, are one thing, but to begin talking concretely about a great array of specific problems is quite another. Time for study, exploration, and analysis is essential."[48]

In its first few months, the new administration therefore launched a lengthy policy review. On the budget, Humphrey and Wilson undertook an intensive effort to make major savings over the next few years, but this predictably ran into opposition from the Joint Chiefs of Staff, who insisted that big cuts would "pose a grave threat to the survival of our allies and the security of the nation."[49] On Korea, Eisenhower and his top advisers moved even more slowly. In December, the president-elect had been exposed to suggestions for escalating the conflict, both from his senior commander in the theater and MacArthur in New York, but he was reluctant to listen to such advice, let alone embrace it. In his first weeks in office, he then faced such a crowded agenda that it was not until February 11 that the NSC first addressed Korea, and then the discussion was confined to the wisdom of launching a relatively small-scale attack around the city of Kaesong. Six weeks later, Eisenhower asked Wilson to assess the cost of a "massive blow" aimed at pushing Communist forces back to the

Korean waist. He also instructed his planning board to reassess all military options. But these directives merely sparked nearly two months of debate, during which time Korean strategy remained in abeyance.[50]

Conclusion

The period between November 1952 and March 1953 did not, therefore, mark a sharp break in US foreign policy. Unlike what would have happened had Taft won the White House, Eisenhower was neither keen to abandon the key elements of the Truman-inspired Cold War consensus nor desperate to move quickly with any smaller changes he thought necessary.

In fact, it was not leadership change in Washington that was most crucial during this period but leadership change in Moscow. In early March, Stalin died. At first glance, even this major event exerted little impact on the slow and deliberate machinery of the Eisenhower administration. Indeed, the president and his secretary of state rejected the notion that a change in Soviet leadership would result in a change in Communist policy. After more than a month of intensive discussions, the president did deliver a speech entitled "The Chance for Peace," which he considered "non-confrontational" in tone. But he called on the new Soviet leadership to undertake concrete actions to demonstrate that it was seizing the "'precious opportunity' afforded by Stalin's death to 'turn the tide of history.'" And even this thin gruel was further watered down by a belligerent Dulles speech two days later that "focused exclusively on containment and deterrence."[51]

Nevertheless, in a roundabout way, Stalin's death was crucial to Eisenhower's unfolding Cold War policy. For a start, it prompted a softening in the Communist position at the stalled Korean War truce talks that led ultimately to the signing of an armistice in July 1953.[52] Then, with the guns silent in Korea, Ike moved to develop his New Look strategy. Although more attuned to the cost of the Cold War than Truman, Eisenhower continued to emphasize the need to contain the Soviets through deterrence. In practice, this translated into a greater emphasis on nuclear weapons in place of expensive ground troops. It also meant getting America's allies to shoulder more of the burden, although here Ike tacked closer to Truman's multilateralism than Taft's unilateralism. Furthermore, by placing allies at the heart of his strategy, he also limited how quickly he could move from pulling back US forces from Europe and Asia; certainly, he would not do so if this meant putting alliance cohesion in danger.[53]

None of these policies sat well with the Republican nationalists. Eisenhower, they grumbled, had agreed to a Korean armistice that sold out Syngman Rhee's dream of uniting the peninsula. The president, they added, had not been serious in seeking to reduce Cold War spending to balance the budget. Even worse, they believed, Ike continued to act as if the president had the dominant, if not sole, voice in the making of foreign policy.

Yet herein lay one of the crucial consequences of Eisenhower's election: nationalist Republican opposition to such policies was remarkably restrained. Before taking office, Ike had been acutely aware of his party's tendency toward fratricide—a tendency exacerbated by spending so long in opposition. Republicans in Congress, he observed, had been so used to a Democrat in the White House that their instinct was to automatically oppose anything that came from the executive branch. "Now that we have a Republican Congress their job is to hold up the hands of the executive departments, but they have not learned that yet. It hasn't become part of their automatic thinking. Their automatic thinking is to tear them down."[54]

In practice, however, because the party had been out of power for so long, even nationalists were prepared to mute their instinctive oppositional traits, not to mention their deep-seated aversion to key elements of Eisenhower's foreign policy agenda. Taft himself performed a valuable service just before succumbing to the illness that would soon kill him. When Senator John W. Bricker introduced a series of amendments that Eisenhower complained would provide "notice to our friends as well as our enemies abroad that our country intends to withdraw from its leadership in world affairs," Eisenhower turned to Taft. At the president's request, Taft agreed to bottle the resolutions up in the Judiciary Committee, giving the new administration time to mobilize effective opposition. Eisenhower used this time to work with Democrats, forging a new bipartisan congressional coalition that would endure, with stresses and strains, for much of the Cold War.[55]

Had Eisenhower not been elected, such a coalition might never have coalesced, but there was an even more significant consequence of both his candidacy and his victory: he prevented a Taft-style challenge to containment from becoming American foreign policy. Although counterfactual reasoning is always fraught with danger, a number of surmises can be made with some confidence. Under Taft, it is unlikely that the Korean War would have been brought to an end without either wholesale US concessions to the enemy or a dangerous escalation of the fighting. It is doubtful that containment would have endured without significant changes aimed at cutting costs, bureaucracy, and even America's relations with its allies. And it is possible that the president might have ceded some of his decision-making responsibilities to the legislature. Under Eisenhower, however, the central components of the Cold War consensus remained safe—certainly far safer than they had appeared to be eighteen months earlier when Truman and Taft had sparred for supremacy.

Notes

1. The amendment was a reaction to Franklin D. Roosevelt's four election victories. It prevented anyone from running for more than two terms as president, except the person holding office at the time of ratification.

2. On the prospects for Taft's campaign, see John R. Greene, *The Crusade: The Presidential Election of 1952* (New York: Lanham, 1985), 86–96; and James T. Patterson, *Mr. Republican: A Biography of Robert A. Taft* (Boston: Houghton Mifflin, 1972), 505.

3. Memo, October 17, 1951, PSF (Political): Taft Folder, box 50, Robert Taft Papers, Library of Congress.

4. *Congressional Record, 1951* (Washington, DC: US Government Printing Office, 1951), 24, 56–58, 94; Patterson, *Mr. Republican*, 475–76; David R. Kepley, *The Collapse of the Middle Way: Senate Republicans and the Bipartisan Foreign Policy, 1948–1952* (New York: Greenwood, 1988), 101–16; Michael Hogan, *A Cross of Iron: Harry S. Truman and the Origins of the National Security State, 1945–1954* (Cambridge: Cambridge University Press, 1998), 100–101, 329, 363–64; Charles R. Gellner, Ellen Clodfelter, and Mary Shepard, "The 'Great Debate' on U.S. Foreign Policy: Hearings and Discussion on the Wherry Resolution" (Washington, DC: Library of Congress Legislative Reference Service, March 12, 1951), 20 (copy in Legislation File: Foreign Resolutions, 82nd Congress, box 295, Tom Connally Papers, Library of Congress).

5. *Congressional Record, 1951*, 4462–64; Drew Pearson, "GOP-MacArthur Friction Noted," *Washington Post*, April 18, 1951.

6. On Taft the conviction politician, see Robert W. Merry, "Robert A. Taft: A Study in the Accumulation of Legislative Power," in *First among Equals: Outstand-*

ing Senate Leaders of the Twentieth Century, ed. Richard A. Baker and Roger H. Davidson (Washington, DC: Congressional Quarterly, 1991), 163–97, esp. 179–80.

7. Robert A. Taft, Speech, March 30, 1952. and NBC Radio Broadcast, June 1, 1952, Speech Material Folder, box 463, Taft Papers. See also "Taft on the Korean War," n.d., Taft Campaign Folder, box 9, Stephen Benedict Papers, Dwight D. Eisenhower Library (hereafter DDEL); and Robert Divine, *Foreign Policy and U.S. Presidential Elections, 1952–1960* (New York: New Viewpoints, 1974), 10.

8. "Some Notes on Republican Campaign Statements regarding Korea," n.d., White House Files, Eisenhower Korean Troops, box 10, David D. Lloyd Papers, Harry S. Truman Library (hereafter HSTL).

9. On "critical elections" and realignment, see James L. Sundquist, *Dynamics of the Party System: Alignment and Realignment of Political Parties in the United States* (Washington, DC: Brookings Institution, 1983). To extend the counterfactual, a Taft presidency would probably have been short-lived as Taft tragically died of cancer in July 1953. But then again, who knows? As Roy Jenkins once observed, in politics "office is normally a preservative," giving new life to politicians who have fulfilled their ambitions. See Roy Jenkins, *Gladstone: A Biography* (New York: Random House, 1995), 231.

10. Eben A. Ayers, Note, March 29, 1952, Politics Folder, box 11, Eben A. Ayers Papers, HSTL.

11. Harry S. Truman, *Memoirs: Years of Trial and Hope, 1946–1952* (New York: Signet, 1965), 561–62.

12. Walter Johnson, ed., *The Papers of Adlai E. Stevenson,* 8 vols. (Boston: Little, Brown, 1974), 4:91; Jeff Broadwater, *Stevenson and American Politics: The Odyssey of a Cold War Liberal* (New York: Twayne, 1994), 76.

13. Johnson, ed., *Stevenson Papers,* 4:viii, 18, 28.

14. Henry Cabot Lodge, "Campaign to Win the Republican Nomination for Eisenhower," n.d., Ann Whitman File: Administration Series, Lodge Folder, box 23, Dwight D. Eisenhower Presidential Papers (hereafter DDEPP), DDEL. Stassen did enter the primaries, largely to block Taft, but also in the hope that, if the convention deadlocked, the party would turn to him. See Bernard Shanley, "The Delaying Action," box 1, Shanley Diary, DDEL.

15. William B. Pickett, *Eisenhower Decides to Run: Presidential Politics and Cold War Strategy* (Chicago: Ivan R. Dee, 2000), 87–88, 97. On Luce's involvement, see Eisenhower to Luce, April 3, 1942, folder 165, box 3, John Shaw Billings: Time-Life-Fortune Papers, South Caroliniana Library, Columbia, SC.

16. Stephen E. Ambrose, *Eisenhower,* vol. 1, *Soldier, General of the Army, President-Elect, 1890–1952,* and vol. 2, *President* (London: Allen & Unwin, 1984), 1:498–99.

17. Lucius Clay to Eisenhower, April 2, 1952, Clay Folder, box 24, DDEPP.

18. "Document 'X,'" n.d., 1952 Campaign and Election Folder, box 10, Robert Humphreys Papers, DDEL; Divine, *Foreign Policy and U.S. Presidential Elections,* 43–44.

19. Republican National Committee, "'52 an Appraisal," PR Director, National Republican Congressional Committee Folder, box 9, Humphreys Papers.

20. There was also Richard M. Nixon's famous "Checkers" speech, when he used television to deny allegations of benefiting from a secret fund.

21. Hope to Eisenhower's Campaign Team, October 2, 1952, 1952 Campaign Folder, box 10, Humphreys Papers; Emmet Hughes, *The Ordeal of Power: A Political Memoir of the Eisenhower Years* (New York: *Atheneum, 1963),* 20–21, 36–37; Divine, *Foreign Policy and U.S. Presidential Elections,* 42–43.

22. Greene, *The Crusade,* 174–75, 204–7.

23. Divine, *Foreign Policy and U.S. Presidential Elections,* 43–44; "Document 'X,'" n.d., Campaign and Election Folder, box 10, Humphreys Papers.

24. Divine, *Foreign Policy and U.S. Presidential Elections,* 50–54; Robert R. Bowie and Richard H. Immerman, *Waging Peace: How Eisenhower Shaped an Enduring Cold War Strategy* (New York: Oxford University Press, 1998), 75.

25. Eisenhower Speeches, September 15, 16, 18, 22, 1952, 1952 Campaign, Speeches and Statements Folder, boxes 1–3, Benedict Papers.

26. Eisenhower Speeches, September 4, 22, 1952, and Notes on Speech Writing Session, August 29, 1952; both in 1952 Campaign: Speeches and Statements Folder, box 1, Benedict Papers; Divine, *Foreign Policy and U.S. Presidential Elections,* 45–46.

27. Johnson, ed., *Stevenson Papers,* 4:67.

28. Sigurd Larmon to William E. Robinson, October 16, 1952, Larmon Folder, box 9, William E. Robinson Papers, DDEL.

29. Robinson to Cake, October 10, 1952, Eisenhower Folder, box 2, Robinson Papers; Eisenhower to Harold Stassen, October 5, 1952, Ann Whitman File, Administration Series, Stassen Folder, box 34, DDEPP.

30. US Department of State, *Foreign Relations of the United States* (hereafter *FRUS), 1952–54,* vol. 15, *Korea* (Washington, DC: US Government Printing Office, 1984), 512–14, 522–25, 533, 537, 545–48, 554–57, 563; Rosemary Foot, *A Substitute for Victory: The Politics of Peacemaking at the Korean Armistice Talks* (Ithaca, NY: Cornell University Press, 1990), 142–50.

31. Walter G. Hermes, *Truce Tent and Fighting Front* (Washington, DC: Center of Military History, US Army, 1992), 303–18; Clay Blair, *The Forgotten War: America in Korea, 1950–1953* (Annapolis, MD: Naval Institute Press, 2003), 970.

32. "Bloodshed in the Hills," *Time,* October 27, 1952; "Then He Was Dead," *Time,* October 6, 1952.

33. "An Old Pattern," *Time,* November 3, 1952. See also "Relationship of Friendly Casualties to Enemy Fire," n.d., copy in Ann Whitman File: Administrative Series, Wilson Folder, box 40, DDEPP.

34. State Department, Office of Public Affairs, "Monthly Survey of American Opinion on International Affairs," January, October, and November 1952, Entry 568L, box 12, Record Group (hereafter RG) 59, National Archives and Record Administration, College Park, MD (hereafter NARA).

35. Samuel Lubell, *Revolt of the Moderates* (New York: Harper & Bros., 1956), 39–40.

36. "Text of Gov. Stevenson's Speech in San Francisco," *New York Times*, September 10, 1952.

37. Johnson, ed., *Stevenson Papers*, 4:115–17, 127.

38. Steven Casey, *When Soldiers Fall: How Americans Have Confronted Combat Casualties, from World War I to Afghanistan* (New York: Oxford University Press, 2014), 134–35.

39. Eisenhower Speech, October 24, 1952, Korea Speech Folder, box 1, Emmet Hughes Papers, Seeley Mudd Library, Princeton University, Princeton, NJ.

40. State Department, Office of Public Affairs, "Daily Opinion Summary," October 27, 30, 1952, Entry 568K, box 4, RG 59, NARA. For analysis, see Martin Medhurst, "Text and Context in the 1952 Presidential Campaign: Eisenhower's 'I Shall Go to Korea' Speech," *Presidential Studies Quarterly* 30, no. 3 (2000): 464–82.

41. Even Nixon, who was the GOP's central attack dog, was careful to distance himself from those who thought Truman had been wrong to intervene in the first place. See State Department, Office of Public Affairs, "Daily Opinion Summary," August 26, 1952, Entry 568K, box 4, RG 59, NARA.

42. Hughes, *Ordeal of Power*, 33. See also Divine, *Foreign Policy and U.S. Presidential Elections*, 76.

43. Greene, *The Crusade*, 224–25; Ambrose, *Eisenhower*, 1:571; Robert G. Kaufman, *Henry M. Jackson: A Life in Politics* (Seattle: University of Washington Press, 2000), 69–70.

44. Merry, "Taft," 189–90.

45. On the motivations behind Eisenhower's appointments, see Robert H. Ferrell, ed., *The Eisenhower Diaries* (New York: Norton, 1981), 226; Dwight D. Eisenhower, *Mandate for Change, 1953–61* (London: Heinemann, 1963), 83–87; and Ambrose, *Eisenhower*, 2:20–24. On the lower-ranking appointments, see Townsend Hoopes, *The Devil and John Foster Dulles* (London: Andre Deutsch, 1974), 146–47, 152–53; and William Stueck, *The Korean War: An International History* (Princeton, NJ: Princeton University Press, 1995), 335.

46. Ambrose, *Eisenhower*, 2:42–43; Herbert S. Parmet, *Eisenhower and the American Crusades* (New York: Macmillan, 1972), 156; Dwight D. Eisenhower, Inaugural Address, January 20, 1953, *The American Presidency Project*, http://www.presidency.ucsb.edu/ws/index.php?pid=9600&st=&st1=.

47. Bowie and Immerman, *Waging Peace*, 79, 84–92.

48. Ferrell, ed., *Eisenhower Diaries*, 226.

49. Bowie and Immerman, *Waging Peace*, 9–108.

50. *FRUS, 1952–54*, vol. 15, pp. 743–45, 769–70; Edward C. Keefer, "President Dwight D. Eisenhower and the End of the Korean War," *Diplomatic History* 10, no. 3 (1986): 267–89, esp. 268, 270–74.

51. Bowie and Immerman, *Waging Peace*, 109–20.

52. Keefer, "Eisenhower and the End of the Korean War," 267–89; Stueck, *Korean War*, 308–47.

53. Bowie and Immerman, *Waging Peace,* 178–209.

54. Minutes, Cabinet Meeting, January 12, 1953, Cabinet Series, box 1, DDEPP.

55. Robert A. Caro, *The Years of Lyndon Johnson: Master of the Senate* (New York: Knopf, 2002), 527–41.

5

When Public Opinion
Does Not Shape Foreign Policy

Suez, Hungary, and Eisenhower
in the 1956 Presidential Election

Scott Lucas

The *New York Times* article on November 5, 1956, was straightforward
in its introduction: "President Eisenhower, troubled about the developing
world crisis but relaxed about tomorrow's voting."[1] While crises and wars
had suddenly flared in Hungary and Egypt, the president enjoyed a large
lead in opinion polls ahead of the same man he had defeated in 1952,
Adlai Stevenson.

The *Times* summary appeared to be borne out the next day. The international conflicts kept Eisenhower busy after he cast his ballot. He considered
whether the United States could make a response to the Soviet invasion of
Hungary, suppressing the uprising that had brought a change of government,
beyond support for Red Cross aid to the victims of tank fire and bullets. He
appealed to British prime minister Anthony Eden for a cease-fire in the Suez
Canal Zone, only twenty-four hours after the first British and French forces
had landed in support of the Israeli assault on Egypt. He fended off a letter
from Soviet premier Nikolai Bulganin suggesting that both Washington and
Moscow send troops to stop the war, warning: "If the Soviets attacked the
French and British directly, we would be in war, and we would be justified in
taking military action even if Congress were not in session."[2]

In contrast, the election was close to an anticlimax. Eisenhower easily swept to victory, taking the Electoral College by 427–73 votes and winning 57.4 percent of the popular vote to Stevenson's 42.0 percent. The president did not lose a single state outside the South, even carrying Stevenson's home state of Illinois. Eisenhower's approach to US foreign policy and international affairs had had little effect—at least negatively—on his electoral fortunes. But was the 1956 presidential ballot just as detached from the administration's policy making, having no effect on Eisenhower and his advisers in a time of sudden crisis?

In 1999, Douglas Foyle published *Counting the Public In: Presidents, Public Opinion, and Foreign Policy,* which used the Eisenhower administration as the focus for an innovative construction of the relationship between policy making and public input.[3] Foyle set up four categories of governance: (1) the delegate, believing that both public input and public support are necessary; (2) the pragmatist, dismissing public input but believing in the need for public support; (3) the executor, accepting public input while not believing that support is essential; and (4) the guardian, rejecting both public input and the necessity of public support. In this model, Eisenhower and his secretary of state, John Foster Dulles, were pragmatists. The president believed that it was essential to educate the public to ensure their support but that, given that general lack of information among the citizenry, policy making could not be held hostage to their wishes: "We can't just let a popular majority sweep us in one direction, because then you can't recover." Eisenhower maintained that the electoral process should not alter that approach: "Only a leadership that is based on honesty of purpose, calmness, and inexhaustible patience in conference and persuasion and refusal to be diverted from basic principles can, in the long run, win out. I further believe that we must never lose sight of the ultimate objectives we are trying to attain. Immediate reaction is relatively unimportant—it is particularly unimportant if it affects only my current standing in the popular polls."[4]

Foyle did not test his hypothesis with respect to foreign policy and the crises around the 1956 election. His four case studies—the 1953 "New Look" strategy, the Vietnamese siege of the French at Dien Bien Phu in 1954, the Formosa Straits of the same year, and the Soviet Union's Sputnik launch in 1957—were deliberately positioned at least a year before a presidential vote to shield his model from "electoral proximity."

When the events of 1956 are examined through public and private records, it is Eisenhower's perspective rather than Foyle's conclusion that is bolstered. The president and his advisers do not easily fit the academic's category of pragmatists, who were not reliant on the public for input but who required public support for their aims and actions. Instead, Eisenhower made clear time and again—to his officials, to correspondents, and to foreign leaders—that he would proceed with what he thought was the right course for US interests, irrespective of the American public's reaction to the policy or to his reelection campaign.

At the same time, the president, always a keen student of psychological warfare, was ready to invoke public opinion in the United States and abroad to try and bend other statesmen to his will. As he told British prime minister Anthony Eden at the start of September, firmly quashing London's hope for military action: "I must tell you frankly that American public opinion flatly rejects the thought of using force until every possible peaceful means of protecting our vital interests have been exhausted without result."[5]

The conclusion that Eisenhower was a pragmatic president is far from novel. The revisionist Eisenhower literature from the 1980s—including biographies such as those by Stephen Ambrose, studies of Eisenhower's approach to operations such as Fred Greenstein's "Hidden-Hand President," and broader examinations such as John Lewis Gaddis's consideration of strategy—all emphasized a capable pragmatism, even if they overstated the president's decisiveness and control of policy making.[6]

However, this notion of the pragmatic is significantly different from Foyle's notion of the pragmatist. It is much wider, with a president assessing the dynamics of American power, geopolitics, relationships with both allies and foes, and economic and military possibilities, burdens, and consequences. It is a pragmatism that Eisenhower expected his officials, to whom he delegated authority for implementation of policy, to share and advance. This conception of Eisenhower the pragmatist overtakes Foyle's narrower definition. In the interest of the pragmatic foreign policy, there were times when the president believed that he had to set aside any attention to public opinion if he believed that this would complicate assessment of the action needed to defend American interests.

This tension between the appreciation of the pragmatic in the executive and the pragmatist as narrowly constructed by Foyle demonstrates how the literature on public opinion and foreign policy needs further development. With general classifications and assertions, the scholarship has not engaged with critical cases in which foreign policy and electoral politics were intertwined. It has failed to deal with both the situation and the man: if the public mattered, it was not as an influence on foreign policy but as a symbol to be deployed on the administration's behalf after strategic and operational decisions had been made.

Two Foreign Policy Crises

Both the Hungarian and the Egyptian crises had lengthy backstories in Washington, even if the plot changes of October 1956 were not anticipated. In the Egyptian case, the United States had wrestled for years between its frustration with the political and military approach of the British, the leading Western power in the area; its desire to steer the Middle East toward an anti-Soviet position; and the irritant of Egyptian-Israeli tensions. It had supported the rise of the military regime, including Colonel Gamal Abdel Nasser, from 1952 and pressed for the departure of the British from the Suez Canal base, finally accomplished in June 1954. It had pursued top-secret shuttle diplomacy between Egypt and Israel from the end of 1954. However, irritated by Nasser's decision to accept military aid from the Soviet bloc, and frustrated by the failure to bring the Egyptian and Israeli leaders to the same negotiating table, it agreed with Britain in March 1956 that Nasser had to be curbed through a series of political, economic, and propaganda measures.

On July 19, 1956, Dulles added to the pressure with the sudden decision to withdraw the offer of funding for the High Aswan Dam, Nasser's dream project for Egyptian progress. Far from accepting the decision, the Egyptian president countered with an ambitious gesture that would also generate revenues for the dam: on July 26, he surprised an enthusiastic crowd in Alexandria with the announcement that Egypt was nationalizing the Anglo-French Suez Canal Company.

Had the British and French launched an immediate military operation to reclaim the canal, the Eisenhower administration might have faced the prospect—uncomfortable given the approaching election—of either acquiescing in a war or standing against two of American's most prominent allies. However, the British were in no position to attack, needing several weeks before an operation could be launched from its Mediterranean ports on Cyprus, more than three hundred miles from the Egyptian coast, and Malta, more than nine hundred miles away. Washington therefore had a window, before the unofficial launch of the presidential campaign after Labor Day, to concentrate on pushing London and Paris toward negotiation of the crisis.

The Hungarian case had a much longer lineage, with the Truman administration putting forth a general aspiration of the "liberation" of Eastern Europe—expressed as the "retraction of Soviet power"—as early as November 1948.[7] The ambition was restated in top-secret blueprints for US foreign policy, including the seminal National Security Council Report 68 in 1950.[8] Eisenhower and Dulles raised liberation to a cutting-edge issue in the 1952 campaign, accusing the Truman administration—despite the confidential guidance and covert operations behind the Iron Curtain—of being soft on communism and abandoning "captive peoples" to Moscow's domination.

However, once Eisenhower took power, he and his advisers were seized by indecision over how far to press for liberation. Faced with uncertainty after the sudden death of Joseph Stalin in March 1953 and the Soviet intervention against the East German uprising in June 1953, they pulled back from military intervention or even public encouragement of uprising. Instead, general statements—Eisenhower's "Change for Peace" speech of April 1953—and initiatives such as a food program in West Berlin, encouraging those from the East to take the assistance as a sign of Western strength, were pursued.[9]

Still, the sweeping aim of retraction of Soviet power was still embedded in US policy, and an organization built up for covert operations looked for an opportunity to exploit. That came in February 1956 with Khrushchev's "Secret Speech," denouncing Stalin, before the Twentieth Congress of the Communist Party. Obtaining a copy of the address from both Israeli and Italian sources, the CIA disseminated parts of it so that they could be broadcast by Radio Free Europe, with the message that publics behind the Iron Curtain should question their own regimes. In June 1956, the National Security Council (NSC) was encouraged when food protests surged in Poznan in Poland. The head of the CIA, Allen Dulles, told the NSC: "The USSR was caught in a dilemma. The Soviets wish to continue their de-Stalinization program and at the same time cut off the debate that is now going on regarding de-Stalinization and the question of freedom. They wish to foster the impression that there is no change in their policy of 'liberalization,' but also wish to close ranks and adopt a 'harder' line, particularly toward the West. They wish to hold the loyalty of the Communist leaders generally in non-Communist countries, and also disavow certain of those leaders. They wish to modify conditions in the satellites, but at the same time 'keep the lid on' and prevent additional riots such as those that recently occurred in Poland."[10]

Suddenly, the liberation of captive peoples, promised by Eisenhower and his advisers but never sought decisively, appeared within reach. At the same time, the risk that the Soviet Union could intervene to put down the marches was ever present.

The Candidates and Foreign Policy

In his speech accepting the Republican nomination on August 23, Eisenhower gave a summary of foreign policy that replaced the 1952 call for liberation with advocacy of cultural interaction: "Good will from our side can do little to reach these peoples unless there is some new spirit of conciliation on the part of the governments controlling them. Now, at last, there appear to be signs that some small degree of friendly intercourse among peoples may be permitted." He then appeared to reject any measures to promote regime change: "My friends, the kind of era [of progress] I have described is possible. But it will not be attained by revolution." Meanwhile, despite the Suez crisis, he made no reference to the Middle East. Instead, he deployed more general rhetoric about the Cold War: "We too must have the vision, the fighting spirit, and the deep religious faith in our Creator's destiny for us, to sound a similar note of promise for our divided world; that out of our time there can, with incessant work and with God's help, emerge a new era of good life, good will and good hope for all men."[11]

Ironically, given the president's own 1952 campaign against the Democrats as weak on communism, the milder approach to Eastern Europe and the elision of Suez gave the Democratic nominee, Adlai Stevenson— the same man who had challenged Eisenhower four years earlier—the opportunity to deride the Republicans as men who had retreated in the face of aggression. Accepting the Democratic nomination a week before the Republican national convention, Stevenson offered the prospect of that condemnation: "The truth is not that our policy abroad has Communism on the run. The truth, unhappily, is not—in the Republican president's words—that our 'prestige since the last World War has never been as high as it is today.' The truth is that it has never been lower." But Stevenson did not lay any specific charges against Eisenhower. He merely chided the "complacent chat," called for leadership, and regretted that "America . . . no longer sparks and flames and gives off new ideas and initiatives."[12] The Democrats' "New America" campaign—focusing on senior citizens, health, education, natural resources, and economic policy—was largely in the domestic realm, while criticism of the administration's foreign policy and military approach was focused almost exclusively on the draft and nuclear weapons tests.

Facing no challenge over its approach to Suez, the administration could maintain its course of encouraging British and French negotiations with Nasser. Before the party conventions, Eisenhower had briefed both Republican and Democratic leaders of Congress. He struck a tough pose: "[I do not] intend to . . . let this one man get away with it. . . . I hope there's no doubt that we will look to our interests." However, he made clear that the administration was pursuing a peaceful resolution. When he invited the congressmen to send two representatives—one Republican and one Democrat—with Dulles to London for the talks, they declined, effectively giving the administration a clear run.[13]

In the discussions, Dulles promoted the Suez Canal Users Association to deprive Nasser of the revenues of nationalization but then stepped away from the idea. British prime minister Anthony Eden claimed to his foreign secretary, Selwyn Lloyd, that Dulles was playing a "game" to "string us along" because of the presidential election. This was, however, one of a series of Eden's disastrous misperceptions during the crisis; the secretary of state was merely implementing Eisenhower's line, defined in late July and set out publicly a week later: "The United States has every hope that this very serious difficulty will be settled by peaceful means. We have stood for the conference method not only as a solution to this problem but in all similar ones." The president effectively ruled out a military response by telling reporters that only Congress could authorize war—and he had no plans to recall legislators for a special session unless Egypt blocked traffic through the canal.[14]

While Eisenhower's stance was not conditioned on public support, the public buttressed the government in opinion polls throughout the summer. Asked in the third week of August whether the United States should respond with "military action" or "economic and political actions" to Egypt's refusal of free passage through the canal, only 33 percent chose the former, against 47 percent for the nonmilitary steps and 20 percent undecided. Two weeks later, those supporting military action had dropped to 27 percent, with 64 percent backing the alternative. And, in late September, respondents rejected the proposal to send US ships and troops if Britain and France attacked Egypt by the wide margin of 55 to 23 percent, with 22 percent undecided.[15]

The president was also undisturbed by events in Eastern Europe. Polish security forces killed scores of protesters in the late June demonstrations in Poznan and had arrested almost 750 people by early August, but the events did not stir the presidential campaign. Between the start of August and mid-October, there was not a single question to Eisenhower on the topic in his press conferences, and he did not raise the specific issue, instead making this general declaration to the People-to-People Conference on September 11: "What we must do is widen every chink in the Iron Curtain and bring the family of Russia, or of any other country behind that Iron Curtain, that is laboring to better the lot of their children—as humans do the world over—closer into our circle, to show how we do it, and then to sit down between us to say, 'Now, how do we improve the lot of both of us?'" Even this sweeping declaration was subordinated to the situation in Egypt and "the Suez problem of today."[16] In his opening campaign press conferences and speeches, Eisenhower did not include Eastern Europe on the checklist of his administration's successes since 1953. Instead, he spoke generally of a shift in Soviet strategy: "They have changed into more of an economic propaganda plan rather than depending on force or the threat of force. This requires intelligent, fast work on our side to put our own case before the world and to operate better, and I think that that change has been made or is being made effectively, and that the Soviets are not doing as well in this plan as they thought they would."[17]

This was a political contest of "neutrals" or of a resistance to "the first great industrial power to challenge the West," rather than a showdown over liberation. Although Eisenhower portrayed the Soviet threat, he did so more as part of the campaign's general theme of the "path to peace" and the "spiritual, intellectual, and economic strength of America."[18] Any specific support for his invocations came from the 1953 cease-fire in Korea, rather than contemporary situations, and he shrugged aside the Democrats' call for a cessation of the testing of nuclear weapons and an end to the draft, insisting that the United States must pursue negotiations with the Soviets from a position of military strength.

There was one notable exception to the approach. On September 26, Eisenhower issued a statement about the trials of those arrested for the Poznan demonstrations. He called for a "genuinely fair and open" process and then expanded the issue beyond the protests for economic reforms: "The basic problem is not what type of economic or social system shall prevail. . . . What is essential is that they be given the opportunity to do so in free and unfettered elections." Still, he stopped short of issuing any encouragement of further protests.[19]

Toward Election Day

By October 12, as Eisenhower stepped up his campaigning, the prospect of either Poland or Suez commanding emergency attention had receded. He told a well-scripted, televised *The People Ask the President* show: "The progress made in the settlement of the Suez dispute . . . at the United Nations is most gratifying. Egypt, Britain, and France had met through their Foreign Ministers, and agreed on a set of principles on which to negotiate; and it looks like here is a very great crisis that is behind us."[20]

Nor was there any apparent reason for concern over the outcome of the election. Eisenhower's eleven-point lead over Stevenson in opinion polls was remarkable for its consistency as well as its size: the fifty-two to forty-one margin was almost unchanged from early August through mid-October. The Democratic nominee's choice of a ban on nuclear testing as his main foreign policy challenge had found little resonance with voters.

Curiously, given that the Suez dispute appeared to move toward a resolution, Stevenson chose this moment to shift his approach and make his first intervention. He seized on the president's declaration of "good news" as duplicity: "I have refrained from now on commenting on the Suez Crisis. . . . Why didn't the President tell us the truth . . . [instead of making] political capital out of a crisis that could engulf the world?"[21]

Unsurprisingly, the jibe had little impact. Stevenson returned to his focus on the nuclear-testing issue, devoting his national television broadcast of October 15 to the subject of "the greatest menace the world has ever known." That challenge was blunted a few days later when Soviet leader Nikolai Bulganin wrote Eisenhower about a ban as "certain prominent public figures in the US" were advocating it. The administration denounced the interference in a US election, with Vice President Richard Nixon describing Stevenson as a "clay pigeon" for Soviet sharpshooters.[22]

Eisenhower appeared on course to an untroubled victory as well as a satisfactory resolution of the Suez crisis. But the calm was suddenly disrupted on October 20 when street protests surged during the meeting of the Central Committee of the Polish Communist Party. Monuments to the Red Army were attacked: red stars and flags were pulled down from roofs of houses, factories, and schools; and portraits of the Soviet military commander Konstantin Rokossovsky were defaced. Eisenhower had to put out a holding statement from a campaign stop in Denver: "Numerous reports have been emanating from Poland which indicate ferment and unrest. These have been accompanied by stories of Soviet troop movements. . . . Naturally, all friends of the Polish people recognize and sympathize with their traditional yearning for liberty and independence."[23]

Three days later, Eisenhower devoted most of his speech to the Brotherhood of Carpenters and Joiners to Poland, using it as a model for others: "A people like the Poles who have once known freedom cannot once and for all be deprived of their national independence and of their personal liberty. That truth applies to every people in Eastern Europe who have enjoyed independence and freedom." Once again, he stopped far short of any encouragement of protests, instead making a general declaration in favor of "freedom-loving people" and promoting free trade and self-government.[24] Events were now overtaking Eisenhower. In Hungary, reports of the Polish events intersected with student demonstrations, and more than 200,000 soon gathered in Budapest with their calls for reforms. Soviet tanks and soldiers answered the Hungarian Communist Party's plea for intervention, and Imre Nagy replaced András Hegedüs as prime minister. On October 25, the president had to put out his second emergency statement in a week, recognizing "a renewed expression of the intense desire for freedom long held by the Hungarian people," and deploring Soviet intervention.[25] Allen Dulles told the NSC the next day: "The revolt in Hungary constituted the most serious threat yet to be posed to continued Soviet control of the satellites. It confronted Moscow with a very harsh dilemma: Either to revert to a harsh Stalinist policy, or to permit democratization to develop in the satellites to a point which risked the complete loss of Soviet control of the satellites."[26]

John Foster Dulles followed up with a speech in Dallas supporting the "aspirations" of the "captive peoples." He reassured the Soviets that "the United States had no ulterior purpose in desiring the independence of the satellite countries" but then encouraged similar demands for reforms inside the Soviet Union: "The peoples who compose the Union of Soviet Socialist Republics . . . too can have hope. The spread of education, and industrial development, create growing demands for greater intellectual and spiritual freedom, for greater personal security through the rule of law, and for greater enjoyment of the good things of life. And there has been some response to those demands."[27]

Then, as the administration was hoping for a significant gain from the uprising, Suez turned from accomplishment to complication. On October 28, a third statement in eight days—interrupting the president's defense of his administration's approach to nuclear weapons—was necessary because of the possibility of a British-French-Israeli agreement to attack Egypt. The Americans did not know of the collusion, agreed on in meetings near Paris on October 22 and 24, but they had indications from British contacts, from the US embassy in Israel, and from aerial surveillance of the area that showed the scale of the Israeli mobilization. In the statement, Eisenhower assured the American people that he had expressed his "grave concern" to Israeli prime minister David Ben-Gurion and that he had requested consultations with London and Paris.[28]

The Israeli invasion of the Sinai Peninsula the next day, followed by an Anglo-French ultimatum to Egypt and aerial attacks, forced Eisenhower to cancel campaign appearances. Instead, he addressed the nation on radio and television on October 31. With a Soviet statement promising a review of its policies and even the withdrawal of "advisers," he hailed the "dawning of a new day" in Eastern Europe—"the people of Poland . . . moved to secure a peaceful transition to a new government"; "a new Hungary is rising"—and drew the line on liberation: "We have . . . sought clearly to remove any false fears that we would look upon new governments in these Eastern European countries as potential military allies." He then turned to Suez and restated the line that the administration had held for three months: "The action can scarcely be reconciled with the principles and purposes of the United Nations to which we have all subscribed. . . . We are forced to doubt that resort to force and war will for long serve the permanent interest of the attacking nations." There would be no special session of Congress to support US involvement in hostilities. Instead, the United States would override the British and French vetoes in the UN Security Council with an appeal to the General Assembly: "There can be no peace without law. And there can be no law if we were to invoke one code of international conduct for those who oppose us and another for our friends."[29] Far from acknowledging any electoral pressure on his decisions, Eisenhower implicitly argued that the twin crises had meant the suspension of party politics. Back on the campaign trial on November 1 in Philadelphia, he asserted: "I have been profoundly encouraged by messages I have received in these past days from congressional members of both political parties. These messages have pledged support—earnest support—of America's decision to choose a path of honor."[30]

Stevenson did not act on the developments in Eastern Europe, but, with a week to go before the election, he tried to seize the opportunity of the Anglo-French-Israeli attack to dent the president's leadership credentials and display his own. Speaking just after Eisenhower's national broadcast, he declared that the world was "on the brink of war again."[31] Two days later, he continued: "We have alienated our chief European allies. We have alienated Israel. We have alienated Egypt and the Arab countries. And in the UN our main associate in Middle Eastern matters now appears to be Communist Russia—in the very week when the Red Army has been shooting down the brave people of Hungary and Poland. . . . I doubt if ever before in our diplomatic history has any policy been such an abysmal, such a complete and catastrophic failure."[32] Finally, he put out a defined challenge. He proposed both a cease-fire and a restoration of a "grand alliance" with Britain and France as well as security for Israel. There would be international oversight of the canal, an initiative on Arab refugees, and economic assistance to the Middle East.

Still, Stevenson's ideas were too muddled and contradictory to have either electoral or foreign policy significance. He could not explain how a grand alliance with London and Paris could be reconciled with their opposition to a cease-fire. He did not set out what he would do about the "dictator of Egypt," President Nasser. And nothing in his plan—in contrast to the actions of the administration—confronted the immediate priority of halting the Israeli invasion and the pretense of Anglo-French "peacekeeping" through bombing and an imminent ground assault.

Eisenhower's campaign easily countered any political threat. It upheld the US-led effort in the United Nations to force a cease-fire. Vice President Nixon was dispatched to cheer the American willingness to stand up to Britain and France as a "declaration of independence that has had an electrifying effect throughout the world"—ironic, given Nixon's later proclamation that the administration had made a grave mistake in not supporting the military operations—and to herald the General Assembly vote as a rebuttal of Stevenson's "preposterous charge" that the United States was alone.[33]

The Democrat appeared to have failed with his final shot. Even while dealing with the Suez crisis, Eisenhower and the NSC could allow themselves to be swept up in optimism over the turn of events in Poland and Hungary. A draft policy paper summarized: "Developments in Poland appear favorable to [our] objective [of a 'national' Communist government]. The Gomulka Government has proclaimed its 'national independence and equality' and has asserted its right to pursue its own internal road to 'socialism.'" In Hungary, the situation was "still fluid": Soviet forces were still in the country, but "the demands of the people on the government have since gone far beyond those originally sought and are now anti-communist as well as anti-Soviet." The policy paper recommended: "Actions taken by the United States and other friendly governments in the present situation should strive to aid and encourage forces in the satellites moving towards US objectives without provoking counter-action which would result in the suppression of 'liberalizing' influences."[34]

The head of the CIA, Allen Dulles, was in no mood for caution. He saw nothing less than the imminent collapse of the Communist system:

What had occurred there was a miracle. Events had belied all our past views that a popular revolt in the face of modern weapons was an utter impossibility. Nevertheless, the impossible had happened, and because of the power of public opinion, armed force could not effectively be used. Approximately 80 percent of the Hungarian Army had defected to the rebels and provided the rebels with arms. Soviet troops themselves had had no stomach for shooting down Hungarians, except in Budapest.

[Prime Minister Imre] Nagy was failing to unite the rebels, and they were demanding that he quit. Somehow a rallying point must be found in order to prevent chaos inside of Hungary even if the Soviets took their leave. In such a heavily Catholic nation as Hungary, Cardinal Mindszenty might prove to be such a leader and unifying force.

Dulles said that discussion of the policy paper was "academic since the situation had largely resolved itself."[35]

But the situation was not resolved, bringing one more twist before the presidential vote. On November 4, two days before the election, the Soviets set aside a review of their policies and invaded Hungary to suppress the uprising. Eisenhower could only express "shock and dismay." After consulting John Foster Dulles, who was in the hospital recovering from an operation for cancer, and then Allen Dulles, he sent a message to Soviet premier Nikolai Bulganin calling for withdrawal of his forces and support of Hungarian self-determination. The Soviets responded by connecting—or diverting—back to Suez, proposing that the United States join them in a peacekeeping force.[36]

So, on Election Day, Eisenhower took himself away from the polls to send important messages, not of celebration over Eastern Europe, but of warning over the Middle East. He told his senior advisers: "If the Soviets attack the French and British directly, we would be in war, and we would be justified in taking military action even if Congress were not in session." He called Prime Minister Eden, forced to halt military operations—in part because of the US refusal to provide essential support for the British pound—only twenty-four hours after the first ground forces landed in the Canal Zone: "I can't tell you how pleased we are that you found it possible to accept the cease-fire."[37]

Keeping Foreign Policy out of Politics

On October 11, after the British and French governments leaked their dissatisfaction with the US stance on Suez to supportive media, Eisenhower was confronted with the charge that "allies [are] apparently feeling that the administration's foreign policy is being inhibited by election-year considerations." He responded: "From the very first day we took up this question there were certain principles that guided us."[38] The record of the administration's deliberations and decisions backs up this firm rebuttal. There is no indication that, even as Eisenhower told his officials that "the question of the Suez [Canal] was probably the Number 1 question in the minds of the American people," its response was shaped by electoral considerations.[39] Instead, when the presidential vote entered White House meetings, it was for Eisenhower to draw a firm line: "In this matter, he does not care in the slightest whether he is re-elected or not. He feels we must make good on our word. He added that he did not really think the American people would throw him out in the midst of a situation like this, but if they did, so be it."[40] The president had held not only to principles but also to his geopolitical and economic assessment of July 31: "We must consider what the end [of force] would be. It might well be to array the world from Dakar to the Philippine Islands against us. . . . The Middle East oil would dry up, and Western Hemisphere oil would have to be diverted to Europe, thus requiring controls to be instituted in the US."[41]

On November 3, as Britain and France—in the guise of peacekeeping—bombed Egypt, Eisenhower faced a challenge in an NSC meeting from Harold Stassen, his special assistant for disarmament:

> Governor Stassen [said] . . . American public opinion [would] be divided if we go on with our plan against Britain, France and Israel. On the other hand, US public opinion could readily be united under a course of action in which we avoided anything except the cease-fire.
>
> Governor Stassen turned to the president and went on to say that he might not succeed in gaining congressional support for his long-term policies if U.S. action in the current crisis divided our people.
>
> The president "responded to Governor Stassen by stating his emphatic belief that these powers were going downhill with the kind of policy that they were engaged at the moment in carrying out. How could we possibly support Britain and France if in doing so we lose the whole Arab world?"[42]

However, Eisenhower's insistence on keeping electoral politics out of foreign policy calculations did not mean that the campaign had no effect. Its significance lay in how foreign governments perceived a possible impact on the president from the impending vote. Bulganin's clumsy attempt to pressure the administration with his letter of support for Stevenson was one example. Far more important, however, were the calculations of Britain and France over the Suez crisis: both countries proceeded with the invasion in part because of a belief that the election would prevent Eisenhower from challenging the operation.

In a letter of July 31 to Eden, the president had tried to remove the American populace as an influence to sway his position: "Public opinion here, and I am convinced in most of the world, would be outraged should there be a failure to make . . . efforts [for a negotiated resolution]."[43] The prime minister was in no mood to heed the warning. Instead, he looked for "information" to prop up his quest to overthrow Egypt's Nasser. He got it initially from his chancellor of the Exchequer, Harold Macmillan. As Eisenhower was warning London against military action, Macmillan was telling the president's envoy, Deputy Undersecretary of State Robert Murphy: "If [Britain] had to go down now, the Government and . . . British people would rather do so on this issue than become perhaps another Netherlands."[44]

Two months later, the chancellor had a series of meetings in Washington with US officials, including Eisenhower and Dulles. He immediately wrote Eden with a misleading interpretation of US policy. Macmillan claimed that Dulles had asked "if Britain could not . . . hold things off until after November 6th [Election Day]." However, rather than taking this as an injunction against military operations, he twisted the conclusion: the Americans would "lay doggo" and not intervene against any attacks before November 6.[45]

Whether from a genuine misunderstanding or a deliberate manipulation of the US position, Macmillan's portrayal of the electoral influence was disastrous. The American threat to the British pound meant that, despite being one of the foremost advocates for war, the chancellor was among the first cabinet ministers calling for a cease-fire: "[I] cannot be responsible for Her Majesty's Exchequer. . . . If sanctions were imposed on us, the country is finished."[46]

Conclusion

Does the case study of Eisenhower and the 1956 election offer a general guide to US foreign policy and electoral influences (or the lack of them) to complement Foyle's model of decision making? Probably not. Both Suez and the Polish and Hungarian crises were special circumstances, coming to a head just as Americans were about to go to the polls. Eisenhower's approach was arguably one based on his specific beliefs: a president acting in the name of peace and the defense of US interests, with decisiveness on the line over military operations against Egypt and caution to the point of hesitation on Eastern Europe and liberation. The electoral situation was also distinctive: with a relatively high popularity rating and a significant advantage in the polls throughout the campaign, the president may have had the luxury of keeping public opinion at a distance. That luxury was also provided by a Democratic opposition that was also nonexistent in its challenge of the administration response to the foreign policy crises until late in the campaign and that then put forth weak arguments that were easily countered by Eisenhower's projection of US strength in the service of peace.

From the standpoint of scholarship on the president and foreign policy, the 1956 case offers reinforcement for the portrayal of the pragmatic executive making its decision on the basis of strategic and tactical evaluations, rather than ideology or electoral calculations. This was particularly effective in the case of Suez, when the president and his advisers stood firmly against allies whose actions threatened the developing US interests in the Middle East. In the case of Eastern Europe, the pragmatism was challenged by the ideological veneer of liberation, which had encouraged working-level officials to pursue political warfare even as the administration was indecisive about the approach, but, after the collapse of the Hungarian uprising, it was reconfirmed as a tactic of "evolution, not revolution," in the Communist bloc. Ole Holsti writes in his leading work on the supposed effect of public opinion on policy making: "Because voters are perceived as punishing incumbent candidates or parties for foreign policy failures . . . or rewarding them for successes . . . decisions by foreign policy leaders may be made in anticipation of public reactions and the probabilities of success or failure."[47] Yet at no point in either the Suez or the East European crises was the Eisenhower foreign policy founded on "anticipation of public reactions," at least in the sense of tailoring that policy to satisfy public opinion. A line was taken. If the US populace did not like it, the line would be maintained, even if there were electoral consequences. The priority was the president's conception of security defined as peace.

An example of anticipation in the Suez crisis is illustrative. In early October, according to his son John, Eisenhower pondered: "If the Israelis keep going—and if the UN says so—I may have to use force to stop them. . . . Then I'd lose the election. There would go New York, New Jersey, Pennsylvania, and Connecticut at least."[48] Yet far from conceding his position—as the British wrongly predicted he would—the president immediately said that he would have to halt the "Israeli aggression" in order to live with his political conscience. He wrote his friend Edward Hazlett during the crisis: "As we began to uncover evidence that something was building up in Israel, we demanded pledges from Ben-Gurion that he would keep the peace. We realized that he might think he could take advantage of this country because of the approaching election and because of the importance that so many politicians in the past have attached to our Jewish vote. I gave strict orders to the State Department that they should inform Israel that we would handle our affairs exactly as though we didn't have a Jew in America. The welfare and best interests of our own country were to be the sole criteria on which we operated."[49]

The historical record backs up Eisenhower's assertion. On October 15, as it looked like Israel might attack Jordan and pursue the breakup of the country, Eisenhower instructed Dulles to warn Israeli ambassador Abba Eban:

No considerations of partisan politics will keep this Government from pursuing a course dictated by justice and international decency in the circumstances, and it will remain true to its pledges under the United Nations.

[Israeli prime minister David] Ben-Gurion should not make any grave mistakes based upon his belief that winning a domestic election is as important to us as preserving and protecting the interests of the United Nations and other nations of the free world in that region.

Eisenhower firmly declared: "I will not under any circumstances permit the fact of the forthcoming elections to influence my judgement. If any votes are lost as a result of this attitude, that is a situation which we will have to confront, but any other attitude will not permit us to live with our conscience."[50] As the secretary of state summarized to Richard Nixon in a phone call on October 31: "[Eisenhower] said throughout he wants to do what is right regardless of the election—he will not sacrifice foreign policy for political expediency."[51]

Douglas Foyle's narrow configuration of pragmatism, with the executive conditioning foreign policy on the assurance of public support, does not hold up in the context of Eastern Europe and Suez between August and November 1956. The president and his advisers were not hostages to the public response to Poland and Hungary; if they were captives, it was to the pace of events, meaning that they were unable to fashion a clear American approach before yet another turn in the political and military situation. Having from summer 1956 set the line of a peaceful resolution of the Suez dispute, the administration held to it—irrespective of public reaction—when London and Paris took the ill-fated move of colluding with Israel in an attack on Egypt. Eisenhower wrote concisely on November 2: "If one has to have a fight, then that is that, but I don't see the point in getting into a fight to which there can be no satisfactory end, and in which the whole world believes you are playing the part of the bully and you do not even have the firm backing of your entire people."[52]

Similarly, having put out a message of liberation in the 1952 presidential campaign, Eisenhower and Dulles did not hold to it over the next four years if events stood in the way of implementation. They had refrained from an aggressive intervention after Stalin's death in March 1953, they pulled back during the East German uprising of June 1953, and they maintained caution while approaching summitry with the Soviets in 1955. When the image of liberation collapsed in November 1956, they quickly reframed US policy to withdraw the concept once and for all, despite public concern over the failure to support those in captive nations.

One can take the lesson beyond a correction of the pragmatic as applied to public opinion and foreign policy. It is also an injunction to those who claim authority in the area to test their general assertions through the revelations of particular cases. In his foundational work, Holsti gives scant consideration to the dynamic during an electoral process beyond the hope that "perhaps the American public, for all its apathy and other well-documented weaknesses, appreciates a generosity of spirit and can be persuaded to support it on election day." His passing attention to the 1956 election asserts that it "took place while the United States was at peace during the interim between the Korean War armistice and escalation of the Vietnam conflict," a misleading statement given the armed conflict and foreign policy crises of Eastern Europe and Suez.[53]

This raises a question mark regarding Holsti's general conclusion: "There is a good deal of evidence that, for better or worse, public opinion had a substantial impact on the foreign policies of recent administrations."[54] Certainly, John Foster Dulles once declared: "We can't get too far ahead of public opinion and we must do everything we can to bring it along with us." But there is no evidence that Eisenhower was constrained in autumn 1956 by a necessity to mobilize public backing for any decision.[55] If public opinion played any role in the administration's policy and implementation, it was not as an objective influence or obstacle but as a lever against troublesome allies, as in Eisenhower's letter to Eden on September 2. While the situation of Eisenhower in 1956 should be treated as a specific case rather than as a guide to the handling of foreign policy in election cycles before and after that date, it offers lines of analysis to be considered. To what extent did the circumstances of foreign policy episodes—for example, the pace of events—shape the US reaction? How much of the response stemmed from the bureaucratic structure set up by the administration? Was the president's personality—notably, his conception of public opinion—the overriding factor? If the opposition had been stronger and timelier in its critiques of Eastern Europe and Suez, would that have changed the dynamic and forced the president to heed public opinion?

In such an examination lies the paradox that, while Eisenhower the general might have told newspaper editors in World War II, "Public opinion wins war," Eisenhower the president and his foreign policy was not going to be bound by that opinion during his quest for reelection.[56] In such an examination is the answer to Holsti's challenge: "Although anecdotal and correlational analyses can make useful contributions towards understanding the foreign policy-public opinion process, they are not an entirely satisfactory substitute for intensive case studies."[57]

Notes

1. Russell Baker, "President Visits Aides: The White House Expects Big Win," *New York Times,* November 6, 1956, 1.
2. US Department of State, *Foreign Relations of the United States* (hereafter

FRUS), *1955–1957*, vol. 16, *Suez Crisis, July 26–December 31, 1956* (Washington, DC: US Government Printing Office, 1990), 1014–15.

3. Douglas C. Foyle, *Counting the Public In: Presidents, Public Opinion, and Foreign Policy* (New York: Columbia University Press, 1999).

4. Quoted in ibid., 32–33.

5. *FRUS, 1955–1957*, vol. 16, pp. 355–58.

6. Stephen E. Ambrose, *Eisenhower,* vol. 1, *Soldier, General of the Army, President-Elect, 1890–1952,* and vol. 2, *President* (London: Allen & Unwin, 1984); Fred I. Greenstein, *The Hidden-Hand Presidency: Eisenhower as Leader* (New York: Basic, 1982); John Lewis Gaddis, *Strategies of Containment: A Critical Appraisal of Postwar American National Security Policy* (New York: Oxford University Press, 1982, 127–97.

7. *FRUS, 1948,* vol. 1, pt. 2, *General: The United Nations* (Washington, DC: US Government Printing Office, 1976), 662–69.

8. National Security Report 68, "A Report to the National Security Council," April 12, 1950, President's Secretary's File, Truman Papers, Harry S. Truman Library,   https://www.trumanlibrary.org/whistlestop/study_collections/coldwar/documents/pdf/10-1.pdf.

9. See Scott Lucas, *Freedom's War: The US Crusade against the Soviet Union, 1945–1956* (Manchester: Manchester University Press, 1999), 163–98.

10. *FRUS, 1955–1957,* vol. 24, *Soviet Union, Eastern Mediterranean* (Washington, DC: US Government Printing Office, 1989), 136.

11. Dwight D. Eisenhower, Address at the Cow Palace on Accepting the Nomination of the Republican National Convention, August 23, 1956, *The American Presidency Project*, http://www.presidency.ucsb.edu/ws/?pid=10583.

12. Adlai Stevenson, Address Accepting the Presidential Nomination at the Democratic National Convention in Chicago, August 17, 1956, *American Presidency Project* http://www.presidency.ucsb.edu/ws/index.php?pid=75172.

13. Minnich Memorandum, August 12, 1956, quoted in Ambrose, *Eisenhower,* 2:353.

14. Dwight D. Eisenhower, The President's News Conference, August 8, 1956, *American Presidency Project*, http://www.presidency.ucsb.edu/ws/index.php?pid=10562.

15. George H. Gallup, *The Gallup Poll: Public Opinion, 1935–1971* (New York: Random House, 1972), 1455.

16. Dwight D. Eisenhower, Remarks at the People-to-People Conference, September 11, 1956, *American Presidency Project*, http://www.presidency.ucsb.edu/ws/?pid=10599.

17. Dwight D. Eisenhower, The President's News Conference, September 5, 1956, *American Presidency Project*, http://www.presidency.ucsb.edu/ws/index.php?pid=10591.

18. Dwight D. Eisenhower, Address at Civic Auditorium in Portland, Oregon, October 18, 1956, *American Presidency Project*, http://www.presidency.ucsb.edu/ws/index.php?pid=10656&st=&st1=.

19. Dwight D. Eisenhower, Statement by the President regarding Trials Following the Poznan Riots in Poland, September 26, 1956, *American Presidency Project*, http://www.presidency.ucsb.edu/ws/index.php?pid=10611&st=&st1=.

20. Dwight D. Eisenhower, Television Broadcast: "The People Ask the President," October 12, 1956, *American Presidency Project*, http://www.presidency.ucsb.edu/ws/index.php?pid=10640&st=&st1=.

21. "Stevenson's Talk Charging U.S. Is 'Misled' on Suez," *New York Times*, October 20, 1956, 12.

22. Porter McKeever, *Adlai Stevenson: His Life and Legacy* (New York: William Morrow, 1989), 380–83.

23. Dwight D. Eisenhower, Statement by the President on the Reports from Poland, October 20, 1956, *American Presidency Project*, http://www.presidency.ucsb.edu/ws/index.php?pid=10661&st=&st1=.

24. Dwight D. Eisenhower, Address at the Anniversary Dinner of the Brotherhood of Carpenters and Joiners, October 23, 1956, *American Presidency Project*, http://www.presidency.ucsb.edu/ws/index.php?pid=10666&st=&st1=.

25. Dwight D. Eisenhower, Statement by the President on the Developments in Hungary, October 25, 1956, *American Presidency Project*, http://www.presidency.ucsb.edu/ws/index.php?pid=10672&st=&st1=.

26. FRUS, *1955–1957*, vol. 25, *Eastern Europe* (Washington, DC: US Government Printing Office, 1990), 295–99.

27. John Foster Dulles Speech, October 27, 1956, *Department of State Bulletin* 35 (November 5, 1956): 697.

28. Dwight D. Eisenhower, Statement by the President on the Middle East Including the Israeli Mobilization, October 28, 1956, *American Presidency Project*, http://www.presidency.ucsb.edu/ws/index.php?pid=10678&st=&st1=.

29. Dwight D. Eisenhower, Radio and Television Report to the American People on the Developments in Eastern Europe and the Middle East, October 31, 1956, *American Presidency Project*, http://www.presidency.ucsb.edu/ws/index.php?pid=10685&st=&st1=.

30. Dwight D. Eisenhower, Address in Convention Hall, Philadelphia, Pennsylvania, November 1, 1956, *American Presidency Project*, http://www.presidency.ucsb.edu/ws/index.php?pid=10686&st=&st1=.

31. Clayton Knowles, "Stevenson Warns of Split in West," *New York Times*, November 1, 1956, 1.

32. Harrison E. Salisbury, "Stevenson Offers a Program to End Strife in Mideast," *New York Times*, November 3, 1956, 3.

33. William M. Blair, "Nixon Hails Break with Allies' Policies," *New York Times*, November 3, 1956, 1.

34. *FRUS, 1955–1957*, vol. 25, pp. 354–58.

35. Ibid., 358–59.

36. *FRUS, 1955–1957*, vol. 16, pp. 976–77, 993–94.

37. Ibid., 1014–15, 1025–27.

38. Dwight D. Eisenhower, The President's News Conference, October 11, 1956, *American Presidency Project*, http://www.presidency.ucsb.edu/ws/index.php?pid=10633.

39. Eisenhower Call to Hoover, October 8, 1956, Anne C. Whitman Series, Eisenhower Diaries, Dwight D. Eisenhower Library.

40. *FRUS, 1955–1957*, vol. 16, pp. 833–39.

41. Ibid., 62–68.

42. Ibid., 902–16.

43. Ibid., 69–71.

44. London to State Department, Cable 550, July 31, 1956, Record Group 59, Central Decimal File, 674.84A/7-3156, National Archives and Records Administration, College Park, MD.

45. Macmillan to Eden, September 25, 26, 1956, PREM 11/1102, National Archives, Kew, London.

46. Quoted in Selwyn Lloyd, *Suez 1956* (New York: Jonathan Cape, 1978), 209.

47. Ole Holsti, *Public Opinion and Foreign Policy* (Ann Arbor: University of Michigan Press, 2009), 60.

48. John S. D. Eisenhower, *Strictly Personal* (New York: Doubleday, 1974), 189.

49. *FRUS, 1955–1957*, vol. 16, pp. 943–45.

50. Ibid., 722–24.

51. Ibid., 884–85.

52. Eisenhower to Gruenther, November 2, 1956, Anne C. Whitman Series, Eisenhower Diaries.

53. Holsti, *Public Opinion*, 288, 49.

54. Ibid., 289.

55. Quoted in Foyle, *Counting the Public In*, 40.

56. "Public Opinion Wins Wars," *Prescott Evening-Courier*, May 4, 1944, 4, http://news.google.com/newspapers?nid=897&dat=19440504&id=ex5TAAAAIBAJ&sjid=5oEDAAAAIBAJ&pg=5553,5303649.

57. Holsti, *Public Opinion*, 62.

6

Leadership Experience in the Cold War

Cuba, Khrushchev, and Quemoy-Matsu in the 1960 Presidential Election Campaign

Sylvia Ellis

The 1960 presidential election was dominated by the leadership question; being "statesmanlike" was especially important given recent Cold War tensions. Indeed, the Republican candidate, Vice President Richard M. Nixon, focused his campaign around his foreign policy credentials. His opponent, Senator John F. Kennedy of Massachusetts, was forced to respond to charges of political immaturity. Was a youthful John Kennedy ready to be the leader of the free world, and could Nixon capitalize on the relative inexperience of the senator from Massachusetts? Answering these questions successfully was a vital part of what was always predicted to be the tightest of elections.

Another decisive part of the winning equation in 1960 was the necessity of adapting to a new era in campaigning. This election was "the first modern campaign," involving new methods, covered widely on television, and featuring two charismatic American political figures.[1] The closeness of the result on November 8—Kennedy won the popular vote by just 120,000 votes out of a record 68.8 million ballots cast—led scholars to ask what tipped the balance in his favor. Studies have examined the Catholic vote, working-class voters in industrial areas, the African American vote, the involvement of organized crime, the farm vote, and regional variations in order to help answer this question.[2] Analysis of the part played by foreign policy has considered whether Kennedy was successful in addressing the issue of his experience, and some attention has been paid to Kennedy's and Nixon's courting of the ethnic vote via foreign policy rhetoric and pledges.[3] However, as Robert Divine pointed out, it is also worth asking why Kennedy did not win more convincingly given recent American defeats abroad. Did he win on image but lose on the issues? Although numerous foreign policy issues engaged the candidates during the 1960 campaign (defense and disarmament, Africa, Latin America, Eastern Europe, the Middle East) and there was agreement on several issues (the struggle against communism, the Berlin problem, summit meetings), three issues dominated the agenda: Cuba, the Soviets, and the tiny offshore islands of Quemoy and Matsu.[4] This chapter will examine all three and show that Kennedy fumbled somewhat in his handling of all of them, but especially Quemoy-Matsu, yet still managed to convince enough of the US electorate that he could be trusted to lead the nation on the world stage. In the process, it also considers the extent to which the foreign policy debate served to educate or obfuscate the issues for the American people in 1960.

The Leadership Question

Long before the party conventions, it was clear that the key issue in the 1960 campaign would be leadership experience, not least because polls showed that American prestige was a major concern for the voters.[5] The Eisenhower administration had suffered a number of setbacks on the world scene between 1957 and 1960, including the launch of the world's first intercontinental ballistic missile by the Soviet Union, the Berlin crisis standoff with Khrushchev, and the coming to power of a Communist-friendly government in Cuba. But perhaps the "greatest blow to American confidence" was the Soviet launch of *Sputnik,* the first artificial earth-orbiting satellite.[6] Democrats took advantage of all these developments, charging that the Eisenhower administration had allowed the Soviets to open up a "missile gap" and was "asleep at the switch." Despite White House denials that this was the case, the issue would not go away, not least because in 1957 the Gaither Report highlighted the vulnerability of the United States to Soviet attack and the inadequacy of its civil defense program.[7] The report was leaked to Chalmers Roberts of the *Washington Post* whose headline on December 20 read "U.S. in Grave Peril."[8] Senator Kennedy joined in the chorus of disapproval from Congress, strategists, scholars, and the public arguing that the United States must invest substantially more of its wealth into the nation's defense capabilities. Working on figures in the public domain that were, as Christopher Preble notes, "estimates . . . based on pure speculation" and passed on to him by the "prophet of the missile gap," the columnist Joseph Alsop, JFK delivered a major speech in the Senate in August 1958 in which he suggested that "by 1960 the United States will have lost . . . its superiority in nuclear striking power" as a result of Eisenhower's willingness to place "fiscal security ahead of national security."[9]

Eisenhower made some inroads into restoring confidence by engaging in personal diplomacy, including meeting Nikita Khrushchev at a Camp David summit in September 1959.[10] But there was still a growing sense of American drift. The veteran journalist Walter Lippmann joined others in asking whether the United States had lost its sense of national purpose, and Eisenhower established the Commission on National Goals in February 1960 to define the nation's objectives for the coming decade.[11] Nixon knew that this context meant that the American electorate would care greatly about the leadership qualifications of the next president and who could best handle the many challenges the United States faced as it entered a new and troubling decade.

Campaign Strategies

In 1960, Nixon ran a positive campaign, Kennedy a negative one.[12] By 1960, the vice president was clear that the "international issue would be No. 1" in the presidential election, telling reporters that the United States must have the will and the resources "to maintain an adequate deterrent."[13] He believed that this was a battleground he could win on. Republicans had long been associated with a strong defense and firm foreign policy leadership.[14] And, in many ways, the Nixon ticket seemed designed to win on that very territory. The vice president chose the Republican senator and former US ambassador to the United Nations Henry Cabot Lodge Jr. as his running mate.[15] But, more importantly, as vice president

Nixon knew that he had several advantages, including being "probably the best known political figure in the country after Eisenhower" who could stress his "superior experience" in the field of foreign policy.[16] Unlike the Democrats, who were tarnished by the so-called loss of China under their watch, he could not be accused of being soft on communism, having been publicly identified with anticommunism through his position on the House Un-American Activities Committee investigations in the late 1940s. Indeed, his spearheading of the prosecution of the suspected spy Alger Hiss made him "into a world figure."[17] His reputation as a vehement anti-Communist was strengthened further during the 1950 Senate race, when he reminded the nation of the accusations that Helen Gahagan Douglas was a Soviet sympathizer by using the term *pink lady* and sending out flyers about her on pink paper.[18] And, unlike earlier vice presidents, who were often seen as mere ornaments, Nixon had the benefit of being the first truly modern vice president. Eisenhower let Nixon chair National Security Council and cabinet meetings in his absence.[19] Nixon's personal interest in foreign affairs meant that he was also happy to undertake numerous, well-publicized overseas visits as vice president. He made great play of these trips during the campaign, being, as Carroll Kilpatrick of the *Washington Post* observed, "an accomplished namedropper": "'As Adenauer said to me.' 'Khrushchev told me.' . . . etc."[20] In all, he embarked on sixty-nine goodwill and official visits, reached all parts of the globe, and met foreign dignitaries on all continents.[21] Although the trips helped foster an image of Nixon as a leader capable of continuing Eisenhower's "peace and prosperity" mission, not all these visits went swimmingly. In the spring of 1958, he visited Latin America, with the tour beginning well in Argentina but ending badly in Caracas, Venezuela, when an angry mob attacked his car. More successfully, and more importantly for the 1960 campaign, in the summer of 1959 he went on a tour of Russia and Poland to support an American trade exposition.[22] Standing in the kitchen of a "full-size model of a middle-class American home . . . full of conveniences that dazzled the Russians," the two leaders engaged in spirited badinage that centered over who was ahead on rockets, washing machines, and quality housing.[23] The photographic image of the "kitchen debate" in Moscow, showing Nixon standing face-to-face with the Soviet leader and jabbing his finger at him as he defended American values, led to a rise in the opinion polls for the vice president, narrowing Kennedy's lead over him (Kennedy was his likely opponent at that stage) to just 4 percent.[24] Eisenhower described Nixon as having "acquitted himself splendidly and in accordance with what you'd expect from a man in high office." As "the man who stood up to Khrushchev," Nixon was now considered "the personification of leadership."[25] Not surprisingly, the photograph was used repeatedly on campaign posters and literature.

Aware of these advantages, Nixon made a decision that proved critical to the outcome of the election. Despite advice to the contrary in some quarters, he chose to run a positive campaign. The *Washington Post* noted that Nixon was out to "confuse his critics" by not fulfilling predictions that the election would be "one of the dirtiest campaigns in recent history." Instead, "Tricky Dick" ran as the "new Nixon," as newspapers observed, noting that his early criticisms of JFK (for attacking the president's leadership) were made "in calm and judicious tones."[26] He believed that he could gain more votes by taking a positive message to the nation—"peace, experience, and prosperity"—and was reluctant to engage in attack politics. Given his reputation as a mean campaigner, this decision to run a "soft campaign" astounded many, especially as the months passed and Kennedy gained ground in the polls.[27] Working with Robert Finch as his campaign manager, Nixon outlined his strategy in his acceptance speech, saying that he would "carry this campaign into every one of the fifty states." Knowing that the election would be tight, he believed that "every vote—and thus every state—would be important." But the schedule for reaching all the states was flexible; he would visit particular states when it was felt to be most opportune. After receiving details of Nixon's "Surefire" campaign plan on foreign policy, aimed at attracting "those non-thinking voters, who, Nixon thinks, will decide [the] election," the Kennedy campaign knew it had to go on the attack.[28] Overall, in terms of campaign rhetoric, Nixon acclaimed more, Kennedy attacked more, and Nixon was forced to defend more.[29]

From the beginning of his campaign for the White House, Kennedy knew that he was behind in the polls on foreign policy and made a concerted effort to address this. Importantly, in 1957, JFK had gained a seat on the Senate Foreign Relations Committee, a powerful position that helped him gain crucial experience. He also made statements in the Senate on foreign policy issues, including calling for an end to the French war in Algeria in July 1957, something that attracted the attention of the national press.[30] The *New York Times* described the speech as "perhaps the most comprehensive and outspoken arraignment of Western policy towards Algeria yet presented by an American in public office."[31] By 1959, JFK was telling the journalist Cyrus Sulzberger that foreign policy would "be the main electoral issue in the sense that the Republicans will be attacked for letting the United States slip back in the power race." And, despite Nixon's credentials, Kennedy believed that his own travels, writings, public addresses, and national service made him a match for the vice president. The Kennedy team briefed campaign workers to stress that their candidate had more foreign policy experience than Nixon: "The truth is that Senator Kennedy was an internationally-recognized authority—and the author of a best-selling book on foreign policy—only three years after Mr. Nixon was graduated from law school."[32] Kennedy's 1940 *Why England Slept,* the published version of his thesis examining the British government's appeasement policy and his wartime service aboard a patrol torpedo boat as well as covering the formation of the United Nations and the Potsdam conference witnessed in a brief spell as a journalist, provided evidence of his patriotism and military experience. His team also stressed that, as a congressman and senator, he had a record of "tough-minded realism" on issues of foreign policy, saying that he "was consistently against proposed reductions in the armed forces prior to Communist aggression in Korea . . . fought for additional defense and research funds . . . [and] played a major role in efforts to put our foreign economic program on a businesslike basis."[33] Kennedy's voting record backed up these claims.[34]

Some of these earlier stands paid dividends in 1960. For instance, his membership in the Latin American Subcommittee of the Senate Foreign Relations Committee and his ten-point program for Latin American development (the Eisenhower administration adopted all ten points) meant that Kennedy had already attracted a substantial number of Latino votes. And, early in 1960, he arranged for Allan Nevins, the distinguished historian, to edit his foreign policy speeches from the 1950s under the title *The Strategy for Peace.* This collection, a 1957 *Foreign Affairs* article entitled "A Democrat Looks at Foreign Policy," alongside his Pulitzer Prize–winning and best-selling *Profiles in Courage* helped raise his profile as a frontrunner in the race for the Democratic nomination in 1960, raised his credibility on foreign policy issues, and showed him to be an orthodox Cold Warrior who favored the defense of South Vietnam, encouragement for the captive peoples of Eastern Europe, and a tough line against the Soviet Union.[35] He focused, in particular, on the administration's lack of understanding of Third World nationalism and called for more economic aid for countries struggling with poverty.[36]

Despite these efforts, Kennedy was still viewed as a relative innocent when it came to foreign affairs, and his campaign team understood that combating this image was essential to his success. This team was run by his close aides Kenneth O'Donnell and Dave Powers and by Lawrence O'Brien as field director. In January 1960, Chester Bowles, a Democratic congressman from Connecticut and former US ambassador to India, became Kennedy's foreign policy adviser, with Adlai Stevenson soon joining him.[37] Portraying JFK as a leader offering "new and dynamic approaches to the country's problems, while tying Nixon to eight years of 'do-nothingism,'" the Kennedy team ran an organized campaign with a planned schedule that included obtaining local detail to allow tailored speeches.[38] It was aided by the use of modern campaigning techniques, not least the use of computer simulations and private, state-by-state polling by Louis Harris.[39] Polls were used throughout the primaries and the general election campaign: sixty-six overall and twenty-six between September and November 1960.[40] Foreign policy issues were not stressed in states where foreign policy was low on the list of priorities for voters and emphasized where it was.[41]

The Campaign Unfolds

From the start of his campaign, JFK adopted an unapologetic, confident manner, but his early speeches avoided specific foreign policy proposals; instead, he concentrated on the general weakness of the US position in the Cold War. In his first major address after announcing his candidacy, Kennedy attacked Eisenhower indirectly by saying that the people "demand a vigorous proponent of the national interest . . . a man capable of acting as the Commander-in-Chief of the grand alliance, not merely a bookkeeper who feels that his work is done when the numbers on the balance sheet come out even." He went on to criticize the current administration on "the growing missile gap, the rise of Communist China, the despair of the underdeveloped nations, the explosive situations in Berlin and in the Formosa Straits, the deterioration of NATO, [and] the lack of an arms control agreement."[42] These criticisms of Ike's foreign policy were, in the early months of 1960, overshadowed as most of the primaries focused on domestic policies.

On May 1, just two weeks before a planned summit meeting between Eisenhower and Khrushchev in Paris to deal with the arms race, Berlin, and Cuba, the U-2 affair changed all that. The shooting down of an American spy plane by the Soviets and Khrushchev's public revelation that the United States had violated Soviet air space for espionage purposes put the Eisenhower administration on the back foot. Khrushchev rescinded an invitation to the president to visit Moscow and withdrew from the summit.[43] The attempt to cover up the incident—by claiming that the U-2 was a lost weather reconnaissance plane—made things even worse. When the Soviet leader revealed the capture of the pilot, Gary Powers, administration officials tried to justify their actions, first saying that Soviet secrecy had pushed them into it, before finally taking responsibility for the act (although never apologizing for this breach of international law). Although the president was supported by the public; the timing of the incident proved costly. With a dark cloud hanging over the summit, Khrushchev demanded that Eisenhower apologize, the president refused (although he had suspended further reconnaissance flights over the Soviet Union), and the summit broke down.[44] Democrats in the House asked for a full explanation of the incident, saying that they were "distressed over the collapse of the Summit . . . and the damage to our prestige and leadership in the world"; Adlai Stevenson accused the administration of "incredible blunders" that provided the Soviets with a "crowbar and sledge hammer" to wreck the Paris summit. Republicans responded by charging Stevenson with making a "reckless speech" and falling "like a ton of bricks for the Khrushchev line," while Nixon argued that foreign policy should not be a campaign issue as national unity was all important when dealing with the Russians.[45] In the middle of this furor, and given Eisenhower's enduring popularity, Kennedy made his first campaign slip on foreign policy. While campaigning in Oregon he asserted that Republican peace and prosperity claims were "blowing up in smoke" and said that "an apology" might have been in order, adding that "regret" would have certainly been a reasonable term. Nixon, who said very little during the controversy, appeared to gain from the crisis. Although, as *Newsweek* put it, "the issue of peace had been blown right out of the Eisenhower

Administration's hands" and "the picture of the Vice President . . . as heir apparent to a successful world policy had been fragmented," Nixon was portrayed by his supporters as an anti-Communist hard-liner (as opposed to Kennedy's apparent "appeasement" of the Soviets); they even argued that the Russian leader hated the vice president and therefore that electing Nixon was sticking it to Khrushchev. A Gallup poll after the collapse of the summit showed that voters felt Nixon would be better at dealing with Russian's leaders than Kennedy, by 57 to 34 percent.[46] In April, Nixon had been behind Kennedy in the polls (46 to 54 percent); he had regained the lead after the crisis (51 to 49 percent) and pulled even farther ahead after the Republican convention (53 to 47 percent).[47] Moreover, pollsters found that 49 percent of the people wanted Nixon to represent the United States at the next summit conference, compared to the only 37 percent who chose Kennedy. The focus on domestic issues and JFK's personal charm and magnetism had been a successful strategy in the primaries, but on matters of national security the question on everybody's lips was whether the young senator could stand up to world leaders.

After what many considered Kennedy's first real foreign policy gaffe, his campaign team battled to portray his foreign policy potential positively. On June 14, JFK made a major Senate speech in which he outlined a twelve-point program to address what he saw as "the lack of a coherent and purposeful national strategy backed by strength."[48] The program included increased defense spending and stronger ties with US allies but essentially boiled down to fighting the Cold War more effectively. This was in line with Kennedy's campaign slogan, "It is time to get this country moving again."[49] Throughout the campaign, there was no disagreement between the two candidates on the goals of American foreign policy, with the result that, after Kennedy's nomination and again after his election, overseas commentators observed that "the general lines of U.S. foreign policy will remain the same."[50] The journalist Roscoe Drummond argued in mid-June that the main issue was "which presidential candidate will the country think best able to mobilize our resources to keep the world at peace and Communist imperialism at bay" and acknowledged that Kennedy was now "addressing himself realistically to what could be one of the weaknesses of his candidacy" by showing in his Senate speech that he would not be soft on communism.[51] By July 1960, Gallup reported that the "overwhelming majority of those interviewed regard relations with Russia and the rest of the world as being the primary problem facing the nation today."[52] And, when pollsters across the country asked whom people would rather have across the bargaining table from Khrushchev, the answer was always heavily in favor of Nixon.[53] Kennedy's recent gaffe had not helped. The "who best to deal with Khrushchev" question continued throughout the campaign, although it reached a peak when the Soviet leader visited New York in September 1960 to speak at the United Nations.

Not that it was plain sailing for Nixon. Eisenhower's foreign policy was less confrontational by the late 1950s, and Nixon followed this record of moderation in the early months of the campaign. This line was soon criticized by his rival for the GOP nomination, Nelson Rockefeller, who wanted a commitment to a strong platform that made the American public aware of the sacrifices needed in order to increase defense spending to meet the Communist threat.[54] The Republicans also faced more bad news on foreign affairs. On June 10, Communist student rioters in Tokyo surrounded a car containing Eisenhower's press secretary, James Hagerty, and the US ambassador to Japan, Douglas MacArthur II. Four days later, angered by the ratification by the Japanese government of the US-Japanese Treaty of Mutual Cooperation and Security and its sanctioning of American air bases in Japan, protesters staged mass demonstrations that led the Japanese to cancel Eisenhower's forthcoming trip to Japan.

After the conventions, Eisenhower invited Kennedy to attend briefings on foreign policy developments. The press surmised that this would result in "a more temperate and constructive discussion of foreign policy issues."[55] This was the case in the late summer, but Nixon was dealt another unexpected blow. On August 24, when asked by Charles Mohr of *Time* magazine whether he could provide an example of a major idea from Nixon that he had adopted, Eisenhower replied: "If you give me a week, I might think of one."[56] The same day, in a speech in Alexandria, Virginia, JFK continued to defend himself against charges of inexperience by going on the attack: "The issue is not merely the experience of the candidates. . . . Mr. Nixon *is* experienced—experienced in policies of retreat, defeat and weakness. . . . Why would anyone point with pride to presiding over successive blows to our security and prestige—Indo-China, Hungary, Suez, Sputnik, the riots in Venezuela, the collapse of the Summit, the riots in Japan, the collapse of the Baghdad Pact, the failure of disarmament, the

U-2 fiasco, and now Cuba and the Congo?"[57] But his opportunity to provide more proof of his suitability for high office came a month later.

The Television Debates

There can be little doubt that the presidential debates had an impact on the outcome of the 1960 election. Indeed, Donaldson argues that "the four televised debates . . . became the decisive events in the 1960 campaigns."[58] In the run-up to the first debate, as Nixon's chief pollster, Claude Robinson, noted how Kennedy tossed into his speeches remarks like "When I visited Moscow" and "I know Khrushchev, too," but he remained perplexed by the Kennedy strategy of continuing "to talk vaguely about 'moving ahead.'"[59] Kennedy's team understood, however, that, by accepting the offer to compete directly with Nixon, JFK had a unique opportunity to counter assertions that he was too young and too green to protect US national interests and could possibly double his exposure. After all, by 1960, 88 percent of American families owned a television.[60] And, in the lead-up to the debates, the polls showed that the two candidates were almost neck and neck (46 to 47 percent).[61] Advised by Eisenhower not to appear, Nixon went ahead because he "relished confrontations" but also because he had confidence in the fact that he was more well-known than Kennedy, had eight years of executive experience, and, as far as he was concerned, had been an "effective spokesman" for the United States. He later acknowledged that giving Kennedy a national platform that placed him on equal status was one of his "biggest mistakes," that he should have insisted on one debate rather than four, and that he should not have allowed the first debate to be on domestic politics.[62] As it turned out, the first debate received the best viewing figures, with over seventy million tuning in, double the number who tuned in for Kennedy's nomination acceptance, and roughly two-thirds of the electorate. And, although the remaining debates averaged around sixty-five million, the first debate had the most impact on the public.[63]

On September 26, in Chicago's CBS studio, the two candidates appeared in the first televised debate. Kennedy addressed his opening and closing statements to the American people and unlike Nixon, appeared "calm and nerveless": "The Vice-President, by contrast, was tense, almost frightened, at turns glowering and, occasionally, haggard-looking to the point of sickness."[64] Kennedy certainly came out looking more states-manlike and healthy; Nixon projected an image of "not one in command but of a schoolyard bully."[65] Both campaign teams closely monitored the impact of the debates on polling. Nixon was the winner with radio lis-teners; Kennedy with television viewers.[66] In the space of a few minutes, Kennedy had addressed the issue of experience head on. However, what was worrying for Nixon was the progress that JFK was making on the issues of peace, dealing with the Russians, and national defense. Gallup polls taken after the first debate showed that Kennedy had jumped 3 per-centage points (46 to 49 percent) in these areas.[67] Harris pollsters, com-missioned by the Kennedy team, concluded that "Kennedy became the leader, Nixon the follower." When respondents were asked about Ken-nedy's positive points, he was described as "forceful, forthright, aggressive (like FDR)," and, although he scored highly on Medicare, education, and helping the farmer, people also felt that he would "deal with Khrushchev firmly." The Nixon campaign's evaluation of the first debate agreed that Kennedy was "proving to be an effective campaigner" who was "making headway in shaking off the idea that he is immature . . . showing his sup-porters that he has political know-how."[68] But voters still largely disagreed that the United States had "become a second rate nation." The vice presi-dent felt that it was "correct to focus on foreign affairs where the ticket is strong, to emphasize experience," as he still had "the advantage," although it was "not as decisive as it was at the outset" of the campaign. Kennedy had "blunted the 'get tough with Russia' issue but had made no in-roads on defense issues or Cuba."[69]

Showing his Naïveté? Kennedy and Quemoy-Matsu

Theodore Sorensen noted in his memoirs that "two . . . foreign policy issues arose in the last three debates, and neither of them worked to Ken-nedy's advantage."[70] Indeed, while popular memory remembers this new element in the presidential campaigning as one that was positive for Ken-nedy, the Democratic contender did not fare so well in these later debates because of Cuba and Quemoy and because Nixon went on the offen-sive by highlighting Kennedy's inexperience and the inconsistencies in his foreign policy statements. With Khrushchev in the United States at the time—on October 12 he gave his infamous shoe-banging talk at the

UN General Assembly—Kennedy and Nixon also clashed again over the collapse of the Paris summit. The Democrat continued to defend his line that an American expression of regret might have saved the conference and that on this occasion the United States had broken international law, something even Lodge had been forced to acknowledge a month earlier during a *Meet the Press* interview. Nixon continued to argue that the U-2 provided vital intelligence that helped maintain US strength, despite knowing that international law experts were giving succor to the Kennedy line that a US apology should have been given. Professor H. Berman of Harvard argued that the flight "violated Soviet air space, and thus violated international law," and that "the standard apology should have been given." Nixon knew he could not put forward "a valid legal argument to counter" such analyses; he could only argue that Khrushchev would not have accepted an apology.[71]

Although considered less decisive in terms of final votes, exchanges in the second debate were more "biting" and "sharp," and Quemoy-Matsu was "one of the high points."[72] Edward Morgan of ABC raised the question of the two Nationalist Chinese islands off the coast of Communist China, asking Kennedy to comment further on his own statement that these were "unwise places to draw our defense line in the Far East." Although there had been a crisis over the Formosa Straits in 1955, few Americans understood the importance of the straits to the nation's foreign policy. In late 1954 and early 1955, China attempted to regain control of several offshore islands from Taiwan but backed down after the Eisenhower administration resorted to what many considered nuclear brinkmanship.[73] But few people appear to have comprehended what was at stake. An opinion poll taken in March 1955 showed that only 10 percent of those questioned knew who owned the islands and that only 14 percent knew how far away the islands were from China's mainland.[74] A second crisis in the Taiwan Straits in 1958—with a similar outcome—did not lead to an enhanced understanding of events. But did a presidential debate enlighten an American public with only a limited knowledge of these islands?

Kennedy certainly attempted to offer some nuance to the discussion. He replied, in a three-minute answer, that he believed "strongly in the defense of Formosa" but argued that the islands were "a few miles . . . off the coast of Red China, within a general harbor area and more than a hundred miles from Formosa" and that Undersecretary of State Christian

Herter and leading military figures such as Admiral Raymond A. Spruance and General Matthew Ridgway had admitted that they were "strategically indefensible." Moreover, he pointed out: "We have never said flatly that we will defend Matsu if it's attacked. We say we will defend it if it's part of a general attack on Formosa." He went on: "If you're going to get into war for the defense of Formosa, it ought to be on a clearly defined line. . . . I believe that we should defend Formosa. We should come to its defense. To leave this rather in the air, that we will defend it under some conditions but not under others, I think is a mistake." While opposed to "withdrawal at the point of a Communist gun," he felt that there was a reduced chance of "being dragged into an unnecessary war" if the Nationalists "could be persuaded to draw the line of defense specifically and exclusively around Formosa." The vice president saw an opening and disagreed "completely with Senator Kennedy" on that point. Indeed, he went beyond the Eisenhower policy of leaving the status of the offshore islands in doubt, saying: "The question is not these two little pieces of real estate; they are unimportant. It isn't the few people who live on them; they are not too important. It's the principle involved. These two islands are in the area of freedom." He continued: "[Kennedy's answer] is the same kind of woolly thinking that led to disaster for America in Korea. I am against it. I would never tolerate it as president of the United States." Indeed, he recalled that South Korea had been judged to be "indefensible as well."[75]

Kennedy's attempt to offer a more sophisticated analysis of the offshore islands question was praised by Theodore White as "probably one of the sharpest and clearest responses of any question of the debates."[76] But, not surprisingly, the Republicans capitalized on this exchange and spent the remaining weeks before the election accusing Kennedy of "appeasement, retreat, and surrender." The *Washington Post* reporter Richard Lyons, traveling with Nixon, said that, during the week after the debate, Quemoy-Matsu was the outstanding fact of Nixon's campaign. As he put it, Nixon "latched onto an issue which he thinks he can clobber Kennedy with." Nixon's audiences were soon "waving signs of 'no surrender.'" One at Long Beach read: "Quemoy and Matsu—Kennedy's Munich." Nixon distorted Kennedy's words when he said that he opposed "handing over to the Communists one inch of free territory," with the implication that JFK might abandon Berlin as well. Chiang Kai-shek also joined in denouncing

Kennedy. While it might have been wise for the Democratic candidate to have abandoned this issue at this stage, he chose not to. Rather, according to one reporter: "[He was] perfectly willing, even eager, to go to bat with Nixon over the Quemoy-Matsu affair, and thus determine who would have the 'peace issue' in the campaign. . . . Kennedy at first felt Nixon had an emotional edge over him with the voter in the Quemoy-Matsu argument . . . [and] he was determined to stick to his position that the 'two rocks' were not worth spilling American blood for."[77] On October 12, Kennedy dedicated an entire speech in New York City to Quemoy and Matsu, pointing out in it that the Eisenhower administration had "long advocated evacuation of these islands" and "had opposed the Nationalist build-up on Quemoy and Matsu—namely, on the grounds that they were 'indefensible.'" He also quoted Admiral Harry E. Yarnell, the former commander of the US Asiatic Fleet, saying that the islands were "not worth the bones of a single American."[78] The speech received relatively little press attention but was described by White as "as fine a campaign discussion of an issue of national importance as this correspondent can remember—yet its impact on the nation was nil."[79]

Eisenhower was not impressed that Nixon had suggested that the administration's policy had shifted—from one retaining some flexibility to one suggesting the islands were part of a definite defense line (the Mutual Defense Treaty of 1955 committed the United States to aid in the defense of Formosa and the nearby Pescadores Islands). And, of course, Nixon was portrayed by Kennedy as "trigger-happy" for even suggesting the possibility of armed conflict.[80] Indeed, he was open to the charge made by Chester Bowles that advocating defense of the two small islands was "painting both himself and the country into a corner."[81] Arthur Krock of the *New York Times* wrote after the second debate that there was a real danger of handing the Communists a significant advantage by that declaring future policy was at the behest of one television reporter's question.[82]

The third debate, on October 14, drew forty-eight million television viewers and four million radio listeners, and, according to Robinson, voters remembered "mostly the argument over Matsu and Quemoy."[83] On this issue, Nixon "scored to 2 to 1." Nixon said that he resented Kennedy's accusation that the administration was "trigger-happy" and suggested that the Democrat would not stand up to dictators, while Kennedy repeated his preexisting stance that the 1955 treaty excluded the two islands.[84] In

the aftermath of the third debate, commentators observed that Quemoy-
Matsu had "become one of the hottest issues in the presidential battle."[85]
In the final debate, on October 21, Kennedy used his opening statement
to further clarify his position on the islands, essentially claiming that
they were not really "an issue in this campaign." He reiterated his vote
in favor of the Formosa resolution in 1955 and his agreement with the
Eisenhower administration's policy: "Mr. Nixon earlier indicated that he
would defend Quemoy and Matsu even if the attack on these islands, two
miles off the coast of China, were not part of a general attack on Formosa
and the Pescadores. I indicated that I would defend those islands if the
attack were directed against Pescadores and Formosa, which is part of the
Eisenhower policy." Nixon pushed him on this, however, by reminding
the viewers and listeners that he could be accused of inconsistency: "[The
senator] voted for the resolution in 1955 which gave the president the
power to use the forces of the United States to defend Formosa and the
offshore islands. But he also voted for an amendment—which was lost,
fortunately—an amendment which would have drawn a line and left out
those islands and denied the right to the president to defend those islands
if he thought it was an attack on Formosa. He repeated that error in 1959,
in the speech that he made. He repeated it again in a television debate."
Kennedy countered by reminding Nixon that Herter had said the islands
were "indefensible," that the Eisenhower administration had tried to persuade Chiang Kai-Shek to withdraw from the islands, and that Nixon
had said: "We should draw a line and commit ourselves, as a matter of
principle, to defend these islands. Not as part of the defense of Formosa
and the Pescadores."[86] Roscoe Drummond cautioned in the *Washington
Post* that it was "profitless and dangerous and confusing" to let the "shout-
ing match roll doing damage every day." His concern was that "what has
been happening is that both have been proclaiming differences which
don't exist and exaggerating whatever differences do exist." Suggesting
that they "rein themselves in," he said that he was "convinced that thus
far the candidates have confused far more than they have clarified the
controversy." Certainly, Nixon had complicated matters by saying that he
was in "exact" agreement with Ike on Quemoy-Matsu when the president
had made it clear that the United States would not "automatically" come
to their defense but would do so if China was about to attack Taiwan,
whereas Nixon suggested an automatic commitment. Likewise, Kennedy

could be criticized for suggesting that he "might well abandon Quemoy and Matsu." As one observer put it, "a hasty reader or listener" might get the impression that Kennedy "favors giving up" the islands while believing that "Nixon favors holding them at all costs" when actually they are both "not so far" from Eisenhower's position.[87]

Although his was the more thoughtful and cautious approach (stressing the dangers of ambiguity in American foreign policy)—and, as Arthur Schlesinger commented, it illustrated his "dislike for rigid interpretations of the cold war"—Kennedy backed down on Quemoy-Matsu in the final days of the campaign.[88] While believing that his position was the correct one, he understood that Nixon's simple refusal to surrender one square inch of free soil would resonate directly with the voters. He was forced to acknowledge that it was a "complex problem, requiring thought not merely rhetoric," and that "in a campaign great care must be used."[89] But he was able to say: "It was in the best interests of national security that Mr. Nixon has now retreated to the Administration's view as contained in the 1955 treaty and resolution which I have supported ever since."[90] After slight adjustments in their positions, the issue was dropped by "mutual consent," according to Sorensen, because both candidates "thought it was harming them."[91] Evidence indicates that it damaged Kennedy more. The election predictor Samuel Lubell found that 47 percent of voters he interviewed agreed with Nixon's argument that "we cannot give in anywhere to communists," compared to 29 percent who backed Kennedy's view that the islands were not worth fighting for. Nixon also saw a comeback in the Gallup polls taken after mid-October.

Castro and Cuba

Perceptions that Quemoy-Matsu had damaged Kennedy led to another campaign slip, this time on Cuba. The Eisenhower administration had appeared impotent in the face of the overthrow of the Batista government and, to Kennedy supporters, to have done little to prevent Cuba's closeness to the Russians. Nixon had met with Fidel Castro for three hours on April 19, 1959, when the Cuban leader visited Washington to speak at the National Press Club.[92] Throughout the campaign, Kennedy had used the growing Communist influence in Cuba as an example of the Eisenhower administration's "standstill" and ineptitude in foreign policy.[93] He called it a "major foreign policy disaster" and asked the Republicans to explain how and why the Communists had been allowed to "roll the Iron Curtain to 90 miles from our shores."[94] During the election campaign, US relations with Castro and Cuba deteriorated further as the new Cuban leader confiscated American property and the United States imposed sugar quotas. Although Nixon was aided by Eisenhower's decision to implement an economic embargo on Cuba, Kennedy called it "too little and too late" and outlined a four-point program of his own that included an "attempt to strengthen the non-Batista democratic anti-Castro forces in exile, and in Cuba itself, who offer eventual hope of overthrowing Castro." Nixon feared that Kennedy had been briefed by Allen Dulles about the CIA's covert training for an exile invasion force—he had not been—but instead this was a generalized anti-Castro program, and he had no specifics in mind. Nixon, aware of the CIA operation, could not, of course, disclose it during the fourth debate and instead criticized Kennedy for proposing an illegal intervention in Cuban internal affairs. And, also, overlooking CIA involvement in Guatemala, he suggested that the quarantine approach had been successful there and could be again in Cuba.[95]

Schlesinger recalled that the "Kennedy staff, seeking to take the offensive after his supposed soft position on Quemoy and Matsu, put out the provocative statement about strengthening Cuban fighters for freedom."[96] Written by the speechwriter Richard Goodwin late one evening, the statement continued: "Thus far those fighters for freedom have had virtually no support from our Government."[97] This was the only policy statement that Kennedy did not approve personally; he was asleep when it was drafted, and he must have wished he had been awake. The press pounced on it, with James Reston writing in the *New York Times* that Kennedy had "made what is probably his worst blunder of the campaign."[98] Nixon was able to portray Kennedy as "shockingly reckless." In preparation for the second debate, Nixon was drilled to emphasize Kennedy's "controlled schizophrenia" on Cuba.[99] Henry Holland, a former assistant secretary for inter-American affairs, advised Nixon to emphasize that "the problems with Cuba and Latin America are problems that arose and were made when the Democrats were in power" and suggested that it was worth emphasizing that "in 1953 there were 11 dictators in Latin America that had grown up during Democratic Administrations; today there are three."[100] Nixon did just that.[101] Kennedy attempted to offer a correction to this, saying: "Of the eleven, eight received substantial military aid from the United States. When the people overthrew these dictatorships, they had to do so against governments having U.S. arms for 'internal security.'"[102] After the third debate, the DNC issued a correction statement to the press, stating what Kennedy had said on Cuba.[103] The final analysis of the debates was offered to Kennedy by Harris. It made uneasy reading. The third debate had narrowed Kennedy's lead (as had the second).[104] Again, both candidates were happy to let the issue fade, and Kennedy did so after explaining "that he was referring not to direct intervention but to stepped-up propaganda and political positions."[105] Overall, the Nixon team was forced to admit that, when averaged, the series of debates were "a draw" but that crucially JFK had "succeeded in creating a victory psychology."[106]

Conclusion

Shortly before election day, the *New York Times* lauded "Senator Kennedy's approach in [the Quemoy-Matsu] case, as in other matters of foreign policy, except for his momentary blunder suggesting intervention in Cuba, a position from which he quickly retreated, seems to us to be more reasoned, less emotional, more flexible, less doctrinaire, more imaginative, less negative than that of the Vice President."[107] Certainly, Kennedy felt confident enough to stress the struggle against communism as the key electoral issue on the eve of the election, in contrast to Nixon, who stressed the strength and stability of the nation, especially in economic terms.[108] The television debates did come to life over the Quemoy-Matsu issue (although most Americans soon forgot about it). But it was an issue that sidetracked the debate on foreign policy. Kennedy learned a harsh lesson: the complexities of foreign policy are not easy to explain to the electorate, especially if your opponent reduces the debate to slogans; a sophisticated analysis of international issues can often be exploited ruthlessly in a presidential campaign. Kennedy attempted to add some subtlety to the presidential debate but was soon forced to back off; it was too narrow an election to risk being misunderstood. The issues of the day—Castro, Khrushchev, and Quemoy-Matsu—were not clarified by this presidential campaign; partisan rivalry would not allow it. On foreign policy, the winner had fallen into a number of traps for his opponent to exploit, with the result that, while foreign policy may not have decided the final result, the likelihood is that it did prevent a more convincing Democratic victory.

Notes

1. Gary A. Donaldson, *The First Modern Campaign: Kennedy, Nixon, and the Election of 1960* (Lanham, MD: Rowman & Littlefield, 2007). See also Edmund F. Kallina Jr., *Kennedy v. Nixon: The Presidential Election of 1960* (Gainesville: University Press of Florida, 2010); W. J. Rorabaugh, *The Real Making of the President: Kennedy, Nixon and the 1960 Election* (Lawrence: University Press of Kansas, 2009); and David Pietrusza, *1960—LBJ vs. JFK vs. Nixon: The Epic Campaign That Forged Three Presidencies* (New York: Union Square, 2008).

2. Robert Divine, *Foreign Policy and U.S. Presidential Elections, 1952–1960* (New York: New Viewpoints, 1974); R. P. Abelson et al., *Candidates, Issues and Strategies: A Computer Simulation of the 1960 Presidential Election* (Cambridge, MA: MIT Press, 1964); T. J. Carty, *A Catholic in the White House? Religion, Politics, and John F. Kennedy's Presidential Campaign* (New York: Palgrave Macmillan, 2004); Shaun A. Casey, *The Making of a Catholic President: Kennedy vs. Nixon 1960* (Oxford: Oxford University Press, 2009); Albert J. Menendez, *The Religious Factor in the 1960 Presidential Election: An Analysis of the Kennedy Victory over Anti-Catholic Prejudice* (Jefferson, NC: McFarland, 2011); Edmund F. Kallina Jr., *Courthouse over the White House: Chicago and the Presidential Election of 1960* (Orlando: University of Central Florida Press, 1988).

3. Laura Jane Gifford, *The Center Cannot Hold: The 1960 Presidential Election and the Rise of Modern Conservatism* (DeKalb: Northern Illinois University Press, 2009).

4. In April 1960, JFK acknowledged that he supported the Eisenhower administration on Cuba, Berlin, and summit meetings. See "Kennedy Assures Ike on Test Ban," *Washington Post*, April 4, 1960, A2.

5. Richard Nixon, *RN: The Memoirs of Richard Nixon* (New York: Simon & Schuster, 1990), 216.

6. Divine, *Foreign Policy and U.S. Presidential Elections, 1952–1960*, 184.

7. See Peter Roman, *Eisenhower and the Missile Gap* (Ithaca, NY: Cornell University Press, 1995); and S. Nelson Drew, "Expecting the Approach of Danger: The 'Missile Gap' as a Study of Executive-Congressional Competition in Building Consensus on National Security Issues," *Presidential Studies Quarterly* 19, no. 2 (1989): 317–35. For more detail on the findings and impact of the Gaither Report, see David L. Snead, *The Gaither Committee, Eisenhower, and the Cold War* (Columbus: Ohio State University Press, 1999).

8. "Secret Report Sees U.S. in Gravest Peril," *Washington Post*, December 20, 1957, A1; "Report U.S. Peril Grave: Secret Study of Red Might Disclosed," *Chicago Tribune*, December 20, 1957, 1.

9. Christopher A. Preble, "Who Ever Believed in the 'Missile Gap'? John F. Kennedy and the Politics of National Security," *Presidential Studies Quarterly* 33, no. 4 (December 2003): 801–26, 804.

10. Divine, *Foreign Policy and U.S. Presidential Elections, 1952–1960*, 184.

11. Henry R. Luce, ed., *The National Purpose* (New York: Holt, Rinehart & Winston, 1960); Divine, *Foreign Policy and U.S. Presidential Elections, 1952–1960*, 188.

12. John W. Malsberger, *The General and the Politician: Dwight Eisenhower, Richard Nixon, and American Politics* (Lanham, MD: Rowman & Littlefield, 2014), 181.

13. "Nixon Rates International Issue First," *Washington Post*, February 7, 1960, A2.

14. "Public Opinion and the 1960 Elections," Political Behavior Report, First Draft, Dr. George Belknap, 1960 Campaign & Transition, General Subject, 1959–1960, John F. Kennedy Library (hereafter JFKL).

15. Iwan Morgan, *Nixon* (London: Arnold, 2002), 60.

16. Martin Plissner, *The Control Room: How Television Calls the Shots in Presidential Elections* (New York: Touchstone, 2000), 130.

17. Stephen A. Ambrose, *Nixon*, vol. 1, *The Education of a Politician* (New York: Simon & Schuster, 1987), 196. For Nixon's own reflections on the Hiss-Chambers affair, see Richard Nixon, *Six Crises* (New York: Doubleday, 1962), 1–7.

18. See Greg Mitchell, *Tricky Dicky and the Pink Lady* (New York: Random House, 1998).

19. Paul Kengor, "The Vice President, Secretary of State, and Foreign Policy," *Political Science Quarterly* 115, no. 2 (2000): 175–99, 176, 181.

20. "Foreign Policy, Economy—Two Major Issues Set Down by Nixon," *Washington Post*, April 17, 1960, A2.

21. Folder: RN—Foreign Dignitaries—Met Here and Abroad by RN, box 11, Subject Files (PPS 77), Campaign 1960, Richard Nixon Library, Yorba Linda, CA (hereafter RNL).

22. Nixon and Khrushchev both discussed the incidents in their published memoirs. See Nikita Khrushchev, *Khrushchev Remembers* (Boston: Little, Brown, 1971), 364–66; and Nixon, *Six Crises*, 235–92.

23. Nixon, *RN*, 208; Rick Perlstein, ed., *Richard Nixon: Speeches, Writings, Documents* (Princeton, NJ: Princeton University Press, 2008), 88–96.

24. Divine, *Foreign Policy and U.S. Presidential Elections, 1952–1960*, 194.

25. Malsberger, *The General and the Politician*, 165.

26. "Nixon to Deal Gently with Opponents, Stress Policies of Administration," *Washington Post*, January 19, 1960, A2.

27. Conrad Black, *The Invincible Quest: The Life of Richard Milhouse Nixon* (London: Quercus, 2007), 406.

28. Memorandum from Alexander Klein to Senator Kennedy, n.d., 1960 Campaign & Transition, General Subject, 1959–1960, Robert F. Kennedy Papers, Pre-Administration Political Files, General Subject File, 1959–1960, box 33, JFKL.

29. William L. Benolt and Allison Harthcock, "Functions of the Great Debates: Acclaims, Attacks, and Defenses in the 1960 Presidential Debates," *Communication Monographs* 66, no. 4 (1999): 341–57

30. *Congressional Record: Proceedings and Debates of the 85th Congress, First Session, Senate,* July 2, 1957, 10782–792.

31. "Kennedy Urges U.S. Back Independence for Algeria," *New York Times,* July 3, 1957, 1, 5.

32. Senator Kennedy's Foreign Policy Record, Papers of President Kennedy (hereafter PPK), Pre-Presidential Papers (hereafter PPP), JFK Campaign 1960, Campaign Literature: Foreign Policy, JFKL.

33. Ibid.

34. *Congressional Quarterly,* May 13, 1960, 849–50.

35. *The Strategy for Peace by Senator John F. Kennedy,* ed. Allan Nevins (New York: Harper & Bros., 1960); John F. Kennedy, "A Democrat Looks at Foreign Policy," *Foreign Affairs* 36, no. 1 (1957): 44–59; "Kennedy Criticizes U.S. Foreign Policy," *New York Times,* September 23, 1957, 3; John F. Kennedy, *Profiles in Courage* (New York: Harper & Bros., 1956).

36. Larry J. Sabato, *The Kennedy Half-Century: The Presidency, Assassination, and Lasting Legacy of John F. Kennedy* (New York: Bloomsbury, 2014), 43.

37. "Kennedy Seeks Bowles as Adviser," *Washington Post,* January 25, 1960, A2; "Rep. Bowles Policy Aide to Kennedy," *Washington Post,* February 24, 1960, A11; "Kennedy Picks Stevenson, Bowles as Advisers," *Washington Post,* July 17, 1960, A9.

38. Lawrence R. Jacobs and Robert Y. Shapiro, "Issues, Candidate Image, and Priming: The Use of Private Polls in Kennedy's 1960 Presidential Campaign," *American Political Science Review* 88, no. 3 (1994): 527–40, 531.

39. Robert M. Elsinger, *The Evolution of Political Polling* (Cambridge: Cambridge University Press, 2003), 86–88.

40. Jacobs and Shapiro, "Issues, Candidate Image, and Priming," 530.

41. Robert McKinney, Off-the-Record Memorandum of Governor John Burroughs' Views concerning Issues of Importance in New Mexico in the Presidential and Vice-Presidential Campaign, September 1, 1960, PPK, PPP, '60 Campaign Issue, Richard Goodwin Working Papers 1958–1960, Schedules—U.S.-Soviet Military Comparison, box 996, File Speech Material and Drafts, 6/8/60–10/31/60, JFKL.

42. John F. Kennedy, The Presidency in 1960—National Press Club, Washington, DC, January 14, 1960, *The American Presidency Project,* http://www.presidency.ucsb.edu/ws/?pid=25795.

43. Michael R. Beschloss, *May-Day: Eisenhower, Khrushchev, and the U-2 Affair* (New York: Harper & Row, 1986); Gary Powers, *Operation Overflight: A Memoir of the U-2 Incident* (Washington, DC: Brassey's, 2004).

44. US Department of State, *Foreign Relations of the United States, 1958–1960,* vol. 9, *Berlin Crisis, 1959–1960, Germany, Austria* (Washington, DC: US Government Printing Office, 1993), 438–52.

45. "Democrats Ask Ike for U-2 Story," *Washington Post,* May 21, 1960, A1, A6; "Adlai 'Fell Like Ton of Bricks' for K's Line, GOP Charges," *Washington Post,* May 22, 1960, A4.

46. "Gallup Check on Issues: Kennedy or Nixon?" *Boston Globe,* May 30, 1960, 32.

47. Nixon, *RN,* 217.

48. "U.S. Policy Shift Urged by Kennedy," *Washington Post,* June 15, 1960, A1; "Text of Kennedy's Speech to Senate Advocating New Approach on Foreign Policy," *New York Times,* June 15, 1960, 32.

49. Theodore C. Sorensen, *Kennedy* (Old Saybrook, CT: Konecky & Konecky, 1965), 178.

50. Special Memorandum, Comment on the Nomination of Senator John F. Kennedy, July 21, 1960, Foreign Broadcast Information Division, Office of Operations, PPK, White House Staff Files, Papers of Pierre Salinger, Pre-Inaugural Correspondence, JFKL.

51. Roscoe Drummond, "Kennedy's Question; Who's Best to Lead," *Washington Post,* June 18, 1960, A11.

52. Robert Dallek, *John F. Kennedy: An Unfinished Life, 1917–1963* (New York: Allen Lane, 2003), 288.

53. "Moves by Ike and K May Be Key to Election," *Washington Post,* October 1, 1960, 5.

54. "Platform Stalls on Foreign Policy," *New York Times,* July 23, 1960, 6.

55. "Foreign Policy Briefings," *Washington Post,* July 18, 1960, A10.

56. Dwight D. Eisenhower, The President's New Conference, August 24, 1960, *American President Project.* http://www.presidency.ucsb.edu/ws/?pid=11915.

57. The Basic Issue: Experience, Address Delivered by Senator John F. Kennedy in Alexandria, Virginia on August 24, 1960, 8/60, PPK, PPP, '60 Campaign, Press and Publicity: Speeches, Statements and Sections 1958–1960, 7/60–11/60, box 1027, JFKL.

58. Donaldson, *First Modern Campaign,* 110.

59. Memorandum from Claude Robinson to Messrs. Nixon, Hall, Finch, September 22, 1960, Campaign 1960, Presidential Debates (PPS 61), box 1, Claude Robinson, Inc.—Evaluation of Debates, RNL.

60. Theodore H. White, *The Making of the President, 1960* (1961; New York: HarperPerennial, 2009), 279, 282.

61. Lydia Saad, "Presidential Debates Rarely Game-Changers," Gallup, September 25, 2008, www.gallup.com/poll/110674/presidential-debates-rarely-gamechangers.aspx.

62. Nixon, *RN,* 217.

63. White, *The Making of the President, 1960,* 178, 283.

64. Ibid., 288–89.

65. Dallek, *John F. Kennedy,* 285.

66. James N. Druckman, "The Power of Television Images: The First Kennedy-Nixon Debate Revisited," *Journal of Politics* 65, no. 2 (2003): 559–71.

67. Lydia Saad, "Presidential Debates Rarely Game-Changers."

68. An Analysis of the First Kennedy-Nixon Debate, September 29, 1960, Louis Harris & Associates, 1960 Campaign & Transition, General Subject, 1959–1960, PPK, PPP, JFKL; Memorandum from Claude Robinson to Nixon, Hall, Finch, October 5, 1960, Campaign 1960, Presidential Debates (PPS 61), box 1, Claude Robinson, Inc.—Evaluation of Debates, RNL.

69. An Analysis of the First Kennedy-Nixon Debate.

70. Sorensen, *Kennedy*, 204.

71. Memorandum from Rita E. Hauser, October 7, 1960, Collection: Campaign 1960, Presidential Debates (PPS 61), box 1, Folder: 4. Relations—Communists, RNL.

72. Rorabough argues: "The three later debates had little impact on the contest." W. J. Rorabough, *The Real Making of the President: Kennedy, Nixon, and the 1960 Election* (Lawrence: University Press of Kansas, 2009), 155. See also "Nixon, Kennedy Step Up Debate," *Washington Post*, October 8, 1963, p. A1; and "Exchanges Sharp," *New York Times*, October 8, 1963, 1.

73. See Bennett C. Rushkoff, "Eisenhower, Dulles and the Quemoy-Matsu Crisis, 1954–1955," *Political Science Quarterly* 96, no. 3 (1981): 465–80; Gordon H. Chang, "To the Nuclear Brink: Eisenhower, Dulles, and the Quemoy-Matsu Crisis," *International Security* 12, no. 4 (1988): 96–122; Robert Accinelli, *Crisis and Commitment: United States Policy toward Taiwan, 1950–1955* (Chapel Hill: University of North Carolina Press, 1996); and Leonard H. D. Gordon, "United States Opposition to the Use of Force in the Taiwan Strait, 1954–1962," *Journal of American History* 72, no. 3 (December 1985): 637–60.

74. American Institute of Public Opinion Poll, March 27, 1955, in Hazel Gaudet Erskine, "The Polls: The Informed Public," *Public Opinion Quarterly* 26, no. 4 (1962): 669–77, 677.

75. Presidential Debate in Washington, DC, October 7, 1960, *American Presidency Project*. http://www.presidency.ucsb.edu/ws/?pid=29401.

76. White, *The Making of the President, 1960*, 292.

77. "Old Issues Dressed Up: 'Peace' Leads Parade," *Washington Post*, October 16, 1960, E1.

78. John F. Kennedy, Speech by Senator John F. Kennedy Prepared for a Dinner Held by the Democratic National and State Committee, Waldorf-Astoria, New York, NY, October 12, 1960, *American Presidency Project* http://www.presidency.ucsb.edu/ws/?pid=25782.

79. White, *The Making of the President, 1960*, 292.

80. "Kennedy Charges Nixon Risks War," *New York Times*, October 13, 1960, 1.

81. "Bowles Calls GOP Blind to Crises," *Washington Post*, October 14, 1960, B8.

82. "In the Nation," *New York Times*, October 14, 1960, 32.

83. Memorandum from Claude Robinson to Nixon, Hall, Finch, October 5, 1960.

84. Presidential Debate Broadcast from New York and Los Angeles, October 13,

1960, *American Presidency Project,* http://www.presidency.ucsb.edu/ws/?pid=29402; Memorandum from Claude Robinson to Nixon, Hall, Finch, October 5, 1960.

85. "Island Is Honeycombed with Defenses," *Philadelphia Inquirer,* October 16, 1960, 10.

86. Presidential Debate in New York, October 21, 1960, *American Presidency Project,* http://www.presidency.ucsb.edu/ws/?pid=29403.

87. Roscoe Drummond, "To the Candidates: Clarifying Quemoy Issue Urged," *Washington Post,* October 19, 1960, A23.

88. Robert B. Norris, "Quemoy and Matsu: A Historical Footnote Revisited," *American Diplomacy,* November 2010, http://www.unc.edu/depts/diplomat/item/2010/0912/comm/norris_quemoymatsu.html.

89. Quemoy-Matsu Statement, Fred Holborn Subject Files, W. W. Rostow, Speeches & Memoranda, PPP, PPK, JFKL.

90. "President Backs Nixon on Quemoy and Matsu," *Washington Post,* October 16, 1964, A1.

91. Sorensen, *Kennedy,* 205.

92. Kengor, *Vice President,* 182.

93. Sorensen, *Kennedy,* 205.

94. "Kennedy Asks Nixon Explain Cuba 'Disaster,'" *Washington Post,* October 16, 1960, A16.

95. Sorensen, *Kennedy,* 205–6.

96. Arthur Schlesinger Jr., *A Thousand Days: John F. Kennedy in the White House* (Boston: Houghton Mifflin, 1965), 225.

97. Richard Goodwin, *Remembering America* (Boston: Little, Brown, 1988), 125.

98. "Washington: The Bees Are Settling along the Potomac," *New York Times,* October 23, 1960, E10.

99. "Kennedy for Peace," October 7, 1960, Collection: Campaign 1960, Series: Presidential Debates (PPS 61), box 1, folder: Foreign Policy, PPP, PPK, JFKL.

100. Telephone Call from Henry Holland to REC—Notes, October 7, 1960, Campaign 1960, Presidential Debates (PPS 61), box 1, RN Debate Preparation, PPP, PPK, JFKL.

101. Presidential Debate in Washington, DC, October 7, 1960, *American Presidential Project,* http://www.presidency.ucsb.edu/ws/?pid=29401.

102. Henry M. Jackson to John F. Kennedy, Corrections, Please! no. 17, October 25, 1960, JFK Campaign 1960, PPP, PPK, JFKL

103. Ibid.

104. An Analysis of the Third Kennedy-Nixon Debate, October 19, 1960, Louis Harris & Associates, 1960 Campaign & Transition, General Subject, 1959–1960, Poll: Third Kennedy-Nixon Debate, PPP, PPK, JFKL.

105. Sorensen, *Kennedy,* 206.

106. Memorandum from Claude Robinson to Nixon, Hall, Finch, October 28, 1960, Campaign 1960, Presidential Debates (PPS 61), box 1, Folder: Claude Robinson, Inc.—Evaluation of Debates, RNL.

107. "The Choice of a Candidate," *New York Times,* October 27, 1960, 36.
108. "The Candidates Fire Election Eve Broadsides," *Washington Post,* November 6, 1960, E1.

7

The Virtues of Moderation

Foreign Policy and the 1964 Presidential Election

Thomas Tunstall Allcock

On July 16, 1964, the newly selected Republican nominee for president of the United States took to the stage of the Cow Palace pavilion in San Francisco to address his party's national convention. Already considered a political outlier by many within the GOP, Arizona senator Barry Goldwater delivered a speech that did little to dispel his reputation as representing the most conservative of Republicans. His address railed against big government, lamented the erosion of law and order in American cities, and excoriated Democratic limpness on foreign affairs. Characterizing his opponents as too weak to defend true American values, he announced his conviction that "extremism in the defense of liberty is no vice . . . moderation in the pursuit of justice is no virtue."[1] It was a sound bite that would come to haunt his campaign. For Goldwater's opponent, President Lyndon Johnson, this public embrace of extremism was a gift. A politician who had long been an expert in locating the politically acceptable middle ground and cross-party consensus building yet was in the midst of pursuing a controversial and divisive program of social reform, Johnson planned a campaign that emphasized his wisdom and restraint in foreign affairs. In contrast to Goldwater's apparent commitment to extremism, the president aimed to maintain his country's global position while avoiding unnecessary provocations. Electorally, this embrace of moderation would be an undeniable success, helping Johnson win one of the greatest victories in American history. The degree to which he allowed these electoral concerns to shape his conduct of foreign affairs would, however, leave a far more complex and troubling legacy.

The election of 1964 has long been of interest to historians, not least because both Johnson and Goldwater are colorful, engaging individuals who have attracted multiple biographical studies of varying quality and academic rigor.[2] As Robert David Johnson recently argued, the 1964 election deserves to be ranked alongside the 1960 and 1968 iterations as a crucial milestone in the development of the modern electoral process. The embrace of television advertising, the dramatic increases in spending, the deliberate linking of race and crime, and the seeds of conservative domination of the Republican Party were all dramatically on display in 1964.[3] Indeed, recent interest in Goldwater's campaign particularly reflects the surge of research into the rise of American conservatism, with the 1964 election cited as a crucial point in the emergence of the modern GOP and its Tea Party–infused fringes.[4]

While rarely focusing on foreign affairs, such studies generally acknowledge that Johnson's decision to position himself as the moderate to Goldwater's extremist was a successful campaign tactic. There is little consensus, however, regarding the degree to which international issues affected the election's outcome. Johnson would win a crushing victory in November, taking all but six states, and accurately judging the electoral impact of various issues is all but impossible. For instance, while one study argues that "the predominant concerns of most voters were related to matters of foreign affairs," another concludes that "domestic issues were the paramount factors" in Johnson's victory.[5] Despite this divergence, contemporary opinion polls do reveal that foreign policy issues—particularly the role of nuclear weapons—did matter to voters, and both candidates took this as a given during their campaigns. There has also been some consideration of the manner in which the election affected US foreign relations, particularly in relation to Vietnam. Most accounts of the conflict will acknowledge the role that Johnson's electoral concerns played in delaying crucial decisions on Southeast Asia, although the unwillingness of policy makers to openly acknowledge this in the documentary record means that this is rarely elaborated on in detail.[6]

This chapter goes beyond previous studies by providing a more holistic assessment of the complex interrelationship of foreign affairs and electoral politics in the 1964 election. As has recently been observed, historians of American foreign relations often appear reluctant to explore these connections, rarely elaborating on the manner in which electoral, as opposed to strategic or economic, concerns shape the nation's interactions with the rest of the world.[7] The predominant realist position embraces the "primacy of foreign policy," yet the 1964 campaign provides a uniquely condensed example of the interplay between foreign and domestic concerns.[8] One of the few historians to tackle the issue in any real depth, Melvin Small, has described a president's first term in office as "six to nine months learning the job . . . [and] a year and a half at most to fashion bold or controversial foreign initiatives" before having to run again on their record, and therefore "they tread cautiously, or pander to popular nationalist sentiments."[9] Thrust into office in tragic and chaotic circumstances in November 1963, Lyndon Johnson condensed that process into less than twelve months, seeking some early modest victories before determinedly following a middle-of-the-road course that might not gain too many votes but would not lose him "more than a bushel."[10] In assessing the manner in which foreign affairs shaped the campaigns of both candidates and examining key examples of how electoral concerns shaped Johnson's thinking on global matters, it is clear that the issues are inseparable. The examples of the crisis in Panama that occurred almost a year before the election and the ongoing deliberations regarding Vietnam both reveal that, even more than has previously been acknowledged, Johnson's electoral worries shaped almost all his decisions regarding major international developments. More importantly, this chapter lays bare the ambivalent impact of this influence, endorsing recent calls for a more detailed understanding through sustained analysis of the relationship of electoral politics to foreign affairs.

The Campaigns

Following his sensitive yet reassuring leadership in the wake of John F. Kennedy's death, Lyndon Johnson began 1964 in enviably good shape for an election. Throughout the year, as his legislative successes, including the Civil Rights Act, the Tax Reduction Act, and the Economic Opportunity Act, mounted, with gross national product on the rise and unemployment standing at less than 5 percent, the likelihood of victory only increased.[11] No complacency would be allowed by a man as insecure or a politician as experienced as Johnson, however. A veteran of bruising electoral battles in his native Texas, Johnson would effectively serve as his own campaign manager, overseeing all major decisions, and fretting over the minor. Long before the identity of his opponent was revealed, he had decided to employ the electoral strategy perfected by his mentor Franklin Roosevelt, which exploited every advantage provided by the presidency and empha- sized his role as the "leader of all the people." Foreign affairs would be use- ful insomuch as they emphasized the president's leadership qualities via a statesmanlike message of peace through strength and restrained power, but they were not envisaged as forming an integral part of the campaign.[12]

Barry Goldwater's successful pursuit of the Republican nomination in July did little to change Johnson's fundamental approach, suggesting only that matters of national security might play a somewhat more prominent role than anticipated. Well before his widely criticized extremism com- ments, Goldwater had established a reputation as an outlier on foreign policy issues. In October 1963, for example, he had celebrated the one- year anniversary of the Cuban Missile Crisis by advocating that NATO field commanders be given the authority to employ tactical or "conven- tional" nuclear weapons as they saw fit. Both his Republican rivals and the Democratic National Committee compiled extensive lists of his more revealing political commentary, including his predictions that without a war the country might be "subjugated" by Communists and his calls for social security to be voluntary.[13] The liberal press in particular reveled in his clumsy verbosity, with the *New York Times* journalist James Reston wryly observing that Goldwater's candidacy offered "rugged individual- ism, jungle economics, and gunboat diplomacy."[14]

Once the campaign began in earnest, Goldwater did little to change the popular perception of his views. The Republican nominee possessed a fiercely loyal support base that had allowed him to triumph at the party convention, but he would struggle to broaden that appeal on the national stage, often badly misjudging his audiences. As Johnson later recalled, Goldwater "proceeded to the heart of Appalachia and criticized the pov- erty program; and then he travelled to Florida, the retirement home of millions of Americans, and denigrated Medicare."[15] Johnson's strategy of Olympian detachment was therefore soon complemented by occasional swipes at Goldwater's gaffes. As the presidential adviser Clark Clifford colorfully phrased it: "Goldwater gave us so many glorious opportunities that from time to time I think we had to stop doing what we were doing in order to take advantage of the fact that he'd pulled his trousers down, bent over, and handed us the paddle."[16]

It was regarding foreign affairs where Goldwater most frequently handed over such paddles, a point the Johnson campaign was quick to grasp. In a memo drafted shortly after the Republican convention, the National Security Council staffer Chester Cooper identified what he described as the "two key relevant elements of this campaign that distinguish it from others." One of these was the potential for racial issues to cause the defection of Democrats to the Republican Party; the other was the chance that "a large (possibly great) number of people who normally vote Republican might be induced to vote Democratic principally on foreign policy grounds."[17] Cooper's analysis reflected the thinking of the campaign team as a whole, and Johnson was soon seeking to instill in the American public a fear of what Goldwater might unleash if granted authority over the nation's nuclear arsenal. In private conversations with journalists, for example, he portrayed this as a solemn responsibility undertaken reluctantly, telling Chalmers Roberts of the *Washington Post* in August: "When you go to talking about this deadly a thing . . . as dropping nuclear weapons, you're going to have to blow the whistle on irresponsibility."[18] Despite this approach paying dividends in negative press coverage of Goldwater's views, it was soon decided that a more direct warning to the public was necessary.[19] As Johnson's aide George Reedy noted, the campaign team needed to "play that atom theme as heavy as we can." "Atom," the president responded. "A.T.O.M., yeah."[20]

The theme was played for all it was worth in the form of one of the most notorious campaign advertisements of the century, one that powerfully dramatized the consequences of a Goldwater victory without ever mentioning the Arizonan by name. The commercial featured a young girl plucking the petals from a daisy before her clumsy counting was jarringly interrupted by a harsh countdown climaxing in the mushroom cloud of a nuclear explosion. "These are the stakes!" Johnson's voice intoned, "to make a world in which all of God's children can live, or to go into the dark," before a final voiceover implored citizens: "Vote for President Johnson. . . . The stakes are too high for you to stay home."[21] While attack ads later became commonplace, the "daisy ad," which aired just once, on September 7, 1964, provoked huge controversy and wide media coverage, precisely as intended.[22] While Johnson could appear as having responsibly withdrawn the commercial, it was replayed on television news programs, discussed in newspapers, and condemned by critics, only serving to widen its reach and impact. Because it focused so much attention on the nuclear issue, the campaign adviser Larry O'Brien viewed the commercial as doing "more to crystallize public opinion against Goldwater than any other single tool we are using."[23]

Following the daisy ad, Goldwater struggled to dispel the suspicion among voters that his election would increase the risk of nuclear war, and his attempts to gain any purchase in the field of foreign affairs floundered. His response to the commercial, for example, included an accusation that John Kennedy had manipulated events during the Cuban Missile Crisis for "maximum domestic political impact."[24] Severely misjudging the public sentiment, he simply provided Johnson with another opportunity to play the dignified statesman, rebuking his opponent without ever mentioning him by name. "It is no tribute to a man's character," the president observed sadly on the second anniversary of the crisis, "to refuse to give John Fitzgerald Kennedy the credit that he is justly entitled to when he is not here to claim it for himself."[25] Goldwater's tendency toward exploitable blunders should not obscure the skill with which the Johnson campaign was able to keep its opponents on the defensive, desperately trying to dispel the image of the Republican challenger as a warmonger. When Goldwater spoke of "conventional" nuclear weapons, for instance, the president was quick to respond: "Make no mistake, there is no such thing as a conventional nuclear weapon."[26] Indeed, a number of observers who spent time on the campaign trail with Goldwater, notably Theodore White, believed the senator to be badly advised and underprepared rather than the caricature that appeared in the press. "Day by day when he read of himself in the papers," White observed, "it was another Goldwater he was reading about, a wild man seeking to abolish Social Security and go to war with Russia."[27] In part, this was due to Goldwater's own failings, but it also owed much to a largely hostile national media and the success of Johnson's tactics.[28] As Reston observed in the *New York Times:* "The world has not been kind [to Barry Goldwater]."[29]

By the closing weeks of the campaign, Goldwater had all but ceased to talk about foreign affairs, unable to find effective leverage against the administration or repair his own reputation. By contrast, Johnson would largely dedicate the crescendo of his campaign to nuclear security, reflecting the dominance he felt over Goldwater on the issue. "The first responsibility, the only real issue in this campaign . . . is 'who best can keep the peace?'" he told a crowd in Los Angeles on October 28. "In the nuclear age the president doesn't get a second chance to make a second guess."[30]

Both campaigns undoubtedly believed that their positions on foreign policy questions mattered to voters, but it is less clear how great an impact such concerns had on the result. While traditionally decisive factors such as economics were of course hugely influential, the inexact science of opinion polls does suggest that the image of Goldwater as potentially dangerous resonated with many voters. In one poll taken in October, for example, 44 percent of respondents believed that the likelihood of nuclear war would increase in the event of a Goldwater victory, while only 8 percent felt the same way regarding Johnson. Similarly, Gallup polls reported that 78 percent disapproved of Goldwater's advocacy of granting nuclear authority to NATO commanders, and more than half of respondents believed that, if elected, Goldwater would either drop an atom bomb in Asia or provoke a war with Cuba.[31] Furthermore, throughout 1964, only "racial problems" consistently scored higher than "international problems" in response to the regularly asked Gallup poll question, "What do you think is the most important problem facing this country today?" And, when asked which party was best placed to deal with such problems, the Democrats were the overwhelming favorite.[32]

Alongside the usual caveats regarding the difficulty of accurately gauging public opinion, there are several reasons to refrain from assigning too decisive a role in Johnson's victory to foreign affairs, however. First, while the possibility of nuclear war was a worry for many voters, there is less evidence to suggest that much public attention was dedicated to the finer points of world affairs. In a poll taken in May, for example, when asked, "Have you given any attention to developments in South Vietnam?" more than 60 percent of respondents admitted they had given "little or none."[33] Media coverage was similarly weighted toward domestic concerns, with one recent study concluding: "Popular references to international issues occurred with only one fourth the frequency of references to domestic happenings."[34] In short, while the 1964 election featured a focus on foreign affairs not commonly seen in presidential elections, the evidence still falls short of convincing that it was a decisive issue. Aside from the usual advantages enjoyed by an incumbent, Johnson had numerous other factors in his favor, including the nation's strong economic performance, favorable treatment from the press, and a remarkable legislative record. While it is likely that fears over Goldwater's foreign policy views contributed to the scale of the president's victory, it is less clear that this was a crucial factor in deciding the victor. Nonetheless, the nature of public debate regarding the nuclear issue in particular and Johnson's determination to portray himself as the moderate help explain why, as will become clear, concern over the November election had a huge influence on the president's conduct of foreign policy from the moment he entered office.

The Panama Crisis

In December 1963, around a month after the assassination of John F. Kennedy, two of Johnson's key advisers on Latin American policy considered how best to respond to charges that the administration's handling of foreign affairs was unduly influenced by electoral worries. Of particular concern was an article by Nathan Miller in the *Baltimore Sun* claiming that Johnson's recent appointment of Thomas C. Mann to oversee his inter-American policy was electorally motivated. "Some diplomatic observers," Miller claimed, "have adopted the view that Mann's major assignment is to 'tranquilize' Latin American problems until after next year's Presidential elections."[35] While the timing of Miller's criticism— just one month after Dallas and still eight months away from even the Democratic national convention—might seem premature, his basic contention regarding the connection of domestic and foreign policy would soon prove accurate. Furthermore, it would also be in Latin America, when riots threatened the US position in Panama, that Johnson would first demonstrate his determination not to let foreign affairs derail his presidential ambitions.

In early January 1964, a dispute between American and Panamanian students in the US-run Panama Canal Zone escalated into rioting and violence that also soon involved the US army and led to almost thirty deaths in four days and dozens more injuries, the majority of them suffered by Panamanian civilians.[36] Reflecting a culmination of years of frustration at American economic dominance of the Canal Zone, the confrontations sparked a furious reaction from the Panamanian government. Foreign Minister Galileo Solis registered a formal protest that blamed "the uncontrollable aggressive acts of the American armed forces" and announced that "diplomatic relations with your distinguished government are broken."[37]

This would be the first major test of Johnson's ability to manage an international crisis, and it was occurring in an area of particular symbolic importance, easily exploitable for political point scoring. Congressman Daniel Flood (D-PA), for example, condemned Panamanian actions as an "audacious, cunning" Soviet plot and urged Johnson to expand the Canal Zone by force. The president's former mentor Richard Russell (D-GA) was less bombastic but privately counseled "a strong stand": "The people of this country are ready for it." And Senate minority leader Everett Dirksen (R-IL) warned: "If we crumble in Panama, the reverberations of our actions will be felt around the world."[38] Hoping to resolve the situation as swiftly as possible, Johnson circumvented diplomatic protocol and telephoned Panamanian president Roberto Chiari directly, only to be informed that the restoration of relations would require "a complete revision of all treaties" regarding the operation of the Canal.[39]

Johnson feared that public opinion was mostly in line with the views of Russell and Dirksen. A Gallup poll taken shortly after the riots revealed that, regarding the canal, of the 64 percent of Americans who had been following events in Panama, almost half urged a "firm policy" while only 9 percent favored concessions.[40] As Richard Scammon, the director of the Bureau of the Census, warned, the American public was unlikely to tolerate a threat to "an area which every grade school history book features with an American flag [and] a snapshot of Teddy Roosevelt." Any show of weakness could therefore provide the Republicans their "first real solid muscled hit at the Administration."[41] When the Democratic stalwart Adlai Stevenson urged Johnson to accede to Panamanian demands in February, commenting that it would result in "resounding applause in an editorial" if he did, the president acknowledged why he felt unable to do so. "I think I would—in the *New York Times*," he conceded irritably. "Then I think the *people* would run me out of the country."[42] Nonetheless, Johnson was acutely aware of the danger of appearing to bully a comparatively tiny neighbor or of provoking further violence. Elements of the international press took particular delight in comparing Johnson's problems to those of other "colonial" powers, but the domestic media and public opinion also posed challenges.[43] While polls reflected opposition to large-scale concessions, government analyses of public opinion also detected widespread sympathy for the Panamanian position and a willingness to enter discussions over the nature of the relationship between the two countries.[44]

The degree to which Johnson's handling of the crisis was guided by these concerns is striking. Unwilling to appear weak or to expose himself to criticism from the Right, Johnson refused to open negotiations over a new canal contract. When Thomas Mann, fresh from an unproductive visit to Panama City, urged him to consider concessions in order to defuse an "explosive situation," he responded that he could not afford to give the impression that foreign nations could burn buildings, "kill soldiers and we will come running."[45] He was, however, willing to enter into wide-ranging "discussions," providing there were no preconditions regarding the canal; an approach that could deflect charges of negotiating under the threat of violence while also appearing reasonable and sympathetic to Panamanian grievances.[46] He seemed to have judged the public mood accurately, with State Department reports noting that this position received widespread editorial support, with most debate reserved for what concessions would be considered acceptable.[47]

Johnson's handling of the Panama crisis was far from universally popular, however. His refusal to budge from the stance of "discussions not negotiations" while Chiari refused to abandon his position of "no relations until negotiations" meant that the impasse dragged on into March.[48] The delay resulted in negative media coverage that alleged divisions within the administration and accused the president of lacking a coherent approach to the crisis.[49] By mid-March, with the benefits of appearing tough outweighed by critical press coverage, Johnson offered a rhetorical olive branch, acknowledging that Chiari's demands reflected a "deeply felt sense of the honest and fair needs of Panama."[50] In the following days, a vaguely worded agreement was hammered out that promised wide-ranging talks, with no preconditions, on US-Panamanian relations. Calling a meeting of key congressional leaders, Johnson ensured that he had an audience for the telephone call to Chiari in which relations were officially reestablished via his personal brand of diplomacy.[51]

In electoral terms, Johnson's handling of the Panama crisis was a success. By striking a moderate path, he gave opponents little to work with in terms of formulating an opposing position; a Republican study group analyzed events shortly after the restoration of relations and largely endorsed Johnson's handling of the crisis, finding little potential political leverage.[52] Johnson also refused to allow the issue to resurface later in the campaign, making few public statements regarding the progress of the discussions until after the election. It was not until December 18 that he would announce that negotiations would begin on an entirely new canal treaty, and by then criticism such as Congressman Flood's claim that this marked the victory of an "international communist conspiracy" could do little damage.[53]

The crisis demonstrated Johnson's determination to take a moderate line in foreign affairs, paying close attention to public opinion, minimizing press coverage of potentially controversial issues, and providing Republican and conservative Democrat opponents with as little ammunition as possible. It was also a diplomatically successful approach, resulting in the peaceful reestablishment of relations while defusing calls for a more aggressive response. In addition, the inconspicuous nature of the subsequent discussions provided the time and space to work out acceptable agreements, announced at a point when Johnson was at his most politically untouchable, which set in motion the process that would eventually result in the granting of the canal to Panama.

If Panama provided an example of the relatively benign impact of electoral concerns on the conduct of foreign affairs, it should be noted that other challenges in Latin America would not respond so well to Johnson's "moderate" approach. In Brazil, for example, long-standing worries regarding President Joao Goulart resulted in US backing for the military coup that saw him overthrown in April 1964. While the general consensus among Johnson's policy-making team had been that it was "preferable if we could waffle through to the next election," worries that Goulart was about to install himself in a Communist dictatorship prompted support for the military plotters. In part because of strategic Cold War concerns, but also because of fears of the domestic political impact of allowing Brazil to "dribble down the drain," a repressive regime that halted Brazilian democracy for decades was warmly endorsed by the president of the United States.[54] Worse was yet to come, however, as another international crisis gradually consumed more of the president's attention. Nowhere would Johnson's electoral concerns shape policy more clearly than in Vietnam or with such deleterious effects.

Vietnam

While the Panama crisis had dragged on longer than Johnson would have liked and the Brazilian coup had come at a less than welcome moment, both appeared relatively resolved by April, squared away well before the election campaign began in earnest. The foreign policy issue that appeared most likely to play a prominent role was the deteriorating situation in South Vietnam. Johnson entered office shortly after the US-sanctioned assassination of South Vietnamese president Ngo Dinh Diem and with around sixteen thousand US military advisers on the ground, both reflecting the depth of the previous administration's commitment to combating the growing insurgency and the reluctance to openly commit combat forces. Although his intentions regarding Vietnam remain a source of substantial debate, Kennedy had certainly been aware of the potential fallout should he withdraw US support, commenting in private: "I can't give up territory like that to the Communists and then get the American public to reelect me!"[55] Whatever his ultimate decision on escalation or withdrawal would have been, he undoubtedly hoped to delay any major choices until after the election, a position fully embraced by his successor. Under Johnson's close watch, Vietnam policy in 1964 would be almost entirely dictated by the November election.

Public interest in Vietnam was galvanized in the early months of 1964 when French president Charles de Gaulle's calls for a neutralization settlement were endorsed by Senate majority leader Mike Mansfield (D-MT), and the challengers for the Republican presidential nomination Barry Goldwater and Richard Nixon began to question American strategy. Further entangling Vietnam with electoral policy, a campaign to draft Ambassador to South Vietnam Henry Cabot Lodge as the Republican presidential nominee also began to gather momentum.[56] Mansfield, Nixon, and Goldwater's comments were a source of irritation for Johnson, but it was Lodge's growing popularity that first revealed the extent to which the president was prepared to shape his strategy in Vietnam to meet domestic political needs. Concerned that any reluctance on the part of his administration to follow Lodge's recommendations might be exploited as evidence of a lack of commitment to the anti-Communist cause, Johnson made it be known that the ambassador's requests were to be met promptly and favorably. He made the point explicitly clear to Secretary of State Dean Rusk, demanding that Lodge be made to feel "he's Mister God, and we're giving him maximum attention."[57] Paranoid that Lodge was compiling a dossier of evidence cataloging the president's lack of commitment, Johnson was willing to authorize requests not because of their merits but because doing so denied the ambassador this imagined advantage.

Johnson's attempts to placate Lodge reflected his desperation to avoid any major decisions or controversies that could provide political traction for an opponent. As the president told National Security Adviser McGeorge Bundy on March 2, he hoped that the combination of American expertise and Vietnamese troops, "fifteen thousand advisers and two hundred thousand people," would be enough to "maintain the status quo for six months."[58] "I'm a trustee. I've got to win an election," Johnson elaborated further on March 4. "Then you can make a decision . . . meantime, let's see if we can't find enough things to do to keep them off base."[59] In essence, it was made clear to all the principal actors on Johnson's foreign policy team that any actions drawing attention to the conflict would not be viewed favorably. When one field commander, for instance, gave an interview deemed too detailed and pessimistic, Johnson raged to Bundy: "We've got a convention and an election going on, and it's not up to the military to go to talking!"[60] Polls suggested that the tactic was working, with a June Gallup poll revealing that events in Southeast Asia did not make the top five concerns of voters.[61]

Johnson's reluctance to make Vietnam a prominent factor in the campaign suggests that it was precisely the kind of issue that Barry Goldwater should have challenged the president on. Indeed, while Johnson's reluctance to discuss Vietnam has on occasion been overstated, Goldwater's acceptance speech at the Republican national convention in July certainly suggested that this was a weakness he would seek to exploit.[62] "Make no bones of this," he warned. "We are at war in Vietnam." Although the fact was somewhat lost among the controversy of his extremism comments, Goldwater accused Johnson and Secretary of Defense Robert McNamara in particular of refusing to admit "whether or not the objective over there is victory" and misleading the American people.[63] With a Gallup poll taken that same month revealing only a 52 percent approval rating for the president's handling of Vietnam policy, Goldwater appeared set to make the president extremely uncomfortable.[64] Then came the drama in the Gulf of Tonkin.

On August 2, US warships providing support for South Vietnamese raids in the Gulf of Tonkin were attacked by North Vietnamese gunboats. A possible second attack was reported by the USS *Maddox* on August 4, although there was substantial confusion and uncertainty over what exactly occurred. Recognizing an opportunity, Johnson nonetheless launched retaliatory air raids against the North and submitted what became known as the Tonkin Gulf Resolution—an open-ended granting of presidential authority over military escalation in Vietnam—to Congress. On the night of August 4, Johnson also delivered a televised address to the nation in which he emphasized his favorite foreign policy message of peace through strength. "Firmness in the right is indispensable today for peace," the solemn president informed the nation, also insisting: "We still seek no wider war."[65] Both houses approved the resolution with only two votes registered in opposition.

The Tonkin Gulf incident was crucial both in shaping the administration's policy in Vietnam—a steady escalation of American involvement without further congressional oversight—and in removing the conflict as a key campaign issue. Following Johnson's statement on August 4, approval of his handling of the conflict jumped to 72 percent, but, even more importantly, when no further incidents occurred, interest in Vietnam swiftly declined.[66] With no public knowledge of the American role in the South Vietnamese raids or the doubts over the second incident, Johnson's response to an apparently unprovoked attack appeared reasonable, proportional, and effective. Considering that doubts had remained over the president's abilities in foreign affairs, this was a substantial fillip, made even sweeter by virtue of the fact that it robbed Goldwater of a potentially productive line of attack. Telephoning the Arizonan shortly before his televised address, Johnson had read the text he intended to deliver and outlined the plans for air strikes on North Vietnamese ports. Given that he had been calling for a tougher stance and greater clarity regarding the US position, Goldwater could do little but tell the president: "I think you've taken the proper action and I'm sure you'll find that everyone will be behind you." After all, he offered: "We're Americans and we stick together." "Alright," a delighted Johnson replied. "Bye fella."[67] Less than ninety minutes later, he was assuring the nation that Senator Gold-water had been contacted: "And I am glad to say that he has expressed his support."[68]

With Congress, the majority of the public, and even his Republican opponent backing his actions, Johnson had succeeded in strengthening his hand on Vietnam. Although the situation on the ground continued to deteriorate, McNamara suggested in September that he thought that they could "squeeze through" until November. He continued, however: "After the election, we've got a real problem on our hands."[69] He would be proved correct on both counts. The administration was able to "squeeze through" to the election largely unscathed, in large part owing to Gold-water's inability to muster an effective critique of policies the administration was desperately hoping would avoid close scrutiny. Although in the closing weeks of the campaign the challenger finally made some attempts to do so, charging that "American sons and grandsons are being killed by Communist bullets and Communist bombs and we have yet to hear a word of truth about why they are dying," they came too late to have any real impact.[70] As Richard Rovere noted in the *New Yorker* in September, through his handling of events the previous month, "Johnson had taken the play away from Goldwater" on Vietnam as a campaign issue.[71]

If Panama demonstrated that the moderating effect of electoral concerns could have a positive impact on Johnson's handling of foreign affairs, then the situation in Vietnam reflected the dangerous nature of such entanglements. Desperate to avoid any kind of controversy, the president delayed decisions regarding escalation or withdrawal and discouraged any form of national debate. Bundy would later recall: "[Johnson] didn't want to take decisions on this issue in an election year . . . there was great frustration because you couldn't get a decision out of him."[72] Even foreign allies such as the British were well aware that major discussions regarding Vietnam were off the table until the following year.[73] In his consideration of a new Panama Canal treaty, Johnson had demonstrated willingness to seek long-term solutions and break from the policies of his predecessors, but, regarding Vietnam, he never deviated from the Kennedy administration's approach, meaning short-term boosts in aid and military advisers that gradually increased the American commitment. Seeking the moderate position, Johnson's public statements on the conflict downplayed the likelihood of dispatching US combat forces but continually reaffirmed his commitment to supporting South Vietnam even as the ability of that nation to sustain itself without those troops dwindled almost daily. In short, the longer the muted commitment to South Vietnam continued, the less likely it became that withdrawal would be viewed as a viable option. In attempting to defer major decisions until after November, Johnson quietly waded deeper into the quagmire. That he was allowed to do so is a major failure of the Goldwater campaign; by not challenging the administration to be more open about its goals and strategies, there would be no public debate regarding the nature of US involvement at a time when Johnson was particularly susceptible to the influence of public opinion. As the Goldwater biographer Robert Goldberg eloquently summarized: "Johnson faced no serious test, no need to justify his course. . . . Americans were not so much deceived about Vietnam during the 1964 election as they were lulled into sleepwalking toward their future."[74]

By October, Vietnam appeared to be of dwindling importance in the campaign. While the Johnson camp was satisfied to air a series of advertisements highlighting Goldwater's more bizarre declarations, their opponents focused on issues closer to home. One potentially fruitful avenue identified by the Republican campaign was the administration's supposed lack of morality. The hitherto most prominent issue in this regard had been the Bobby Baker scandal, which had exposed the illegal financial dealings of Johnson's former Senate aide and drawn attention to the president's own personal wealth. While the Baker case had ultimately done little damage to the president, in early October a new scandal threatened to erupt when one of Johnson's closest aides, Walter Jenkins, was arrested in a YMCA bathroom with another man and charged with "disorderly conduct." The story soon reached the press and was given added weight when it was revealed that Jenkins had been arrested on a similar charge in 1959. Given the prevailing attitude toward homosexuality in the early 1960s, the Jenkins incident provided an opportunity for Goldwater to renew his attacks on the morals of the men running the nation, and he would indeed make occasional allusions to what he termed Johnson's "curious crew." His campaign also made efforts to keep the story alive in the press and produced campaign paraphernalia that referenced the incident, but Goldwater himself was reluctant to pursue the issue too vigorously, finding it unseemly.[75] Any likelihood that the scandal would become the biggest news story in the run-up to Election Day, however, was eliminated when a series of dramatic events pushed foreign affairs to the forefront once again. On October 14, Soviet leader Nikita Khrushchev was deposed, the following day a new Labour government was voted into power in the United Kingdom, and, on October 16, the People's Republic of China carried out its first successful nuclear test.

The result of those three remarkable days was made clear to Johnson when discussing the Jenkins situation with his friend Donald Cook shortly afterward. "How much is this going to hurt us?" asked the president, referring to the impact of the Jenkins arrest on the election. "I don't think it's going to make any appreciable difference," replied Cook, who noted a surprisingly sympathetic reaction from much of the press corps and then continued: "The Russian thing came along, and the Chinese thing. It's been pushed very quickly and very far into the background."[76] Again recognizing a golden opportunity, Johnson dramatically left the campaign trail for consultations with his foreign policy team before making a televised address to the nation. A furious Goldwater charged that the speech was "political" and attacked the Federal Communications Commission for allowing free broadcasting on the major networks.[77] Fully exploiting the incumbent's advantage, Johnson's October 18 speech painted the president as the consummate peace candidate, calmly responding to international challenges with a restraint born of confidence and strength. The nuclear test came as "no surprise," the Chinese were a long way from developing effective delivery systems, and the administration would continue to promote the limited test ban treaty and oppose nuclear proliferation. Johnson also welcomed his new British allies and reaffirmed his position on the Soviet Union: "We intend to bury no one, and we do not intend to be buried."[78]

In certain respects, Johnson's speech was an accurate reflection of his foreign policy positions. He was, for example, far more serene regarding the prospect of a nuclear China, which he considered inevitable, than his predecessor had been, although his genuine conviction about the danger of nuclear proliferation was consistently on show throughout the campaign.[79] Nonetheless, Goldwater was correct that the speech was intended to both distract from the Jenkins arrest and strengthen the president's position as the moderate candidate in contrast to his blustering and dangerous opponent. Once again, Goldwater struggled to counter, with his accusations that the government had been caught "flat-footed" by world events failing to have much impact.[80] Sensing an opportunity to drive home his advantage, Johnson focused more than ever on foreign affairs in the final days of the campaign as a despondent Goldwater struggled to counter. At the climax of a whirlwind speaking tour, the president addressed a packed Madison Square Garden on October 31, hammering home the principle on which his campaign and his handling of foreign affairs had been run. "Extremism in the pursuit of the Presidency is an unpardonable vice," he warned, "and moderation in the affairs of the Nation is the highest virtue."[81]

Conclusion

The 1964 presidential election is notable for a variety of reasons, not least the scale of Johnson's victory, which was a landslide rarely matched before or since. In a contest where the incumbent could point to sustained economic growth, legislative successes, and a relatively balanced budget, foreign policy was one of the few areas likely to give his opponent any substantial traction, yet Goldwater spectacularly failed to take advantage of this opening. In part, this was due to Johnson's ability to keep Goldwater on the back foot, defending his own clumsily articulated positions rather than challenging the president's, but it was also down to the Republican campaign's failings. Although Goldwater accused Johnson of lying regarding the depth of American involvement in South Vietnam, he also supported the Gulf of Tonkin resolution and associated reprisals and largely disregarded the issue for much of the contest. Ultimately, Goldwater's commitment to extremism, gleefully exploited by his opponent, undermined his credibility on foreign affairs. In the first election since the Cuban Missile Crisis of October 1962, Johnson's successful portrayal of himself as moderate and restrained yet capable of strength and decisiveness at times of crisis was far more appealing than Goldwater's at best bombastic and at worst reckless approach to world affairs. The lack of a serious challenge to his policies meant that Johnson was able to continue on a dangerous path unchecked when it was undeniably clear that he was acutely sensitive to public opinion. Foreign affairs played a role in the election, but in the form of Johnson's effective exploitation of Goldwater's reputation, not in any genuine debate regarding the direction of national policy.

Of greater importance, the 1964 campaign demonstrates that domestic political concerns can rarely be overstated as a factor in foreign policy decision making, becoming ever more crucial as an election draws closer. While the case of Panama reveals that this can occasionally be a relatively benign influence, other examples in Brazil and Vietnam reflect the damaging consequences of following the path of least electoral resistance. On the matter of public opinion, Johnson famously declared: "Everybody worries about war and peace. Everything else is chickenshit."[82] This is typical Johnsonian overstatement, yet it reflects his awareness of the simple truth that foreign affairs affect elections and therefore that elections affect foreign affairs. The unique circumstances of Johnson's first year in the presidency meant only that this was more starkly on display in 1964 than in other years. While his delaying of major decisions and downplaying of American global commitments would have serious long-term consequences, in the short term it was an effective electoral strategy. Johnson had, for better or worse, proved the virtues of apparent moderation.

Notes

1. "Barry Goldwater's 1964 Acceptance Speech," *Washington Post,* http://www
.washingtonpost.com/wp-srv/politics/daily/may98/goldwaterspeech.htm.
2. Examples include Robert Caro, *The Years of Lyndon Johnson,* 4 vols. (New York: Knopf, 1982–2012); Robert Dallek, *Flawed Giant: Lyndon Johnson and His Times* (Oxford: Oxford University Press, 1998); Randall Woods, *LBJ: Architect of American Ambition* (Cambridge, MA: Harvard University Press, 2007); Robert Alan Goldberg, *Barry Goldwater* (New Haven, CT: Yale University Press, 1995); and Rick Perlstein, *Before the Storm: Barry Goldwater and the Unmaking of American Consensus* (New York: Hill & Wang, 2001).
3. Robert David Johnson, *All the Way with LBJ: The 1964 Presidential Election* (Cambridge: Cambridge University Press, 2009), 12.
4. For a good overview, see Kim Philips-Fein, "Conservatism: A State of the Field," *Journal of American History* 98, no. 3 (2011): 723–43.
5. David Myers, *Foreign Affairs and the 1964 Presidential Election in the United States* (Meerut: Nishkam, 1972), 1; Melvin Small, *Democracy and Diplomacy: The Impact of Domestic Politics on U.S. Foreign Policy, 1789–1994* (Baltimore: Johns Hopkins University Press, 1996), 118. Other accounts tend to range between the two perspectives, assigning substantial but not necessarily decisive weight to foreign affairs. See, e.g., Johnson, *All the Way with LBJ;* Theodore H. White, *The Making of the President, 1964* (London: Cape, 1965); Dallek, *Flawed Giant,* 122–85; Woods, *LBJ,* 539–57; Goldberg, *Barry Goldwater,* 181–37; and Perlstein, *Before the Storm,* 372–515.

6. See Frederik Logevall, *Choosing War: The Lost Chance for Peace and the Escalation of War in Vietnam* (Berkeley and Los Angeles: University of California Press, 1999), 237–51; and Brian VanDeMark, *Into the Quagmire: Lyndon Johnson and the Escalation of the Vietnam War* (Oxford: Oxford University Press, 1991), 18–29.

7. In particular, the "modest plea to restore politics, and political struggles, to our understanding of American foreign relations," in Thomas Alan Schwartz, "'Henry, . . . Winning an Election Is Terribly Important': Partisan Politics in the History of U.S. Foreign Relations," *Diplomatic History* 33, no. 2 (2009): 173–90, 189.

8. Douglas Kriner, "Presidents, Domestic Politics, and the International Arena," in *The Oxford Handbook of the American Presidency*, ed. George Edwards and William Howell (Oxford: Oxford University Press, 2009), 668–88. For a relevant exploration of similar issues regarding German history, see Brendan Simms, "The Return of the Primacy of Foreign Policy," *German History* 21, no. 3 (2003): 275–91.

9. Small, *Democracy and Diplomacy*, xii.

10. Dallek, *Flawed Giant*, 97.

11. Statement on the Economy by Walter Heller, August 18, 1964, Abe Fortas Papers, Series no. 4, box 159, Yale University Library, New Haven, CT (hereafter YUL).

12. Johnson, *All the Way with LBJ*, 10.

13. "What Goldwater Said," July 1964, Abe Fortas Papers, Group no. 858, Series no. 4, box 159, YUL.

14. Quoted in Johnson, *All the Way with LBJ*, 67.

15. Lyndon Baines Johnson, *The Vantage Point: Perspectives of the Presidency, 1963–1969* (London: Weidenfeld & Nicolson, 1972), 102.

16. Clark M. Clifford Oral History Interview IV, August 7, 1969, by Joe B. Frantz, Lyndon B. Johnson Library, Austin, TX (hereafter LBJL).

17. Chester Cooper to McGeorge Bundy, "Thoughts on the Task Ahead," July 16, 1964, in *Declassified Documents Reference System* (Farmington Hills, MI: Gale, 2014).

18. Lyndon Johnson and Chalmers Roberts, August 14, 1964, Tape WH6408.22, Citation no. 4962, Recordings of Telephone Conversations, Miller Center Presidential Recordings, Miller Center, University of Virginia (henceforth MCPR).

19. For a detailed analysis of press coverage during the election, see Myers, *Foreign Affairs and the 1964 Presidential Election*, 26–52.

20. Lyndon Johnson and George Reedy, August 20, 1964, Tape WH6408.29, Citation no. 5047, MCPR.

21. "Peace, Little Girl," 1964 Presidential Campaign Television Spot, LBJL, http://www.lbjlib.utexas.edu/johnson/media/daisyspot.

22. For further details, see Lawrence F. O'Brien Oral History Interview IX, April 9, 1986, by Michael L. Gillette, Internet Copy, LBJL; Richard Goodwin, *Remembering America: A Voice from the Sixties* (Boston: HarperCollins, 1988), 304–

6; and Kathleen Hall Jamieson, *Packaging the Presidency: A History and Criticism of Presidential Campaign Advertising* (1984), 3rd ed. (Oxford: Oxford University Press, 1996), 169–221.

23. O'Brien Oral History Interview IX, LBJL.

24. Paul R. Hengeller, *In His Steps: Lyndon Johnson and the Kennedy Mystique* (Chicago: Ivan R. Dee, 1991), 146–47.

25. Lyndon B. Johnson, Remarks at the Municipal Park, South Gate, California, October 11, 1964, *The American Presidency Project*, http://www.presidency.ucsb.edu/ws/?pid=26588.

26. Perlstein, *Before the Storm*, 420.

27. White, *The Making of the President, 1964*, 110.

28. Myers, *Foreign Affairs and the 1964 Presidential Election*, 26–52.

29. Quoted in Johnson, *All the Way with LBJ*, 259.

30. Lyndon B. Johnson, Remarks at City Hall in Los Angeles, October 28, 1964, *American Presidency Project*, http://www.presidency.ucsb.edu/ws/?pid=26680.

31. Myers, *Foreign Affairs and the 1964 Presidential Election*, 22–24.

32. George H. Gallup, ed., *The Gallup Poll: Public Opinion, 1935–1971* (New York: Random House, 1972), 1864–1910.

33. Ibid., 1882.

34. John H. Aldrich, Christopher Gelpi, Peter Feaver, Jason Reifler, and Kristin Thompson Sharp, "Foreign Policy and the Electoral Connection," *Annual Review of Political Science* 9, no. 1 (2006): 477–502, 488.

35. Martin to Gordon (and attached copy of *Baltimore Sun* article), December 28, 1963, National Security File, Country File (henceforth NSF, CF), Brazil, box 9, LBJL.

36. "Chronology of Events Relating to Flag Controversy," NSF, CF, Panama, box 64, LBJL; Walter LaFeber, *The Panama Canal: The Crisis in Historical Perspective* (New York: Oxford University Press, 1978), 140.

37. Translation of Solis Message to Rusk, January 10, 1964, NSF, CF, Panama, box 64, LBJL.

38. Woods, *LBJ*, 498; Lyndon Johnson and Richard Russell, January 10, 1964, Tape WH6401.10, Citation no. 1303, MCPR; LaFeber, *Panama Canal*, 143.

39. Lyndon Johnson and Roberto Chiari, Transcript of Telephone Conversation, January 10, 1964, NSF, CF, Panama, box 64, LBJL.

40. Gallup, ed., *Gallup Poll*, 1864.

41. LaFeber, *Panama Canal*, 143.

42. Lyndon Johnson and Adlai Stevenson, Transcript of Telephone Conversation, February 26, 1964, in *Taking Charge: The Johnson White House Tapes, 1963–64*, ed. Michael Beschloss (New York: Simon & Schuster, 1997), 251.

43. USIA Report, "Foreign Reaction to Panama Situation," January 13, 1964, NSF, CF, Panama, box 64, LBJL.

44. State Department American Opinion Summary, January 13, 1964, NSF, CF, Panama, box 64, LBJL.

45. Lyndon Johnson and Thomas Mann, January 14, 1964, Tape WH6401.14, Citation no. 1360, MCPR.

46. Copy of President's Statement on Panama Crisis, January 23, 1964, Office Files of Bill Moyers, box 105, LBJL.

47. State Department Public Opinion Summary, January 24, 1964, NSF, CF, Panama, box 63, LBJL.

48. Alan McPherson, *Yankee No! Anti-Americanism in U.S.–Latin American Relations* (Cambridge, MA: Harvard University Press, 2003), 111.

49. "Mann's Role Disputed in Confusion on Canal," *Evening Star,* March 19, 1964, Thomas Mann Papers, box 329, Texas Collection, Baylor University, Waco, TX; Johnson, *All the Way with LBJ,* 43.

50. Copy of President's Statement on Panama Crisis, March 21, 1964, Office Files of Bill Moyers, box 105, LBJL.

51. Memo of Conversation, "NSC Meeting with Congressional Leaders," April 3, 1964, Lyndon Johnson and Roberto Chiari, Transcript of Telephone Conversation, April 3, 1964, and "Senator Morse Reports," all NSF, NSC Meetings File, box 1, LBJL; Tad Szulc, "U.S. and Panama Sign Agreement to Restore Ties," *New York Times,* April 4, 1964.

52. Mark A. Lawrence, "Exception to the Rule? The Johnson Administration and the Panama Canal," in *Looking Back at LBJ: White House Politics in a New Light,* ed. Mitchell B. Lerner (Lawrence: University Press of Kansas, 2005), 37.

53. Quoted in LaFeber, *Panama Canal,* 146.

54. Bundy to Johnson, March 28, 1964; Memo of Conversation, Bundy, Goodpaster, Helms et al., March 28, 1964, both NSF, Country File, Brazil, Box 9, LBJL.

55. Quoted in Small, *Democracy and Diplomacy,* 117.

56. For details of Lodge's failed bid for the nomination, see Johnson, *All the Way with LBJ,* 66–113.

57. Lyndon Johnson and Dean Rusk, Transcript of Telephone Conversation, March 2, 1964, in Beschloss, ed., *Taking Charge,* 262.

58. Lyndon Johnson and McGeorge Bundy, Transcript of Telephone Conversation, March 2, 1964, in Beschloss, ed., *Taking Charge,* 263.

59. Lyndon Johnson and McGeorge Bundy, Transcript of Telephone Conversation, March 4, 1964, in Beschloss, ed., *Taking Charge,* 267.

60. Lyndon Johnson and McGeorge Bundy, Transcript of Telephone Conversation, July 14, 1964, in Beschloss, ed., *Taking Charge,* 456.

61. Gallup, ed., *Gallup Poll,* 1882; Mitchell Lerner, "Vietnam and the 1964 Election: A Defense of Lyndon Johnson," *Presidential Studies Quarterly* 25, no. 4 (1995): 751–66, 762.

62. Mitchell Lerner has argued that Johnson was much clearer regarding his intentions than is commonly acknowledged. See Lerner, "Vietnam and the 1964 Election."

63. Goldwater's 1964 Acceptance Speech, WashingtonPost.com, http://www.washingtonpost.com/wp-srv/politics/daily/may98/goldwaterspeech.htm.

64. Dallek, *Flawed Giant,* 147.

65. Lyndon B. Johnson, Radio and Television Report to the American People Following Renewed Aggression in the Gulf of Tonkin, August 4, 1964, *American Presidency Project,* http://www.presidency.ucsb.edu/ws/?pid=26418.

66. Johnson, *All the Way with LBJ,* 156.

67. Lyndon Johnson and Barry Goldwater, August 4, 1964, Tape WH6408.06, Citation no. 4715, MCPR.

68. Johnson, Radio and Television Report to the American People, August 4, 1964.

69. Lyndon Johnson and Robert McNamara, Transcript of Telephone Conversation, September 24, 1964, in *Reaching for Glory: Lyndon Johnson's Secret White House Tapes, 1964–1965,* ed. Michael Beschloss (New York: Simon & Schuster, 2002), 41.

70. Goldberg, *Barry Goldwater,* 232.

71. Quoted in Johnson, *All the Way with LBJ,* 157.

72. Dallek, *Flawed Giant,* 148.

73. Logevall, *Choosing War,* 224.

74. Goldberg, *Barry Goldwater,* 216.

75. Woods, *LBJ,* 549–52.

76. Lyndon Johnson and Donald Cook, October 17, 1964, Tape WH6410.12, Citation no. 5902, MCPR

77. Myers, *Foreign Affairs and the 1964 Presidential Election,* 60.

78. Lyndon Johnson, Radio and Television Report to the American People on Recent Events in Russia, China, and Great Britain, October 18, 1964, *American Presidency Project,* http://www.presidency.ucsb.edu/ws/?pid=26627.

79. William Burr and Jeffrey T. Richelson, "Whether to 'Strangle the Baby in the Cradle': The United States and the Chinese Nuclear Program, 1960–64," *International Security* 25, no. 3 (2000/2001): 54–99; Thomas Schwartz, "Moving Beyond the Cold War: The Johnson Administration, Bridge-Building and Détente," in *Beyond the Cold War: Lyndon Johnson and the New Global Challenges of the 1960s,* ed. Francis Gavin and Mark Atwood Lawrence (Oxford: Oxford University Press, 2014), 76–96, 80.

80. Myers, *Foreign Affairs and the 1964 Presidential Election,* 69.

81. Lyndon Johnson, Remarks in Madison Square Garden, October 31, 1964, *American Presidency Project,* http://www.presidency.ucsb.edu/ws/?pid=26700.

82. Quoted in Perlstein, *Before the Storm,* 412.

8

Every Way Out

Vietnam, American National Identity, and the 1968 Presidential Election

Sandra Scanlon

The night before polls opened on November 5, 1968, the presidential hopefuls Hubert Humphrey and Richard Nixon held four-hour live telethons broadcast on rival television networks from Los Angeles. Throughout 1968, Nixon had tried to avoid direct discussion of the Johnson administration's policy on the Vietnam War, preferring to play a safe hand by declaring that there could only be one president at a time and maintaining that he did not want to jeopardize peace initiatives by offering alternative military strategies. By the dawn of the election, however, he had used private back channels to discourage the Republic of Vietnam's (South Vietnam) President Nguyen Van Thieu from engaging with the peace talks taking place in Paris and now publicly highlighted the negative consequences of the administration's most recent development, a halt to the bombing of the Democratic Republic of Vietnam (North Vietnam). He stated that he had learned that the North Vietnamese were moving "tons of supplies along the Ho Chi Minh Trail and [that] our bombers are not able to stop them." Claiming to be quoting from a UPI report from Saigon, he argued that the Democratic candidate "doesn't know what's going on," following Humphrey's charge that he was being "irresponsible." Humphrey also asserted that it would not help negotiations for the GOP candidate to "falsely accuse." Nixon revealed the dif-

ficulty of maintaining an ambiguous policy on Vietnam by first telling
viewers that hopes for peace in Vietnam had been "gravely diminished"
since the bombing pause while then claiming that, "as long as the bombing pause may bring the war to an honorable end, we should be for it."
Humphrey, continuing his close relationship with the policies of President Lyndon Johnson, simply labeled the president's decision to initiate a
bombing pause "courageous" and argued that Americans had "to be willing to take some risks for peace."[1]

The telethons provided a weak substitute for a direct confrontation
between the two main party candidates; Nixon had consistently refused
his main opponent's request for a live debate. This back-and-forth war of
words on the eve of the election was indicative, however, of the vague ways
in which foreign policy was discussed throughout much of 1968. Humphrey's long-standing reputation as a "flaming liberal" was diminished
somewhat by the time he ran for president, but voters could clearly dis-
cern distinctive differences between his domestic policy preferences and
those of either Nixon or the independent candidate, former Alabama governor George Wallace.[2] Nixon's early political reputation had been built
on his hardline foreign policy credentials and particularly his image as a
champion of exposing domestic subversion. But all three candidates in
1968 adhered to the basic principles of the Cold War consensus, especially
with regard to the containment doctrine. With regard to the increasingly
unpopular war in Vietnam, each promised policy alternatives that would
bring the war to a successful conclusion, but none identified a coherent
strategy for ending the war on terms that would secure the basic goals of
providing for South Vietnam's independence and upholding US credibility. Furthermore, there was little of significance to truly distinguish the
positions of Humphrey and Nixon on Vietnam, while Wallace fell back
on the familiar refrain that he would simply hand management of the
war over to the armed forces and thereby end US involvement quickly.
The candidates' ambivalence reflected public opinion; while a majority of
Americans polled believed that US military intervention had been a mistake, only a very small minority countenanced withdrawal should it lead
to a North Vietnamese takeover of the South. The war clearly informed
daily discourse on the most important threats facing the nation, and, as
this chapter will argue, it played a key role in defining who was deemed
most competent when it came to managing the nation's problems. But,

given the lack of difference in policy terms between Nixon and Humphrey, the war's function in determining how people voted on Election Day is more difficult to gauge.

Scholars have championed the relevance of foreign policy to the 1968 presidential election, but there is no consensus as to its meaning on Election Day. Melvin Small declared 1968 "the foreign policy election of the twentieth century." "Vietnam," he asserted, "was the central issue in the campaign, defining the terms of battle for the nominations and the trajectory of political discourse."[3] Small acknowledged that it had "always been clear that the 1968 election was not a referendum on the war," but he maintained: "The fact that Americans did not vote on the war on Election Day did not mean that the war was not the overriding issue in the run-up to the November showdown."[4] Julian Zelizer also posited that "discord over Vietnam shaped the presidential election of 1968" and signaled the "imperiled" condition of both the Democratic Party and its liberal internationalist agenda.[5] The Tet Offensive of January 1968, Walter LaFeber suggested, "marked the turning point of both the war and the U.S. presidential campaign of 1968."[6] The centrality of Vietnam to this presidential election was signaled by early accounts, most notably Lewis Chester, Godfrey Hodgson, and Bruce Page's opinion-shaping *An American Melodrama,* published in 1969. "Nothing is clearer," the British journalists stated, "than the imperative that an account of the politics of 1968 must start with Vietnam, the progress of which dominated the struggle for the Presidency from first to last." Yet they further posited: "The nature of its effect was not always agreed upon; it was often more oblique than was supposed; the war was perhaps not the simple and overriding moral issue that many honest crusaders perceived it to be."[7]

Certainly, a great many events occurred in 1968 supporting the contention that Vietnam dominated the election. Senator Eugene McCarthy's emergence as a contender for the Democratic nomination during the early primaries was conditioned by his opposition to the war, while the president's near loss to McCarthy in the New Hampshire primary was based on Democrats' disenchantment with Johnson's handling of the war. Senator Robert F. Kennedy's candidacy was in practical terms predicated on his opposition to the Johnson administration's handling of Vietnam. Indeed, the president's dramatic decision not to run again in the aftermath of the Tet Offensive signaled perhaps the clearest evidence that the war conditioned who ran for the Democratic nomination. On the Republican side, Richard Nixon, as Andrew Johns highlighted, built his return to politics after 1962 on publicly challenging the Democrats' record on Vietnam, while George Romney's chances of securing the nomination were virtually devastated by his careless assertion in August 1967 that, on his return from Vietnam in 1965, he had supported the war because he had been subject to "the greatest brainwashing that anybody can get."[8] George Wallace's third-party challenge was fundamentally undermined by his choice of running mate, General Curtis LeMay, who infamously and embarrassingly asserted that he would use "anything we could dream up" to force North Vietnam's surrender.[9] Even ignoring the impacts of the war on American society and the breadth of support for the Cold War consensus, Vietnam clearly affected who ran for the presidency and why their campaigns gained or lost partisan and public support.

Other factors affected the fate of individuals' electoral chances. Nixon secured the nomination in large part because he built important alliances with southern conservatives more preoccupied with civil rights than Vietnam. Despite the attention paid to Romney's brainwashing comment, support for his candidacy had already dropped quite dramatically from its high point in November 1966, when he enjoyed a short-lived eight-point lead over other Republican contenders. Romney lacked a well-organized campaign team or strategy, and, as Governor Jim Rhodes of Ohio famously quipped: "Watching George Romney run for the presidency was like watching a duck try to make love to a football."[10] In *The Deadly Bet*, LaFeber presented a detailed analysis of how Vietnam affected politics during 1968, but he firmly asserted that, by the time of Martin Luther King's assassination in April, "the 1968 campaign was turning into an examination of the national soul that went far beyond Vietnam."[11] Social historians such as David Farber have further maintained that racial disorder, rather than polarization over Vietnam, determined voter behavior in 1968.

Michael Flamm is perhaps the most determined critic of seeing 1968 as an election that was dominated by foreign policy issues, particularly in attempting to understand what motivated voter behavior. Law and order was "arguably the decisive factor," he asserted, in determining Nixon's narrow victory.[12] Voters may have overwhelmingly declared Vietnam the most significant threat facing the nation, but Flamm contended that the war was "a distant, impersonal concern." In October 1968, *Time* magazine claimed that law and order had "virtually anesthetized the controversy over Vietnam." Writing in 1970, Ben Wattenberg and Richard Scammon supported this contention when they resolutely declared that the war "was *not* the essential issue on which votes swung yea or nay."[13] A 1974 assessment of press coverage of the 1968 election declared a "startling difference" between the emphasis that the news media placed on Vietnam's importance and the significance attached to foreign policy by voters.[14] Polls conducted shortly after Election Day also supported this position; when asked to account for their vote, only 3 percent of respondents named "Vietnam" as decisive, while 2 percent named "other foreign policy." The main reasons named were "experienced and qualified," at 12 percent, and "for a change" and "did not like the other candidates," at 10 percent each.[15]

Scholars who argue that foreign policy defined the 1968 election do not, however, insist that voters consciously chose their preferred candidate on the basis of his Vietnam policies. This chapter argues that the Vietnam War was central to the character and outcome of the 1968 presidential election precisely because most people asserted that Vietnam was the most pressing problem facing the nation and precisely because a majority of voters insisted that the Democratic administration had failed in its efforts to deal with this problem. Vietnam was, furthermore, as much a domestic problem as an international one, and thus 1968 was more similar to than different from other election cycles in which foreign policy was not decisive. While all three candidates promised that they would end the war—with differing degrees of emphasis on how peaceful the final settlement would be—each constructed his policies with quite distinctive interpretations of American identity and American purpose in the Cold War. Humphrey's emphasis on taking risks for peace clearly contrasted with Wallace's commitment to a military solution. But Humphrey's position was also distinctively different from that of Nixon, whose allusion to "peace with honor" included the possibility that a settlement would be secured by threat of force. Perhaps more importantly, Nixon was more successful in aligning his views on the meaning of the war in terms of American sacrifice and patriotism than were his opponents. Party identification may have played the decisive role in determining the outcome of the 1968 presidential election, but Nixon's interpretation of Vietnam as a domestic social issue and his commitment to the politics of polarization meant that he enjoyed a far greater ideological victory than his narrow electoral victory suggested.

Johnson, Humphrey, and Public Opinion, 1967–1968

During late 1967, Johnson recognized that resolving the war in Vietnam was vital to securing his domestic policy agenda and his personal credibility. "By somehow scaling down the war," LaFeber notes, "he could more easily find resources to deal with crimes, turmoil in the inner cities, and the growing economic dilemma."[16] The administration's solution to domestic criticism of its Vietnam policies—which by this time stemmed more from fellow Democrats than Republicans—was a significant propaganda drive designed to enhance positive images of the administration's military strategies. General William Westmoreland, the commander of US forces in Vietnam, was temporarily recalled to Washington, DC, to deliver the positive message that the "end begins to come into view." While nonspecific about an end date to the war, he claimed that the "enemy's hopes are bankrupt" and asserted that the following year a "new phase" of the war would commence in which the South Vietnamese would take on "an ever-increasing share of the war."[17] The administration's strategy reflected the public mood, which revealed discontent about the drawn-out nature of the conflict but a continued commitment to securing a successful settlement.

Much of the public had already become disillusioned with the war, with 45 percent polled in early December 1967 asserting that it was a mistake to send troops to Vietnam in the first place.[18] At the same time, a far greater number of Americans—66 percent—described the president as a hawk. Polling revealed public confusion about prominent individuals' positions on the war, with Johnson being perceived as significantly more hawkish than Republicans such as Nixon or California governor Ronald Reagan.[19] In early February, while 61 percent of polled Americans described themselves as hawks and 70 percent supported a continuation of the bombing of North Vietnam, only 35 percent approved of the president's handling of the war.[20] Popular hostility to Johnson grew during the early months of 1968 as the public became increasingly pessimistic about the opportunities afforded by hawkish military strategies.

Such pessimism preceded the Tet Offensive of January 30, 1968, but the domestic fallout from the large-scale military attacks on South Vietnamese cities exacerbated public dissatisfaction with the president's handling of the war. By late February, there was only a slight increase in the number of Americans who thought it had been a mistake to send troops to Vietnam, while a majority continued to believe that the United States was not losing ground in its military campaign.[21] But the number of those who described themselves as hawks had by early April dropped dramatically to 41 percent and now equaled the number identifying as doves.[22] The national scene thereby proved a forbidding environment for Johnson, and public discontent with his handling of the war contributed to his decision to propose peace talks in Paris that included the North Vietnamese and the National Liberation Front and to dramatically announce that he would not seek a second term as president. As David Schmitz discussed, however, Johnson's decision was in large part based on the change in opinion that occurred among his staff and associates rather than on wider public opinion.[23] It was not clear in March 1968 that public opinion favored any particular course of action in Vietnam other than perhaps a greater acceptance of the idea that the South Vietnamese should assume a larger share of the military burden. It was certainly clear that the public had not embraced the idea of an American withdrawal that would lead to the North Vietnamese takeover of the South.

Popular frustration with Johnson's handling of the war was demonstrated during the Democratic primary in New Hampshire, which took place on March 12, 1968. By this time, Senator Eugene McCarthy of Minnesota represented the most significant antiwar challenger to the president. He had been recruited during fall 1967 by the antiwar activists Allard Lowenstein and Curtis Gans of Americans for Democratic Action, and he announced his campaign on November 30. As Michael Nelson noted: "McCarthy was not Lowenstein and Gans's second choice to take on Johnson, much less their first." They had approached Kennedy during the spring of 1967, following his March 2 Senate speech in which he called for a bombing halt. That speech may have received praise from antiwar activists, but its wider reception was more negative. He realized that "every public disagreement with Johnson on the war or any other issue would be portrayed in the media as the latest installment in their personal rivalry." Having been rejected by Kennedy, Lowenstein and Gans turned to Senator George McGovern of South Dakota. Despite his personal objection to the war, he refused to challenge Johnson because he was running for reelection to the Senate that year. McCarthy, McGovern recommended, was the most suitable candidate given that he was not up for reelection. McCarthy was, furthermore, privately considering a challenge to Johnson in order to act as a protest candidate.[24] While McCarthy became the standard bearer for the antiwar cause in Congress as a result of his challenge to Johnson, the results of the New Hampshire primary were more ambiguous than antiwar activists were prepared to acknowledge publicly. McCarthy came within seven points of defeating Johnson, but those New Hampshire Democrats who identified as hawks outnumbered doves by three to two among McCarthy supporters. Polls revealed that more than half the state's Democrats did not even know McCarthy's name; they were simply voting for the candidate who was not Johnson.[25] Philip Converse, Warren E. Miller, Jerrold G. Rusk, and Arthur C. Wolfe concluded in 1969 that the vote McCarthy "drew in New Hampshire could scarcely be labelled a 'peace vote,' despite the fact that such a conclusion was frequently drawn."[26] McCarthy thereby served his goal as a protest candidate, but perhaps not in the ways he had intended.

Johnson's near loss provided a political opportunity for others, especially Kennedy, who announced his own candidacy soon thereafter. The political commentators Roland Evans and Peter Novak reflected the mood in Washington, DC, when they wrote that Johnson and his closest political advisers were "in a state of near shock" as a result of the primary results. Leading Democrats in Wisconsin and California, the most important upcoming primary states, were rapidly reviewing their support of the president. New York's party leaders privately warned that the party would lose the State Assembly and congressional seats "unless the President bowed out (scarcely conceivable) or changed his war policy." While there appeared little confidence that McCarthy could win the nomination, the New Hampshire result stimulated a significant rise in party support for Kennedy's potential challenge. "Many LBJ loyalists," Evans and Novak wrote, "are now convinced he must soften his war policy—at the least, dropping his long-planned tactic of campaigning as patriot President, at most shifting somewhat his war policy—to keep down McCarthy and stave off Kennedy."[27]

Kennedy had been considering a nomination challenge for some time but was concerned about appearing unpatriotic by openly denouncing the president's war policies. Speaking with Clark Clifford on March 14, however, he made it known that, with regard to Vietnam, he "felt that the policy was a failure": "Both because of his conscience and pressure from others, he felt compelled to take action in this regard." While indicating that he would support the president should he agree to issue a statement that he was establishing a commission to reevaluate US policy in Vietnam "in its entirety," Kennedy made it known that he was seriously considering a run.[28]

This hardly came as a surprise to the White House, where disdain for Kennedy's Vietnam proposals was regularly expressed from early 1967. Walt Rostow commented to the president in November 1967 that, while it agreed with the administration's position that neither a withdrawal nor a purely military solution was acceptable, Kennedy's article in *Look* magazine "includes some misstatements of fact or interpretation, particularly concerning our past negotiating efforts and positions, but also including our military objectives and the course of political developments in the South."[29] In February 1968, General Earle Wheeler commented on Kennedy's recent remarks about dealing with corruption in South Vietnam and his proposal that an enclave strategy be substituted for the search-and-destroy policy. Wheeler remarked that the enclave policy would "in effect result in abandonment of a large portion of Vietnam to the control of the enemy" and noted that "much of the progress to date in building a viable Vietnamese nation would be nullified." He concluded that Kennedy's proposals were "neither feasible nor desirable."[30] Such frustrations reflected a more widespread view among administration officials that Kennedy was misrepresenting official policy on Vietnam for his personal political gain. One White House official had earlier noted that Kennedy's February 8, 1967, speech on Vietnam "is hard to come to grips with since it contains a minimum of fact and a maximum of tone, attitude and innuendo."[31] Kennedy's long-standing recommendation called for a cessation of the bombing of North Vietnam as a means of encouraging negotiations, a position that was deemed naive by key officials such as Maxwell Taylor and already tried and tested by Rostow. Kennedy therefore demonstrated a willingness to defy the administration on foreign policy throughout 1967, and Johnson's fear of a Kennedy political challenge certainly influenced his decision not to seek the nomination. It was only with the dramatic domestic fallout from the Tet Offensive and the New Hampshire primary that Kennedy became an official nominee, however. As such, foreign policy, more than any other issue, determined who ran for the Democratic presidential nomination in 1968. Yet, despite the prominence of antiwar opinion among the field of Democratic nominees that had emerged by April 1968, the antiwar camp enjoyed only limited official success.

The battle over the foreign policy plank at the Democratic national convention revealed the continued dominance of the political establishment and particularly Johnson's persistent influence. Humphrey may well have had reservations about the efficacy of administration policy during early intervention in Vietnam, but, by the midterm elections of 1966, he was advising Democrats to "run on Vietnam" and had become a vocal advocate for Johnson's foreign policies. "His reward," Nelson noted, "was to be portrayed on the cover of *Esquire*'s November issue as a ventriloquist's dummy sitting in Johnson's lap."[32] Humphrey proved singularly unwilling to break with the president on Vietnam until late in his campaign. As vice president and a key figure among the party's political establishment, he was the most probable candidate to win the nomination despite McCarthy's and especially Kennedy's appeal among key demographic groups. He realized that it was unnecessary to enter the primaries when he received the vast majority of Pennsylvania's 103 delegates, despite the fact that McCarthy received 71.7 percent of votes cast in the primary.[33] Given the majority status of the Democratic Party, he could reasonably have expected to enjoy a straightforward road to victory. Throughout much of 1968, however, he polled significantly behind his Republican rival. One cause was his dysfunctional campaign team and its failure to develop a successful strategy. Nelson commented that Humphrey failed to realize that he could not induce younger voters to abandon McCarthy or Kennedy. Instead, he appointed Walter Mondale and Fred Harris as campaign chairs, neither of whom was "young, cool, or anti-war enough to appeal to youth": "Neither was experienced in national elections; neither liked sharing the job with the other; and both had full-time responsibilities in the Senate."[34] Of greater importance was his campaign's inability, or dogged refusal, to break with the president on Vietnam. On August 1, Humphrey suggested differences with Johnson on Vietnam when he publicly stated: "I'm trying to make my views compatible with the government of the United States—and I'm having a little trouble with that." He quickly rejected any major difference with Johnson, however, when he insisted: "I do not want to run for the presidency by turning my back upon those who have stood with me and repudiating the good works of my party, my President, and my predecessors."[35] Regardless of public opinion about the best means of bringing America's involvement in the unpopular war to a conclusion, a majority of Americans regarded the administration's competence in foreign policy as poor. Sticking to the administration line—despite the fact that Humphrey and his key supporters among unions, businessmen, and southerners supported the war—therefore had a deleterious effect on his campaign.

Divisions among Democrats played out in front of television cameras during the floor fight at the national convention over the party's Vietnam plank. Humphrey had earlier tried to signal his intent to take US policy in a new direction once elected, using his campaign's foreign policy adviser, the former ambassador to the UN George Ball, to publicly champion the point that Humphrey would reassess Vietnam policy "pretty radically." Ball also sharply criticized McCarthy's proposal to meet with negotiators in Paris as "mischievous interference" and lambasted his assertion that the American people would accept a unilateral withdrawal. Instead, he promised "an honorable settlement in Viet Nam" should peace talks be permitted to reach fruition.[36] In a mid-August interview, Humphrey snapped his fingers and stated that the "bombing would be stopped like that" if there was a sign that it would lead to peace. He argued that the "war has propelled us to reassess our entire foreign policy." But his image as Johnson's underling remained intact, and he further noted that the Democratic platform would not repudiate Kennedy's and Johnson's decisions on the war.[37] Unable to persuade Johnson to countenance a suggestion that the bombing should be stopped, Humphrey acquiesced with the establishment line. As the Democratic Party Platform Committee hardened in its opposition to any criticism of Johnson, Humphrey denounced doves' stop-the-bombing plank.[38] Senator Edmund Muskie, who was considered a strong contender as Humphrey's vice presidential nominee, tried to assuage doves' frustrations. "Sometimes in the emotion of the debate on Viet Nam," he stated, "we overemphasize our differences." He claimed that all sides wanted peace in Vietnam, but this offered little to disgruntled doves and nothing to voters in terms of specific policy options.[39] Bitterness and divisiveness among Democrats, coupled with scenes of intense violence on the streets of Chicago, ensured that Humphrey officially entered the presidential campaign on the back foot. His campaign staff, furthermore, appeared to have made no plans for the final election prior to the convention, despite the fact that it was abundantly clear for some time that he would win the nomination.[40]

Humphrey trailed his Republican rival, Richard Nixon, by twelve points in early September. His early strategy was to appear more dovish than his opponents while maintaining a strong stance against extremists at home. By the end of the month, the campaign team accepted that he also needed to distance himself from the charges of incompetence and intransigence associated with the Johnson administration. On September 26, he delivered a speech in San Francisco in which he outlined "a new strategy for peace." While campaign officials continued to argue that the speech was not a break with the president on foreign policy, Humphrey had earlier explained to reporters over lunch that a change in leadership would inevitably result in a change in policy: "If you plan on staying in business, you never expect the other fellow's inventory when you take over a store, even if it's your best friend." He emphasized the role of the United Nations in maintaining international peace and insisted that the United States "cannot play the role of global gendarme." With regard to Southeast Asia, he offered three basic guidelines for future policy: "self-help; regional and multilateral responsibility; and selective American assistance."[41] Such vague pronouncements were insufficient to move public opinion, but Humphrey's announcement three days later had a more dramatic effect.

"Only in the face of looming political disaster and personal humiliation," Nelson writes, "did Humphrey realize that he had no choice but to chart a different course on Vietnam." On September 30, he delivered a speech in Salt Lake City in which he called for a halt to the bombing of North Vietnam. He had phoned the president fifteen minutes before delivering the speech, but he did not request (or anticipate) Johnson's support. While the proposal was fairly modest, Ball encouraged the news media to present it as a major break with the administration. Privately, he told reporters: "What he's privately saying is that he'd pull the troops out and try to end the war January 21, 1969."[42] Peace Democrats cautiously embraced the candidate's new rhetoric, while many of the party faithful who were disgruntled by the administration's handling of the war embraced the opportunity to rally behind the party's standard bearer. Humphrey thereby enjoyed a late surge in support. As Terry Sanford, the national chair of Citizens for Humphrey-Muskie announced in late October: "[There] is no doubt about the upsurge. The only question is whether it's enough."[43] Humphrey had belatedly recognized the importance of establishing distance between his potential presidency and that of Johnson, and he presented his policies with regard to the long-standing goal of securing an honorable peace in Vietnam. Democratic voters increasingly supported his candidacy because he promised an alternative policy in Vietnam, but not one that represented a fundamental break with the narrative of American exceptionalism and anticommunism. Like his rivals, Humphrey remained firmly committed to the Cold War consensus. But, despite a belated upsurge of support for his candidacy, the Democratic Party continued to lose support overall, opening the door for Nixon in particular to begin the process of building a Republican majority. This majority was, in no small part, built on the GOP candidate's ability to define Vietnam in positive terms that resonated with traditional concepts of national purpose in the world.

Nixon, Wallace, and the Forging of a Great Silent Majority

During the presidential primaries in March 1968, Nixon reportedly confided to his aides Richard Whalen, Patrick Buchanan, and Ray Price that he believed "there's no way to win the war" because of the domestic backlash that would ensue once the military strategies required to force North Vietnam's surrender were implemented. Whalen later reported that Nixon stated that, although he no longer believed military victory to be possible, "we have to seem to say the opposite, just to keep some degree of bargaining leverage."[44] The extent to which Nixon truly rejected a military solution to the war has most recently been challenged by David Schmitz, who convincingly argues that, on entering office, Nixon intended to use military means to force North Vietnam to accept an American settlement: "He believed that through a covert expansion of the war into Cambodia, escalation of the bombing through his 'madman strategy,' implementation of the Nixon Doctrine and the policy of Vietnamization, and successful manipulation of public opinion, he could gain the political time necessary to force concessions from Hanoi militarily and bring about an end to the war that achieved his goals."[45] Nixon abandoned this strategy only following the failure of the Cambodian incursion in May 1970. As president, he sought to redefine the meaning of victory in the popular imagination so that his far more limited settlement would indeed accord with "peace with honor."[46] Throughout 1968, however, he tried above all else to appear ambiguous on Vietnam. He certainly did not abandon his strong commitment to challenging Communist expansion and remained a concerted advocate of the Cold War. But his presidential campaign gave the impression that he had a unique ability to manage the war effort because of his experience in foreign policy. By refusing to propose specific policies, he created the impression that he had plans to end the war that differed from those of Johnson but that he could not reveal for fears of upsetting the president's peace initiatives. As such, he remained a hawk to those who desired stronger military action and a potential dove to those who simply wanted the war to end.

While he was the favored candidate by the summer of 1968, Nixon faced a potential upset in the person of Governor Ronald Reagan of California and therefore needed to walk a fine line with conservative Republicans at the convention. He secured the active support of Senator Strom Thurmond of South Carolina because of his private commitments to stand firm on civil rights, but he could not discount the importance of foreign policy in securing support from the burgeoning conservative movement. His statement to the Republican National Committee's Committee on Resolutions, in which he declared that the Johnson administration had "wasted" the "massive military superiority" of the United States in Vietnam, was interpreted by the conservative journal *Human Events* as an indication of his preference for a military solution to the stalemate.[47] Referring to the management of the war, Nixon stated simply: "The fact is that our men have not been out-fought; the Administration has been out-thought."[48] During a meeting with southern Republicans at the convention, he stated that, with regard to Vietnam, he would follow Eisenhower's means for ending the Korean War: "We'll be militarily strong and diplomatically strong."[49] Reiterating his recent attack on the administration's "failure to train and equip the South Vietnamese, both for fighting their own war now and for the task of defending their own country after the war is settled,"[50] he highlighted his plans to prepare the South Vietnamese to take over much of the fighting and to induce the Soviets to be more cooperative in reducing tensions in Vietnam and elsewhere. Strength in diplomacy, he made clear, was to be founded on military and economic power: "What we've got to do is walk softly and carry a big stick and we can have peace in this world. And that is what we are going to do."[51] This rhetoric was hardly unexpected; throughout the year, Nixon had been arguing that "in quarantining North Viet Nam we would have to take a much closer look at all the military options available," and he continuously maintained that "real leadership in this field, which has been lacking, uses the threat of military power as a diplomatic weapon."[52] Nixon thereby secured the support of both conservative and moderate Republicans and handily won the nomination while maintaining his standard line that the administration lacked competence in managing the war but he possessed vast experience in foreign policy. His choice of vice president, Governor Spiro Agnew of Maryland, also did nothing to reveal his foreign policy preferences. As LaFeber noted: "[The] Republican candidates opened the final stretch of the campaign with their hands free to deal with the subject of Vietnam."[53]

While avoiding public commentary, Nixon took private steps to derail the peace negotiations in Paris. Through the medium of a Republican activist, Anna Chennault, he urged President Thieu not to endorse the negotiations until after the November election.[54] Henry Kissinger, Governor Nelson Rockefeller's former foreign policy adviser, also provided a back channel of information on the Paris Talks through his contacts with Richard Allan and John Mitchell, leading figures in the Nixon campaign team.[55] Johnson became aware of Nixon's activities but did not make the issue public. Had Nixon's activities become publicly known, they almost certainly would have cut into his lead over Humphrey, which in September stood at 43 to 31 percent. At 19 percent, Wallace continued to enjoy significant support at this time.[56] Nixon's cautious approach to Vietnam—at least his cautious public stance—helped solidify his standing in the polls throughout September and early October. Much of his support in this area rested on two assumptions. The first was that his experience in foreign policy afforded him greater credibility in managing international affairs than either Humphrey or Wallace. The second was that he had a secret plan to end the war. Nixon had never in fact made any reference to a secret plan, but he allowed this misrepresentation of his position to serve his political goals.[57] By carefully refusing to be drawn on the issue, he avoided having to disabuse his varied supporters of their interpretations of his Vietnam strategies.

Although cautious and determined not to appear as a hawk, Nixon did not ignore the political benefits of attacking his opponent's record on the war. Indeed, a core part of the Nixon campaign strategy was to continuously repeat the message that, while Johnson may have had good intentions, he was relying on "old, tired men" who were making mistakes. Speaking on the eve of the campaign, Nixon stated that, while his hopes for peace had been "tremendously high" only days before, he was now discouraged. "If we are going to avoid what could be a diplomatic disaster," he warned Republican activists in Los Angeles, "it is going to be necessary to get new men and a more united front in the United States of America." "Fresh ideas, new men, and new leadership" were essential.[58] Attacking the Johnson administration clearly had political utility among voters disillusioned with the current handling of the war effort, but Humphrey's apparent about-face in late September threatened to undermine the value of this strategy. Nixon's position held sway and was ultimately significant in determining the broader understanding of the meaning of Vietnam in the years that followed because he did more than simply attack Democrats' positions on the war. He reflected on Vietnam as a domestic, social problem, one that was deeply connected to conflicts at home, most notably violent unrest in black ghettos and radical antiwar activism.

Writing of his speech to the Congress of American Industry and National Association of Manufacturers in January 1968, Walter Trohan of the *Chicago Tribune* commented that, instead of focusing on Vietnam, Nixon chose to speak of the war at home. He duly spoke of how law and order was under attack, especially by black activists making war plans for summer rioting; activists had been inspired by the grandiose promises of change put forth by the Johnson administration, promises that had not been kept. Nixon regularly utilized the image of black radicalism to highlight the breakdown of law and order, frequently noted as an issue of primary concern to voters. But, in Nixon's rhetoric, the separation between the war at home and the conflict in Vietnam was not as great as Trohan suggested. "The ultimate testing-place of America is America itself," Nixon stated. "All our power and prestige and ability to keep the promises that keep the peace—everything we stand for and dream of— rest, in the end, on the unity and strength of America. If we are divided, if we default on the promise we have made to ourselves, the foundation on which we are attempting to build a better future will crumble."[59] Nixon presented his candidacy as one based on the concept of bringing America together, one designed to rebuild a recently lost consensus. In reality, his rhetoric was exclusionary, intended to further define what constituted appropriate dissent and, by extension, core American values. Humphrey suffered more at the hands of antiwar protestors than either of his rivals, but, as Colin Dueck notes, Vietnam's association with social unrest at home "redounded against the Democrats, since this disorder had occurred on their watch, and was widely resented even by millions of their core constituents."[60] Such unrest and resentment ultimately weakened Humphrey's electoral chances, just as Nixon's stance on Vietnam helped cement his image as a champion of order.

In large part, Nixon's success in solidifying his position as a champion of opposing domestic unrest was based on factors extraneous to his campaign. Certainly, Agnew utilized the kind of red-baiting rhetoric that had once been part of Nixon's repertoire. But, in 1968, Nixon's own critiques of dissent were more subtle. He built on the campaigns of grassroots supporters of the war to frame Vietnam as a moral or social issue for Americans. And supporting the troops became the primary framework for achieving this goal. These grassroots campaigns began with pro-Johnson demonstrations in 1965, but, in response to antiwar protest, they assumed a new character and were designed to associate traditional American values of loyalty and patriotism with opposition to dissent. The most dramatic exhibition of support for the troops serving in Vietnam took place in May 1967 with the mammoth rally We Support Our Boys in Vietnam.[61] Raymond Gimmler, a New York Fire Department chief and an active member of the American Legion, became the face of the large-scale patriotic parade, stating that he was motivated by his disgust at the "peaceniks" and "anti-Americans" protesting the war. The parade's committee stated that the event was designed to challenge "attacks on our nation and the impression given to the world of a people who oppose their country": "Above all we are striving to assure our fighting men in Vietnam that they have the full respect, love, prayers and backing of the American People." The committee was convinced that its efforts represented Americans' "authentic voice."[62]

The *New York Times* estimated that as many as seventy thousand people marched in the parade in a "forest of American flags" while tens of thousands more watched from the sidelines and PBS broadcast thirteen hours of live footage of the event. Many who appeared in the parade carried signs urging the use of greater force. Indeed, several of the signs carried by marchers implored the administration to "Bomb Hanoi." The *Times* reported that the "usual atmosphere" of the parade was "belligerent": "It showed clearly in such signs as: 'Down with the Reds,' 'My country right or wrong,' 'Hey, hey, what do you say; let's support the USA,' 'Give the boys moral ammo,' . . . 'God bless us patriots, may we never go out of style,' and 'Escalate, don't capitulate.'" The parade was mainly orderly. Still: "A dozen times paraders or their sympathizers attacked individuals displaying signs urging the end of the war or expressing such sentiments. A man who was said to be a bystander was smeared with tar and feathers." [63]

While demonstrations such as this parade were not anti-administration in tone, Humphrey was unable to create an attachment to such activists. He was neither entirely part of the administration, nor separate from it, and his focus on "law and justice," rather than law and order, failed to fully repudiate antiwar protest. Wallace echoed many of the sentiments expressed by these demonstrators, but his caustic language alienated those whose focus was on honor, sacrifice, and harmony. On the other hand, Nixon's message—his call for national unity coupled with his reputation as an ardent anti-Communist—did resonate with such grassroots activists. This fact did not necessarily translate into electoral support for the Republican's presidential bid. But his message helped condition public attitudes toward dissent, and popular acceptance of his message of law and order discredited antiwar protest. His message in 1968 affected how many Americans understood Vietnam thereafter: as a war fought between Americans rather than between competing political forces in Vietnam. Unintentionally, his message also limited his policy options when it came to fighting the Vietnam War. His promises of peace led inexorably to the pursuit of Vietnamization, while his focus on the domestic environment led the administration to publicly prioritize such populist issues as concern for American prisoners of war. As antiwar protests declined after 1970, so did popular acceptance of the national security imperatives at stake in Vietnam.

Polling suggests that there was very little direct correlation between the candidates' specific policies regarding Vietnam and the outcome of the election. As Robert Mason notes: "Nixon's minority share of the electorate did not represent a coherent vote for confidence in a Republican future."[64] As such, it is difficult to gauge the practical effect of Nixon's rhetorical association between foreign policy and domestic values. What is clearer, however, is the great extent to which Nixon and Wallace succeeded in undermining the Democratic majority, in large part by drawing links between the administration's failed Vietnam policies and domestic turmoil. Nixon thereby reflected popular beliefs that a positive outcome to the war—however ambiguously such an outcome was defined—was correlated with American ideals. The foundations of Nixon's Silent Majority strategy were laid during the 1968 election and ultimately bore considerable fruit.

The October "Surprise"

From the time that he made his dramatic announcement in March, Johnson assured his vice president that he was working to secure significant steps toward peace before the November election. In October, he informed Humphrey that it "looks like Hanoi has moved," although there was still a lot to be discussed before any substantive measures could be taken.[65] By the end of the month, the administration was poised to take a step that added significant weight to the candidate's earlier call for a bombing halt. On October 31, Johnson announced that he had "ordered that all air, naval and artillery bombardment of North Vietnam cease as of 8 a.m., Washington time, Friday morning." All parties had reached the stage, he claimed, whereby "productive talks can begin."[66] The halt was predicated on enemy assurances regarding the reestablishment of the Demilitarized Zone, a pledge that cities in the South would not be attacked, and an agreement to enter productive negotiations with the government of South Vietnam. Deciding whether to pursue the halt in order to stimulate negotiations at Paris had not been easy for the administration. Now the Johnson White House faced the additional quandary of attempting to ensure that the move was not construed as merely a "political stratagem."[67] Secretary of Defense Clark Clifford described the fear of Senator Richard Russell of Georgia that the halt would be understood by friend and foe as simply a political move to shore up Democratic support. Clifford denied that Russell's fears were justified, arguing instead that the public would interpret the halt as a sound attempt to negotiate an end to the war. As Johnson rightly feared, the administration's opponents were unlikely to allow the administration to push this message without opposition. Thurmond, for instance, issued a press release in which he emphasized the possible political motivations underscoring the move: "Many will view this unilateral cessation of bombing with suspicion and question why the Administration waited until five days before the election to announce this action."[68]

Reflecting the lack of distinctions between the candidates' Vietnam strategies, neither Nixon nor Wallace was willing to be so bold. Wallace stated simply that he hoped the president would be successful and that "we have an honorable peace in Southeast Asia." Nonetheless, he further remarked that it was "unfortunate, probably, that it all comes right on the eve of the election." "There are those who will say that it's politically inspired. I don't say that because I'm not fully aware of the facts," he concluded.[69] Nixon chose a more strident tactic, praising the president's pursuit of peace while repeating "in harsher language" an earlier assertion that Johnson had allowed a "security gap" to develop in the military strength of the United States relative to that of the Soviet Union. Despite administration attempts to refute Nixon's claim, the GOP candidate found welcome support for his arguments among Republican voters. Nixon accused Humphrey of being one of those "fuzzy thinkers" and "false prophets" who "profess to believe that keeping America strong is somehow being against peace." "They will," he proclaimed to a cheering crowd in San Antonio, "get America into war, not because they want war but because they don't understand how to keep the peace."[70] Yet, in light of Humphrey's surge following his announcement of support for a bombing halt, Nixon's team feared the effects of the president's latest policy shift. The New York Times reflected his staff's mood when it declared that, although the new policy was likely to have "no more than a limited effect on voter behavior," a small shift in support to Humphrey jeopardized Nixon's chances of taking key battleground states such as New York, Pennsylvania, and Michigan.[71] Nixon attempted to defuse the issue by again emphasizing the overall incompetence of the Democrats in securing international peace. His tone became harsher, especially once the momentum toward peace was thwarted when Saigon refused to accept the new terms for entering substantive negotiations. Peace remained elusive in early November 1968, despite each candidate's promises to use every means necessary to honorably end US involvement in Vietnam. Voters had little more to inform their decisions than such vague promises and assessments of the candidate's character and competence.

Conclusion

The extent to which the Vietnam War influenced how people voted on Election Day is therefore ambiguous. Humphrey's late surge in support drew largely from former Wallace supporters, who were consistently less interested in Vietnam than supporters of the other two candidates. Most were traditional Democrats who were disenchanted with Wallace by November and moved more by Humphrey's willingness to break with Johnson than by the specific details of his assertion of independence. Nixon lost votes to Humphrey in the North but gained backing from Wallace supporters in the South. Humphrey also took the 7–8 percent of voters who were undecided in early October.[72] As Nelson discusses, however, given the Democrats' overall eighteen-point lead over Republicans in party identification, Humphrey's near parity with Nixon was a dramatic blow.[73] If Vietnam did not determine the outcome of the election, the debates that raged during 1968 regarding foreign policy reoriented American politics and contributed to the national identity polarization of the 1970s that enhanced conservative political gains.

The 1968 election possibly best reveals how politicians are affected by foreign policy and how they try to make use of it in elections, more than it does how individual voters or groups of voters responded to foreign policy in deciding how to vote. Furthermore, it reveals how international players (in this case South Vietnam and President Nguyen Van Thieu most clearly) have tried to utilize the American electoral cycle to secure favorable relations or terms. But the election itself also revealed something important about how Nixon would later present his foreign policies to the public and why he succeeded in sustaining American involvement in Vietnam for four more years. Unlike Humphrey, Nixon actively utilized positive polarization and framed the Vietnam War as an American domestic struggle, rather than an international one. The roots of the Silent Majority speech of November 1969 were clearly evident in his 1968 campaign, a campaign that presented Nixon with a far greater ideological triumph than his narrow victory would suggest.

Notes

1. UPI Report, "Nixon, Humphrey, Give Their Views in Four-Hour Telethons from California," *Bend (OR) Bulletin*, November 5, 1968, 6.

2. Bruce Biossat, "Hubert Humphrey, a 1948 Liberal Earnestly Seeking a 1968 Identity," *Victoria (TX) Advocate*, August 27, 1968, 4.

3. Melvin Small, "The Election of 1968," *Diplomatic History* 28, no. 4 (2004): 513–28, 513.

4. Melvin Small, "Response to Commentaries," *Diplomatic History* 28, no. 4 (2004): 577.

5. Julian Zelizer, *Arsenal of Democracy: The Politics of National Security—from World War II to the War on Terrorism* (New York: Basic, 2009), 214.

6. Walter LaFeber, *The Deadly Bet: LBJ, Vietnam, and the 1968 Election* (Lanham, MD: Rowman & Littlefield, 2005), 24.

7. Lewis Chester, Godfrey Hodgson, and Bruce Page, *An American Melodrama: The Presidential Campaign of 1968* (Harmondsworth: Penguin, 1969), 39.

8. Andrew Johns, "A Voice from the Wilderness: Richard Nixon and the Vietnam War, 1964–1966," *Presidential Studies Quarterly* 29, no. 2 (1999): 317–35, 318. George Romney quoted in Andrew Johns, "Achilles' Heel: The Vietnam War and George Romney's Bid for the Presidency, 1967 to 1968," *Michigan Historical Review* 26, no. 1 (2000): 1–29, 13.

9. Dan T. Carter, *The Politics of Rage: George Wallace, the Origins of the New Conservatism, and the Transformation of American Politics* (Baton Rouge: Louisiana State University Press, 1995), 359.

10. Theodore H. White, *The Making of the President, 1968* (London: Jonathan Cape, 1969), 54.

11. LaFeber, *Deadly Bet*, 91.

12. Michael Flamm, *Law and Order: Street Crime, Civil Unrest, and the Crisis of Liberalism in the 1960s* (New York: Columbia University Press, 2007), 2.

13. Both quotes from Flamm, *Law and Order*, 162.

14. Doris A. Graber, "Press Coverage and Voter Reaction in the 1968 Presidential Election," *Political Science Quarterly* 89, no. 1 (1974): 68–100, 88.

15. Alfred E. Eckes, "Commentary," *Diplomatic History* 28, no. 4 (2004): 569–71, 570.

16. LaFeber, *Deadly Bet*, 19.

17. General William Westmoreland quoted in Associated Press, "Late News Roundup," *Prescott (AZ) Courier*, November 16, 1967, 1.

18. George H. Gallup, ed., *The Gallup Poll, 1935–1971* (New York: Random House, 1972), 2099.

19. Ibid., 2101.

20. Ibid., 2105.

21. Ibid., 2108.

22. Ibid., 2124.

23. David F. Schmitz, *The Tet Offensive: Politics, War, and Public Opinion* (Lanham, MD: Rowman & Littlefield, 2005), xv.

24. Michael Nelson, *Resilient America: Electing Nixon in 1968, Channeling Dissent, and Dividing Government* (Lawrence: University Press of Kansas, 2014), 75–77.

25. LaFeber, *Deadly Bet*, 45.

26. Philip Converse, Warren E. Miller, Jerrold G. Rusk, and Arthur C. Wolfe, "Continuity and Change in American Politics: Parties and Issues in the 1968 Election," *American Political Science Review* 63, no. 4 (1969): 1083–1105, 1092.

27. Roland Evans and Peter Novak, "Johnson and New Hampshire," *Free-Lance Star* (Fredericksburg, VA), March 16, 1968, 4.

28. Clark Clifford, Memorandum of Conversation with Senator Robert Kennedy and Theodore C. Sorenson, March 14, 1968, Special Files, White House Famous Names, box 8, Folder: Kennedy, Robert F., 1968 Campaign, Lyndon Baines Johnson Presidential Library, Austin, TX (hereafter LBJL). Kennedy recommended that the commission include Edwin Reischauer, Kingman Brewster, Roswell Gilpatric, Carl Kaysen, Senator Robert Kennedy, General Lauris Norstad, General Matthew Ridgway, Senator Mike Mansfield, Senator John Sherman Cooper, and Senator George Aiken. President Johnson rejected the recommendation.

29. Walt W. Rostow, Memorandum for the President, Analysis of Senator Robert Kennedy's Article on Viet-Nam in *Look,* November 16, 1967, National Security Files, Country File, Vietnam, box 102 (1 of 2), Folder: Vietnam 7F (1) 1/66–11/67, Congressional Attitudes and Statements (1 of 3), LBJL.

30. General Earle Wheeler, Memorandum for the President, Subject: Senator Kennedy's Views on South Vietnam, February 3, 1968, National Security File, Country File, Vietnam, box 102 (1 of 2), Folder: Vietnam 7F (2)a 12/67–3/69, Congressional Attitudes and Statements (1 of 2), LBJL.

31. Memorandum, Subject: Comments on Senator Robert Kennedy's 8 February Speech, February 9, 1968, National Security File, Country File, Vietnam, box 102 (1 of 2), Folder: Vietnam 7F (2)a 12/67–3/69, Congressional Attitudes and Statements (1 of 2), LBJL.

32. Nelson, *Resilient America,* 65.

33. Ibid., 94.

34. Ibid., 94. The *Chicago Tribune* commented in October 1968 that Humphrey's personal staff was "considered by many to be the least impressive group in the entire Humphrey entourage." "The Humphrey Brain Trust," *Chicago Tribune,* October 20, 1968, H64.

35. "Vietnam Barb Balanced by Humphrey," *The Blade* (Toledo, OH), August 1, 1968, 3.

36. "Ball against Gene's Peace Talks Plans; Leave Negotiators Alone He Says," *Chicago Tribune,* July 1, 1968, 10.

37. UPI Report, "Peace Hint Needed to Stop Bombs," *Chicago Tribune,* August 18, 1968, 6.

38. David Farber, *Chicago '68* (Chicago: University of Chicago Press, 1988), 165.

39. "Viet Doves Lost Battle for Viet Plank," *Chicago Tribune,* August 29, 1968, 1.

40. The *Chicago Tribune* reflected widespread public commentary when it noted that there was a "propensity among the personal staffers for openly jostling for influence with the boss." "The Humphrey Brain Trust."

41. Russell Freeburg, "Hubert Tells Strategy for Peace," *Chicago Tribune,* September 27, 1968, 3.

42. Nelson, *Resilient America,* 194.

43. Tom Wicker, "Humphrey Surge Is Offering Aides a Hope for Upset," *New York Times,* October 27, 1968, 1.

44. Richard Nixon, Statement to Richard J. Whalen, Ray Price, and Patrick Buchanan, March 29, 1968, quoted in Richard Whalen, *Catch the Falling Flag: A Republican's Challenge to His Party* (Boston: Houghton Mifflin, 1972), 137.

45. David Schmitz, *Richard Nixon and the Vietnam War: The End of the American Century* (Lanham, MD: Rowman & Littlefield, 2014), 45.

46. Sandra Scanlon, *The Pro-War Movement: Domestic Support for the Vietnam War and the Making of Modern American Conservatism* (Amherst: University of Massachusetts Press, 2013), chap. 4.

47. "Richard Nixon: Republican Candidate," *Human Events,* September 28, 1968, 3–8.

48. Richard Nixon, Speech before the Committee on Resolutions, Republican National Convention, August 1, 1968, cited in "Richard Nixon: Republican Candidate," 7.

49. Richard Nixon cited in tape transcription of meeting with southern Republicans, August 6, 1968, in "What Dick Nixon Told Southern Delegates," *Miami Herald,* August 7, 1968, reprinted in Jeffrey Kimball, *The Vietnam War Files: Uncovering the Secret History of Nixon-Era Strategy* (Lawrence: University Press of Kansas, 2004), 64.

50. Richard Nixon, Speech before the Committee on Resolutions, Republican National Convention, August 1, 1968, quoted in "Richard Nixon: Republican Candidate," 6.

51. Kimball, *The Vietnam War Files,* 64–65.

52. Chesly Manly, "Leadership Crisis Big Issue, Nixon Asserts," *Chicago Tribune,* February 12, 1968, 6.

53. LaFeber, *Deadly Bet,* 112.

54. See Larry Berman, *No Peace, No Honor: Nixon, Kissinger, and Betrayal in Vietnam* (New York: Touchstone, 2001), 32–36; Kimball, *The Vietman War Files,* 56–62; and Anthony Summers, *The Arrogance of Power: The Secret World of Richard Nixon* (London: Penguin, 2000), xiv, 298–305.

55. Kimball, *The Vietnam War Files,* 58.

56. Robert Mason, *Richard Nixon and the Quest for a New Majority* (Chapel Hill: University of North Carolina Press, 2004), 32.

57. Sarah Katherine Mergel, *Conservative Intellectuals and Richard Nixon: Rethinking the Rise of the Right* (Basingstoke: Palgrave Macmillan, 2010), 35. Andrew Johns notes: "[A] memorandum in the files of the Republican National Committee acknowledges that Nixon did indicate that he had definite ideas on how to end the war through what would become known as Vietnamization. Yet he did not reveal his thoughts to even his closest confidants." Andrew Johns, *Vietnam's Second Front: Domestic Politics, the Republican Party, and the War* (Lexington: University Press of Kentucky, 2010), 198. Kimball elaborated: "For doves and moderates, he [Nixon] spoke less of escalating military measures and protecting vital interests and more of taking *non-military* steps toward *peace;* for hawks and conservatives, he continued to talk about putting *pressure* and *winning* the peace. For all Americans, he spoke of a peace with *honor*." Kimball, *The Vietnam War Files,* 41.

58. Russell Freeburg, "Nixon Vows Peace in Windup; Hubert Defends Stand on Viet," *Chicago Tribune,* November 5, 1968, 1.

59. Walter Trohan, "Report from Washington: Nixon Speech Focuses on Domestic Ills," *Chicago Tribune,* January 7, 1968, 2.

60. Colin Dueck, *Hard Line: The Republican Party and Foreign Policy since World War II* (Princeton, NJ: Princeton University Press, 2010), 148.

61. See Scanlon, *Pro-War Movement,* chap. 5.

62. We Support Our Boys in Vietnam Parade Committee Statement, Issues Early May 1967, We Support Our Boys in Vietnam, Inc. Archive, Hoover Institution Archives, Stanford, CA, box 7, Folder: Letters, 1967–1968.

63. "70,000 Turn Out to Back U.S. Men in Vietnam War," *New York Times,* May 14, 1967.

64. Mason, *Richard Nixon,* 35.

65. Lyndon Johnson Telephone Conversation with Hubert Humphrey, October 1968, Miller Center, University of Virginia, Presidential Recordings Program, Tape WH6810.11, Conversation no 13621.

66. Lyndon B. Johnson, The President's Address to the Nation upon Announcing His Decision to Halt the Bombing of North Vietnam, October 31, 1968, *The American Presidency Project,* http://www.presidency.ucsb.edu/ws/?pid=28772.

67. Telephone Conversation between Clifford and President Johnson, October 22, 1968, *Foreign Relations of the United States, 1964–1968,* vol. 7, *Vietnam, September 1968–January 1969* (Washington, DC: US Government Printing Office, 2003), document 106.

68. Senator Strom Thurmond, Press Release (on the cessation of bombing in Vietnam), October 31, 1968, Thurmond Papers, Speeches Subseries A, box 31, Folder: Press Release, Washington, DC, October 31, 1968, Clemson University Libraries, Clemson, SC.

69. Anthony Ripley, "Wallace Told of Johnson Action; Hopes for Honorable Peace," *New York Times,* November 1, 1968, 55.

70. E. W. Kenworthy, "Nixon Links Rival to 'Security Gap,'" *New York Times,* November 2, 1968, 1.

71. Tom Wicker, "Impact on Campaign; Bombing Halt Likely to Aid Humphrey Only a Little, but That May Be Crucial," *New York Times,* November 1, 1968, 51.

72. Nelson, *Resilient America,* 207.

73. Ibid., 224.

9

The Peace Candidate

Richard Nixon, Henry Kissinger, and the Election of 1972

Thomas Alan Schwartz

On Election Day, November 3, 1970, the journalist Marilyn Berger called Richard Nixon's national security adviser, Henry Kissinger, in the early evening. Kissinger started their conversation by saying, "What are you taking me away from, a Republican landslide?" When she asked whether he was serious, he replied, "I can't see it."[1] The midterm elections were a huge disappointment to the Nixon White House. The president could take some comfort in the defeat of a few of his adversaries in the Senate, such as Charles Goodell in New York, Joseph Tydings in Maryland, and Albert Gore in Tennessee. But most of the candidates he campaigned for had lost, including George Murphy in California and George H. W. Bush in Texas. The Republican attempt to capitalize on violent protests against Nixon had backfired. The Democrats, with their spokesman Senator Edmund Muskie, the frontrunner for the Democratic presidential nomination, doing a television appearance on the eve of the election, received favorable commentary for the calm and sincere image they presented to the electorate. Muskie was leading Nixon in one-on-one polls for 1972, and the election results seemed to confirm this trend. Republicans did gain two seats in the Senate but lost nine House seats and eleven governorships—the overall Democratic margin in House elections increased from 1.1 million votes in 1968 to 4.5 million in 1970.[2]

Nixon was shaken by the results, writing later: "It seemed possible that I might not even be nominated for re-election in 1972."[3] Although there was never a strong challenge from within his party, the president's overall popularity was slipping below 50 percent, the economy was sluggish, and Americans were unhappy with the increasing levels of crime and domestic disorder. Nixon was particularly incensed when a Gallup poll showed that Americans thought the country's prestige abroad had fallen during his presidency. "We are not getting credit for foreign policy," he angrily told his chief of staff, H. R. Haldeman.[4] In a long memorandum in early December 1970, he told Haldeman that he wanted a meeting with the special counsel Dick Moore, the speechwriter William Safire, and Henry Kissinger. He had "reluctantly concluded that [the] entire effort on the public relations front has been misdirected and ineffective." What was needed in his view was "to get across those fundamental decencies and virtues which the great majority of Americans like—hard work, warmth, kindness, consideration for others, willingness to take the heat and not to pass the buck and, above all, a man who always does what he thinks is right, regardless of the consequences." Nixon knew that Haldeman might wonder about including Kissinger in this group for such a public relations–oriented meeting, but his reason was straightforward and captured Kissinger's unique position within the White House hierarchy: "The reason is that he will love sitting in such a meeting. He will keep it absolutely confidential; he will not contribute anything on how to get the ideas across, but above everything else, he is our big gun in the area where we have had our greatest success, and while he does not know it, he is the one who has been measured the favorite."[5]

Although the judgment that Kissinger would keep things "confidential" seems very naive, the more interesting point is why Nixon believed Kissinger to be "the favorite." In his conspiratorial view, the Eastern establishment media—the television networks and the liberal newspapers—had anointed Kissinger as the wise man of the administration, the Harvard professor and one of their own, and the only colorful figure among the bland white men in the Republican administration. For political reasons, Nixon believed that it was now important for the administration to use that popularity with the establishment to get his administration's message across. His people had been cautious about having Kissinger on television, thinking that his German accent might alienate middle America, but Nixon delighted in a flattering October 1970 *60 Minutes* profile of his adviser and now encouraged him to do more television appearances. Others in the administration's press office reacted with the same enthusiasm. Safire told Kissinger: "That was the most fantastic show I have ever seen; it not only reflected well on you, but also on the President and the administration." The British television personality David Frost now wanted Kissinger on his program, and the *Today* show's Barbara Walters arranged an interview. Kissinger's appearance on the national news shows announcing his resignation from Harvard in January 1971 was a part of this new media campaign, connected to Nixon's larger strategy of turning around his political fortunes.[6] Nixon recognized how important success in foreign policy—and getting the personal credit for that success—would be for his reelection. The best bet for those political benefits was using Kissinger, with his singular loyalty to the president and his skill in outmaneuvering the bureaucracy. Kissinger was now, as Haldeman told him, "indispensable to the President, and both he and the President know it, and he's got to stay here."[7]

In this chapter, I argue that Richard Nixon—often thought of as the quintessential foreign policy president—worked diligently to craft the narrative of "peace candidate" in the run-up to the 1972 presidential election. There would be bumps along the way—especially Vietnam—but the president's opponents misread his military moves there and underestimated his determination to get out of Vietnam by the time of the election. In shaping his image as the peace candidate, Nixon deliberately used Henry Kissinger, ironically helping create Kissinger's own cult of celebrity as well. The two men undertook steps in foreign policy, particularly their trifecta—the opening to China, the Strategic Arms Limitation Talks (SALT) agreement with the Soviet Union, and the negotiations to end the Vietnam War—with a strong sense of their impact on Nixon's domestic political standing. Although all these moves could be justified for foreign policy reasons, it is clear that their timing and choreography were designed for maximum domestic political effect. Nixon was determined to be reelected, and every priority in his administration—especially foreign policy—was subordinate to that purpose.

Two Foreign Policy Challenges: Vietnam and China

With Nixon's blessing, Kissinger assumed a role that was foreign policy adviser with an eye on domestic politics. This is reflected in his advice about Vietnam, the issue that Nixon believed was central to his reelection. The president was growing increasingly impatient and determined to rid himself of the albatross of the war. He had hoped to end it quickly after he took office, using a combination of military threats and high-level diplomacy with the Soviet Union. Neither of these approaches worked, and Nixon resorted to following the advice of his defense secretary, Melvin Laird, and pursuing Vietnamization—the slow withdrawal of American forces and increased training of the South Vietnamese—coupled with secret peace talks led by Kissinger in Paris. Nixon's decision to invade Cambodia in April 1970 set off a national uproar, and, despite a quick withdrawal and a continuing decline in American casualties, the war continued to sap his popularity. In December 1970, Nixon told Kissinger that he wanted to go to Vietnam in April 1971, tour the country, give speeches touting the achievements of Vietnamization and President Thieu, and then make "a basic end of the war announcement." Kissinger, sounding more political than his boss, told him that, if the United States pulled out all its forces in 1971 and South Vietnam came under attack in 1972 and collapsed: "We'll have to answer for [it] at the elections."[8] This blunt political argument seemed to sway Nixon, although he asked Kissinger to draw up plans that might allow him some type of popular move later in 1971, such as announcing that no more draftees would be sent to Vietnam. He knew, as he would grudgingly admit publicly, that he expected "to be held accountable by the American people" should he fail to end American involvement in the war.[9]

Ironically enough, this hope to end the war more quickly led Nixon to authorize a South Vietnamese offensive into Laos to cut the Ho Chi Minh Trail. Launched at the end of January 1971, Lam Son 719 suffered from a combination of intelligence failures and poor military leadership, and the result was disaster.[10] Army of the Republic of Vietnam (ARVN) forces beat a chaotic and hasty retreat, with American television showing demoralized South Vietnamese soldiers clinging to helicopter skids as they sought to escape Laos.[11] Determined to change this perception, Nixon gave a nationally televised speech on April 7, 1971, and insisted that the Laotian operation proved that Vietnamization was working successfully and that therefore he could increase the rate of American troop withdrawals.[12] But, despite his speech, polls showed that almost 73 percent of Americans wanted the United States out by the end of 1971, 60 percent wanted withdrawal even if the South Vietnamese government collapsed, and 58 percent believed it morally wrong for the United States to fight in Vietnam.[13]

In the midst of the negative assessment of Laos, the Nixon administration received some good news. The Chinese government decided to make its own move in the game of diplomacy by having its champion ping-pong team, following its victory during a competition in Japan, invite the American team to visit China. The news of the invitation came on April 7, 1971, the same day as Nixon's Laos speech, as if the Chinese had timed their invitation as a response to Nixon's announcement that the United States was withdrawing even faster from Vietnam. Over the next ten days, "ping-pong diplomacy" dominated the television news coverage, with favorable images of China and positive assessments of the "thaw" in relations between the United States and China.[14] *Time* magazine entitled its coverage "The Ping Heard Round the World" and speculated that "China has finally decided to turn outward again."[15] Haldeman noted: "The big thing now is to make sure we get credit for all the shifts in China policy, rather than letting them go to the State Department."[16] Kissinger even told Nixon that the extensive media attention was a needed "diversion from Vietnam" and something needed for the "game with the Soviets."[17]

Nixon had been interested in making an overture to China from the very beginning of his presidency. His famous *Foreign Affairs* article of October 1967 made the case for taking a new approach to China, and during the first two years of his presidency he gave numerous indications of his interest in the country, even telling *Time* magazine in October 1970: "If there is anything I want to do before I die, it is to go to China."[18] But the China of the Cultural Revolution, led by the mercurial Mao Zedong, was slow to respond and gave conflicting signals of its intentions. It was not until the invitation to the American table tennis team that things seemed to begin moving. On April 27, 1971, the Pakistani ambassador, Agha Hilaly, who had been serving as an intermediary between the two nations, called to request a meeting with Kissinger with an urgent message from the Chinese government. China was now prepared "to receive publicly in Peking a special envoy of the president of the U.S. (for instance Mr. Kissinger) or the U.S. Secretary of State or even the President of the U.S. himself for direct meeting and discussions."[19]

Nixon and Kissinger knew the importance of the message they received—it "spoke for itself," Kissinger wrote in his memoirs, also calling it "the most important message an American President had received since World War II."[20] Nixon called Kissinger to discuss possible envoys, including Kissinger's great patron, Nelson Rockefeller, as well as David Bruce and George H. W. Bush. In a rather bizarre moment, Nixon even mentioned Thomas Dewey, the Republican presidential candidate from the 1940s, who had died the month before. Although Kissinger said in his memoirs that "originally there was no thought of sending me," this is disingenuous at best since he had already suggested himself back in December and the Chinese note suggested him by name. The only other possibility Kissinger warmed to was Rockefeller because on foreign policy Rockefeller "would take [Kissinger's] advice," and he praised the idea as "original" and Rockefeller as a "tough" negotiator. But he also subtly agreed with a Nixon comment that Rockefeller would have great "visibility" and that the Chinese would "jump" at the possibility, thereby encouraging the suspicion in Nixon's mind that Rockefeller might steal away the president's thunder.[21] In his memoirs, Kissinger says that Nixon's "overriding" motive for selecting him was that he best understood the foreign policy of the administration and what Nixon sought to achieve. But he also acknowledges what is clear in retrospect—the domestic political motives Nixon had. As Kissinger himself noted: "Of all the potential emissaries I was the most subject to his control. . . . [M]y success would be a Presidential success."[22] Nixon instinctively knew, as he told Kissinger, that "we played a game and we got a little break" and that this break could have a tremendous political impact.[23]

But only if the "game" was handled correctly. Nixon and Kissinger wanted to keep their initiative a secret, which had already required cutting out the foreign policy bureaucracy of the government. Nixon initially tried to dampen speculation about changes in China policy—as he put it: "What we have done has broken the ice; now we have to test the water to see how deep it is."[24] But he also wanted to keep other American politicians from stealing his thunder, particularly Democrats like Mansfield and rivals like Edward Kennedy. Kissinger asked Hilaly to convey to the Chinese as his own idea that "President Nixon will find it more difficult to move quickly in the matter if American politicians come into it."[25] Nixon and Kissinger wanted the preparation for Nixon's visit to be handled in a "preliminary *secret* meeting" between Kissinger and Zhou or another high-level Chinese official.[26] The original Chinese message indicated a preference for a public visit, and Kissinger said that he later learned that the Chinese were suspicious about the American demand for secrecy, perhaps considering it as a way to allow for the United States to change its mind abruptly. Kissinger argued that secrecy would protect the initiative against hostile forces within the bureaucracy or from other countries.[27] No doubt there were real advantages to secret diplomacy in the case of two so long-estranged countries like the United States and China. But the real danger in public knowledge would be diminishing the psychological and political impact of the announcement of the visit, something that would catch Nixon's political opponents completely offguard and strengthen his claim to be the "peace" candidate in 1972.[28]

Two Successes: The Soviet Union and China

In the first half of 1971, peace was the theme Nixon wanted to push at all times. In March 1971, he gave a speech in Newport at the Naval War College in which he criticized "new isolationists" but also tried—unsuccessfully—to encourage the renaming of America's armed forces as the "peace forces" of the country and repeatedly praised the officers for their service in the "peace forces."[29] He told Kissinger that even the "selfish and partisan" liberal journalists, indeed, "any guy with any sense of decency is interested in world peace."[30] Along with the China initiative, Nixon recognized that progress with the Soviets would be central to his campaign. As Kissinger was still sorting out the details of the China trip, the White House was preparing to announce a "procedural breakthrough" in the SALT, which had been under way since late 1969. The background of this issue was less convoluted than of China but still captured the mix of foreign policy and domestic politics that drove the Nixon White House. Both Nixon and Kissinger came into office with an understanding of the importance of relations with the Soviet Union—it was the key to the concept of linkage and to their plan for a Vietnam settlement—and Nixon regarded his management of US-Soviet relations as central to the success of his presidency. In setting up the backchannel relationship between Kissinger and Soviet ambassador Anatoly Dobrynin, Nixon hoped for dramatic results—bargains between the two superpowers on issues like arms control, Vietnam, and the Middle East. He was rather quickly disappointed, especially at the lack of Soviet interest in an early summit meeting in 1970 that Nixon hoped might boost Republican chances in the midterm election.[31]

By January 1971, Nixon knew that arms control—a subject he frequently disparaged as reflecting the "pathetic idealism" of Americans—was now a political and economic imperative, necessary because "it's important to people" and there was little domestic support for increased defense spending.[32] He sent Kissinger to see Dobrynin to suggest the outline of a possible SALT agreement in which he was prepared to bargain the defensive antiballistic missile (ABM) system provided the Soviets would link such an agreement to a "freeze" on offensive land-based weapons. Nixon, who had little interest in the technical details of arms control, nevertheless knew that "the SALT thing would be enormously important" to his political prospects.[33] For their part, the Soviets also believed that Nixon might be ready to deal, largely for the same American domestic political reasons. When Senator Muskie planned a trip to Moscow in January 1971, Kissinger told Dobrynin: "President Nixon hopes that Moscow will not do anything to make these trips a big issue in the purely internal contest within the U.S." Dobrynin recognized Nixon's anxiety and suggested to his superiors: "It is important that the incumbent President constantly remain alert (but without excessively annoying him personally) to the fact that we can still play a role in the upcoming 1972 U.S. presidential election campaign, especially if he ignores our interests or directly opposes them."[34] He also recognized that Nixon still wanted the fanfare and publicity of a summit meeting to finalize any agreements he made with the Soviets. He told the Politburo how Kissinger remarked once again at the end of their talks that Nixon "continues to attach a great deal of importance to his meeting with the Soviet leadership."[35]

On May 20, 1971, Nixon and the Soviet leadership jointly announced that the United States and the Soviets would now strive for an ABM agreement and at the same time begin consideration of limits on offensive weapons. Not surprisingly, it was the featured news item on all three networks, with the CBS commentator Eric Sevareid noting directly how it would improve Nixon's chances for reelection.[36] Nixon called Kissinger the evening of the announcement and praised his negotiations with Dobrynin, telling him that he "couldn't have handled it better." He was pleased at the "hell of a television wallop" the announcement got.[37] In the days after the SALT announcement, Kissinger repeatedly told Nixon that, after some briefings and meetings with him, reporters were now writing how "you're creating a whole new era of American foreign policy, one of the most significant in 20 years."[38] A few days later, Kissinger told Nixon: "In terms of achievements—this sounds self-serving—but who has had a 3-year period like this? If you had said on January 20th that you would get 400,000 troops out of Vietnam in 2 years, open the way to a visit to Peking, a visit to Moscow, a SALT Agreement, you'd have all of that done at the end of your third year. . . ." Nixon interrupted: "That'd be incredible, wouldn't it?" Kissinger added: "They would have said, That's insanity."[39]

After the successful SALT announcement, Kissinger prepared for his secret trip to China. When he met with Nixon on July 1 before leaving for Asia, the president told him to be tough with the Chinese, but, true to his domestic political concerns, he reminded Kissinger again to tell the Chinese that "we expected them to institute a severe limit on political visitors" prior to his own visit.[40] He also told Kissinger that he wished him "not to indicate a willingness to abandon much of our support for Taiwan until it was necessary to do so," and he closed their meeting by mentioning again that "six thousand of our troops in Taiwan were directly related to our conduct of the war in South Vietnam so that as that issue was solved the requirement for these troops would disappear."[41]

Kissinger's stature in Washington was prominent enough that the American media covered his trip, and the false report of his stomachache in Pakistan merited attention on the CBS Evening News.[42] His meeting with the Chinese began awkwardly, with Zhou offering cigarettes to the nonsmoking Americans and Kissinger apologizing for reading a prepared statement. He again explained the reasons for secrecy, this time emphasizing that the president wanted it so "we can meet unencumbered by bureaucracy, free of the past, and with the greatest possible latitude."[43] However, at the end of the two-day visit, he described the talks in enthusiastic terms to Nixon as "the most searching, sweeping and significant discussions I have ever had in government." He assured the president that he and Zhou "have laid the groundwork for you and Mao to turn a page in history" and that, if the United States could handle its dealings with the Chinese with "reliability, precision, and finesse, . . . we will have made a revolution."[44]

By the end of the discussions in China, Kissinger even delved directly into American politics, explaining to his Chinese counterparts the "China lobby" and its opposition to the Nixon administration's policies. But he also made an argument that would later become a cliché of American politics: "President Nixon, precisely because his political support comes from the center and right of center, cannot be attacked from that direction, and won't be attacked by the left in a policy of moving toward friendship with the People's Republic of China." The Chinese even agreed to a Thursday evening, July 15, simultaneous announcement to allow the Americans to get the most publicity from the weekly news magazines like *Time* and *Newsweek*. Kissinger made sure to put forward Nixon's request that the Chinese not invite other American politicians and taught the Chinese an American expression by asking them to prevent the issue from becoming a "political football."[45]

Still, the secret was so well handled that, when Nixon asked for television time from the networks for the evening of July 15, they all speculated that his speech would have something to do with a breakthrough in the Vietnam peace talks.[46] Instead, he announced that he would visit China to "seek a new relationship with the People's Republic of China," but "not at the expense of our old friends." Hoping to assuage Moscow's fears, he added: "[Our action] is not directed against any other nation." He also came back to the central theme he wanted to reinforce on every occasion, his role as a peacemaker: "I will undertake what I deeply hope will become a journey for peace, peace not just for our generation but for future generations on this earth we share together."[47] This announcement received an overwhelmingly favorable reception from the media. Commentators fell over themselves seeking historical analogies, with Howard K. Smith of ABC calling it "the most dramatic development in international affairs since the Hitler-Stalin pact," and others calling it "stunning," "unbelievable," and "incredible." Nixon's own news summary reported that "there has not been a Presidential action which has brought such wide comment and speculation," most of which was favorable.[48] Negative comments came from conservatives like Barry Goldwater and William Buckley, but the overwhelming national and international approval heartened Nixon, and, as Haldeman noted, he asked him to conduct a poll.[49] One showed the public approved of his trip by a 68 to 19 percent margin.[50] Others had him leaping ahead of Muskie for the first time in over a year, a clear indication that the good news in foreign policy was translating into political support.[51]

Nixon continued to defend the move toward China in electoral terms, explaining to Kissinger: "If we hadn't done something and we'd been tossed out, everything would have come apart at the seams, and all we're doing is to frankly buy some time and to turn around if we can still turn around." Not forgetting the geopolitics involved, he added that he wanted the United States to continue to "play an Asian role," and Kissinger agreed: "We can't roll over for the Chinese." But, in the midst of reassuring themselves that they would remain strong and be even stronger when reelected, Nixon could not resist coming back to the powerful political impact of the China opening: "The way this thing has shocked . . . particularly our usual critics . . . the left—the liberals, the peacenik types—they are just up a wall. They don't know what to do with this. . . . The mood really in the country has significantly changed."[52]

Foreign Policy and Domestic Politics

By the beginning of 1972, and despite his success with China and the Soviet Union, Nixon was concerned that Vietnam remained an issue. With the presidential election now only ten months away, polls showed Nixon tied with or with only a narrow lead over his Democratic opponents. His diplomatic achievements had led *Time* to name him "Man of the Year" and pronounce his leadership "refreshingly flexible and disconcertingly unpredictable."[53] But Vietnam still hung like an albatross across his political prospects, with some opponents like Senator George McGovern calling him a "liar" for saying that he had offered an American withdrawal in return for the release of the prisoners of war (POWs).[54] President Thieu's unopposed "reelection" in September 1971 was another embarrassment to the administration. Even Kissinger acknowledged to Nixon that "no one gives a damn" about Thieu, even though both men still refused North Vietnamese demands that the Americans overthrow the South Vietnamese leader as a part of the settlement.[55] Public support for the war now hinged almost exclusively on gaining the return of American POWs. Nixon already planned another January announcement of troop withdrawals from Vietnam, but he considered doing something more to neutralize Vietnam as a political issue, at least temporarily. He hoped that the revelation of Kissinger's secret talks and his offer to withdraw all US troops six months from the signing of an agreement and a cease-fire would buy him time with the American public, indicating that he had indeed gone the extra mile in trying to bring about an end to the war. As his speechwriter William Safire put it: "Nixon [wanted to answer] the doves at home who were berating him for not having made the offer of a date certain for U.S. withdrawal in return for a cease-fire and a prisoner of war exchange. By getting out of that squeeze he hoped to put a world opinion squeeze on the North Vietnamese to break the impasse."[56]

On January 25, 1972 Nixon gave a nationally broadcast speech, outlining a proposal for a cease-fire, American withdrawal, the return of the POWs, and new elections. The speech also highlighted the role of "Dr. Kissinger" as the president's "personal representative"; he traveled secretly to Paris twelve times to negotiate. The focus on Kissinger's role became one of the lead stories over the next week.[57] Both *Time* and *Newsweek* featured him on their covers with the title "Nixon's Secret Agent." Not all the coverage was positive. Eric Sevareid saw Kissinger's role in a raw political light—as an emissary of the president who was not accountable to the Congress and could be used as a way to defuse Vietnam as a political issue.[58] But others like Howard K. Smith praised Kissinger for exactly this reason and thought that the Democrats would now find it "hard to make a political issue" of Vietnam.[59] Nixon's Vietnam speech gave him a brief boost in the polls, and, temporarily at least, Vietnam was not the major political issue.

Nixon's "journey for peace" to China in February 1972 competed successfully for media coverage with the Democrats' early primary campaigns. Television coverage proved critical to the presentation of the China trip, both in preaching the foreign policy symbolism of the reconciliation of former enemies and in making the domestic political point that it was Richard Nixon who was doing this. Kissinger at first evinced something approaching a snobbish disdain for the "obsessive single-mindedness of the advance men" who accompanied him on his planning trips to China, comparing them to past "barbarians" with whom the Chinese had dealt.[60] But China offered a particular bonus for American television coverage as early evening events could be transmitted live on American morning programs, while morning events in China could headline the evening news. In an era before the 24-7 media environment, when there were basically two news windows, Nixon's advance team, led by Dwight Chapin but under Haldeman's close and painstaking supervision, carefully choreographed events to ensure maximum coverage. They made sure that both Nixon's arrival and his departure from China occurred in prime viewing hours and that such events as the welcoming banquet, the meeting with Mao, Nixon's trip to the Great Wall, and Mrs. Nixon's tours of schools and collective farms fit the timing of television news.[61] The television networks heavily dominated within the 155-member press delegation, often at the expense of the print media, and with the result that one critic observed: "Nixon was finally getting the kind of 'p.r.' he had sought for more than three years."[62] By the end of the week, Gallup registered an awareness of the visit at 98 percent, a record at the time, and public approval of Nixon's trip to China was 84 percent, a remarkable achievement in and of itself.[63]

The only substantive issue that Nixon and Kissinger had with the Chinese was the status of Taiwan, and Nixon handled it in a characteristically political fashion. He had already made it clear that he was determined to reduce American forces on the island. He now told Zhou that this was a major political issue for him with conservatives in the Republican Party and that the two countries needed "to find language which will meet your need yet does not stir up the animals so much that they gang up on Taiwan and thereby torpedo our initiative."[64] After long hours of negotiation, the final communiqué used an unusual formulation: it affirmed that the United States did not "challenge" the belief of all Chinese that there was but one China and that Taiwan was part of China. It affirmed as well that a peaceful resolution of the Taiwan question would allow for an American withdrawal from the island. Although there was some criticisms and charges of a "sellout" of Taiwan, the media coverage remained favorable. The television networks broadcast reports on the Shanghai communiqué and Kissinger's briefing, as well Nixon's toast, with his extravagant claim that "this was the week that changed the world."[65] Kissinger thought that the controversy about the communiqué was subsumed by the very television coverage he had once disdained. "Pictures overrode the printed word," he wrote, adding: "The public simply was not interested in the complex analyses of the document after having watched the spectacle of an American president welcomed in the capital of an erstwhile enemy."[66]

As Nixon basked in the glow of his China trip and looked forward to his summit meeting in Moscow, North Vietnam launched its Spring-Summer Offensive, known to Americans as the Easter Offensive. The North Vietnamese feared that their Chinese and Soviet allies would once again pressure them to accept the division of their country because they wanted to pursue good relations with the United States.[67] They also believed that antiwar public opinion in the United States would act as another restraint and thought that Nixon would not risk escalating the war with a presidential election in November.[68] The first days of the Easter Offensive went well for the Communist forces, and they made significant gains against the ARVN units. When Kissinger actually raised the prospect of military defeat, Nixon reacted strongly. "If the ARVN collapses a lot of other things will collapse around here." He emphasized: "If they were going to collapse, they had to do it a year ago. We can't do it this year, Henry." He made his view clear to Kissinger: "We're playing a much bigger game. We're playing a Russian game, a Chinese game, an election game."[69] Throughout the discussions, Nixon equated defeat in Vietnam with his political defeat in the United States, and he was determined to use almost every element of his power to prevent this.[70] Kissinger shared these sentiments up to a point but believed that the United States could differentiate "our pressures against Moscow, Peking, and Hanoi so as to isolate North Vietnam and demoralize it."[71] Nixon worried that Kissinger did not fully share his central priority, and he was more suspicious than Kissinger of Russian policy toward North Vietnam. He also suspected that Kissinger was more interested in the personal glory attendant on another secret mission—this one to Moscow—that was planned for late April. "Henry, with all of his many virtues, does seem too often to be concerned about preparing the way for negotiations with the Soviets," he wrote in his diary, noting that Kissinger seemed to believe that, even if the United States failed in Vietnam, "we can survive politically." Nixon, however, "had no illusions whatever on that score." Not only would the United States not have "a credible foreign policy," but defeat in Vietnam would also spell the end for his reelection efforts. He told Kissinger: "I'm willing to throw myself on the sword. We are not going to let this country be defeated by this little shit-ass country."[72]

Kissinger went to Moscow for the planning of the summit trip but was unable to get any cooperation from the Soviets on slowing the North Vietnamese offensive. When the North Vietnamese took the South Vietnamese district capital of Quang Tri on May 1 and threatened the imperial city of Hue, Nixon believed that he now needed to take strong military action, both in authorizing bombing raids on Hanoi and Haiphong and in taking a step that even Lyndon Johnson had shied away from—mining the harbor at Haiphong. Because the North's conventional military offensive relied so heavily on a daily flow of fuel for its tanks and armored vehicles in the South, a disruption in the supply could have serious effects in a way that Johnson's Operation Rolling Thunder had not. But mining Haiphong meant the possibility of direct interference with Soviet shipping. It put into jeopardy the Moscow summit and posed the question of whether the United States should cancel it before the Soviets did. Nixon was inclined to cancel it, but, even before Kissinger got back to Washington, he asked Haldeman to run a poll to determine popular reaction if he did. He made it clear that there was no way he could attend the summit, make agreements with the Soviets, trade toasts, and drink champagne while the North Vietnamese, armed with Soviet tanks and weaponry, marched into Hue or Kontum. The poll results came back indicating that 60 percent favored going ahead with the summit in spite of the invasion. Nixon believed that the American public was more likely to be influenced by failure and military defeat than a successful summit, but he decided to gamble and let the Russians make the decision on whether to cancel the summit.[73]

Media reaction to Nixon's decision reflected the gloomy atmosphere of Washington as well as the intense unpopularity of the war.[74] Marvin Kalb remarked that the move was a "frontal challenge" to the Soviet Union and placed the summit "very, very much in jeopardy."[75] The political reaction from the Democrats was passionate and even vitriolic. McGovern called the move "reckless, unnecessary, and unworkable, a flirtation with World War III." Edward Kennedy said that it "demonstrates the desperation of the president's Indochina policy."[76] But Nixon's gamble worked, with the Russians showing the limits of their solidarity with Hanoi.[77] The Soviets did tell Nixon that, because of Vietnam, there would be a more "subdued"

public welcome, but, compared to the empty streets of Beijing, reporters estimated about 100,000 Muscovites came out to see Nixon's motor-
cade. The American network anchors went out of their way to talk about
how "remarkable" it was that the summit was occurring at all given what
had happened in Vietnam.[78] The signing of agreements, timed for each
nightly newscast, also highlighted the contrast with the China summit,
stressing the "substance" of these meetings as opposed to the symbolism
of the China trip. The networks duly noted the environmental and health
agreements on the first night and presented the agreement on cooperation
in space as a true "21st century" achievement of the summit.[79] They gave
considerable broadcast time to ceremonial events, including Nixon placing a wreath at the grave of the unknown soldier, attending the Bolshoi
Ballet, and speaking directly to Russians over Soviet television. In the
background of many of these stories was Kissinger, referred to by John
Chancellor, NBC's anchor, as "the second most important American" at
the summit. Kissinger used his briefings with journalists to encourage
them to recognize the historic importance of the meetings as the two
superpowers were "learning to be equal partners in the preservation of
peace."[80] He also encouraged them to portray the meetings as a true turning point in history, possibly "the end of the Cold War," and a "healthy
and civilized" way for the two superpowers to deal with each other.[81]

The signing of the SALT agreement was followed by the final act of
the summit, the "Basic Principles" agreement defining relations between
the superpowers. Hailed as the fulfillment of Nixon's inaugural pledge to
move from an era of confrontation to an era of negotiations, the document proclaimed that the two countries "will proceed from the common
determination that in the nuclear age there is no alternative to conducting
their mutual relations on the basis of peaceful coexistence."[82] Accepting
the Soviet term *peaceful coexistence* was a substantial American concession,
acknowledging the Soviet Union's status as an equal, and accepting the
legitimacy of the superpower rivalry. But the idea that the nuclear-armed
superpowers would now exercise restraint, consult with each other, and
move toward disarmament was a politically powerful way to wind up the
summit, leading to the euphoric tone of the media coverage. The CBS
anchor, Walter Cronkite, declared that Nixon's trip exceeded expectations
and that, although there had been no final deal on trade and no agreement on Vietnam, that "paled into insignificance" compared to SALT

and the Basic Principles agreement. All this was "the personal accomplishment of President Nixon's diplomacy" as he had, along with Kissinger, created a basis of mutual respect and friendship with the Soviet leaders.[83] Nixon's dramatic return to the United States, landing in a helicopter on the steps of the Capitol to report to Congress and a live national audience on his visit, added further to the treatment of the summit as historic by the commentators.[84] The rhetoric in the speech was not restrained; Nixon called for seizing this "unparalleled opportunity to build a new structure for peace" and for America "to lead the world up out of the lowlands of constant war, and onto the high plateau of lasting peace."[85]

Vietnam and the Election

When William Safire and Henry Kissinger strolled through downtown Warsaw, reflecting on the results of the Moscow summit, Safire remarked: "Been one hell of a week, Henry. What does the President do for an encore?" Kissinger didn't hesitate: "Make Peace in Vietnam."[86] But Nixon and Kissinger were still not certain it could be achieved before the election. When they discussed Vietnam in early August, both expressed pessimism about South Vietnam's long-term viability, but Nixon's basic concern was that the Saigon regime would remain intact until the November election. With the domestic political implications foremost in his mind, Nixon emphasized: "We also have to realize, Henry, that winning an election is terribly important. It's terribly important this year." Kissinger agreed, and, in response to Nixon's question of whether the United States could have a "viable foreign policy" if North Vietnam conquered South Vietnam in a year or two, he added that, if they could get a proper settlement by October, "by January 74 no one will give a damn."[87] Although this conversation is frequently cited to demonstrate the "decent interval" thesis, it also reflects the mixture of domestic politics and foreign policy issues the two men weighed as they contemplated the Vietnam endgame. Kissinger was more optimistic about the negotiations than Nixon was, and his own personal investment in them and pride in his role as negotiator led him to see more progress than Nixon did. Nixon also worried more about raising expectations among voters within the United States each time Kissinger met with the North Vietnamese in Paris as disillusionment could be harmful politically.[88] But he did not stop his National Security

Council deputy, and Kissinger continued his meetings in Paris, even asking the president to let him put forward a proposal at his September meeting that Saigon had not approved.

The North Vietnamese could read the American opinion polls as well as anyone else, and they recognized by mid-September that their favored candidate, George McGovern, was far behind. This led Hanoi, under pressure from both Moscow and Beijing, to drop its demand that Thieu resign as part of a peace settlement, clearing the way to an agreement.[89] But, as Kissinger was successfully concluding his negotiations in Paris, Nixon's rival, Senator George McGovern, delivered his own Vietnam plan in a nationally televised paid political broadcast. McGovern declared that, on inauguration day, he would halt the bombing of North Vietnam and halt all aid to South Vietnam. He would then withdraw American forces within ninety days and expect that this would lead to the return of the POWs. His speech made it clear that McGovern still believed that there was political gain in a strong antiwar stance and that the Nixon administration's commitment to the survival of the Thieu regime was a domestic political vulnerability. Along with the Watergate scandal—the *Washington Post* ran a front-page story on Republican espionage against Democratic candidates the same day as McGovern gave his speech—Vietnam remained one of the only issues still working against Nixon's prospective landslide. But McGovern was now asking so much less from the North Vietnamese than they had already indicated they were prepared to grant to Nixon—if Kissinger could get Thieu to accept the agreement.

Kissinger was certain that Thieu would accept the agreement, arguing: "The settlement he's got is the best Thieu is ever going to get and, unlike '68, when Thieu screwed Johnson, he had Nixon as an alternative. Now he has McGovern as an alternative, which would be a disaster for him, even worse than the worst possible thing that Nixon could do to him."[90] Nixon assured Kissinger that he would do whatever he could to convince Thieu, although, shortly before Kissinger left, he again reminded him: "We cannot have a collapse in South Vietnam prior to the election." Kissinger assured Nixon that that would not happen. Nixon ultimately told Kissinger: "If you can make the deal, do it now. If you can't, do the next best thing." Kissinger then asked: "Politically it'd be better for you to do the latter?" Nixon replied: "Henry, don't even think of the politics. Let me say: either has an advantage."[91] Nixon was thinking of the politics involved but believed that he was far enough ahead in the polls that either result could be spun in a way that favored his candidacy. (And he made sure he had a poll conducted to check this!)[92] He thought that the settlement Kissinger had negotiated was the best they could do, but, if Thieu refused to go along now, he was prepared to wait until after the election. Kissinger for his part desperately wanted a settlement before the election.

Thieu and his government completely rejected Kissinger's agreement, demanding numerous changes, including the withdrawal of North Vietnamese forces. A bitterly disappointed Kissinger left Saigon, never to return. The Communist leaders of North Vietnam were outraged as well, believing that they had been betrayed by the American imperialists. On the morning of October 26, Radio Hanoi began broadcasting the contents of this agreement, hoping to win the battle of public opinion. Kissinger was ready. His press conference, with his famous line, "We believe that peace is at hand," was covered by all three networks live and then led the evening news. Kissinger's words had an electric effect across the country, with commentators like Dan Rather remarking that they guaranteed Nixon's landslide, while others also remarked on Kissinger's centrality in negotiating the peace agreement.[93] Haldeman, who often worried about Kissinger upstaging Nixon, was pleased with Kissinger's press conference and called it "the best lucky break of the campaign" because it "takes the [Watergate] corruption stuff off the front pages, totally wipes out any other news."[94] Nixon called Kissinger later that evening and jokingly began by saying: "I understand that all the three network news shows were about Vietnam and I wonder why." Kissinger chuckled and responded by noting that he had talked to Chuck Colson, the president's political adviser, who believed that "we had wiped McGovern out now." Kissinger added that he thought it brilliant that the president was now getting the credit without the agreement being finalized. Nixon was very pleased, telling Kissinger that he was glad he made the announcement since, if he himself had made it, people would think it was a political move.[95] In this simple statement, Nixon made clear how useful Kissinger's actions were to advancing his political position.[96]

But his "peace is at hand" would soon become a target for critics who questioned why an agreement seemed to be still out of reach. Senator McGovern appeared on *Meet the Press* on October 29 to argue that Kissinger's statement was all about electoral politics, and then, at a campaign rally on November 5, he accused Kissinger of lying and added: "Peace is not at hand; it is not even in sight." Kissinger did worry that the North Vietnamese might publicly break off the talks when the agreement was not signed on October 31, which had been the original schedule. But he doubted that they would take such an action "unless they think they can keep us from bombing again."[97] Even though he had sent some messages to Hanoi earlier that the agreement could be considered complete, he told Haldeman: "We'll just have to brazen that one out." He recognized that Nixon wanted to continue to encourage optimism, telling Haldeman that he knew that Nixon "was a little flakey about you now destroying hopes." He encouraged the idea of using Vice President Agnew to blast McGovern for his statements about the war, thereby allowing Nixon to continue to profess a more hopeful message.[98] Nixon's final campaign speeches underscored this careful blend of optimism and strength: "We are going to sign the agreement when the agreement is right, not one day before. And when the agreement is right, we are going to sign, without one day's delay."[99]

Conclusion

On Election Night, when Nixon arrived back at the White House, he found a handwritten note from Kissinger on the pillow of his bed. It saluted his "historic achievement"—"to take a divided nation, mired in war, losing its confidence, wracked by intellectuals without conviction, and give it a new purpose and overcome its hesitations"—and thanked him for his "unfailing human kindness and consideration" and for the "privilege of the last four years."[100] Nixon's overwhelming electoral victory—forty-nine states and 60.7 percent of the popular vote—was a remarkable personal achievement in which Kissinger had played a decisive role. Kissinger called Nixon late on Election Night to congratulate him, extending his "warmest congratulations" as Nixon harshly described McGovern as a "prick" for what he regarded as an ungracious concession speech. Kissinger agreed, calling the South Dakota senator "ungenerous, unworthy," and, playing to all Nixon's prejudices, reminded him that the media and "all the intellectuals" were against him but that he triumphed nevertheless.[101]

It was a short-lived triumph. The Vietnam negotiations in Paris stalled again, and Nixon resorted to using B-52s to bomb Hanoi over Christmas

1972 in order to persuade both Hanoi and Saigon to accept the fragile peace agreement. The Paris Peace Treaty allowed the withdrawal of American forces and the return of POWs, but it did not end the war, which dragged on for another two years until Hanoi's victory. Soon after the treaty, the Watergate scandal broke into the open, crippling Nixon's power, and ultimately dooming his presidency. Ironically enough, Kissinger was largely spared this ordeal, being seen by many as the real genius behind American foreign policy. He became secretary of state and guided American foreign policy until the election of Jimmy Carter in 1976.

Nixon's ability to use foreign policy triumphs for domestic political purposes remains unmatched in recent American history, but it also serves as a cautionary tale. The perception of foreign policy success can win votes and even turn an election. Reality reasserts itself, however, and foreign policy success is often transitory, unlikely to lead to the kind of durable electoral transformation that presidents and their political parties may seek. Nixon the peace candidate did succeed in pushing the Democratic Party further to the left, contributing to the perception of many Americans that the Republicans were the party of national security. It was ironic, given the Cold War presidencies of Truman, Kennedy, and Johnson, but there is no doubt that it has had a lasting legacy in American politics.

Notes

1. Telcon, Kissinger and Berger, November 3, 1970, Nixon Presidential Materials Staff (NPMS), National Archives and Records Administration, College Park, MD (hereafter NARA).

2. Richard Reeves, *President Nixon* (New York: Simon and Schuster, 2001), 272.

3. Richard Nixon, *RN: The Memoirs of Richard Nixon* (New York: Grosset & Dunlap, 1978), 497.

4. Nixon to Haldeman, December 1, 1970, Memoranda from the President, President's Personal File, Nixon Materials Project, box 2, folder 4, NARA.

5. Memorandum, Nixon to Haldeman, December 4, 1970, Memoranda from the President, President's Personal File, Nixon Materials Project, box 2, folder 4, NARA.

6. CBS Evening News, January 16, 1971, Vanderbilt Television News Archive (VTNA).

7. H. R. Haldeman, *The Haldeman Diaries* (New York: Putnam's, 1994), December 12, 1970, 262.

8. Ibid., December 21, 1970, 267.

9. Richard Nixon, Address to the Nation on the Situation in Southeast Asia, April 7, 1971, *The American Presidency Project,* http://www.presidency.ucsb.edu/ws/index.php?pid=2972&st=&st1=.

10. The best treatment of the invasion is in John Prados, *The Blood Road: The Ho Chi Minh Trail and the Vietnam War* (New York: Wiley, 1998), 311–79, esp. 359–60.

11. The reports are captured in these segments on NBC Evening News: March 21, 22, 1971, VTNA.

12. Nixon, Address to the Nation on the Situation in Southeast Asia, April 7, 1971, VTNA.

13. The NBC newscast on May 3, 1971, had these scenes. NBC Evening News, May 3, 1971, VTNA. The polling data come from Mark D. Harmon, "Historical Revisionism and Vietnam War Public Opinion," *Peace Studies Journal* 3, no. 2 (August 2010): 15–32, 20.

14. One representative is a lengthy CBS report from April 17, 1971, that has interviews with the US players extolling the Chinese. CBS Evening News, April 17, 1971, VTNA.

15. "The Ping Heard Round the World," *Time,* April 26, 1971, http://www.time.com/time/magazine/article/0,9171,902878,00.html.

16. Haldeman, *Haldeman Diaries,* April 12, 1971, 327.

17. Telephone Conversation between President Nixon and Henry Kissinger, April 14, 1971, http://nixontapes.org/hak/1971-04-14_Nixon_001-091.mp3.

18. Richard Nixon, "Asia After Vietnam," *Foreign Affairs* 46, no. 1 (1967): 113–25; "The Mid East: Search for Stability," *Time,* October 5, 1970. "Asia After Vietnam" is reprinted in *Foreign Relations of the United States* (hereafter *FRUS*), *1969–1976,* vol. 1, *Foundations of Foreign Policy, 1969–1972* (Washington, DC: US Government Printing Office, 2003), 10–21.

19. *FRUS, 1969–1976,* vol. 17, *China, 1969–1972* (Washington, DC: US Government Printing Office, 2006), 301.

20. Henry Kissinger, *The White House Years* (New York: Little, Brown, 1979), 715.

21. Telephone Conversation between President Nixon and Henry Kissinger, April 27, 1971, 002–052, Nixontapes.org, http://nixontapes.org/hak/1971-04-27_Nixon_002-052.mp3. There is a transcript in *FRUS, 1969–1976,* vol. 17, pp. 303–38.

22. Kissinger, *White House Years,* 717.

23. *FRUS, 1969–1976,* vol. 17, p. 304.

24. Richard Nixon, The President's News Conference, April 29, 1971, *American Presidency Project,* http://www.presidency.ucsb.edu/ws/index.php?pid=2993#axzz1zlfeJbcK.

25. *FRUS, 1969–1976,* vol. 17, p. 313.

26. Ibid., 318.

27. Kissinger, *White House Years,* 725.

28. Kissinger called Nixon's attention to a *Washington Post* article that labeled him the "peace candidate." *FRUS, 1969–1976,* vol. 7, *Vietnam, July 1970–January 1972* (Washington DC: US Government Printing Office, 2010), 674.

29. *FRUS, 1969–1976,* vol. 1, p. 305.

30. Telephone Conversation between President Nixon and Henry Kissinger, May 21, 1971, 003–114, Nixontapes.org, http://nixontapes.org/hak/1971-05-21_Nixon_003-114.mp3.

31. MemCon, Dobrynin to Politburo, July 9, 1970, in *Soviet-American Relations: The Détente Years, 1969–1972,* ed. David C. Geyer and Douglas E. Selvage (Washington, DC: US Government Printing Office, 2007), 175. This was, of course, Dobrynin's interpretation of the American interest in a summit meeting, but it probably is not far off the mark.

32. *FRUS, 1969–1976,* vol. 32, *SALT I, 1969–1972* (Washington, DC: US Government Printing Office, 2010), 403.

33. Ibid., 476. See also Raymond Garthoff, *Détente and Confrontation* (Washington: Brookings Institution, 1994), 30.

34. MemCon, Dobrynin to Politburo, January 9, 1971, in Geyer and Selvage, eds., *Soviet-American Relations,* 250–51.

35. Ibid., 263.

36. NBC Evening News, May 20, 1971, VTNA.

37. Telephone Conversation between President Nixon and Henry Kissinger, May 21, 1971, 003–110, Nixontapes.org, http://nixontapes.org/hak/1971-05-21_Nixon_003-110.mp3.

38. Ibid.

39. *FRUS, 1969–1976,* vol. 32, p. 510.

40. *FRUS, 1969–1976,* vol. 17, pp. 355–56.

41. Ibid., 357.

42. CBS Evening News, July 10, 1971, VTNA.

43. *FRUS, 1969–1976,* vol. 17, p. 361.

44. Ibid., 453–55.

45. Ibid., 414–15.

46. NBC News July 15, 1971, VTNA.

47. Margaret MacMillan, *Nixon and Mao* (New York: Random House, 2007), 202.

48. Annotated News Summary, July 19, 1971, President's Office Files, box 32, President's Office Files, Nixon Library.

49. Haldeman, *Haldeman Diaries,* July 16, 1971, 388.

50. *Washington Post,* September 20, 1971, A6.

51. Robert Mason, *Richard Nixon and the Quest for a New Majority* (Chapel Hill: University of North Carolina Press, 2004), 137.

52. *FRUS, 1969–1976,* vol. 13, *Soviet Union, October 1970–October 1971* (Washington, DC: US Government Printing Office, 2011), 874–75.

53. *Time,* January 3, 1972.

54. Rick Perlstein, *Nixonland: The Rise of a President and the Fracturing of America* (New York: Scribner, 2008), 618.

55. Telephone Conversation between President Nixon and Henry Kissinger, January 1, 1972, 017–125, Nixontapes.org, http://nixontapes.org/hak/1972-01-01_Nixon_017-125.mp3.

56. William Safire, *Before the Fall: An Insider's View of the Pre-Watergate White House* (Garden City, NY: Doubleday, 1975), 400.

57. Dan Rather reported on CBS, highlighting Kissinger's role, and then noting the strange White House rule that prevented the news organizations from playing the audio of Kissinger's briefing. CBS Evening News, January 26, 1972, VTNA.

58. Sevareid would remain skeptical about Kissinger, using an editorial on February 7, 1972, about the death of Tommy Thompson to criticize his style of diplomacy. See CBS Evening News, February 7, 1972, VTNA. After Watergate began, he became far more sympathetic to Kissinger's position.

59. Walter Isaacson, *Kissinger* (New York: Simon & Schuster, 1992), 397–98.

60. Kissinger, *White House Years,* 774–75.

61. Chapin's approach was painstaking and deliberate. He outlined it in a conference in 2010. See "The Week That Changed the World: The Inside Story of Richard Nixon's 1972 Journey to China," November 10, 2010, University of Southern California US-China Institute, http://china.usc.edu/week-changed-world-inside-story-richard-nixon%E2%80%99s-1972-journey-china.

62. Seymour Hersh, *The Price of Power* (New York: Summit, 1983), 495.

63. MacMillan, *Nixon and Mao,* 121.

64. *FRUS, 1969–1976,* vol. 17, p. 699.

65. NBC's coverage of Nixon's toast interspersed shots of Zhou as well as Kissinger listening attentively. NBC News, February 22, 1972, VTNA.

66. Kissinger, *White House Years,* 1092.

67. Lien-Hang T. Nguyen, *Hanoi's War: An International History of the War for Peace in Vietnam* (Chapel Hill: University of North Carolina Press, 2012), 241.

68. Stephen P. Randolph, *Powerful and Brutal Weapons: Nixon, Kissinger, and the Easter Offensive* (Cambridge, MA: Harvard University Press, 2007), 28–29.

69. *FRUS, 1969–1976,* vol. 8, *Vietnam, January–October 1972* (Washington, DC: US Government Printing Office, 2010), 168–69.

70. The only two measures Nixon excluded were the use of nuclear weapons and sending American combat troops back into Vietnam. The nuclear weapons issue is controversial since he did raise it in a conversation with Kissinger on April 25, 1972. However, the context of this conversation and several other references to nuclear weapons that appear on the tapes indicate that this was never a serious possibility. For an excellent discussion of this, see Richard A. Moss, "Behind the Back Channel: Achieving Détente in U.S.-Soviet Relations, 1969–1972" (Ph.D. diss., George Washington University, 2009), 339.

71. Kissinger, *White House Years,* 1113.

72. *FRUS, 1969–1976*, vol. 14, *Soviet Union, October 1971–May 1972* (Washington, DC: US Government Printing Office, 2006), 434.

73. Richard Nixon, Address to the Nation on the Situation in Southeast Asia, May 8, 1972, *American Presidency Project*, http://www.presidency.ucsb.edu/ws/index.php?pid=3404&st=&st1=.

74. Safire captures the very negative response. See Safire, *Before the Fall*, 428.

75. The postspeech analysis can be found at CBS, Richard Nixon Speech Re. Vietnam War (Post-Speech Analysis Only), May 8, 1972, VTNA.

76. Stephen Ambrose, *Nixon*, vol. 2, *The Triumph of a Politician, 1962–1972* (New York: Simon & Schuster, 1989), 540–41.

77. Vladislav M. Zubok, *A Failed Empire: The Soviet Union in the Cold War from Stalin to Gorbachev* (Chapel Hill: University of North Carolina Press, 2007), 220–21.

78. Both the ABC and the NBC broadcasts of Nixon's arrival noted the crowds and how remarkable it was that the summit was taking place. ABC Evening News, May 22, 1972, and NBC Evening News, May 22, 1972, VTNA.

79. This was particularly the case with CBS News, Walter Cronkite being a space enthusiast. See CBS Evening News, May 24, 1972, VTNA.

80. Bernard Kalb and Marvin Kalb, *Kissinger* (Boston: Little, Brown, 1974), 314.

81. John Chancellor made the reference to the meeting as possibly meaning the end of the Cold War in his May 22 newscast. See NBC Evening News, May 22, 1972, VTNA.

82. Richard Nixon, Text of the "Basic Principles of Relations between the United States of America and the Union of Soviet Socialist Republics," *American Presidency Project*, http://www.presidency.ucsb.edu/ws/index.php?pid=3438&st=&st1=.

83. Cronkite, although a liberal Democrat, expressed this enthusiasm in the CBS broadcast on May 29. See CBS Evening News, May 29, 1972, VTNA.

84. The idea for such a dramatic return came from a legendary public relations man, Tex McCrary, who had mentored both the Nixon speechwriter William Safire and the Nixon advance man Dwight Chapin. Charles J. Kelly, *Tex McCrary: Wars, Women, Politics: An Adventurous Life across the American Century* (Lanham, MD: Hamilton, 2009), 195.

85. *FRUS, 1969–1976*, vol. 1, p. 399; CBS, Richard Nixon Address to Congress Re. His Trip to the USSR, June 1, 1972, VTNA.

86. Safire, *Before the Fall*, 459. Nixon stopped first in Iran and then in Poland after the Moscow summit.

87. "Nixon, Kissinger and the 'Decent Interval,'" Miller Center, University of Virginia, http://millercenter.org/presidentialclassroom/exhibits/nixon-kissinger-and-the-decent-interval.

88. Kissinger, *White House Years*, 1319.

89. *FRUS, 1969–1976*, vol. 9, *Vietnam, October 1972–January 1973* (Washington, DC: US Government Printing Office, 2010), 25.

90. Haldeman, *Haldeman Diaries*, 630.

91. *FRUS, 1969–1976,* vol. 9, pp. 144–53.

92. Haldeman, *Haldeman Diaries,* October 22, 1972, https://www.nixonlibrary.gov/virtuallibrary/documents/haldeman-diaries/37-hrhd-audiocassette-ac26a-19721022-pa.pdf.

93. CBS Evening News, October 26, 1972, VTNA.

94. Haldeman, *Haldeman Diaries,* October 26, 1972, 638.

95. Telephone Conversation between President Nixon and Henry Kissinger, October 26, 1972, Nixontapes.org, http://nixontapes.org/hak/1972-10-26_Nixon_032-063.mp3. This conversation is particularly revealing in how well the two men understood the domestic political implications of this step. In his memoirs, Kissinger remarks blandly: "Nixon and I did not discuss the domestic political implications." Kissinger, *White House Years,* 1398.

96. In one of his rare misreadings of the evidence, Isaacson says that Nixon was "enraged" by Kissinger's pronouncement. See Isaacson, *Kissinger,* 460.

97. *FRUS, 1969–1976,* vol. 9, p. 317.

98. Ibid., 329–31.

99. Richard Nixon, Address to the Nation: "Look to the Future," November 2, 1972, *American Presidency Project,* http://www.presidency.ucsb.edu/ws/index.php?pid=3682&st=&st1=#axzz2gPUnWeev. See also Kalb and Kalb, *Kissinger,* 387.

100. Nixon, *RN,* 715.

101. Telephone Conversation between President Nixon and Henry Kissinger, November 8, 1972, Nixontapes.org, http://nixontapes.org/hak/1972-11-08_Nixon_033-060.mp3.

10

Dealing with Defeat

Gerald R. Ford, Foreign Policy, and the 1976 Election

Andrew Priest

The 1976 presidential election took place in highly unusual circumstances. The incumbent, Gerald R. Ford, ran for office as an unelected president who had succeeded Richard Nixon following Nixon's decision to resign in August 1974 over the Watergate scandal, an unprecedented event. Ford himself had been an unelected vice president appointed by Nixon in 1973 following the resignation of Vice President Spiro Agnew for financial misdemeanors. Then, as president, Ford experienced a serious challenge for the Republican nomination from Ronald Reagan, the former actor and California governor who successfully marshaled a right-wing revolt that came close to derailing Ford's primary campaign. By this time, President Ford's difficulties had been compounded by the emergence of a strong Democratic challenger, Jimmy Carter, previously governor of Georgia, who had been virtually unknown to the vast majority of Americans at the start of the year. Yet, because of Watergate, Carter's outsider status and lack of experience in Washington endeared him to the American people and made his nomination possible. As Carter himself summarized in his acceptance speech at the Democratic national convention, 1976 was "not . . . a year of politics as usual."[1]

Yet in many ways the election campaign itself was fairly conventional.

President Ford represented the tarnished Republican administration, in office for eight years and containing several key Nixon holdovers (most notably Henry Kissinger), while Carter's ability to tap into the American people's cynicism about post-Watergate Beltway politics was a standard, albeit unusually intense, electoral tactic designed to distance him from the sitting president's positions. Moreover, Carter was able to appeal to independents and moderate Republicans by focusing on traditional concerns about domestic politics—and especially the economy—that remained the dominant campaign issues. As a Gallup poll conducted in October 1976 illustrated, when Americans were asked what they thought was the most important problem facing the country today, 43 percent of respondents said inflation, the economic situation, the high cost of living, and high prices, 33 percent said unemployment and the recession, and a mere 7 percent said international problems, foreign aid, and foreign affairs.[2] The era of foreign policy–dominated elections was, it seemed, finally over.

Much of the election cycle, however, also revolved around the issues of presidential authority and credibility, and in these areas foreign policy was crucial. At the end of April 1975, Americans saw the South Vietnamese capital, Saigon, fall to Communist forces in the most humiliating of circumstances, ending a divisive and debilitating war that left bitter legacies and made many Americans suspicious of political leaders who might make hasty commitments of troops overseas. Combined with Watergate, the disaster of the Vietnam War fundamentally challenged American beliefs in its constitutional system of government and contributed to the sense of what the sociologist Daniel Bell has called "the end of American exceptionalism."[3] Moreover, the process of détente was being challenged at home, and, as Sarah Snyder has recently shown, relations with the Soviet Union, the promotion of human rights within the Soviet sphere, and attendant questions about morality in American foreign policy were important issues for voters in establishing and undermining presidential credibility.[4] Unrest in the Middle East also continued to have a direct impact on the American people, causing rising fuel prices and fuel shortages at home, while there is evidence that Ford's policies in Southern Africa negatively affected the African American vote.[5] The candidates therefore spent a good deal of time trying to appeal to the electorate on foreign policy issues, sometimes with considerable success—for example, Carter and human rights—and sometimes with unforeseen failure, such as Ford's infamous gaffe that there was no Soviet domination of Eastern Europe. As Thomas Schwartz puts it: "The 1976 election may not have turned on foreign policy, but it certainly played a role in Ford's defeat."[6]

That Ford came so close to snatching the election in the final days and weeks of the campaign suggests that foreign policy could have made the difference and that his refusal or inability to exploit Republican foreign policy positions and divisions between his policies and those of his opponents hampered his ability to develop a winning campaign. Ultimately, Ford appeared to be incoherent and lacked a clear narrative, while Carter was able to craft a more consistent and convincing line despite his obvious shortcomings.

The Ford Problem

When Gerald Ford took office in August 1974, he faced a daunting challenge. The country was reeling from the shock of the first presidential resignation as well as a stagnant economy, high unemployment, and rampant inflation caused at least in part by the debilitating effects of the long war in Vietnam and the rising price of oil. Added to this, the combined impact of the Watergate scandal and the Vietnam conflict had undermined the authority of the office of the presidency itself. The new president therefore had to convince Americans that their "long national nightmare" was over, as he put it on his first day in office.[7]

Somewhat paradoxically, these conditions also offered President Ford opportunities. He may have self-deprecatingly joked that he was "a Ford and not a Lincoln," but throughout his brief presidency members of his team continued to believe that he could win election in his own right.[8] They encouraged him to draw on popular perceptions of the Civil War a century before to invoke the idea of binding up the nation's wounds to banish the twin traumas of Watergate and Vietnam to the past while demonstrating that he was a credible leader who could take the country forward.[9] However difficult the fall of Saigon was in the spring of 1975, it at least allowed the president to claim that the war was over for Americans, that the United States was now at peace, and, that, as the country approached its bicentennial, it could look with optimism toward its third century as a nation.[10]

His inner circle believed that he could gain a particular edge over potential rivals because of his experience in international affairs. Foreign policy offered the opportunity for the president to present himself as a strong political figure and to reassure the American people about the direction of the country. "I have said before, and continue to firmly believe," the special adviser Robert Goldwin told the president's deputy chief of staff, Richard B. Cheney, in March 1975, "the man who can *make Americans proud of themselves again as Americans* will deserve and get the admiration and gratitude of the American people." Demonstrating the moral character of American foreign policy, Goldwin suggested, would both show the coherence of Ford's foreign policy and illustrate that Ford was a worthy leader at home and abroad.[11]

Yet this would not be easy. As Ford's campaign recognized, the American electorate was in an unusually cynical mood about its political institutions and leaders at this time.[12] Ford's decision to leave in place important personnel from the Nixon administration—notably Secretary of State and National Security Adviser Henry Kissinger—compounded such views, reinforcing the notion that it was business as usual in the White House. So too did the president's decision to pardon his predecessor—in September 1974, just one month after he entered office—to prevent any prosecution arising out of the Watergate affair. Ford also faced a Congress that was increasingly assertive in the wake of Watergate and Vietnam, and the 1974 midterm elections saw large majorities returned for the Democrats in both houses. In particular, many members of the legislature were desperate to ensure that nothing was done to lead the United States into another major commitment of troops in an area of the world that was not vital to American interests.

The president also had an image problem. He was a regional politician thrust into office at the highest level with no experience of campaigning nationally. Voters knew little about him, but those who took the time to find out generally perceived him to be competent, honest, and friendly, traits that were important at a time of great instability and served him well in stabilizing the presidency. Republican supporters especially were pleased that he wanted to maintain a strong defensive posture without being drawn into another conflict like Vietnam. Yet these same characteristics meant that many outside the party regarded him as being mediocre—a mainstream Republican whose carefully crafted position as manager of the transition from the era of the "imperial presidency" also made him appear to be dull and uninspiring.[13] By late 1975, the campaign strategist Robert Teeter argued that Ford had gone some way to restoring people's faith in the office of the presidency but worried that support for the president was "soft."[14] Few voters saw him as a strong foreign policy president, and many members of the media treated him as being something of a dunce, despite his strong academic record and history of achievement in Congress. Ford's bullish press secretary, Ron Nessen, despaired at the way in which the president was portrayed on television and often openly sparred with journalists about it. One reporter, pressing the president on his foreign policy credentials, even ended an interview by asking: "You are aware there is a world out there?"[15]

Incumbency was therefore a powerful weapon, although one that was also not without its disadvantages. Ford's decision to pardon Nixon notwithstanding, during the first months of 1975 the president appeared to be riding out the controversies of the previous administration and, in his own modest way, to have mastered the important aspects of his brief and gone some way toward restoring people's confidence in the presidency. A Harris poll conducted in June revealed that Ford would defeat any Democrat challenger in an election.[16] In particular, Ford successfully contrasted his own approach with that of the increasingly unpopular Democratic Congress, which people blamed for the country's economic woes and which saw its approval rating languishing at 20 percent while the president's climbed above 50 percent. Yet even this tactic of attacking Congress was also not without risk as columnists accused President Ford of giving too much license to his vice president, the liberal multimillionaire Nelson Rockefeller—himself a controversial choice for office—and risking a backlash from the opposite wing of the party. "The 1976 threat to the Ford Administration lies on the Right, and not on the Left," warned *The American Political Report* of February 1975.[17] And so it proved.

The Reagan Challenge

President Ford later claimed that he seriously underestimated the challenge posed by Ronald Reagan for the Republican nomination. By late 1975, he believed that his campaign committee was functioning well, that it had succeeded in recruiting many supporters of the putative candidate Reagan, and that the country was now in a much better shape than it had been just one year before. He was therefore surprised when in November Governor Reagan called him to say that he was about to announce his candidacy.[18] In fact, Ford's campaign team had been preparing for the Reagan challenge for some time; what they were slow to realize was how successful it would be.

Simply put, Reagan built his campaign on dissatisfaction with the policies of the Nixon-Ford administration, preempting Jimmy Carter in campaigning as a political outsider to exploit Ford's long congressional career and to suggest that the president was part of the problem rather than its solution.[19] Reagan claimed that Ford was a key exponent of the insular Washington politics that ignored the plight of struggling American workers and simultaneously made the United States more vulnerable abroad. He also successfully used the media, particularly television, to convey his message. In contrast, Ford came across poorly on television. By attacking Ford on a few key issues (as well as riding his luck), Reagan won the North Carolina primary at the end of March 1976, picking up support from the conservative Democrat George Wallace, who had by then effectively been removed from the race. Then, as White House staff secretary James E. Connor put it, he "blitzed" the president in Texas and won in Indiana in early May. By this stage, there was something close to panic among Ford's supporters, who worried that Reagan's success meant that Republicans were starting to see the president as a loser, leading to further erosion at the grassroots level and to other candidates joining the fray.[20] By the spring and early summer of 1976, the Ford team's early confidence was crumbling.

Reagan especially excelled at exploiting the president's positions on issues of national security and defense, areas he increasingly focused on as the primary season progressed.[21] The Ford team privately admitted that they struggled to respond effectively to this tactic, although it was perhaps the manner rather than the substance of the attack that concerned them. Connor complained that almost regardless of the charge—whether it was about negotiations over the status of the Panama Canal, US defensive capabilities vis-à-vis the Soviets, or the need for reform in Washington— their response was "defensive and bureaucratic."[22] Reagan, in contrast, was brash and dynamic. He accused the administration—and Henry Kissinger in particular—of weakening the United States with its détente policies and found much support in doing so. By December 1975, Teeter reported on a Gallup poll indicating that the White House now had what he called a "serious momentum problem" following Reagan's announcement of his candidacy. He noted that this was unlikely to be arrested "without a Mayaguez or something comparable that we don't see in the immediate future" or a major foreign policy change to wrest the initiative from Reagan.[23] The *Mayaguez* incident had involved the capture of a US container ship by Khmer Rouge gunboats immediately after the end of the Vietnam War in May 1975. The decision to attempt to rescue the crew had been popular despite a high death toll because the public perceived the president to have acted decisively, and he consequently received a significant upturn in his approval ratings.[24] Without such an unforeseen development, the media campaign team now argued that the president needed to cast Reagan as an irresponsible, ambitious, naive politician who threatened to commit US forces to another war like Vietnam and risked confrontation with the Soviet Union. "In a nutshell, we must go for the jugular and *eliminate* the credibility of the Reagan candidacy," opined Ford's campaign manager, Rogers Morton.[25]

Reagan was also successful in campaigning on specific issues, especially the president's policies on the Panama Canal and Southern Africa. On the latter, while Ford faced an infinitely complex and fluid situation in dealing with the transition of Mozambique and Angola to postcolonial states, revelations about his provision of millions of dollars in secret funds for anti-Communist forces in the bloody Angolan Civil War led directly to congressional involvement in late 1975 and to the president agreeing to greater oversight of the American intelligence community.[26] While Ford may have wanted to show that he was striking out on an independent but assertive foreign policy in dealing with the situation in Angola, to many this seemed more like a continuation of the politics of the Vietnam era, especially because the side the Americans supported lost. Yet Reagan's charge was that the president had not done enough in Angola, and this had resulted in the worst possible scenario: "We gave just enough support to one side to encourage it to fight and die but too little to give them a chance of winning. Now we're disliked by the winner, distrusted by the loser and viewed by the world as weak and unsure."[27] Ford was also unable to capitalize on Reagan's gaffe in saying that, if asked, he would consider sending troops to Rhodesia, another former European colony in Southern Africa struggling to make the transition to independence, so

Reagan's momentum grew.[28] While Ford's team fretted that this augured badly for the president's chances of obtaining the nomination, they further feared that, if Reagan won the Republican nomination, the chosen Democratic candidate could outflank him in the presidential campaign by drawing attention to his bellicose rhetoric, which was appealing to many, and accusing him of being trigger happy toward the Soviets and risking another war like Vietnam.[29]

Reagan also had other organizational advantages over President Ford. Partially, these were the result of changes to presidential campaign rules in the wake of Watergate as Congress passed new federal finance laws to limit the possible abuse of funds by candidates and their organizations. This meant that, as long as another potential Republican candidate might challenge the president for the party's nomination, the Republican National Committee (RNC) could not become involved in campaigning for the president. Another separate organization, the President Ford Committee (PFC), was therefore established.[30] These legislative revisions gave an advantage to candidates who were unable to raise large amounts of money from a few wealthy donors, while other developments at state level and within the Republican Party itself further eroded Ford's position as the automatic nominee.[31]

More than this, however, the Republican electoral machine was in disarray. Staff in the White House and on the PFC and RNC failed to agree among themselves or to coordinate with each other.[32] This was damaging to the president because, as his campaign strategy document put it, "bickering within the Administration contributes to the perception that the President is not really in control, thus not a leader."[33] Such problems were exemplified by the clumsy attempt to remove Vice President Rockefeller from the ticket, which began when the right-wing head of the PFC—and so Ford's first campaign manager—Howard "Bo" Callaway, publicly undermined the vice president's position in discussion with reporters in June 1975. While Ford initially assured Rockefeller of his position, he ultimately dropped him from the ticket in October, adding to Reagan's sense that Ford was vulnerable.[34] In February 1976, Ford's longtime confidant Jack Stiles offered a frank assessment of the challenges that the campaign faced, which included Callaway's poor temperament for such a struggle and the bloated campaign's weak organizational structure. The result, Stiles suggested, was chaos and low morale.[35] Soon after,

Callaway was forced to leave following reports about a conflict-of-interest case in Colorado, and Rogers Morton replaced him.[36]

In contrast, the Reagan campaign was slick, efficient, and organized. It was able to exploit a loose coalition of different groups that had diverse aims but were united in their disillusionment with the current political scene and the Ford administration in particular. While Reagan was often desperate for money throughout the primaries season—because his supporters were not campaigning for him specifically but rather raising issues with which he was sympathetic—they were able to raise funds outside the stricter post-Watergate campaign rules and target sympathetic voters who would not normally be motivated to participate in the primaries. As one analysis complained, this meant that Ford's team was "in real danger of being out-organized by a small number of highly motivated right wing nuts, who are using funds outside of the Reagan campaign expenditure limits."[37]

Going into the Republican national convention in Kansas City in August, therefore, the result still hung in the balance. The candidates were virtually neck-and-neck, and only a few delegates had not declared. In the end, Reagan may only have undone his campaign by making the tactical error of announcing his vice presidential running mate—the liberal Pennsylvanian Senator Richard Schweiker—before the convention began.

Despite Ford's eventual victory—he gained 52.5 percent of the delegates—the Kansas City convention had a distinctly conservative flavor. Even in defeat, Reagan was heavily influential in Ford's decision to add the conservative Robert Dole from Kansas as the vice presidential candidate, and the convention adopted a number of important policy positions that appeared to be critical of the president's conduct in office. Perhaps most significantly, delegates agreed on a plank insisting on the need for morality in foreign policy, criticizing the president's refusal to meet with the Soviet dissident writer Alexander Solzhenitsyn. They also chided Ford about his policies of détente with the Soviet Union, especially the Helsinki Accords, and called for openness in making diplomatic agreements, the latter effectively an overt attack on Secretary of State Kissinger.[38] The delegates thus appeared to undermine Ford's claims even to represent his own party and provided ammunition for the Democrats as the final stages of the contest began.[39]

Throughout the campaign, members of the Ford camp had been trying to convince themselves that the president could achieve a Harry Truman–style comeback like 1948 when the president had been consistently trailing the polls but managed to squeak home on Election Day. By midsummer, however, such optimistic assessments were starting to tarnish as Ford had proved that he was no Harry Truman on the campaign trail. Although the official campaign strategy document continued to assert that the president could still win, it also confessed that he faced "a unique challenge": "No President has overcome the obstacles to election which you will face."[40]

The Carter Factor

In contrast to the Republicans, the Democrats showed a remarkable degree of unity in endorsing Jimmy Carter, a candidate who had emerged from an initially crowded field to triumph with ease at the convention. That the party endorsed its chosen candidate on the first ballot was surprising enough, but that he was a one-term governor from the Deep South unknown to most in the party a year before made it even more so. The Democrats had also successfully avoided contentious and divisive issues, so their platform appeared to be coherent and their party united. This was exemplified by the singing of the civil rights anthem "We Shall Overcome" at the end of the convention.[41] By August, Carter was ahead by twenty points in the polls.[42]

As expected, Carter focused his campaign on the failures of the Nixon-Ford era, especially the economy, but also Vietnam and Watergate and the need to unite the country after years of division. He wanted to maintain or increase the role of the government in the nation's economic affairs, particularly to ensure full employment, control inflation, and overhaul the tax regime, closing loopholes and cutting taxes for the poorest. This set him clearly against policies that Ford had already established as president that looked to cut the federal budget and gave him an advantage with voters disillusioned by the apparently still stagnant—or at least sluggish—economy. Carter also hinted that he might cut parts of the defense budget in order to fund such programs, a prospect Ford and his team pounced on.

Yet it was in the area of foreign policy reform that Governor Carter really made his mark with his call for honesty, morality, and ethics to be brought center stage. He connected the crisis in US foreign policy with the one in domestic affairs.[43] He said that he had traveled all over the country in his campaign for the presidency and talked to many people about what he called their "deep hurt" with the present state of affairs. Using his outsider status, he attacked the loss of integrity in recent Nixon-Ford foreign policy, especially the secrecy in which it had been conducted and support for authoritarian regimes in such nations as Chile, Pakistan, and Angola. He excoriated Henry Kissinger's brand of personal diplomacy, claiming that, if elected president, he was "not going to exclude the American people" from the diplomatic process, "as Mr. Ford and Kissinger have done."[44] Yet, while he said that he wanted to advance the Strategic Arms Limitation Talks, he also assailed Ford and Kissinger for not being tougher with the Soviets in negotiations over the Helsinki Accords and promised to take stronger action against Arab nations if faced with another oil boycott. In one sense, this was a risky strategy, leading to accusations of incoherence, but, as Henry Plotkin has suggested, it meant that Carter could successfully appeal to both conservatives and liberals.[45] As the Republican convention had illustrated, détente was unpopular with the many voters who believed that it gave too much away to the Soviets. The country had arguably become more hard-line on relations with the Soviet Union in recent times, and many voters saw the president as being further to the Left than they were on issues such as détente.[46] Moreover, what mattered was that, as the challenger, Carter took a stand to undermine the authority of the president and claim a strong moral position.

As with Reagan during the primaries, Ford struggled to counter this assault and articulate a moral vision of his own. In contrast to Carter's born-again Christianity, which meant that he wore his religious heart on his sleeve, Ford rarely discussed his religious views, and this was a major handicap when the people wanted moral guidance. As his adviser George Van Cleve noted, the presidency had always been viewed as a place of quasi-religious leadership, and the American people justified their actions, and wanted those of the United States in the world to be justified, in explicitly religious and moral terms. Carter's success was therefore partially explained by Americans looking for a spiritual leader, but there was more to why it was particularly important in 1976:

> The answer, or at least a large part of the answer, to that question
> has to do with the pervasive feeling that we have lost our sense

of national purpose. And, in my view, the single most important set of events which contributed to this belief were [*sic*] the events surrounding the war in Viet Nam. That war was the first war in modern times [in] which many Americans felt it was wrong or even immoral to fight. From beginning to end, it was a war which many supported, and many opposed, without knowing why. *Never* did the nation's leaders come forward with an explanation for our actions sufficient to silence the dissent. And the events surrounding the close of the war left wounds in the national spirit which have not healed.[47]

Van Cleve urged the president to think and talk in these kinds of moralistic terms. While he suggested that the American people would not necessarily agree on ideas about justice and freedom in global affairs, the president could and should articulate a vision and stick to it.

Ford failed to do so largely because of his adherence to a rigid and traditional mind-set. All but ignoring the previous decade of war, which he claimed was now firmly in the past, the president made speeches suggesting that the cornerstone of American foreign policy had always been peace and that the previous six presidents had maintained the foundations of American foreign policy to ensure American security, even though all were in some way tainted by association with the Vietnam quagmire. Ford also claimed that his opponent was proposing to make a fundamental change in the direction and conduct of US foreign policy. Carter's doctrine of human rights was, he suggested, untested and potentially dangerous with "a strong flavor of isolationism" about it.[48] For Ford, those voices calling for a reduction in American global commitments had to be resisted so that the United States did not let its guard down.[49] The president also objected to the very idea that Vietnam should cause the United States to take stock. He said Carter's suggestion that the United States had lost power, respect, and standing because of Vietnam and that it should therefore refuse to become involved in another conflict was "slandering the good name of the United States." This, he claimed, discouraged America's allies and encouraged its adversaries.[50]

Furthermore, Ford's refusal to grant an amnesty to the tens of thousands of Vietnam draft dodgers and deserters—announced almost as soon as he became president—may have been initially popular, but it looked hypocritical when he claimed that he wanted the people to put the war behind them and because he followed it so quickly with his announcement that he would grant a pardon to former president Nixon over Watergate.[51] As the peak of the election campaign approached, close Ford associates recommended giving a blanket amnesty, but the president insisted that this could not happen and created a Presidential Clemency Board to which people had to apply.[52] In contrast, Governor Carter said that he wanted to be more lenient but insisted that as president he would have to issue a pardon rather than an amnesty because a pardon implied that the perpetrators would be forgiven regardless of whether what they did was right or wrong. He could easily contrast President Ford's swift pardon of Nixon with his refusal to forgive those from the Vietnam era. This, he suggested, looked like the political classes protecting their own kind, and he compared it to white-collar criminals getting away with their crimes while the poor and uninfluential went to jail.[53]

Yet, more than any of this, Ford's inability to connect with ordinary Americans hamstrung the campaign. This reached a crisis point at the end of the summer as various members of his team sought a reassessment of their strategy. Teeter subsequently summarized that they "had found in the primaries that when the president campaigned regularly, he was not effective," but at the time the chief strategist, Stuart Spencer, was far less delicate, telling Ford directly: "Mr. President, as a campaigner, you're no fucking good!"[54] A decision was therefore made to stop him from receiving "continuous media exposure which is staged simply for the benefit of exposure."[55] The so-called Rose Garden strategy, whereby Ford would stay in Washington carrying out the duties of office rather than jetting round the country, was intended to remind voters that he was in charge and that he should remain in that position. This brought Ford some considerable success during the final weeks of the campaign. He reduced the massive deficit built up over the summer as both he and Carter dealt with a series of setbacks. Carter's were, however, more significant, and he struggled to shake off charges that he was too inexperienced to be president.

By September, therefore, the Ford team's optimism was growing and increased further as they approached the presidential debates—the first since the infamous Kennedy-Nixon encounters of 1960—at the end of the month.[56] Ford's agreement to participate was based on the idea that he essentially had nothing to lose, and his fine performance in the first contest reinforced his sense of momentum, despite a technical glitch that meant the loss of sound for some twenty-seven minutes as both candidates stood in awkward silence. He went on the offensive and looked presidential in contrast to an ill-prepared and apparently intimidated Carter. The race was back on.

By the time of the second debate on foreign affairs, held in San Francisco on October 6, Ford's people were starting to believe that they could win against all the odds as Carter came under increased scrutiny about his lack of foreign policy credentials. Carter was an unknown quantity whose judgment had not been proved and at times appeared to be questionable, as he had shown with his infamous comments about lust and adultery in an interview with *Playboy* magazine published in mid-September. In unguarded comments with freelance reporters, he stated that, in trying to resist temptation and sin, he was "human" and "tempted." Most notoriously, in talking about Christ's teachings on adultery, he said: "I've looked on a lot of women with lust. I've committed adultery in my heart many times." He also used the word *screw*. Although the interview was wide-ranging, these comments were, perhaps understandably, the most widely reported in the weeks leading up to the election.[57]

The Ford campaign attempted to exploit this by showing how, for example, Governor Carter had consistently argued in favor of the war in Vietnam, including Richard Nixon's bombing of Cambodia, despite his subsequent condemnation of it.[58] He was consistently accused of being "fuzzy" on foreign issues, and the president had already had opportunities to attack him for looking to make cuts in defense in order to fund other programs.[59] His inexperience also meant that he had to rely on others to advise him: "While Jimmy Carter is obviously an intelligent man, no one has ever accused him of being an expert on the economy or foreign policy," opined George Van Cleve. The range of views among Carter's advisers, some of whom had as little in common as "Machiavelli and Woodrow Wilson," meant that his policy groups were simply "a front, a publicity game, and little else."[60] As Van Cleve had suggested earlier in the summer, while the success of Ford's candidacy undoubtedly rested on his ability to convince people that he had a suitable response to domestic challenges, "perceptions of relative foreign policy ability and expertise will affect public views of the candidates."[61]

This statement proved to be prophetic, although in exactly the opposite way to what Van Cleve intended. On October 6, in the second presidential debate, which dealt specifically with issues of foreign affairs, it was Ford's disastrous gaffe on the status of Eastern Europe that was the memorable line and the one that sunk the Ford presidency. At the end of a response to a question on relations with the Soviet Union, Ford infamously declared: "There is no Soviet domination of Eastern Europe, and there never will be under a Ford administration."[62] While this was bad enough, he compounded it by refusing to back down either during the remainder of the debate or in the days that followed. Although the postdebate news conference was dominated by the mistake, the campaign team was initially hopeful that the substance of the rest of the debate would carry them through. A survey of views from one hundred law students at George Washington University, for example, gave Carter a slight lead but focused on Ford's style in the debate rather than the error. Later analysis suggested that very few voters considered the gaffe to be a major issue, but media attention in the hours and days afterward changed this, and voters' assessments of his performance plummeted.[63] It is significant that this faux pas became one of the most important developments of the campaign, undermining Ford's claims that he was a competent leader who could sail the United States through the presently choppy waters. It stalled the Ford resurgence, and on Election Day Carter squeezed home, winning the Electoral College 297–240 and the popular vote by 50.1 to 48 percent, or less than 1.7 million ballots out of a total of almost 80 million cast.[64]

Conclusion

With hindsight, it is difficult to imagine a Gerald Ford victory in the 1976 presidential election. The economy was in a desperately poor state, Americans were disillusioned with the era of Vietnam and Watergate, and President Ford was tainted by association with the disgraced Richard Nixon (especially after his quick decision to pardon him). More than this, Ford also faced a perception problem that made his prospects more difficult. As one postelection analysis put it, he was a "*half incumbent*" in that he was "perceived as an incumbent but was also a *challenger*," who then had to campaign for the presidency in his own right against a challenger with many advantages, particularly being a naturally good television performer.[65]

Yet Jimmy Carter's narrow margin of victory shows that the result was not a foregone conclusion. While Carter was largely successful in utilizing his image as a Washington outsider to exploit public disillusionment with Republican policies at home and abroad, he was also vulnerable to charges of inexperience at the national level and poor judgment. This explains his massive early lead in the summer of 1976 when he was able to attack the Republican platform in broad terms and also the whittling away of that lead as the election approached and the arguments became more specific. This vulnerability was particularly pronounced when it came to international affairs, of which he had little knowledge or experience. Carter's charges of diplomatic secrecy, military adventurism, and unwarranted interference in other nation's affairs conducted by the Ford administration therefore certainly hit home and made his promise of prioritizing human rights more attractive. Yet his attack on the policies of détente appeared to be too much like political opportunism, and the Ford campaign's focus on foreign issues gave them an opportunity to demonstrate the president's credentials in an area in which he had already had some success.

In the end, it might have worked had it not been for the second debate gaffe. As it was, rather than enhancing Ford's credibility—a central focus of his presidency and the election—this small mistake and the feeble White House response to it exposed voters to what they perceived to be deeper problems with his leadership. While the Rose Garden strategy may have succeeded in accentuating the positives of Ford's claim to the presidency, the essentially negative nature of this approach relied on the president showing that he was clearly in charge and had the answers to the important questions. The Eastern Europe error sowed enough seeds of doubt to suggest that he was not and did not.

Conversely, Carter, like Ronald Reagan, was able to project an image of someone—and something—new and positive. While he had to take a risk to do this and saw his lead almost vanish in the final weeks of the campaign, it was his only option if he was going to win. Ultimately, just enough voters saw specific qualities in Carter—strength, decisiveness, and morality—to convince them that he should be the new occupant of the White House. Jimmy Carter had narrowly succeeded in convincing a majority of Americans that he had the necessary political authority in domestic and foreign policy to be elected president, while Gerald Ford had not.

Notes

1. Jimmy Carter, "Our Nation's Past and Future": Address Accepting the Presidential Nomination at the Democratic National Convention in New York City, July 15, 1976, *The American Presidency Project,* http://www.presidency.ucsb.edu/ws/?pid=25953.

2. Gallup Poll, Roper Center, http://ropercenter.cornell.edu/polls/us-elections/presidential-elections/1976-presidential-election.

3. Daniel Bell, "The End of American Exceptionalism" (1975), reprinted in Daniel Bell, *Sociological Journeys: Essays, 1960–1980* (London: Heinemann, 1980), 245–71. See also Trevor B. McCrisken, *American Exceptionalism and the Legacy of Vietnam: US Foreign Policy since 1974* (Basingstoke: Palgrave Macmillan, 2003), esp. 20–39.

4. Sarah B. Snyder, "Through the Looking Glass: The Helsinki Final Act and the 1976 Election for President," *Diplomacy and Statecraft* 21, no. 1 (2010): 87–106.

5. Carl Peter Watts, "Dropping the F-Bomb: President Ford, the Rhodesian Crisis, and the 1976 Election" (paper presented at the annual meeting of the Society for Historians of American Foreign Relations, Lexington, KY, June 2014). I am extremely grateful to Carl Watts for sending me a copy of this paper.

6. Thomas Alan Schwartz, "'Henry, . . . Winning an Election Is Terribly Important': Partisan Politics in the History of U.S. Foreign Relations," *Diplomatic History* 33, no. 2 (2009): 173–90, 189.

7. Gerald R. Ford, Remarks on Taking the Oath of Office, August 9, 1974, *American Presidency Project,* http://www.presidency.ucsb.edu/ws/?pid=4409. While this was a direct reference to the wounds of Watergate, which he claimed were "more painful and more poisonous than those of foreign wars," Ford subsequently applied similar ideas to consigning Vietnam to the past. See Robert McMahon, "Contested Memory: The Vietnam War and American Society, 1975–2001," *Diplomatic History* 26, no. 2 (2002): 159–84, 164–65.

8. Gerald R. Ford, December 6, 1973, quoted in Richard Reeves, *A Ford, Not a Lincoln: The Decline of American Political Leadership* (London: Hutchison, 1976), 39.

9. See, e.g., David W. Belin to the President, "Projecting Leadership and Statesmanship—Some Major Opportunities," February 13, 1976, 3, box 36, Folder: Presidential Handwriting File, Political Affairs—Ford (3), Robert T. Hartmann, "Speech Suggestions," July 14, 1976, Robert T. Hartmann Files, box 7, Folder: Nomination Acceptance Speech, 8/19/76 Memoranda, Hartmann to the President, July 13, 1976, Hartmann to Max Friedersdorf, July 15, 1976, and Ron Neeson to Hartmann, July 20, 1976, Robert T. Hartmann Files, box 7, Folder: Nomination Acceptance Speech 8/19/76, all Gerald R. Ford Presidential Library, Ann Arbor, MI (hereafter GRFL).

10. Gerald Ford, Address at a Tulane University Convocation, April 23, 1975, *American Presidency Project,* http://www.presidency.ucsb.edu/ws/?pid=4859.

11. Robert Goldwin to Donald Rumsfeld, March 14, 1975, 3, James E. Connor

Files, Staff Secretary Subject Files, box 7, Folder: Campaign—Ford Constituency, GRFL.

12. Campaign Strategy for President Ford, n.d. [1976], 31, Dorothy E. Downton Files, box 1, Folder: Presidential Campaign: Campaign Strategy Program (1) GRFL.

13. Ibid., 52.

14. Robert Teeter to Richard Cheney, November 12, 1975, Robert Teeter Papers, box 63, Folder: 11/12/75, GRFL.

15. Ron Nessen, *It Sure Looks Different from the Inside* (Chicago: Playboy, 1978), 164.

16. Reeves, *A Ford, Not a Lincoln,* 182. See also, e.g., "Themes," April 21, 1976, Connor Files, Staff Secretary Subject Files, box 7, Folder: Campaign—Planning 1976.

17. *The American Political Report,* February 21, 1975, Connor Files, Staff Secretary Subject Files, box 7, Folder: Campaign—Early Efforts.

18. Gerald R. Ford, *A Time to Heal: The Autobiography of Gerald R. Ford* (New York: Harper & Row, 1979), 331–32.

19. See, e.g., Statement by the Hon. Ronald Reagan, November 20, 1975, Ron Nessen Papers, box 39, Folder: Reagan—Announcement of Candidacy, 11/20/75, GRFL; Text of Governor Ronald Reagan's Nationwide Television Address, March 31, 1976, Nessen Papers, box 39, Folder: Reagan—Nationwide TV Address.

20. Connor's Notes on Ronald Reagan, May 5, 1976, 1, Connor Files, Staff Secretary Subject Files, box 7, Folder: Campaign—Planning 1976.

21. See Michael Brenes, "Making Foreign Policy at the Grassroots: Cold War Politics and the 1976 Republican Primary," *Journal of Policy History* 27, no. 1 (2015): 93–117; and Jonathan Moore and Janet Fraser, *Campaign for President: The Managers Look at '76* (Cambridge, MA: Ballinger, 1977), 46–47.

22. Connor's Notes on Ronald Reagan, May 5, 1976, 2, Connor Files, Staff Secretary Subject Files, box 7, Folder: Campaign—Planning 1976.

23. Teeter to Bo Callaway, December 11, 1975, Teeter Papers, box 63, Folder: 12/11/75.

24. Gallup poll (n. 2 above); Gergen to Cheney, June 21, 1976, 4, Presidential Handwriting File, box 42, Folder: Public Relations—Public Opinion Polls, GRFL.

25. Rogers Morton to Bruce Wagner, April 7, 1976, President Ford Committee Records, box B4, Folder: Advertising—Primary Campaign (1), GRFL.

26. John Robert Greene, *The Presidency of Gerald R. Ford* (Lawrence: University Press of Kansas, 1995), 112–16.

27. Text of Governor Ronald Reagan's Nationwide Television Address, March 31, 1976, 13, Nessen Papers, box 39, folder: Reagan—Nationwide TV Address.

28. Greene, *The Presidency of Gerald R. Ford,* 168; Watts, "Dropping the F-Bomb."

29. See David Gergen, "President Ford: 10 Reasons Why He Should Carry the GOP Banner in November," June 11, 1976, 3, Michael Raoul-Duval Papers, box 15, Folder: Ford Electability, GRFL.

30. See Red Cavaney to Connor and Jack Calkins, January 21, 1976, Connor Files, box 7, Folder: Airline Transport to Cheney, Richard (1), Campaign—Early Efforts.

31. Gerald M. Pomper, "The Nominating Contests and Conventions," in *The Election of 1976: Reports and Interpretations,* ed. Gerald M. Pomper (New York: Longman, 1977), 1–34, 2–5.

32. Jerry H. Jones to Rumsfeld and Cheney, August 26, 1975, Jerry Jones Files, box 23, Folder: President Ford Committee (2), GRFL; Connor's Notes on Ronald Reagan, May 5, 1976, 3, Connor Files, Staff Secretary Subject Files, box 7, Folder: Campaign—Planning 1976.

33. Campaign Strategy for President Ford, 51.

34. Greene, *The Presidency of Gerald R. Ford,* 158–60.

35. Jack Stiles, Campaign Report, February 24, 1976, Downton Files, box 1, Folder: Presidential Campaign: Campaign Report.

36. See Callaway to the President, March 29, 1976, Nessen Papers, box 32, Folder: Callaway, Howard H.

37. "An Explanation of the Reagan Victories in Texas and the Caucus States," n.d., May 1976, Jones Files, box 25, Folder: Reagan, Ronald (2).

38. It is notable that Ford openly began to distance himself from Kissinger as his term progressed, excluding him from aspects of decision making on Vietnam in the spring of 1975, and relieving him of his position as national security adviser in November. See Robert D. Schulzinger, "The End of the Vietnam War," in *Nixon in the World: American Foreign Relations, 1969–1977,* ed. Frederik Logevall and Andrew Preston (Oxford: Oxford University Press, 2008), 211; Greene, *The Presidency of Gerald R. Ford,* 140; and Reeves, *A Ford, Not a Lincoln,* 179–80.

39. Pomper, "Nominating Contests," 18–27; Moore and Fraser, *Campaign for President,* 57–58.

40. Campaign Strategy for President Ford, 2.

41. Pomper, "Nominating Contests," 31–32.

42. Greene, *The Presidency of Gerald R. Ford,* 175.

43. Jimmy Carter, *Why Not the Best?* (Eastbourne: Kingsway, 1977), 178.

44. Carter, "Our Nation's Past and Future"; Presidential Campaign Debate, October 6, 1976, *American Presidency Project,* http://www.presidency.ucsb.edu/ws/index.php?pid=6414.

45. Henry Plotkin, "Issues in the 1976 Campaign," in Pomper, ed., *Election of 1976,* 35–53, 50–51.

46. Teeter to Cheney, December 24, 1975, Foster Chanock Files, box 4, Folder: Teeter, Robert—Memoranda and Polling Data, GRFL.

47. Barbara Koelb to Gergen, September 29, 1976, with Enclosure from Van Cleve to Gergen, David Gergen Files, box 2, Folder: Campaign—General Strategy, GRFL.

48. Gerald Ford, Remarks and a Question-and-Answer Session with Members of the Pittsburgh Economic Club in Pittsburgh, Pennsylvania, October 26, 1976, *American Presidency Project,* http://www.presidency.ucsb.edu/ws/?pid=6539.

49. Gerald Ford, Remarks upon Receiving the Golden Helmet Award from the American Veterans of World War II, October 19, 1976, *American Presidency Project,* http://www.presidency.ucsb.edu/ws/?pid=6488.

50. Gerald Ford, The President's News Conference, October 14, 1976, *American Presidency Project,* http://www.presidency.ucsb.edu/ws/?pid=6462.

51. Greene, *The Presidency of Gerald R. Ford,* 37–52.

52. David W. Belin to the President, "Projecting Leadership and Statesmanship—Some Major Opportunities," February 13, 1976, 5–6, box 36, Folder: Presidential Handwriting File, Political Affairs—Ford (3), GRFL.

53. See, e.g., Presidential Campaign Debate, September 23, 1976, *American Presidency Project,* http://www.presidency.ucsb.edu/ws/index.php?pid=29404.

54. Robert M. Teeter quoted in Moore and Fraser, *Campaign for President,* 118. See also Jules Witcover, *Marathon: The Pursuit of the Presidency, 1972–1976* (New York: Signet, 1977), 564; and James A. Baker III with Steve Fiffer, *Work Hard, Study . . . and Keep Out of Politics: Adventures and Lessons from an Unexpected Public Life* (New York: Putnam's, 2006), 39.

55. Gergen to Cheney, August 10, 1976, Connor Files, box 7, Folder: Campaign—Planning 1976; Van Cleve to Gergen, Subject: Politics and the Presidency, July 1, 1976, Gergen Files, box 2, Folder: Campaign—General Strategy.

56. See Gergen to Cheney and Mike Duval, September 18, 1976, Raoul-Duval Papers, box 31, Folder: Strategy; and Opening Comments by Edwin Newman, Presidential Campaign Debate, September 23, 1976.

57. See Robert Scheer, "*Playboy* Interview, Nov. 1976," in *Conversations with Carter,* ed. Don Richardson (Boulder, CO: Lynne Reiner, 1998), 58.

58. "Carter on the Vietnam War," Note by Gergen [?], n.d., Gergen Files, box 17, Folder: Debate Background—Vietnam War.

59. David W. Belin, "The Election of President Ford," September 7, 1976, esp. 8–9, Raoul-Duval Papers, box 12, Folder: Belin, David—Strategy Papers; Belin to President, October 1, 1976, White House Central Files, Subject Files, box 14, Folder: PL/Ford (Exec.) 11/18–24/76, GRFL.

60. Van Cleve to Gergen, Subject: Destroying Carter's Credibility: Stage One, July 1, 1976, Gergen Files, box 2, Folder: Campaign—General Strategy. For a discussion of Carter's foreign policy advisers, see Betty Glad, *An Outsider in the White House: Jimmy Carter, His Advisors, and the Making of the American Foreign Policy* (Ithaca, NY: Cornell University Press, 2009), 7–40.

61. Van Cleve to Gergen, July 5, 1976, Raoul-Duval Papers, box 13, Folder: Campaign Strategy—Suggestions (2).

62. Gerald Ford, Presidential Campaign Debate, October 6, 1976.

63. Press Conference by Richard B. Cheney et al., October 6, 1976, Raoul-Duval Papers, box 17, Folder: Press Conferences—Campaign Advisers. See also Frederick Steeper, "The Public's Response to Gerald Ford's Statements on Eastern Europe during the Debate," Market Opinion Research, Revised Version of Paper

Originally Given in May 1977, 23–24, Teeter Papers, box 62, Folder: Post Election Analysis Speeches and Reports (5).

64. Election of 1976, *American Presidency Project,* http://www.presidency.ucsb.edu/showelection.php?year=1976.

65. Notes from Fred Currier 1976 Post Election Speech at the Economic Club, n.d., Teeter Papers, box 62, Folder: Post Election Analysis—Speeches and Reports (3).

11

The Domestic Politics of War and Peace

Jimmy Carter, Ronald Reagan, and the Election of 1980

Robert Mason

On October 28, 1980, Jimmy Carter and Ronald Reagan met in Cleveland, Ohio, for the only presidential debate of the campaign between the two major-party candidates. Election Day was just a week away, and opinion polls suggested that both had a chance of victory. According to the latest Gallup poll, the president had moved ahead of the former California governor by 45 to 42 percent; the Louis Harris poll had the same numbers but Reagan ahead of Carter.[1] In both camps (especially the president's), there were aides who were not sure that participation in the debate was a wise move, but both candidates were confident in their ability to outperform their opponent.[2]

It would be Reagan whose confidence proved to be the more prescient. In his closing statement, he memorably pushed forward two key charges against Carter's record, one based on economic performance, and one involving foreign policy. "Are you better off than you were four years ago?" Reagan asked Americans. He alluded to inflation and mentioned unemployment—two pressing problems at home. He looked overseas as well: "Is America as respected throughout the world as it was? Do you feel that our security is as safe, that we're as strong as we were four years ago?" Just as memorably, in trying to advance one of his main arguments against Reagan—that Reagan was unlikely to be effective as president in maintaining peace—Carter had misfired, noting that he had asked his thirteen-year-old daughter Amy what "the most important issue" was; her response, the president said, was "nuclear weaponry and the control of nuclear arms."[3] Carter's supporters in the audience groaned; a panel of voters convened by the *New York Times* to discuss the debate erupted in laughter.[4]

At the polls a week later, Americans gave the victory to Reagan, unexpectedly by a landslide. In the popular vote, his margin over Carter was 50.8 to 41.0 percent; John B. Anderson, a disillusioned liberal Republican running as an independent, picked up 6.6 percent. Republican success in winning control of the Senate for the first time since 1952, together with gains in the House of Representatives, further encouraged the view that the 1980 elections marked a turn toward conservatism, perhaps even a realignment and the start of a new Republican-dominated era in American politics. This was an election in which foreign policy played a complex role, wrapped in perceptions of American decline. First, the background to the contest was a significant shift in public opinion on foreign policy, which became more supportive of interventionism. Second, the Carter years witnessed a conservative revitalization that was partly grounded in a critique of apparent decline. And, third, as the White House incumbent at a time of economic challenges, Carter saw foreign policy as presenting his most promising case for reelection. All these factors boosted the significance of foreign policy in the presidential contest even if the domestic dimension of decline—such as high unemployment and high inflation—probably retained more influence on the outcome. This did not amount to an electoral realignment, but it did signal a desire for a new direction both at home and overseas.

Foreign Policy in 1980

Election Day in 1980 was the one-year anniversary of a landmark event for the United States overseas. On November 4, 1979, a group of Iranian students took sixty-six Americans hostage at the US embassy in Tehran; a year later, as Americans went to the polls to choose among Carter, Reagan, and Anderson, fifty-two hostages remained in captivity. It was against the backdrop of the hostage crisis that the 1980 presidential campaign took place. The crisis at first fostered support for Jimmy Carter in a striking example of the rally-'round-the-flag effect but in time raised questions about his leadership.[5] Vividly and painfully exemplifying the limits of US power overseas, the hostage crisis fed a resurgence in patriotic sentiment. As they followed the events, "most [Americans]," the historian David Farber writes, "became increasingly certain of one thing: the United States had lost its way—economically, culturally, politically, and even militarily." Despite the political cynicism that had taken hold during the 1970s in the shadow of Vietnam and Watergate, "Americans demonstrated both a sometimes fierce, even xenophobic nationalism and an emotional bond to their fellow Americans held captive in Iran."[6]

As Farber's observation suggests, setbacks in foreign policy were far from the only aspect of the country's problems under debate during the 1980 campaign. The fortunes of the economy were especially salient. In real terms, family income on average was 5 percent lower in 1980 than it was on Carter's arrival in the White House.[7] Inflation was high (running at more than 12 percent for 1980), and so was unemployment (eight million), together generating the challenge of "stagflation"; in early 1980, the "misery index" that added together the inflation and the unemployment rates reached its highest level since 1932, before easing somewhat. Under Carter, moreover, the country had experienced "the highest interest rates since the Civil War," Reagan noted, and the prime rate stood at 15.5 percent on Election Day. Especially because of the energy crisis— which involved a new dependence on foreign oil and which Carter labeled "the moral equivalent of war"—these economic challenges had a foreign dimension.[8]

Despite the personal impact of stagflation for many Americans, foreign policy was frequently at the forefront of political debate in 1980. Reagan often observed: "What this Administration has done to the domestic economy is infinitesimal [compared] to what has been done on the international scene to this country of which we were once so proud."[9] Such charges promoted the significance of foreign policy, but Carter and his supporters also played an important role in this regard, believing that this was a debate that favored their cause. "Foreign policy was involved more prominently throughout the campaign than inflation," noted the scholar Jonathan Moore soon after the election, "and it played a more explicit role in the behavior of candidates and the media."[10] The economic challenges facing the United States nevertheless ensured that the salience of unemployment and inflation eclipsed that of foreign policy.[11] A Reagan aide remarked: "The media are more interested in [the war-and-peace issue] than the people themselves are."[12] Still, this is not to say that international questions were unimportant. A University of Michigan study of public opinion reported that, while 56 percent of voters said that the most important issue was the economy, almost one in three named defense as the most important issue—a much higher proportion than in 1976.[13] According to Stephen Hess and Michael Nelson, a survey of presidential elections from 1952 to 1984 suggests that the 1980 contest was one of three in which foreign policy played "a significant role in the electorate's decision process," even if nonforeign issues were more important.[14]

It was not only the hostage crisis that fed this concern about foreign policy; in December 1979, the Soviet Union invaded Afghanistan, creating a situation that Carter named "the most serious foreign-policy crisis since World War II."[15] In making such a comment, Carter succumbed to hyperbole, but the invasion's political consequences were indeed significant. "The invasion of Afghanistan and its political aftermath," notes the historian Julian Zelizer, "ended a decade-long quest among Democrats and moderate Republicans for a centrist national security agenda."[16] That quest had first, under Richard Nixon and then Gerald Ford, involved détente and a stress on negotiation with the Soviet Union; on the Democratic side, it then extended to Jimmy Carter's emphasis on human rights as a defining characteristic of American foreign policy after Vietnam. "The defeat of the center in national security politics during the 1970s," Zelizer concludes, "was a defining moment in the history of modern conservatism."[17] This moment had implications for party politics and for policy making; while divisions on foreign policy deepened within the Democratic Party, the decline of détente fostered new unity among Republicans.

The post-Vietnam years had been a period of transition in public opinion on foreign policy if also a period of public unconcern, relatively speaking, about international and defense matters.[18] The Vietnam War had generated wariness of and skepticism toward American intervention overseas, but the foreign policy challenges of the Carter years encouraged a shift from dovishness to hawkishness. Hostility toward the Soviet Union, concern about the Cold War standing of the United States, and support for higher spending on defense were all on the increase. Polls suggested, for example, that in 1973 only about one in five Americans held a highly unfavorable view of the Soviet Union, but the proportion was one in three by 1980. "By the time of the 1980 presidential election," the pollsters Daniel Yankelovich and Larry Kaagan noted, "fearing that America was losing control over its foreign affairs, voters were more than ready to exorcise the ghost of Vietnam and replace it with a new posture of American assertiveness."[19] When Carter's pollster Patrick Caddell conducted interview research about attitudes on arms limitation, he reported "a general concern" about foreign and defense questions: *Nothing in our structured quantitative research prepared us for the below surface anxiety and concern over these issues that the open end interviews revealed,*" he wrote.[20] Yet, although Carter's record in foreign policy and his management of the hostage crisis in particular fostered dissatisfaction with his administration, most Americans remained generally supportive of his measured and cautious approach to that crisis. An October poll, moreover, gave him a 53 to 52 percent edge over Reagan as the candidate "best able to keep us out of war."[21]

While the hostage crisis in Iran and the Soviet invasion of Afghanistan encouraged public concern about America's world standing, these developments did not initiate but merely confirmed a conservative trend in opinion on foreign policy that had been building during the second half of the 1970s. "For those who wish to argue that the 1980 election really was preceded by a shift to the right," writes the political scientist William G. Mayer, "attitudes about foreign policy must clearly rank as Exhibit A."[22] For Mayer, this evolution in public opinion is significant especially because a rightward shift is not similarly visible in other policy areas, such as economic/welfare issues and social issues. According to Gallup, the number of voters describing themselves as right of center was no higher in 1980 than in 1976, and Louis Harris noted a decline since 1968 in the number of self-identified conservatives.[23]

The Conservative Resurgence

Concerns about American weakness overseas, together with economic and cultural themes, helped inform the organizational and intellectual resurgence of conservatism during the 1970s. Staunch anticommunism had been a founding characteristic of modern American conservatism during the 1950s, and then Barry Goldwater's quest for the presidency in 1964 partly rested on a fundamental critique of existing Cold War policy—which his opponents (among Republicans as well as Democrats) branded, all too successfully, as dangerous and irresponsible. During the Nixon administration, conservative dissatisfaction with the policies of détente and especially with the opening to China was great enough that a group of leading figures on the Right supported an insurgent challenge, by Representative John Ashbrook of Ohio, to Nixon's renomination in 1972. Four years later, Ronald Reagan found that attacks on détente energized Republican support for his challenge to Gerald Ford for the presidential nomination more powerfully than did other issues.[24]

Among Reagan's most wounding attack lines targeting Ford in 1976 was one that questioned the administration's negotiations on the future of the Panama Canal Zone. "When it comes to the Canal," Reagan said, "we built it, we paid for it, it's ours, and we should tell [Panamanian dictator Omar] Torrijos and Company that we are going to keep it!" In November 1977, Richard Viguerie, a leading figure of the "New Right," called the question of the Canal treaty's ratification, somewhat hyperbolically, "the most electrifying issue conservatives have ever had."[25] New Right organizations energetically pursued an antiratification campaign that added 400,000 names to the lists that Viguerie maintained to support their signature tactic of direct mail. Anticommunism also mobilized conservative evangelicals and fundamentalists; criticizing the Strategic Arms Limitation Talks (SALT)—which led to the SALT II Treaty, signed in June 1979—Sandra Ostbyu of Christian Voice explained that this was a position that formed "part of our attitude toward godless communism."[26] The decline of détente and the foreign policy travails of the Carter administration not only buoyed the organizational revitalization of conservatism but also fostered unity on the Right both within and beyond the Republican Party. Whereas moderate Republicans had opposed Goldwater on Cold War policy and conservative Republicans had challenged Nixon on détente, a new degree of agreement was now visible.[27]

Grassroots mobilization in support of a conservative foreign policy alternative found voice when in 1978 the New Right supported challenges to congressional supporters of the Canal treaties, both in primaries and in general elections. This signature issue of a new conservatism in foreign policy apparently proved less powerful than its promoters claimed, however. It seemed significant only in Gordon Humphrey's defeat of Senator Tom McIntyre in New Hampshire and, later, in 1980, in John P. East's defeat of Senator Robert B. Morgan in North Carolina.[28] As the political scientist Byron Shafer notes, the presidency has more relevance to foreign policy than Congress does, and this institutional fact has consequences for electoral politics—diminishing the likelihood that a question of foreign policy shapes outcomes in congressional elections while maximizing its impact in contests for the White House.[29]

Among the sternest critics of Carter's foreign policy were neoconservatives. Neoconservatives were in most cases formerly loyal Democrats who now believed that, in the aftermath of Vietnam, the party was drifting toward a policy of weakness against the expansionist threat of communism. The Coalition for a Democratic Majority, established at the end of 1972 in the aftermath of Richard Nixon's landslide victory, sought to mobilize centrist Democrats against the "New Politics" associated with McGovern. While neoconservatism had first emerged mostly in criticism of Great Society liberalism at home, in the 1970s neoconservatives increasingly concentrated on foreign policy. The historian Justin Vaïsse identifies a fivefold agenda that pushed them to dissent during the Carter years, despite the post–Afghan invasion turn to toughness: to defend democracy; to promote human rights; to assert America's military power; to support Israel; and to attach less significance to multilateralism and the United Nations. This led to what Vaïsse labels a "'migration' to the right," against Carter and in support of Reagan on foreign policy, within neoconservatism. Neoconservatives did not necessarily voice this support publicly, and some would return to the Democratic fold, but the transition was consequential in the long term for conservatism and for the Republican Party's approach to foreign policy.[30] Although neoconservative dissatisfaction with Carter was an elite response to trends within the Democratic Party, in fashioning an appeal to a wider public Reagan harnessed the claim that the administration—"dominated . . . by the McGovernite wing of the party"—had turned away from Democratic Party tradition. "I do not believe," he said, "this administration's defense policies are representative of the thinking of millions of rank-and-file Democratic Party members."[31]

Yet the new conservatism carried dangers as well as advantages. The ardent anticommunism that inspired conservative activism threatened to alienate voters of a more moderate stripe. As he prepared his presidential campaign, Ronald Reagan was careful to restrain his rhetoric; in mid-1979, the *New York Times* noted that he offered "a calm, reasoned, and even dull speech."[32] The goal to avoid an extremist tag animated the Reagan campaign. Reagan's pollster Richard Wirthlin wrote in March 1980: "We must position the Governor, in these early stages, so that he is viewed as less dangerous in the foreign affairs area, more competent in the economic area, more compassionate on the domestic issues and less of a conservative zealot than his opponents and the press now paint him to be."[33] On the campaign trail, Reagan projected a message of "peace through strength" that synthesized the case for military buildup with the claim that such policies made war less likely, not more likely.[34] A study by Kiron K. Skinner, Serhiy Kudelia, Bruce Bueno de Mesquita, and Condoleezza Rice concludes that Reagan's message posed a challenge to existing assumptions of Cold War policy: "Reagan was campaigning on the radical notion that the American conventions of containment and deterrence were wrongheaded and had relegated the country to second-place status."[35] The Carter administration, Reagan said, was "totally oblivious" to Communist expansionism, offering a response "of weakness, inconsistency, vacillation and bluff." What he promised instead was a "prudent and measured" buildup of national defenses, alongside an emphasis on the need for negotiation with the Soviet Union.[36] He stressed, too, a commitment to "a balanced and equitable arms limitation agreement," which stronger defenses would facilitate: "The way to avoid an arms race is not simply to let the Soviets race ahead."[37]

Carter's Foreign Policy Challenges

If Reagan used his candidacy to advance an argument about Cold War policy, then the administration's difficult record shaped Jimmy Carter's quest to retain the White House. In 1979, Carter reached new depths of popularity, his Gallup ratings even worse than Richard Nixon's had been just before his resignation.[38] The focus of public dissatisfaction involved the country's economic travails—high unemployment, high inflation, high energy prices—together with the perception that Carter was a weak, ineffectual leader. Foreign policy was not, directly, a factor. Yet the CBS/*New York Times* poll only once reported majority approval of Carter's conduct of foreign policy, which was in response to the Camp David accords of September 1978.[39] Paradoxically, pollsters reported support for the constituent elements of Carter's foreign policy, including not only Middle East peace efforts but also talks on arms limitation with the Soviet Union, increases in defense spending, and diplomatic recognition of China. Connected with this dissatisfaction was a widespread belief that America's standing in the world was poor and weakening.[40] Believing that the Democrats' old New Deal coalition was crumbling, Carter thought that conservative aspects of his agenda, including increased spending on defense, might complement its liberal aspects, including arms control and his human rights focus, and offer "hopes of building upon the old Democratic coalition and broadening it somewhat."[41]

Carter's response to foreign policy challenges delivered electoral benefits in boosting his ability to withstand a challenge to his renomination from Senator Edward M. Kennedy of Massachusetts. Formally launching his candidacy just two days after the seizure of the hostages, Kennedy first experienced difficulty in criticizing Carter, who was initially the beneficiary of a significant rally-'round-the-flag effect. When, in early December, Kennedy questioned Carter's decision to allow Mohammad Reza Pahlavi, the deposed shah, to enter the United States for medical treatment, the public response was hostile. Carter announced that he would not engage in nomination politics and instead concentrate on his White House duties; while initially the results were beneficial in boosting his ratings for presidential leadership, over time, as overseas crises and domestic problems persisted and accumulated, the Kennedy challenge gained force. He won a series of states that included Michigan, New York, and Pennsylvania, adding, on the last day of primary season, California and New Jersey.[42] Even though Carter survived the Kennedy challenge, the wounds inflicted by party division were lasting. "My main handicap for re-election," Carter later said, "came from the liberal wing of the Democratic party"—mobilized by the Kennedy candidacy.[43] According to the Carter aide Hamilton Jordan, that candidacy "was the single critical factor in [Carter's] defeat."[44]

The challenges in foreign policy that Carter faced encouraged him to move away from his stress on human rights and toward an emphasis on toughness. Soon after the Afghan invasion, he withdrew the controversy-beset SALT II agreement from Senate consideration. Then, in

July 1980, he signed Presidential Directive 59 (PD-59), which called for a buildup in nuclear arms and sought to replace the doctrine of mutually assured destruction that had long informed the country's nuclear policy as a response to the Soviet Union's enhanced ability to engage in limited warfare against military targets. Soviet officials interpreted PD-59 as one among other developments signaling a new era of confrontation in the Cold War; at home, some saw it as a political response to the charge in the Republican platform that administration policy offered "a Hobson's choice between mass mutual suicide and surrender."[45] Even though the president now supported increased spending on defense, a position in line with public sentiment, many believed that he did not—exemplifying the depth of the perception that he was weak on defense.[46]

An incumbent's bid for reelection usually relies on, most of all, a referendum on the record. Because voters saw the president's record as weak, the Carter campaign sought to define the contest not as a referendum but as a choice between two candidacies, stressing that the Republican challenger was unqualified for the White House. The effort to place Reagan's putative inadequacies at the heart of the campaign often involved foreign policy because this was potentially the most wounding attack on his qualifications to be president. Although Carter's response to overseas crises had boosted his standing, by summer 1980 this hardly represented a strong argument for his reelection. "To the public," Caddell noted in June, "American foreign policy appears in disarray—the hostages are still captive, the Russians seem on the move and while there is a deep apprehension over armed conflict, a sense of political and military decline pervades the public mood."[47] Polls conducted after the Republican national convention in July gave Reagan a two-to-one edge over Carter.[48] Yet, if Carter succeeded in pushing Reagan on the defensive over the issue of peace and war as "the central issue of the campaign, the guy loses big," an aide said in September—by which time Carter had taken the lead.[49] Surveying presidential contests between 1956 and 1988, the political scientist John Kenneth White notes that Carter's success in achieving better poll ratings on foreign policy than his Republican rival was unusual for a Democrat during the Cold War era—an achievement bettered only by Lyndon Johnson in 1964.[50]

Carter's acceptance speech, at New York's Madison Square Garden in August, signaled the thrust of attack. He said that victory for Reagan posed "the risk of an uncontrollable, unaffordable, and unwinnable nuclear arms race" and an "alarming, even perilous destiny." On the campaign trail, he made the point yet more starkly, observing that the election "will help to decide *whether we have war or peace*," and noting that voters faced "an awesome choice."[51] Opening his campaign against Reagan on Labor Day in Tuscumba, Alabama, he connected the message with an effort to maintain the support of his native South. "We southerners believe in the nobility of courage on the battlefield," he said. "And because we understand the costs of war, we also believe in the nobility of peace."[52] Reagan's policies, he said in early October, were "an excellent way to lead our country toward war."[53] Carter claimed that Reagan showed a "repeated habit" of advocating American military intervention "when the obvious judgment made by [Carter himself] and by Nixon and Ford and Johnson and Kennedy and Eisenhower and Truman has been to avoid conflicts."[54] Complementing this "trigger-happy" charge was the claim that, as president, Reagan would also foment division at home.[55]

The aggression of Carter's anti-Reagan rhetoric seemed counterproductive, precipitating a charge of meanness, and helping undermine the positive personal evaluations that were among his strengths. According to Reagan, Carter was "reaching a point of hysteria that is hard to understand"; he said that he "was deeply saddened . . . that the President would stoop so low." According to Richard Wirthlin: "If we had tried to use our advertising to depict him as dishonest and mean, we could not have done the job he did on himself."[56] Yet Carter seemed to have few other options; fostering doubt about Reagan on foreign policy was a key strand of his strategy. Nevertheless, when leading Carter surrogates had attempted to carry the message, the efforts had secured little attention and therefore had had little impact. While the meanness charge elicited a pledge from Carter that he would speak "with more reticence" in future, opinion polls suggested that the strategy was hitting its target, despite some cost for popular evaluations of the president.[57] According to polls, by mid-October Carter had won back support among skeptical Democratic and independent voters to achieve parity in the race with Reagan. Not only had his attack impetus fostered concerns about Reagan's ability to maintain peace, but it was also apparently hindering his effort to reap the electoral advantage of dissatisfaction with the state of the economy.[58] "The suburban mommies don't want their little boys to go to war, so they won't vote for Reagan," said one Democrat.[59] Exemplifying such opinion, a woman in the Detroit suburbs commented: "Reagan might end the recession real fast, but we'd be in World War III quickly."[60]

Confronting the Reagan campaign, Richard Wirthlin noted, was "the perceptual dilemma that large numbers of voters now wrestle with": "On the one hand, Reagan would be a strong and decisive leader in foreign affairs (which 'we' applaud), but on the other hand, he would be too quick to push the nuclear button (which 'we' fear and abhor)." He counseled a stress on peace.[61] As the New York Times journalist Hedrick Smith noted, the campaign sought to project Reagan as a pragmatic, "compassionate" Republican, as "strong but not trigger-happy, firm but not belligerent, positive but not divisive, calm but in command."[62] In his acceptance speech, Reagan emphasized peace alongside an attack on the administration's record. "Never before in our history have Americans been called upon to face three grave threats to our very existence, any one of which could destroy us," he said. "We face a disintegrating economy, a weakened defense and an energy policy based on the sharing of scarcity." He added: "Today, a great many who trusted Mr. Carter wonder if we can survive the Carter policies of national defense."[63]

A series of missteps and gaffes threatened to reinforce Carter's case that Reagan lacked presidential ability. Notably, before the Veterans of Foreign Wars convention in August, he referred to the Vietnam War as a "noble cause." Hindsight suggests that the phrase astutely connected with a desire to recover pride in the American mission, yet contemporaries usually saw the comment as "an attempt to open up national wounds that had scarcely healed," as the journalists Jules Witcover and Jack Germond observed.[64] The impetus of the Carter campaign, as notably exemplified by its commercials, sought to push home the advantages of incumbency and the doubts about Reagan by emphasizing the weighty responsibilities of the White House and the responsibility for nuclear warfare in particular. According to the Reagan aide Lyn Nofziger: "We're running against Carter on the economy, and we're trying to make Reagan into a man of peace."[65] That strategy achieved perhaps its greatest success during the television debate with Carter. "Reagan mentioned 'peace' so often it sounded like he had invented the word," wrote the journalist Lou Cannon.[66]

After the debate, Reagan's poll ratings improved, but volatility remained a characteristic of the campaign. This was a campaign in which many Americans fixed their voting choice at an unusually late point in the campaign; the Gallup postelection poll suggested that as many as 37 percent made their decision during the last week, and for one in ten this was on Election Day itself.[67] The last days of the campaign were especially volatile when, in the aftermath of the Carter-Reagan debate, there was a potential breakthrough in the quest to secure the release of the hostages. The columnist William Safire, supportive of the Republicans, stingingly wrote that Iran's leader, Ayatollah Khomeini—"the religious fanatic who hates us all"—"has cast his vote for Jimmy Carter, seeking to swing the US election to a man he knows he can continue to control."[68] Carter believed that this was a crucial moment. "Now my political future might well be determined by irrational people on the other side of the world over whom I had no control," he wrote in his memoirs. "If the hostages were released, I was convinced my reelection would be assured; if the expectations of the American people were dashed again, there was little chance that I could win."[69] Caddell's polling for Carter supported the view that end-of-campaign events proved crucial in the defeat: "The debate aftermath and the reentrance of the hostages issue focused critical attention on the Carter administration, specifically, for many previous uncertain voters, on economic management."[70] The effort to escape a referendum on the administration's overall performance through a foreign policy–oriented campaign, especially focusing on Reagan's deficiencies, had failed. In the Reagan camp, Wirthlin agreed that the election represented a referendum on Carter's record, especially with respect to the economy, though he disagreed that the president had a chance to win reelection until the breakthrough in the hostage crisis proved abortive.[71] Reagan aides had nevertheless long feared that an "October Surprise"—resolving the hostage crisis—might ruin their candidate's chances.[72]

It was not only the fast-moving events of the campaign year that lent volatility to the Carter-Reagan contest. A key reason for this volatility was the failure of both Carter and Reagan to inspire much enthusiasm among many voters. "The 1980 presidential election," noted the political scientist Thomas Cronin, "is being treated as almost as unwelcome an event as the attack on Pearl Harbor."[73] Gallup reported that, in October, just 23 percent of poll respondents had a "highly favorable" opinion of Reagan and that Carter's favorability rating was little better, at 30 percent. According to a Roper postelection poll, only 21 percent of Carter voters and 43 percent of Reagan voters reported "a good deal of enthusiasm" for their candidate.[74]

Supporting the views of Caddell and Wirthlin, pollsters for the candidates, most analysis of the 1980 presidential election emphasizes dissatisfaction with the Carter record as the key factor explaining Reagan's victory. Such analysis, moreover, usually attributes more electoral power to economic factors than to issues of foreign policy. This is not to suggest, however, that ideas about foreign policy did not distinguish Reagan voters from Carter voters. The *New York Times* exit poll found that a majority of respondents favored a tougher line against the Soviet Union, even if increasing the risk of war; of this group, 70 percent voted for Ronald Reagan, while Carter had a 64 percent share of the minority that disagreed.[75] Moreover, polls suggested that voters perceived greater differences between Carter and Reagan on foreign issues than on domestic issues.[76] Modeling presidential approval ratings between 1977 and 1987, the political scientists Miroslav Nincic and Barbara Hinckley assert that a 1 percent increase in a president's overall rating was the product of a 1.5 percent increase in approval on economic policy and of a 3 percent increase in approval on foreign policy. This is a conclusion that acknowledges the greater impact of public opinion on the economy but nevertheless underlines the significance of foreign policy in influencing a president's popularity. As a result, according to Nincic and Hinckley, most observers "underestimated the impact of foreign policy evaluations, which we now see was sizable." They furthermore note that the hostage issue was more likely to influence Carter's approval ratings among Democratic supporters, whereas, for Republican and independent voters, relations with the Soviet Union were more important.[77] Another study in political science, by John H. Aldrich, John L. Sullivan, and Eugene Borgida, similarly concludes that the existence of large differences on foreign policy between the candidates coincided with a context of high salience for such issues in 1980, overall generating a large effect on the election.[78]

Conclusion

The 1980 election results showed that Carter's effort to hold together the Democratic coalition had failed, though his success in remaining competitive through the campaign and sometimes in achieving a lead in the polls was an impressive achievement, given that the context for the incumbent was the least promising since Herbert Hoover sought reelection in 1932.[79] Perhaps the most notable demographic shift in voting behavior was one for which foreign policy seemed important: the movement of men toward the Republican Party.[80] The 1980 presidential election marked the emergence of the modern gender gap in American politics, sometimes interpreted then as a transient phenomenon, but soon consolidated as an enduring aspect of electoral behavior; the CBS/*New York Times* exit poll reported that 56 percent of male voters but only 47 percent of female voters supported Reagan.[81] It was a trend that had been noticed during the campaign, inviting strategic responses. Reagan pledged to nominate the first female Supreme Court justice, a pledge designed to tackle the gender disparity in support that opinion polls were revealing.[82] Carter's pollster Pat Caddell identified "human issues—peace, human rights, women's rights, justice for minorities"—as "'*feminine*' *issues*," and he argued that they involved an area of strength for the president; conversely, "*a perceived lack of Presidential decisiveness on masculine issues*" was a weakness.[83] Two sets of issues seemed important in explaining Reagan's relative lack of appeal among women; the first involved antifeminism, epitomized by the party's failure to embrace a platform commitment to the Equal Rights Amendment, and the second involved his warmonger image.[84] Yet analysis of exit polling downplayed the former in favor of the latter, suggesting that issues of war and peace primarily informed the appearance of the gender gap.[85] Such an insight was in line with earlier manifestations of gender disparities in voting that had involved greater support among women for Republican candidacies, often connected with foreign policy and defense.[86] This was probably, at least in part, a misperception; aides in the Reagan White House soon concluded that views on the economy and the welfare state as well as on foreign policy informed the gender gap.[87] In summer 1982, Richard Wirthlin noted that approval ratings for Reagan's foreign policy were at 62 percent among men but just 45 percent among women, but he subsequently discovered both that the gender gap seemed volatile and that the contribution of foreign policy, as distinct from other issues and concerns, was relatively minor.[88]

More broadly, the Reagan years saw the revitalization of the Republican Party. Even if Reagan did not succeed in mobilizing enduringly an electoral majority in support of his party, Republicans achieved what Wirthlin labeled "parity" status with the Democrats.[89] Reagan pursued military buildup, increasing spending on defense while making cuts elsewhere, but he also pursued negotiation with the Soviet Union, proving to be more pragmatic than his tough words sometimes suggested. "While the Iran-Contra scandal and several of the Reagan administration's other adventures in the third world, as well as the massive deficits accrued by the herculean defense buildup, gave liberal critics ample ammunition for battling Reagan's conservative national security legacy, the American public, by and large, believed in Reagan's big picture: America was the world's 'indispensable' superpower," writes David Farber. Moreover, Farber adds: "Reagan's presidency gave conservatives a national security platform they were thrilled to build on."[90] Reagan's America, furthermore, involved a celebration of patriotism, perhaps especially evident at the Los Angeles Olympics of 1984 and in Reagan's reelection campaign.[91] Foreign policy contributed to Reagan's popularity as president.[92] Yet the rightward trend in public opinion on foreign policy of the late 1970s did not last long. "The *trend* in foreign policy attitudes," notes William Mayer, "was clearly in a liberal direction through most of the 1980s." The Reagan years witnessed a decline in the proportion of Americans who saw the Soviet Union as enjoying military superiority, and support for more spending on defense declined. It is a trend that can be interpreted as a signal of public support for the Reagan agenda on the Cold War in tackling the insecurities of the late 1970s.[93]

The election of 1980, then, was a watershed in American politics, marking the rejection of Jimmy Carter rather than an electoral embrace of Ronald Reagan and the Republican Party. During that election year, foreign policy often dominated the headlines, yet the electoral salience of hard times still eclipsed that of overseas challenges. Even though public opinion on foreign policy was moving rightward, especially under the shock of "America's first encounter with radical Islam" and an apparent advance by the Soviet Union in the Cold War, the president saw a foreign policy–grounded appeal as offering his best chance of retaining the White House.[94] Yet Reagan managed to escape the effort to cast him as a dangerously trigger-happy conservative, in the mold of Barry Goldwater, on his road to victory.

Notes

1. Adam Clymer, "Carter and Reagan to Meet Tonight in Debate That Could Decide Race," *New York Times,* October 28, 1980, A1, A24.

2. Elizabeth Drew, *Portrait of an Election: The 1980 Presidential Campaign* (New York: Simon & Schuster, 1981), 311–12.

3. Jack W. Germond and Jules Witcover, *Blue Smoke and Mirrors: How Reagan Won and Why Carter Lost the Election of 1980* (New York: Viking, 1981), 281, 280.

4. Lou Cannon, "Reagan Blasts Carter for 'Ineptitude' as He Seeks to Avoid Any of His Own," *Washington Post,* October 31, 1980, A2; Bernard Weinraub, "Area Panel's Scorecard on the Debate," *New York Times,* October 30, 1980, B20.

5. One analysis of forty-one foreign policy crises between the 1950s and the mid-1980s quantified the hostage crisis as being one among four that exhibited the greatest rallying effect, in terms of its impact on presidential approval. John R. Oneal and Anna Lillian Bryan, "The Rally 'round the Flag Effect in U.S. Foreign Policy Crises, 1950–1985," *Political Behavior* 17, no. 4 (1995): 379–401.

6. David Farber, *Taken Hostage: The Iran Hostage Crisis and America's First Encounter with Radical Islam* (Princeton, NJ: Princeton University Press, 2005), 2, 152.

7. Gerald M. Pomper, "The Presidential Election," in *The Election of 1980: Reports and Interpretations,* by Gerald M. Pomper et al. (Chatham, NJ: Chatham House, 1981), 65–96, 76.

8. Henry A. Plotkin, "Issues in the Presidential Campaign," in Pomper et al., *The Election of 1980,* 38–64, 39, 42–51; Walter Dean Burnham, "The 1980 Earthquake: Realignment, Reaction, or What?" in *The Hidden Election: Politics and Economics in the 1980 Presidential Campaign,* ed. Thomas Ferguson and Joel Rogers (New York: Pantheon, 1981), 98–140, 107; "Reagan: 'Working Together We Can Make America Great . . . Again,'" *Washington Post,* October 12, 1980, A2.

9. Howell Raines, "Reagan Seeks to Stress Arms Issue without Seeming 'Trigger-Happy,'" *New York Times,* June 2, 1980, B10.

10. Jonathan Moore, ed., *The Campaign for President: 1980 in Retrospect* (Cambridge, MA: Ballinger, 1981), xii.

11. Warren E. Miller and J. Merrill Shanks, "Policy Directions and Presidential Leadership: Alternative Interpretations of the 1980 Presidential Election," *British Journal of Political Science* 12, no. 3 (1982): 299–356, 317–18.

12. Drew, *Portrait of an Election,* 321.

13. Kiron K. Skinner, Serhiy Kudelia, Bruce Bueno de Mesquita, and Condoleezza Rice, *The Strategy of Campaigning: Lessons from Ronald Reagan and Boris Yeltsin* (Ann Arbor: University of Michigan Press, 2007), 202.

14. Stephen Hess and Michael Nelson, "Foreign Policy: Dominance and Decisiveness in Presidential Elections," in *The Elections of 1984,* ed. Michael Nelson (Washington, DC: Congressional Quarterly Press, 1985), 129–54, 143. The other two contests were 1952 and 1972.

15. Drew, *Portrait of an Election,* 52.

16. Julian E. Zelizer, "Conservatives, Carter, and the Politics of National Security," in *Rightward Bound: Making America Conservative in the 1970s,* ed. Bruce J. Schulman and Julian E. Zelizer (Cambridge, MA: Harvard University Press, 2008), 265–87, 265.

17. Zelizer, "Conservatives," 286.

18. John H. Aldrich, John L. Sullivan, and Eugene Borgida, "Foreign Affairs and Issue Voting: Do Presidential Candidates 'Waltz Before a Blind Audience?'" *American Political Science Review* 83, no. 1 (1989): 123–41, 131.

19. Daniel Yankelovich and Larry Kaagan, "Assertive America," *Foreign Affairs* 59 (1980): 696–713, 696.

20. Andrew Z. Katz, "Public Opinion and the Contradictions of Jimmy Carter's Foreign Policy," *Presidential Studies Quarterly* 30, no. 4 (2000): 662–87, 679.

21. Everett Carll Ladd, "The Brittle Mandate: Electoral Dealignment and the 1980 Presidential Election," *Political Science Quarterly* 96, no. 1 (1981): 1–25, 23.

22. William G. Mayer, *The Changing American Mind: How and Why American Public Opinion Changed between 1960 and 1988* (Ann Arbor: University of Michigan Press, 1992), 45–72, 45.

23. Stanley Kelley Jr., *Interpreting Elections* (Princeton, NJ: Princeton University Press, 1983), 185.

24. Robert Mason, *Richard Nixon and the Quest for a New Majority* (Chapel Hill: University of North Carolina Press, 2004), 137–39, 219–23.

25. Richard A. Viguerie, *The New Right: We're Ready to Lead* (1980), rev. ed. (Falls Church, VA: Viguerie, 1981), 65.

26. Daniel K. Williams, *God's Own Party: The Making of the Christian Right* (New York: Oxford University Press, 2010), 167.

27. Sandra Scanlon, "Building Consensus: The Republican Right and Foreign Policy, 1960–1980," in *Seeking a New Majority: The Republican Party and American Politics, 1960–1980,* ed. Robert Mason and Iwan Morgan (Nashville: Vanderbilt University Press, 2013), 143–59, 154–56.

28. Robert Mason, "Foreign Policy and the Republican Quest for a New Majority," in ibid., 160–78, 173.

29. Byron E. Shafer, "The Notion of an Electoral Order: The Structure of Electoral Politics at the Accession of George Bush," in *The End of Realignment? Interpreting American Electoral Eras,* ed. Byron E. Shafer (Madison: University of Wisconsin Press, 1991), 37–84, 48–51.

30. Justin Vaïsse, *Neoconservatism: The Biography of a Movement,* trans. Arthur Goldhammer (Cambridge, MA: Belknap Press of Harvard University Press, 2010), 86, 96–147, 180–86 (quotation 180).

31. "Reagan: 'Working Together We Can Make America Great . . . Again.'"

32. Skinner, Kudelia, Bueno de Mesquita, and Rice, *Strategy of Campaigning,* 141.

33. Drew, *Portrait of an Election,* 353.

34. Douglas E. Kneeland, "Reagan Calls Peace His First Objective in Address to Nation," *New York Times,* October 20, 1980, A1, D10.

35. Skinner, Kudelia, Bueno de Mesquita, and Rice, *Strategy of Campaigning,* 140.

36. Lou Cannon, "Reagan: 'Peace through Strength,'" *Washington Post,* August 19, 1980, A1, A4.

37. Kneeland, "Reagan Calls Peace His First Objective," D10.

38. Austin Ranney, "The Carter Administration," in *The American Elections of 1980,* ed. Austin Ranney (Washington, DC: American Enterprise Institute for Public Policy Research, 1981), 1–36, 30.

39. Katz, "Public Opinion," 663–64.

40. Burton I. Kaufman and Scott Kaufman, *The Presidency of James Earl Carter Jr.,* 2nd ed., rev. (Lawrence: University Press of Kansas, 2006), 185.

41. Interview with Jimmy Carter, November 29, 1982, 45–46 (quotation 46), Carter Presidency Project, Miller Center, University of Virginia, web1.millercenter.org/poh/transcripts/ohp_1982_1129_carter.pdf.

42. Peter G. Bourne, *Jimmy Carter: A Comprehensive Biography from Plains to Postpresidency* (New York: Scribner, 1997), 456–62.

43. Interview with Jimmy Carter, 44.

44. Interview with Hamilton Jordan, with Landon Butler and Thomas Donilon, November 6, 1981, 81, Carter Presidency Project, web1.millercenter.org/poh/transcripts/ohp_1981_1106_jordan.pdf.

45. Zelizer, "Conservatives," 282–84; Kaufman and Kaufman, *The Presidency of James Earl Carter Jr.,* 220–21 (quotation 221).

46. Martin P. Wattenberg, *The Rise of Candidate-Centered Politics: Presidential Elections of the 1980s* (Cambridge, MA: Harvard University Press, 1991), 111.

47. Drew, *Portrait of an Election,* 389.

48. Ladd, "Brittle Mandate," 8.

49. Edward Walsh, "Carter to Return to 'Peace or War' Issue," *Washington Post,* September 28, 1980, A2; Ladd, "Brittle Mandate," 8.

50. John Kenneth White, *Still Seeing Red: How the Cold War Shapes the New American Politics* (1997), updated and expanded ed. (Boulder, CO: Westview, 1998), 144.

51. Germond and Witcover, *Blue Smoke and Mirrors,* 250, 244.

52. Walsh, "Carter to Return to 'Peace or War' Issue."

53. Skinner, Kudelia, Bueno de Mesquita, and Rice, *Strategy of Campaigning,* 190.

54. Terence Smith, "Carter Reiterates Doubt about Reagan," *New York Times,* September 24, 1980, A26; Hedrick Smith, "Examining What President Says on Reagan and War," *New York Times,* October 28, 1980, A24.

55. James Reston, "Carter's Curious Campaign," *New York Times,* October 8, 1980, A27.

56. Howell Raines, "Reagan's Camp Sees Carter as His Own Worst Enemy," *New York Times,* October 12, 1980, 32.

57. Germond and Witcover, *Blue Smoke and Mirrors,* 262.

58. Hedrick Smith, "Poll Shows President Has Pulled to Even Position with Reagan," *New York Times,* October 23, 1980, A1, B14.

59. Rowland Evans and Robert Novak, "'Antidote' for Reaganemia," *Washington Post,* October 29, 1980, A23.

60. Rowland Evans and Robert Novak, "'Meanness' Backlash," *Washington Post,* October 13, 1980, A19.

61. Drew, *Portrait of an Election,* 374–75.

62. Hedrick Smith, "At Center Stage, Reagan Takes His Biggest Role," *New York Times,* July 14, 1980, A9.

63. "Text of Reagan's Speech Accepting the Republicans' Nomination," *New York Times,* July 18, 1980, A8.

64. Germond and Witcover, *Blue Smoke and Mirrors,* 214.

65. Theodore H. White, *The Transformation of American Politics: The Making of the President, 1956–1980* (New York: Harper & Row, 1982), 395.

66. Lou Cannon, *Reagan* (New York: Putnam's, 1982), 295.

67. Ladd, "Brittle Mandate," 9.

68. William Safire, "Stealing an Election?" *New York Times,* November 3, 1980, A23.

69. Jimmy Carter, *Keeping Faith: Memoirs of a President* (London: Collins, 1982), 565–66.

70. Patrick H. Caddell, "The Democratic Strategy and Its Electoral Consequences," in *Party Coalitions in the 1980s,* ed. Seymour Martin Lipset (San Francisco: Institute for Contemporary Studies, 1981), 267–303, 272.

71. "Reagan Pollster Says Carter's Leadership Was Key Issue," *New York Times,* November 6, 1980, A26.

72. Dick Wirthlin with Wynton C. Hall, *The Greatest Communicator: What Ronald Reagan Taught Me about Politics, Leadership, and Life* (Hoboken, NJ: Wiley, 2004), 70–73.

73. Thomas E. Cronin, "Our Hate Affairs with the Candidates," *Los Angeles Times,* November 4, 1980, C5.

74. Ladd, "Brittle Mandate," 5, 7. In the Gallup poll, no pair of major-party candidates had been rated more weakly since 1952, when Gallup started to ask the question.

75. Burnham, "1980 Earthquake," 123.

76. Aldrich, Sullivan, and Borgida, "Foreign Affairs and Issue Voting," 132.

77. Miroslav Nincic and Barbara Hinckley, "Foreign Policy and the Evaluation of Presidential Candidates," *Journal of Conflict Resolution* 35, no. 2 (1991): 333–55, 341–47 (quotation 347).

78. Aldrich, Sullivan, and Borgida, "Foreign Affairs and Issue Voting," 135–36.

79. Andrew E. Busch, *Reagan's Victory: The Presidential Election of 1980 and the Rise of the Right* (Lawrence: University Press of Kansas, 2005), 127–28; Cheryl Hudson and Gareth Davies, "Reagan and the 1980s," in *Ronald Reagan and the 1980s:*

Perceptions, Policies, Legacies, ed. Cheryl Hudson and Gareth Davies (New York: Palgrave Macmillan, 2008), 1–15, 5.

80. While contemporary discussion of the gender gap usually focused on the voting behavior of women as unusual, it was in the voting behavior of men that change was more visible. Louis Bolce, "The Role of Gender in Recent Presidential Elections: Reagan and the Reverse Gender Gap," *Presidential Studies Quarterly* 15 (1985): 372–85.

81. Ladd, "Brittle Mandate," 15; Jane J. Mansbridge, "Myth and Reality: The ERA and the Gender Gap in the 1980 Election," *Public Opinion Quarterly* 49, no. 2 (1985): 164–78, 165.

82. Douglas E. Kneeland, "The Republican Defends Stance on Equal Rights and War Accusations," *New York Times,* October 15, 1980, A1, A24.

83. Drew, *Portrait of an Election,* 419, 433–34.

84. Edward Walsh, "Reagan Is Still the Women's Second Choice," *New York Times,* October 16, 1980, A1, A3.

85. Kathleen A. Frankovic, "Sex and Politics—New Alignments, Old Issues," *PS* 15, no. 3 (1982): 439–48.

86. Robert Mason, *The Republican Party and American Politics from Hoover to Reagan* (New York: Cambridge University Press, 2012), 95, 179.

87. Memo, Adis M. Vila to Elizabeth H. Dole, October 22, 1982, "Women—Gender Gap (2)," box 77, Elizabeth H. Dole Files, Ronald Reagan Presidential Library, Simi Valley, CA.

88. Memo, Richard B. Wirthlin to Edwin Meese III, July 15, 1982, "Polling Data—1982 (1)," box 45, and memo, Richard B. Wirthlin to Ron Hinckley, November 12, 1982, "Women—Gender Gap (2)," box 77, Dole Files.

89. Mason, *The Republican Party and American Politics,* 247–81.

90. David Farber, *The Rise and Fall of Modern American Conservatism: A Short History* (Princeton, NJ: Princeton University Press, 2010), 206.

91. Gil Troy, *Morning in America: How Ronald Reagan Invented the 1980s* (Princeton, NJ: Princeton University Press, 2005), 147–74.

92. Clyde Wilcox and Dee Allsop, "Economic and Foreign Policy as Sources of Reagan Support," *Western Political Quarterly* 44, no. 4 (1991): 941–58.

93. Mayer, *Changing American Mind,* 45–73 (quotation 62).

94. The phrase is David Farber's. It is the subtitle of Farber, *Taken Hostage.*

12

1984, Regional Crises, and Morning in America

The Predawn of the Reagan Era

David Ryan

In the election of 1984, the economy was very important as the country emerged from the recessionary years of the early 1980s, but foreign policy issues also played a crucial role. Primarily, the Reagan administration had to change the image of the Cold Warrior in US culture. By late 1983, Americans were worried about the hard-line aspects of Reagan's character. They feared that he just might be the candidate who would act on his aggressive rhetoric and get the United States involved in a regional conflict or that he might press the Soviet Union too hard. His campaigners were keen to defuse the negative aspects of his foreign policy. The year 1984 would be recast as one of peace, with Reagan as the candidate of peace and constructive engagement. Yet one of Reagan's favorite issues, support for the contras in Nicaragua cut against this broader objective.

The year 1984 instantly evokes the dystopian novel by George Orwell and its infamous aphorism: "He who controls the past controls the future." For Reagan, the immediate objective was to secure a second term. As far as foreign policy issues were concerned, this meant that his warmongering image—which both attracted and repelled certain constituencies—had to be temporarily rewritten, the character recast. In 1985, at least insofar as the problematic issue of Nicaragua was concerned, Reagan was unleashed. The United States passed a national emergency in May because the Sandinistas posed an unusual and extraordinary threat to US foreign policy. The contras were canonized as the moral equivalent of the Founding Fathers, and Charles Krauthammer identified the putative Reagan Doctrine: to roll back left-wing governments around the world. But all this had to be muted in 1984.

The campaign also provided the administration with the opportunity to rejuvenate the metanarrative of US history and foreign policy. The campaign advertisement epitomized the theme of dawn, renewal, and a nostalgic return to a country of conservative certainty. "It's morning again in America," the voiceover related. More people would go to work, interest rates were half the record high of 1980, more would buy new homes, more would get married, inflation was low, the future could be viewed with a new confidence, the country was "prouder and stronger and better." There was little reason to return to the country of four years ago—to go back, it was implied but never stated, to the Carter years of stagflation, uncertainty, and malaise—as the new images of tractors, taxis and the paper boy, weddings and flags hoisted in backyards kindled a yearning for a contemporary iteration of Norman Rockwell's America.

This morning in America was juxtaposed not only against Carter but also against the nightmare of the Vietnam War. Reagan represented the new dawn. The narrative sought to transform the mood and confidence of the country.[1] Reagan, the dream catcher, had to neutralize two potential foreign policy nightmares that reawakened images and narratives of Vietnam: Nicaragua and Lebanon. Both invited memories and fears of another Vietnam.

The Reagan administration therefore crafted a set of atmospherics that tried to portray the president as taking reasonable steps, without appearing weak, toward a less belligerent stance toward the Soviet Union, China, and Nicaragua. In Lebanon, he was faced with recuperating after the Beirut bombings of the marine barracks in October 1983. The administration had deployed troops there as part of the multilateral peacekeeping initiative as a demonstration of an American presence, yet their vulnerable position also threatened the administration with unwanted negative stories in 1984 unless they were redeployed to safe locations—offshore, out of Beirut.

At a time when Reagan has moved through the proverbial canonization and into the company of the greats among US presidents, and at a time when the historiography has credited him with too much strategic foresight, another antidote is still necessary. After the Cold War scholars reinterpreted his presidency, Michael Schaller writes: "Reagan's once-ridiculed naiveté was recast as sincerity; his laziness presented as inner calm; his disinterest in details proof of his mastery of the big picture."[2] This chapter examines the negative influences of two regional crises on the prospects for Reagan's reelection. More, it examines the measures taken by the administration to offset the polling data demonstrating that the public both feared intervention and regarded Reagan as a warmonger. It was imperative to allay such fears and to reassert the wider and more comforting narratives of the nation and to use the 1984 election campaign to reunite the country after the Vietnam War.

Reagan and Central America: The Making of a Crisis

Reagan's candidacy and victory in 1980 were presented as a complete repudiation of the past. Where Carter was presented as indecisive, Reagan was resolute. Reagan also distanced himself from his Republican predecessors, reinjecting US foreign policy with values such as democracy promotion where Nixon, Kissinger and Ford were too concerned with realism, US interests, and power. Both visually and rhetorically, the Reagan people rekindled a traditional dreamscape of an America that comforted after the upheaval of the 1960s and 1970s. Reagan aligned himself with an ultraconservative vision of the United States reengaging with the world and reasserting its power. His character and candidacy played into the widespread nostalgic mood of the period.[3] Such euphoria, according to Wolfgang Schivelbusch in his study of defeat, is not unusual after a national defeat in war; a "dreamland," a condition of unreality, frequently emerges. The past is repudiated. "The more popular the revolt," he argues, "and the more charismatic the new leadership, the greater the triumph will seem."[4] With confidence, the nation turns to the future, guided by a mythical past. Though Reagan has subsequently been attributed with wondrous powers of leadership, his initial years—indeed, his entire presidency—were filled with controversy and disagreement, especially in the areas of intervention and foreign policy.[5] Despite Reagan's desire to use Central America and Nicaragua in particular as a site to exhibit the rejuvenation of US power, the majority of the American public was consistently skeptical, and Congress was perennially inconsistent on and indecisive about support for the contras.

Reagan was an optimist and an ambitious cold warrior who believed strongly in American exceptionalism; he wanted to rewrite the American narrative after the Vietnam War and reengage US power.[6] He represented the public image of the Vietnam revisionist and spoke out against the "Vietnam syndrome."[7] Within his divided administration, the ideologues fed him extremist advice on Soviet and Cuban machinations, especially in Central America.[8] Though several principals did not share these visions, they believed that something needed to be done to address the malaise of the 1970s. Nicaragua was not only an area that could demonstrate US resolve; it was also considered vital to US credibility. Reagan's national security adviser, Robert McFarlane, at one point argued: "If we could not muster an effective counter to Cuban-Sandinista strategy in our own backyard, it was far less likely that we could do so in the years ahead in more distant locations. . . . We had to win this one."[9] Moreover, Reagan's rhetoric in the early years of his administration characterized the situation in such extreme terms that, once he had committed himself to the cause, it would be difficult to back off without invoking questions on his credibility.

Reagan viewed the world through a Manichaean prism that set the Sandinistas on the wrong side of the Berlin Wall. Because the lessons of Vietnam were ignored, regional conflicts were situated within this global outlook that overlooked local complexities; the regional experts within the US Foreign Service were removed from their posts in Central America, replaced by men who had served in some capacity in Vietnam.[10] Nicaragua could provide an antidote to Vietnam.[11]

Among the principals, Reagan's first secretary of state, Alexander Haig, wanted to take the war to the region and draw a line in El Salvador to demarcate the limits of the Soviet advance.[12] He questioned whether the United States had the will to act while it still enjoyed "the freedom of action [Reagan] had won at the polls."[13] His views were opposed by other principals who did not view Central America as strategically vital. Secretary of Defense Caspar Weinberger worried that the region and El Salvador in particular might become another Vietnam; US interests were not extensive there, but, if the United States got involved, it would find it difficult to extricate itself, and lives, resources, and reputation would be spent.[14] Weinberger argued: "One of the principal lessons I had learned from the whole Vietnam experience was that we could not suddenly explode upon the American people a fully-fledged war and expect to have their support." Americans would have to believe that US interests demanded a war, and, if that was the case, the war would then have to be prosecuted "with all the resources and will to win that we possessed."[15] Internally, the administration considered the applicability of the Vietnam analogy and debated the dangers posed by the Sandinistas and the Salvadoran rebels (FMLN).[16] Others tried to allay Weinberger's concerns and derided his fears that some Americans might get killed in the region.[17]

Reagan's attachment to the contras and to prevailing in Nicaragua was unconditional, though it had to be tempered in 1984. Though the faltering attempt to roll back the Sandinista revolution had been ongoing since 1981, it was only after the 1984 elections—early in 1985—that the Reagan Doctrine was identified and announced. In *Time* magazine, Charles Krauthammer described it as that effort to support "those who are risking their lives on every continent from Afghanistan to Nicaragua to defy Soviet-supported aggression and secure rights which have been ours from birth."[18] The contras were both devastating tactically and ineffective strategically, impelling further US support and engagement.[19]

Congress remained divided on contra aid and on Central America more generally. The polls were generally negative. The *New York Times* criticized Reagan's ability to learn from the past, opining: "The same fears about impotence and credibility were the stuff of a thousand speeches justifying American involvement for a generation in the lost war in Indochina."[20] Yet the administration went to extremes: the CIA mined the harbors of Nicaragua, an act for which the United States was found guilty at the International Court of Justice in 1986; Reagan described the contras as "our brothers, these freedom fighters . . . the moral equivalent of the Founding Fathers and the brave men and women of the French Resistance."[21] A declaration of national emergency was signed on May 1, 1985, because the Sandinistas "posed an unusual and extraordinary threat to US foreign policy."[22] Eventually, the whole project unraveled with the revelations associated with the Iran-Contra scandal.[23] But, in 1984, Reagan was still ambitious, the public wary and skeptical, and his advisers aware of the potential for damage at the polls.

Opinion polls demonstrated that generally Americans did not share Reagan's concerns with the Sandinistas as a threat to the United States. A study of public opinion concluded: "During Reagan's first year in office, opinion formed in opposition to the administration's policy and despite concerted efforts by the President and his chief foreign policy spokespersons, it has remained deeply critical ever since. . . . The public does not believe that US interests at stake in the region are as vital as the administration has portrayed them, and they are fearful that US involvement will lead to 'Another Vietnam.'"[24] Overall support for Reagan's policies on Nicaragua remained low. But, given his commitment and the importance of the anti-Communist rhetoric and atmosphere of the early 1980s, in the context of the putative "second Cold War," in certain years the president was able to convince wavering congressional representatives to switch their votes on contra aid.[25]

Yet Reagan was rarely able to convince wider sections of the US public. Support in the early years hovered around mid–20 percent approval; in October 1983, it reached 26 percent. Public wariness was galvanized by the ongoing large-scale military maneuvers conducted in Honduras throughout 1983 that situated US troops in the proximity of the violence. The Beirut bombing of October 1983, in which 241 Americans were killed, was followed shortly by the US invasion of Grenada, leading to a temporary but limited spike in favorable opinion of Reagan's handling of Nicaragua. Approval rose from 26 to 36 percent. According to Sobel: "[The] increased support . . . vanished as quickly as it had appeared." Two months later, just 28 percent of Americans approved of Reagan's handling of Nicaragua.[26] It is not unusual that short foreign policy crises have a strong and positive impact on presidential popularity while longer-term engagements have profound negative effects.[27]

The White House pollster Richard Wirthlin argued that there was a "sharp" difference in public opinion on foreign policy and domestic issues. On foreign policy, public attitudes changed "much more rapidly" than they did on domestic issues. In his words: "Americans in essence are willing to give the president much more room in terms of almost a leap of faith." Yet, when it comes to negative foreign policy stories, the "disillusion and disappointment" can be rapid.[28]

The Juxtaposition of Lebanon:
The Deployment and the Disaster

The Grenada operation provided the Reagan administration with a temporary boost in public opinion, but the ongoing US presence in Lebanon proved to be a far more problematic and divisive issue. The administration was internally divided on whether that presence should be maintained. It was not just about the safety of US forces but also about the secretary of state's desire to maintain the presence to demonstrate US staying power and credibility. This was set against the concerns for US safety and the public inclination to disengage, which was a vital consideration in the election cycle.

The participation in the Lebanese operations was a far different issue from the central pillars of the Reagan Doctrine and the fear of potential intervention in Nicaragua. Reagan frequently argued that, without contra aid, the United States might be required to take more direct action, though that proposition was always presented as a worst-case scenario. But the potential for intervention was clearly seen in the negative context of public opinion and its impact on the 1984 elections. By late 1983, Lebanon required consideration in terms of a US withdrawal, and Nicaragua mandated keeping the US troops out; moreover, the administration also wanted to keep the stories out of the press. For instance, on November 7, 1983, the *Baron Report* identified the salient issues: Reagan was still considered too "trigger-happy" and too blindly, "ideologically, anticommunist" to pragmatically deal with the Soviets, and, at least within the US rhetorical depiction, Nicaragua was a key outpost of Soviet influence. The *Baron Report* argued that elections usually center on economics, with foreign policy a third in voters' priority: "That's been assumed to be good for Reagan, since foreign policy has always been his weakest point with the public. . . . The change in Reagan's image on foreign policy has clearly reduced GOP fears of it becoming a central issue in the campaign." Grenada provided an antidote, "most critically, of course, [because] 'we won'—or appeared to—which has not happened often since World War II."[29]

The secretary of state, George Shultz, and Caspar Weinberger were deeply divided on the presence of US troops in Beirut as part of the multinational force (MNF) injected to oversee the withdrawal of Israeli, Syrian, and other forces from Lebanon. Shultz felt it imperative to have a US presence in the MNF and on the ground in Lebanon; it related to US credibility and leadership. He argued the case extensively throughout the meetings of 1983 and 1984, but he stated the case most succinctly in his memoirs: "I was [in August 1983], if anything, even more convinced than the president that we must stand firm in Lebanon, for worldwide as well as for Lebanese considerations." He was gratified by the House and Senate vote in September 1983 that authorized the deployment of marines in Lebanon for an additional eighteen months. He recounted: "It let everyone know that the United States had staying power."[30]

Weinberger and his deputy at the Department of Defense, Colin Powell, were skeptical. Weinberger later reflected: "My own feeling was that we should not commit American troops to any situation unless the objectives were so important for American interests that we had to fight, and that if those conditions were met, then we had to commit, as a last resort, not just token forces to provide an American presence, but enough forces to win and win overwhelmingly."[31] The friction between the two principals was played out through the exchange of documents and the minutes of the National Security Planning Group (NSPG), which was dealing with the crisis. Weinberger argued that the staff was excessively worried about US credibility: "Only if we stayed in Lebanon would we demonstrate our manhood or secure any of our objectives."[32] For Shultz, the Reagan administration was in a typical post-Vietnam dilemma. He wrote to the president on October 5, 1983: "In effect, the choice is one of accepting the strategic costs of getting out soon or the possible political costs of staying in." Lebanon was the new "litmus test" of US credibility.[33] For Weinberger, the reduction of the US presence was both necessary and desirable. From an offshore position, the US forces would not be the targets that they had become *in* Beirut, and they would be able to deploy additional gunfire: "Thus, we would not be weakening our commitment to help secure peace in the Mid East, but would actually strengthen it in terms of fire power."[34] Weinberger's arguments were centered on the safety of the troops, the achievements of specific objectives, and not the strategic and symbolic maintenance of a presence.

The CIA eventually came to support Weinberger's position; the Marines were not safe, and they were increasingly a concern for the US public, Congress, and the press. Reagan did not need such concerns and negative media in the run-up to an election year. Yet Shultz was still determined to "stay the course." He cabled US ambassador Reginald Bartholomew on October 24, 1983: "Our commitment to a united, sovereign, and independent Lebanon remains unshakeable. Now, more than ever, we will stay the course. That commitment included the continuing presence of U.S. forces in the MNF."[35]

Shultz's views were not shared by the US public. When the Soviets shot down flight KAL 007 on September 1, 1983, Reagan again benefited from a temporary boost in public opinion, but he failed to sustain that response. Americans were not fully comfortable with the US presence, though there was a short-term positive reaction; still, an even larger majority believed that the marines had no clear purpose in Lebanon.[36] More broadly, a slight majority felt that Reagan was too quick to get US military forces involved in international problems, and 52 percent were uneasy about his approach.[37]

By late 1983, the administration's report to Congress was sent with a cover letter from the president noting the importance of congressional support and that US interests were served by the US participation in the MNF. Still, internal memoranda in preparation for the congressional report indicated: "Premature withdrawal of the MNF would damage seriously the international credibility of the United States and its partners and call into question the resolve of the West to carry out its responsibilities to help the free world defend itself. Such action would certainly bring about a return to full scale hostilities in Lebanon and regional instability threatening vital U.S. interests."[38] Yet the recommendations from the Pentagon were compelling. By the end of the year, Weinberger laid out options for Reagan on the next steps in Lebanon. To minimize damage to US credibility, the administration could pressure the Lebanese government to indicate that the MNF was no longer needed. Or it could adapt the Nixon Doctrine and strengthen the Lebanese army. Further, it could announce continued support and accelerated deliveries of equipment, but, most crucially, Weinberger recommended moving US forces to offshore amphibious ships.[39]

Days later, on January 3, 1984, Reagan's talking points for the NSPG meeting illustrated the impact of the public debate and its influence on foreign policy, which by that stage had become an election-year concern.

The president opened the meeting with the observation that there were strong feelings within his administration on the issue: "But I have to say I am pretty mad about the way we have been backed into a situation so that we are reduced to considering redeployment of our forces in Lebanon in response to a public debate stimulated by leaks from within our government." The Long Commission report on the Beirut bombings had been leaked, as had the Joint Chiefs of Staff proposals on US redeployment. Reagan insisted on a unified statement by lunchtime and insisted that the leaks stop.[40] The "Non-Paper" for the meeting noted that "domestic support [was] unraveling." Further, it noted: "Virtually all of the serious press has turned against us—some because they seek quick withdrawal; others because they argue we are not pressing Syria hard enough." Yet escalation and increased pressure on the Syrians potentially produced their own problems. The Syrians might take direct action against the MNF or US ships. Failure to induce further Syrian flexibility "would have dangerous consequences for our relations with the moderate Arabs, the Europeans, and the Congress, and would strengthen arguments that we have no strategy, that we are falling further into the 'quagmire,' and that our military responses are not likely to bring about results."[41] Therefore, it was considered imperative that the United States find a way to withdraw without appearing weak. The Lebanon Group of the Crisis Management Center (National Security Council) argued that the problem was not Lebanon or the Lebanese government but how to get US troops out. Scanning the horizons, and looking at the scenario for the next nine months, group members did not see any prospect for a political settlement. Moreover: "Reagan can't have the MNF in there in July to give the Democratic candidates a shot at the MNF. The polls will show unhappiness due to Lebanon. There will be informal Republican pressure also."[42]

Still, in an interview with the *Wall Street Journal* on February 2, 1984, Reagan indicated that the administration could not surrender given the import of the situation and the prospects for disintegration in Lebanon. He told the *Journal:* "Now, can the United States, in the face of this, can the United States suddenly up and—regardless of our allies in the multinational force or anything else—say, 'Well, we're going to get out?' And if we get out, that means the end of Lebanon. And if we get out, it also means the end of any ability on our part to bring about an overall peace in the Middle East. And I would have to say that it means a pretty disastrous result for us worldwide."[43] Within days the United States was getting out. Reagan's statement of February 7, 1984, announced the redeployment of the US troops to the ships. It was presented in terms of providing extra leverage and a "reconcentration" to address "decisive new steps." The statement confirmed the points of the "Next Steps" document, which echoed the Nixon Doctrine. Yet for Reagan: "These measures, I believe, will strengthen our ability to do the job we set out to do and to sustain our efforts over the long term."[44]

On February 9, 1984, George Gallup noted growing public approval for Reagan's handling of the economy, but, at the same time, Reagan appeared to be increasingly vulnerable on foreign policy issues when America's concern over the threat of war had grown to its highest point since the Vietnam War: 49 percent of Americans disapproved and 38 percent approved of Reagan's overall handling of foreign policy. On Central America, 49 percent disapproved of his stance, while 28 percent approved. On Lebanon, 59 percent disapproved, against 28 percent who approved. By mid-January 1984, Reagan had delivered a speech with the theme "A Year of Peace," and he would soon announce the redeployment of US troops out of Beirut. "Once we pulled the troops out of Lebanon, it was never close again," White House political director Ed Rollins said years later. "We knew the troops were a major, major obstacle."[45]

1984: The Broad Context of the Peace Initiatives

Though foreign policy was clearly seen as of secondary importance for the 1984 elections, the administration knew two things. First, the public still perceived Reagan as too much of an ideologue and perhaps not the candidate to deal most effectively with the Soviets. Second, should regional issues such as Lebanon or Nicaragua get out of control, they could easily become a liability and potentially revive memories of the Vietnam War, images of the proverbial quagmire, a US defeat, or a questioning of US credibility. Overall, Reagan's approval was high—59 percent—but the polls also indicated that he was vulnerable on Lebanon and Central America.[46]

The withdrawal from Lebanon had been managed to some extent. There was little prospect that the United States would become an effective partner to the MNF or to the longer-term and wider prospects for Middle

East peace. Crucially, Lebanon had been defused as a US election-year issue.

The moderates in his administration and Nancy Reagan, despite her desire that her husband not pursue a second term, also clearly realized that the president had to recast his identity and craft a character that was more the candidate for peace. Even if his policies and platform advanced nothing specifically new, atmospherics were important, and he was lucky, above all, to face a relatively weak opponent. Despite the previous three years of bellicose rhetoric, for 1984 Reagan would be the candidate of firm peace—a peacemaker and a statesman. The ideologues had lost out to the moderates within the administration, and there were few who opposed the new message and image. Moreover, the troubling aspects of foreign policy had to be defused: Lebanon, Nicaragua, and the ideologically driven anti-Communist rhetoric.

In January 1984, while delivering a speech to the nation, Reagan declared "a year of opportunities for peace." As LeoGrande writes: "He spoke not of the 'Evil Empire' but of 'our fellowship as members of the human race, our oneness as inhabitants of the planet.'"[47] He promised to talk with the Soviets; he visited China in April; he appeared the elder statesman in June 1984 at the economic summit of Western leaders; and, for all its visual impact, the D-Day speech delivered at Normandy reiterated similar messages at a poignant location.[48] His speech to the United Nations of September 1984 further advanced the reflection on constructive engagement, peace, and negotiations.[49] He spoke of a constructive and realistic relationship with the Soviet Union. The tone was set early in 1984 in the famous address to the nation. Reagan indicated: "There is no rational alternative but to steer a course which I would call credible deterrence and peaceful competition. And if we do so, we might find areas in which we could engage in constructive cooperation. Our strength and vision of progress provide the basis for demonstrating with equal conviction our commitment to stay secure and to find peaceful solutions to problems through negotiations. That's why 1984 is a year of opportunities for peace."[50]

Even if the troops had been pulled out of the immediate circle of danger in Lebanon, the prospects of getting troops into Nicaragua was still a political concern, as was the possibility that the region might erupt during the campaign. When Tony Motley replaced Thomas Enders as assistant secretary of state for inter-American affairs in July 1983, he was told by White House chief of staff James Baker and Shultz that "his main job was to prevent Central America from becoming a campaign issue." In his memoirs, Reagan's attorney general, Edwin Meese, recollected that, given the negative polls, the administration was aware that ongoing association with the cause would tarnish his reputation. Meese wrote: "For this reason, the political shop was averse to having the President go on television to fight for Contra aid, particularly in 1983–84, and supported the State Department approach, which basically promised to 'negotiate' the Sandinista problem under the rug until after the election."[51]

Nicaragua was also a problem. The White House pollster Richard Wirthlin was especially worried about contra aid, which his numbers told him was "pure poison" with the electorate. In late 1983, Wirthlin's polls found: "Only 37 percent of the public had heard or read anything about Nicaragua. But of those who had, only 18 percent supported Reagan's handling of the issue." Some 70 percent of those polled feared that the war in Nicaragua would lead the United States into another Vietnam.[52]

By spring 1984, Reagan walked a political tightrope between resolute action to advance Central American policy and repeated denials that he had any intention of sending US troops to war. Ironically, after the success of Grenada, his denials were less credible; perhaps he would be tempted to intervene directly yet again. Moreover, after Grenada, the power of the Vietnam syndrome in the Pentagon was somewhat reduced.[53] Further, after the United States had mined the harbors of Nicaragua in early 1984, senior administration figures indicated that they had in fact drawn up contingency plans for the possible use of US combat forces in the region.[54]

Given the division between Shultz and Weinberger on Lebanon, public unity of purpose was deemed important on Central America even though it did not exist in private. To that end, Shultz, Weinberger, William Casey, and McFarlane—the administration's foreign policy principals—released a joint press release to "state emphatically that we have not considered nor have we developed plans to use U.S. military forces to invade Nicaragua or any other Central American country." They reconfirmed their position: that the United States did not seek to destabilize or overthrow the government of Nicaragua.[55]

Yet concurrent military operations undermined these assertions. Extensive US military exercises were still being conducted in the region.

Big Pine II and Granadero I saw the deployment of thirty-five hundred troops in the spring of 1984. The navy held another exercise, Ocean Venture, in the Caribbean with thirty thousand US personnel. But, crucially, once these operations were completed, the Pentagon took a lower profile in the region until after the US election.[56] Still, smaller exercises continued.[57]

The principals also reiterated their support for the Contadora peace process, the regional attempt to find a negotiated solution. They stated that they endorsed the twenty-one Contadora objectives but focused entirely on the requirements made on Nicaragua. The Sandinistas had to terminate the export of subversion, which had stopped in 1981. They had to reduce the size of their military, implement democratic commitments made to the Organization of American States, and remove Soviet and Cuban personnel.[58] I have argued elsewhere that in fact the Reagan administration was doing what it could to undermine these negotiations and the other diplomatic options. The principals' statement said nothing about the commitments that Contadora required of the US allies in the region. Had El Salvador, Honduras, or Guatemala faced these conditions, the risk of US policy unraveling was too great.[59]

Conclusion

Foreign policy was not the crucial issue for the election; though potential damage control was very much a part of the planning and the campaign management.[60] Richard Wirthlin's polls in 1984 showed consistently that the administration was potentially vulnerable on its Central America policy.[61] By February 1984, George Gallup noted growing public approval of Reagan's handling of the economy, and, at the same time, Reagan appeared to be increasingly vulnerable on foreign policy issues when America's concern over the threat of war had grown to its highest point since the Vietnam War. By midyear, given the opposition, campaign strategists knew that Reagan would not be defeated unless he did something to undermine his own position. One of their key concerns was to keep the candidate on script, especially after the August 11 quip on radio that he was outlawing the Soviet Union and would bomb within five minutes, which produced a negative reaction.[62]

The Reagan acceptance speech of August 1984 was filled with a nostalgic and elegiac evocation of a United States untroubled by the world.

The difficult areas were dealt with briefly. They prompted memories of the nightmare too readily identifiable in the polls and in Congress. Reagan's morning in America was filled with sweet dreams.

In November 1984, Reagan won 59 percent of the popular vote; few others in US history had achieved the forty-nine-state landslide. Of the 535 Electoral College votes available, Reagan won 525, Mondale a mere 10. Mondale won only his home state, Minnesota, and the District of Columbia.

On the issues, Reagan was not a particularly strong candidate. In the first presidential debate in Louisville on October 7, he appeared lost in details that he could not convey effectively. Nancy Reagan thought he was "tense, muddled, and off-stride." Questions on his age, his health, and his competence were raised in the media.[63] These appeared, albeit briefly, as though there might be an electoral contest; by contrast, Mondale was relatively youthful and on point, but his points were off target. Within a couple of weeks, Reagan recovered, entering the second debate with a much lighter touch and tone, remembered most famously for the quip on age. He responded to questions on his ability to serve a second term with: "I will not make age an issue of this campaign. I am not going to exploit, for political purposes, my opponent's youth and inexperience."[64] Even Mondale joined in with the laughter and later acknowledged that he knew he had lost the election at that point.

Though much has been made of the "Reagan as a reckless war monger, and Mondale as a feckless weakling," thesis, the former proposition had been somewhat tamed by 1984, even if Mondale's fight presented few big worries. The Reagan people were indeed most happy when Mondale picked on the traditional image of Reagan the warmonger who threatened not only to bring confrontation with the Soviet Union but also to potentially bankrupt the United States with excessive defense spending. These attacks they could withstand and to some extent relish because to some audiences they also represented an attack on American defense and security. They were least comfortable when the president's competence was called into question. Indeed, Reagan's convoluted response to the question on the CIA's "assassination manual" distributed in Nicaragua brought on considerable disdain. Yet the campaign memoranda made clear that the president should be represented as an idealized personification of a mythical America: "Paint Reagan as the personification of all that is right with or heroized by America. Leave Mondale in a position where an attack on Reagan is tantamount to an attack on America's idealized image of itself."[65]

Richard Darman had identified what he called "mythic America," which Reagan seemed to embody. By 1984, much of the negativity associated with the economy had been left behind, and the campaign captured the tone in the "morning in America" advertisement. Cannon relates that *Newsweek* depicted Reagan as the "America as it imagined itself to be—the bearer of the traditional Main Street values of family and neighborhood, of thrift, industry and charity instead of government intervention where self-reliance failed."[66] When Mondale's campaign attacked Reagan, inadvertently he seemed to be attacking something more cherished, albeit something akin to a fairy tale.

When, in July 1984 at the Democratic national convention, Mondale belabored the arms race, Reagan's "unfair" economic policies, and the budget deficit and made the infamous promise, "He'll raise taxes" (for both arms and the deficit), continuing, "So will I. He won't tell you, I just did," he was *briefly* lauded for dealing head on with the issue of the deficit. But his promise of increasing taxes and reducing defense spending to the tune of $30 billion, the savings to be diverted into social programs, education, and the environment, indicated that he clearly misunderstood the mood of the electorate. He could not effectively couch his message in the optimistic frame of liberal justice and thus came across as, in Jeane Kirkpatrick's characterization of him, "bad news Fritz."[67] He represented an old form of liberalism in an increasingly conservative age.

Even though Nicaragua and Lebanon were very negative issues at the polls, the overall relationship with the Soviet Union had been somewhat ameliorated. Much has been made of the influence of Nancy Reagan on the president's turn or that of George Shultz. Beth Fischer rejects the notion that the turn came about because of electoral concerns or those related to public opinion. Apart from the famous January 1984 speech, the audiences were frequently European or indeed Soviet. And, indeed, National Security Decision Directive 75 of January 1983 had outlined: "The US must demonstrate credibly that its policy is not a blueprint for an open-ended, sterile confrontation with Moscow, but a serious search for a stable and constructive long-term basis for US-Soviet relations." Indeed, the memoirs of George Shultz emphasize the point that the military buildup of the early period could facilitate the "realistic reengagement with the Soviets."[68] The point is that they sought realistic engagement, *not* a hostile and risky attempt to end the Cold War. Still, public opinion lagged behind the changed message; polls indicated some fear in response to Reagan's overall approach to foreign policy. Yet despite the ongoing and continuous negativity surrounding Nicaragua, once troops were pulled out of Lebanon at least one of the foreign policy issues to register was effectively removed.

Notes

1. Ronald Reagan Television Ad: "It's Morning in America Again," Paid for by Reagan-Bush '84, YouTube, http://youtu.be/EU-IBF8nwSY.

2. Michael Schaller, *Right Turn: American Life in the Reagan-Bush Era, 1980–1992* (New York: Oxford University Press, 2007), 75.

3. Michael Kammen, *Mystic Chords of Memory: The Transformation of Tradition in American Culture* (New York: Vintage, 1993), 655–63.

4. Wolfgang Schivelbusch, *The Culture of Defeat: On National Trauma, Mourning, and Recovery* (New York: Henry Holt, 2001), 10–11.

5. See Dinesh D'Souza, *Ronald Reagan: How an Ordinary Man Became an Extraordinary Leader* (New York: Touchstone, 1999). Very favorable memoirs include Edwin Meese III, *With Reagan: The Inside Story* (Washington, DC: Regnery Gateway, 1992); and Michael K. Deaver, *A Different Drummer: My Thirty Years with Ronald Reagan* (New York: Harper Collins, 2001). Memoirs of the other principals are more rewarding. For more recent work on Reagan, see Sean Wilentz, *The Age of Reagan: A History, 1974–2008* (New York: Harper, 2008), John Patrick Diggins, *Ronald Reagan: Fate, Freedom, and the Making of History* (New York: Norton, 2008); James Mann, *The Rebellion of Ronald Reagan: A History of the End of the Cold War* (New York: Penguin, 2010); and Will Bunch, *Tear Down This Myth: How the Reagan Legacy Has Distorted Our Politics and Haunts Our Future* (New York: Free Press, 2009). Otherwise, see Lou Cannon, *President Reagan: The Role of a Lifetime* (New York: Simon & Schuster, 1991). See also Robert Dallek, *Ronald Reagan: The Politics of Symbolism* (Cambridge, MA: Harvard University Press, 1999); and Garry Wills, *Reagan's America: Innocents at Home* (New York: Doubleday, 1987).

6. Trevor McCrisken, *American Exceptionalism and the Legacy of Vietnam: US Foreign Policy since 1974* (London: Palgrave, 2003).

7. For a historiographic outline, see Gary R. Hess, *Vietnam: Explaining America's Lost War* (Malden, MA: Blackwell, 2009).

8. The Committee of Santa Fe, L. Francis Bouchey, Roger Fontaine, David C. Jordan, Lieutenant General Gordon Sumner, and Lewis Tambs, *A New Inter-American Policy for the Eighties* (Washington, DC: Council for Inter-American Security,

1980), 1, 3, 46, 52; David Ryan, *US-Sandinista Diplomatic Relations: Voice of Intolerance* (London: Macmillan, 1995), 1–3.

   9. Peter Kornbluh, "The US Role in the Counterrevolution," in *Revolution and Counterrevolution in Nicaragua*, ed. Thomas W. Walker (Boulder, CO: Westview, 1991), 323–349, 325. See also David Ryan, "The Peripheral Center: Nicaragua in US Policy and the US Imagination at the End of the Cold War," in *Foreign Policy at the Periphery: The Shifting Margins of US International Relations since World War II*, ed. Bevan Sewell and Maria Ryan (Lexington: University Press of Kentucky, 2017); Ronald Reagan, Address before a Joint Session of Congress, April 27, 1983, *Public Papers of Ronald Reagan, 1983*, Ronald Reagan Presidential Library, https://www.reaganlibrary.archives.gov/archives/speeches/1983/42783d.htm; and William M. LeoGrande, *Our Own Backyard: The United States in Central America, 1977–1992* (Chapel Hill: University of North Carolina Press, 1998).

   10. Raymond Bonner, *Weakness and Deceit: US Policy and El Salvador* (London: Hamish Hamilton, 1985), 244–54; Lars Shoultz, *National Security and United States Policy towards Latin America* (Princeton, NJ: Princeton University Press, 1987), 9–10, 63; Ryan, *US-Sandinista Diplomatic Relations*, 8–9; LeoGrande, *Our Own Backyard*, 75–80.

   11. LeoGrande, *Our Own Backyard*, 126, 348; Ryan, *US-Sandinista Diplomatic Relations*, 88–106.

   12. Juan de Onis, "State Department Says Salvador Rebels Get Fewer Arms," *New York Times*, February 24, 1981; John Goshko and Don Oberdorfer, "Haig Calls Arms Smuggling to El Salvador 'No Longer Acceptable,'" *Washington Post*, February 28, 1981.

   13. Alexander M. Haig, *Caveat: Realism, Reagan, and Foreign Policy* (London: Weidenfeld & Nicolson, 1984), 131.

   14. See Ronald Reagan, Parallel between El Salvador and Vietnam, February 24, 1981, *American Foreign Policy Current Documents*, no. 671 (Washington, DC: Department of State, 1984), 1237; and Reagan, Parallels between El Salvador, Vietnam and Afghanistan, March 3, 1981, *American Foreign Policy Current Documents*, no. 677 (Washington, DC: Department of State, 1984), 1277. Apart from the coverage in the *New York Times* and the *Washington Post*, see also "Vietnam and El Salvador," *Baltimore Sun*, February 26, 1981; Max Lerner, "Salvador Offers U.S. Opportunity," *Southeastern Missourian*, February 27, 1981; UPI, "Déjà Vu? Aid to El Salvador Fuels Viet Memories," *Beaver County Times* (Beaver, PA), March 2, 1981; "House Members Protest Involvement of Military Advisors in El Salvador," *Lakeland (FL) Ledger*, March 3, 1981; NYT Service, "Ronald Reagan Foresees No Vietnam," *Milwaukee Journal*, March 4, 1981; AP, "Reagan Doesn't Foresee Troops in El Salvador," *Herald Journal*, March 4, 1981; and Times Poll, "Majority Fears El Salvador May Be Another Vietnam," *Los Angeles Times*, March 22, 1982.

   15. Caspar Weinberger, *Fighting for Peace: Seven Critical Years at the Pentagon* (London: Michael Joseph, 1990), 22.

   16. Robert L. Schweitzer and Roger Fontaine, Memorandum for Richard V.

Allen, NSC Meeting February 25, and SIG Paper on El Salvador, February 24, 1981, El Salvador, vol. 1, OA 91363, Ronald Reagan Library (hereafter RRL).

17. Ibid.

18. *New York Times,* February 24, 1985, cited in Norman A. Graebner, Richard Dean Burns, and Joseph M. Siracusa, *Reagan, Bush, Gorbachev: Revisiting the End of the Cold War* (Westport, CT: Praeger Security International, 2008), 76; Charles Krauthammer, "The Reagan Doctrine," *Time,* April 1, 1985.

19. See Peter Kornbluh, *Nicaragua: The Price of Intervention* (Washington, DC: Institute of Policy Studies, 1987), and "The Covert War," in *Reagan versus the San-dinistas: The Undeclared War on Nicaragua,* ed. Thomas W. Walker (Boulder, CO: Westview, 1987), 21–38.

20. Editorial, *New York Times,* January 23, 1984, cited in Graebner, Burns, and Siracusa, *Reagan, Bush, Gorbachev,* 72.

21. International Court of Justice (ICJ), *Nicaragua v. The United States of America* (The Hague: ICJ, June 27, 1986), 137–41; Ronald Reagan, Remarks at the Annual Dinner of the Conservative Political Action Conference, March 1, 1985, *The American Presidency Project,* http://www.presidency.ucsb.edu/ws/index.php?pid=38274&st=&st1=.

22. Ronald Reagan, Executive Order 12513, "Prohibiting Trade and Certain Other Transactions Involving Nicaragua," May 1, 1985, *Public Papers of Ronald Reagan, 1985,* http://www.reagan.utexas.edu/archives/speeches/1985/50185a.htm.

23. John Tower, Edmund Muskie, and Brent Scowcroft, *The Tower Commission Report: Full Text of the President's Special Review Board* (New York: Bantam, 1987); US Senate Select Committee on Secret Military Assistance to Iran and the Nica-raguan Opposition, US House of Representatives, Select Committee to Investigate Covert Arms Transactions with Iran, *Iran-Contra Affair,* 100th Cong., 1st sess., SR 100-216/HR 100-433 (Washington, DC: US Government Printing Office, November 17, 1987); Lawrence E. Walsh, *Final Report of the Independent Counsel for Iran/ Contra Matters,* 3 vols. (Washington, DC: US Court of Appeals, August 4, 1993).

24. William M. LeoGrande, *Central America and the Polls: A Study of US Public Opinion Polls and US Foreign Policy towards El Salvador and Nicaragua under the Reagan Administration,* Special Report (Washington, DC: Washington Office on Latin America, March 1987), 41–42. See also Richard Sobel, *The Impact of Public Opinion on U.S. Foreign Policy since Vietnam: Constraining the Colossus* (New York: Oxford University Press, 2001).

25. Fred Halliday, *The Making of the Second Cold War* (London: Verso, 1983); Sobel, *The Impact of Public Opinion,* 99.

26. Sobel, *The Impact of Public Opinion,* 103.

27. Nonetheless, there is considerable evidence that dramatic foreign policy events have a strong and generally positive effect on presidential popularity as the public "rallies 'round the flag," though the longevity of the effect is short. John E. Mueller, *War, Presidents and Public Opinion* (New York: Wiley, 1973). Long-term crises, such as the Korean and Vietnam Wars, the Iranian hostage crisis, and

the Iran-Contra scandal, may have more profound negative effects. Lee Sigelman and Pamela Conover, "The Dynamics of Presidential Support during International Conflict Situations: The Iranian Hostage Crisis," *Political Behavior* 3, no. 4 (1981): 303–18, cited in Clyde Wilcox and Dee Allsop, "Economic and Foreign Policy as Sources of Reagan Support," *Western Political Quarterly* 44, no. 4 (1991): 941–58.

28. Shoon Kathleen Murray, "Private Polls and Presidential Policymaking: Reagan as a Facilitator of Change," *Public Opinion Quarterly* 70, no. 4 (2006): 477–98. Murray writes: "Given that Reagan's pollster held these views, it is not hard to imagine that the president and his top aides felt more room to maneuver on foreign policy issues and less need to heed the public's policy preferences." Ibid., 487.

29. *The Baron Report*, November 7, 1983, Lebanon/Grenada, Ronald Reagan's Speech 10/27/83, OA 11244, Barody Files, RRL.

30. George P. Shultz, *Turmoil and Triumph: My Years as Secretary of State* (New York: Scribner's, 1993), 227.

31. Weinberger, *Fighting for Peace*, 111.

32. Ibid.

33. Memorandum for the President from George P. Shultz, "Our Middle East Policy," October 5, 1983, Executive Secretariat NSPG, Box 2, 91306, NSPG 0072, October, 14, 1983, RRL.

34. Memorandum for the Assistant to the President for National Security Affairs from Secretary of Defense, "US Policy in Lebanon and the Middle East," October 21, 1983, Executive Secretariat NSC Country File Near East and South Asia, box 38, Subject File 41, Lebanon Chronology (1), RRL.

35. Telegram for Ambassador Bartholomew from the Secretary of State, "After the Attack: Talking to Factional Leaders," October 24, 1983, Executive Secretariat NSC Country File Near East and South Asia, box 38, Subject File 41, Lebanon Marine Explosion 10/23–11/3/83 (5), RRL.

36. David Shribman, "Poll Shows Support for Presence of U.S. Troops in Lebanon and Grenada," *New York Times*, October 29, 1983.

37. Shribman, "Poll Shows Support for Presence of U.S. Troops in Lebanon and Grenada."

38. Memorandum for Donald P. Gregg, Charles Hill, Colonel John Stanford, Roger Clegg, Alton Keel, and Brigadier General George A. Joulwan from Robert M. Kimmitt, "Lebanon Report to Congress," December 14, 1983, Vice President George Bush Office of NSC, Gregg, Donald P., Subject File 19775-1, Lebanon, George Bush Library.

39. Memorandum for the President, "Next Steps in Lebanon," December 30, 1983, Executive Secretariat NSC Country File Near East and South Asia, box 38, Subject File 41, Lebanon Chronology (2), RRL.

40. Memorandum for the President from Robert C. McFarlane, "Talking Points for NSPG on the Next Steps in Lebanon," January 3, 1984, The Reagan Files, http://www.thereaganfiles.com/8413-nspg-meeting-talking.pdf.

41. Memorandum for the President from Robert C. McFarlane, "NSPG Meet-

ing on Next Steps in Lebanon," n.d., "NSC Non-Paper: Next Steps in Lebanon" attached, Executive Secretariat NSC Country File Near East and South Asia, box 38, Subject File 41, Lebanon Chronology (2), RRL.

42. Lebanon Group, January 18, 1984, Crisis Management Center CMC, NSC Records 1982–1985, box 1, 90929, Lebanon Documents 4 January 1984, Rumsfeld Cables 2 (6 of 9), RRL.

43. Ronald Reagan, Interview with Robert L. Bartley and Albert R. Hunt of the *Wall Street Journal* on Foreign and Domestic Issues, February 2, 1984, www.reagan .utexas.edu/archives/speeches/1984/20284j.htm.

44. Ronald Reagan, Statement on the Situation in Lebanon, February 7, 1984, *Public Papers of the Presidents of the United States: Ronald Reagan, 1984*, Ronald Reagan Presidential Library, https://www.reaganlibrary.archives.gov/archives/ speeches/1984/20784d.htm.

45. Cannon, *President Reagan,* 510.

46. LeoGrande, *Our Own Backyard,* 347.

47. Ibid., 347–48.

48. Remarks at a Ceremony Commemorating the 40th Anniversary of the Normandy Invasion, D-Day, June 6, 1984, *The American Presidency Project,* http://www .presidency.ucsb.edu/ws/index.php?pid=40018&st=&st1=.

49. Ronald Reagan, Address to the 39th Session of the United Nations General Assembly in New York, New York, September 24, 1984, *American Presidency Project,* http://www.presidency.ucsb.edu/ws/index.php?pid=40430&st=&st1=.

50. Ronald Reagan, Address to the Nation and Other Countries on United States–Soviet Relations, January 16, 1984, *American Presidency Project,* http://www .presidency.ucsb.edu/ws/index.php?pid=39806&st=&st1=.

51. Meese, *With Reagan,* 235.

52. Jane Mayer and Doyle McManus, *Landslide. The Unmaking of the President, 1984–1988* (London: Fontana, 1988), 34–35. See also David Shribman, "Poll Finds a Lack of Public Support for Latin Policy," *New York Times,* April 29, 1984.

53. LeoGrande, *Our Own Backyard,* 248.

54. Richard Halloran, "U.S. Said to Draw Latin Troops Plan," *New York Times,* April 8, 1984.

55. Joint Statement by Secretary of State George Shultz, Secretary of Defense Caspar Weinberger, DCI William Casey, and NSA Robert McFarlane, in *American Foreign Policy: Current Documents, 1984* (Washington, DC: US Government Printing Office, 1985), 1052–53 (document 516).

56. Richard Halloran, "Pentagon; Arms and the Election Year," *New York Times,* June 29, 1984, http://www.nytimes.com/1984/06/29/us/pentagon-arms-and-the-election-year.html.

57. LeoGrande, *Our Own Backyard,* 348.

58. Joint Statement by Shultz, Weinberger, Casey, and McFarlane, 1052–53.

59. Ryan, *US-Sandinista Diplomatic Relations.*

60. Evan Thomas, "Local Politics, Global Power," *Time,* April 9, 1984.

61. Cannon, *President Reagan,* 384.

62. Ibid., 535–36.

63. Ibid., 495; Schaller, *Right Turn,* 58.

64. Reagan-Mondale Debate, October 21, 1984, YouTube, https://www.youtube.com/watch?v=CKEWxTK7L0w.

65. Cannon, *President Reagan,* 501; Wilentz, *The Age of Reagan,* 173.

66. Cannon, *President Reagan,* 494.

67. Schaller, *Right Turn,* 58; Wilentz, *The Age of Reagan,* 174.

68. Beth A. Fischer, *The Reagan Reversal: Foreign Policy and the End of the Cold War* (Columbia: University of Missouri Press, 1997), 51–68; NSDD 75, "U.S. Relations with the USSR," Memorandum from William P. Clark to the Vice President, January 17, 1983, National Security Decision Directives, Ronald Reagan Presidential Library, https://reaganlibrary.archives.gov/archives/reference/Scanned%20NSDDs/NSDD75.pdf; Shultz, *Turmoil and Triumph,* 463–86.

13

Ending the Cold War without Debate

Foreign Policy and the 1988 Election

Robert A. Strong

The contest for the American presidency in 1988 should have been a campaign with lively discussions and debates about international politics. It was not. The foreign policy dog did not bark in an election held on the eve of the end of the Cold War. Explaining why may raise important questions about the role of foreign affairs in American presidential politics.

In 1988, the world was on the cusp of radical revolutions in Eastern Europe, dramatic transformations in the Soviet Union, an end to apartheid in South Africa, demands for democracy in China, the toppling of dictators in numerous nations, and the emergence of new or more powerful regional economic and trade associations. It was a year full of major foreign policy issues, and first among them was the future of relations between the United States and the Soviet Union.

Evidence that the Cold War might be coming to an end was evident throughout the late 1980s. Mikhail Gorbachev, the dynamic Soviet leader, was introducing economic and political ideas and reforms that no other Communist leader had ever contemplated. In 1985, he announced a unilateral Soviet moratorium on nuclear weapons testing. In 1987, he made a public commitment to withdraw Soviet forces from Afghanistan. In the same year, he worked with Ronald Reagan to finalize the terms for the Intermediate-Range Nuclear Forces (INF) agreement. This was not a treaty like earlier arms control agreements, which simply capped or regulated the military hardware used to deliver nuclear weapons. Instead, it eliminated an entire category of such weapons. The two superpowers promised to dismantle the modern medium-range missiles that had destabilized European security and produced political controversy for more than a decade. Before signing the INF agreement, Gorbachev and Reagan met in Iceland and actually talked about the possibility of eliminating all nuclear-armed missiles. These were dramatic developments. At the end of 1988, within weeks of the conclusion of the American presidential campaign, Margaret Thatcher would declare that the Cold War was over.[1] George Shultz, Ronald Reagan's secretary of state in his second term, had reached the same conclusion.[2] Even Reagan admitted, when visiting Moscow in the summer of 1988, that his labeling of the Soviet Union as an "evil empire" was a statement that belonged to a "different era."[3]

American voters in 1988 should have expected their presidential candidates to talk about the Cold War, its possible conclusion, and what that conclusion might mean.[4] That did not happen. Nor did the candidates engage in serious and substantive discussions of significant domestic policy problems. Instead, voters endured a campaign that is widely remembered as among the most vapid and vicious in modern experience.[5]

Large numbers of Americans responded to the campaign by not voting. In 1988, barely half the voting age population completed a ballot to select the next president. It was the lowest participation in a presidential election the nation had seen since 1924.[6] In all the presidential elections since 1988 voter turnout has been higher.

The Democratic nominee was the sitting governor of Massachusetts, Michael Dukakis, who outlasted a large field of primary contenders by making fewer mistakes than his opponents. He had an inspiring personal story about his family's immigrant origins and success as a Northeast governor. But he also had a low-key technocratic manner that rarely generated genuine public enthusiasm. He suggested that voters should set ideological differences aside and choose the more competent of the candidates.

The Republican nominee, Vice President George Bush, had briefly served in the House of Representatives in the late 1960s but failed in two statewide campaigns for a Senate seat in Texas. In the 1970s, he held appointed posts in the party, in the cabinet, and overseas but then spent eight years hidden in the very large shadow cast by Ronald Reagan. Bush was a loyal vice president, widely known and liked by party regulars, but not a prominent independent figure on the national political stage. He lacked Reagan's rhetorical skills and strong ideological convictions. An infamous *Newsweek* magazine cover, published in the week Bush declared his presidential candidacy, questioned whether the vice president was a "wimp."[7] Neither candidate in 1988 struck voters as the stuff of which a Mt. Rushmore visage might be made.

When Dukakis emerged from the Democratic national convention in midsummer, he had a two-digit lead in the polls; a few months later, Bush held a comparable lead over his Democratic rival. Nothing happened to the economy or to national security in the intervening weeks to explain the swing in poll results. It almost certainly occurred because support for both candidates was shallow and large numbers of potential voters were genuinely undecided.

Neither campaign provided much in the way of policy substance by which the undecided might make up their minds. The Bush campaign identified a number of minor Dukakis positions that were broadly unpopular. The governor had vetoed a Massachusetts law requiring public school teachers to lead their students in the Pledge of Allegiance. He did so for the understandable reason that the Supreme Court had declared such laws unconstitutional.[8] There was very little discussion in the campaign about any of the arguments the courts had considered in rendering that judgment and endless superficial messaging implying that Dukakis was unpatriotic or un-American for his opposition to the flag and the pledge. Later, there were false rumors that Dukakis's wife had burned a flag at a political protest.[9] It did not help Dukakis that his campaign managers were slow and ineffective in responding to Republican attacks. As two astute observers have noted, having declared that the election should be about competence, not ideology, Dukakis proceeded to run an utterly incompetent campaign in which he allowed his opponent to define the ideological positions of the Democratic nominee as excessively liberal and out of touch with most Americans.[10]

Dukakis made more mistakes. In the second of two presidential debates, he delivered a weak performance.[11] In the very first question, he was asked if he would want a mandatory death penalty for a criminal who raped and murdered his wife, Kitty. Dukakis was a declared opponent of the death penalty. A question about that public policy issue was

completely fair. Framing such a question in connection to a hypothetical violent crime committed against a candidate's spouse was not. It gave
Dukakis a chance to show some passion. He might have criticized the
reporter for posing an inappropriate question. Or he might have made
the point that we have a legal system instead of vigilante justice precisely
because victims and their loved ones can be blinded by anger and devastated by grief in the aftermath of a violent crime. He did neither of those
things. Instead, he responded in a relaxed, bland, and matter-of-fact fashion, quickly changing the subject to the war on drugs that he hoped to
carry out if elected. He missed the point, and pointedness, of the question
and confounded the expectations of the audience listening to his answer.

Earlier, the Dukakis campaign released a photograph and some video
footage of the candidate riding in a tank that was supposed to convey the
message that Dukakis was a veteran knowledgeable about military affairs
and national defense. It had a different effect. The picture of the Massachusetts governor in an oddly shaped helmet peering from the hatch at
the top of a tank made him look strange and small. The pictures and the
video were mildly comical, and the Bush campaign circulated them far
and wide.

And the Bush campaign managers did much more than that. The
political advertising in 1988 included attack ads that were widely regarded
as both racist and effective.[12] While Dukakis was serving as governor, an
African American inmate named Willie Horton was temporarily released
from prison in a furlough program that had been created by the state
legislature under a previous governor. Horton committed a rape and an
assault while on furlough, and the Bush campaign used the image of a
revolving door at the gate of a prison in one of its commercials to send the
message that Dukakis was weak on crime. Because of the media coverage
and controversy the ad generated, voters in 1988 could be forgiven if they
went to the voting booth knowing more about Willie Horton than they
did about the two vice presidential candidates, Dan Quayle and Lloyd
Bentsen.

The campaign of 1988 is most often remembered for its nasty and
negative advertising and could easily be analyzed and criticized on those
grounds alone. But, as we have already noted, there is an additional reason
to be concerned about what happened in this presidential election cycle.
The contest for the White House in 1988 took place just before some of

the most dramatic changes in and challenges to the international system that any modern presidency has ever known. It would have been good, and might have been expected, that presidential candidates in that year would spend considerable time and energy discussing and debating those emerging changes. That debate could have educated voters about what was coming and might have informed them about how the candidates hoped to respond.

The debate did not occur. Toward the end of the campaign, the editors of the *New York Times* observed that, "on foreign relations, both men have had remarkably little to say" and that neither had appreciated the "the opportunities and risks" associated with Gorbachev and changes taking place in the Soviet Union.[13] Therein lies the central problem in any serious consideration of foreign policy and the 1988 presidential election.

The Primaries

It might have been different. At the outset, in the primary contests in the two political parties, there was some expectation that attention might be given to at least some aspects of the changing national security and international affairs landscape. Gary Hart, an early frontrunner in the Democratic field, was a senator who had expertise and interest in arms control, military policy, and Pentagon reform. In 1986, Richard Nixon predicted that Hart would be the party's nominee in 1988 and the likely winner in a contest with George Bush.[14] Had his candidacy not been consumed by first speculation and then evidence of marital infidelity, Hart might well have made national security an important topic in the campaign.[15] In 1987, before the media coverage regarding his personal conduct, he wrote essays and delivered speeches that clearly indicated his intention of making military reform and foreign policy major issues in his forthcoming campaign.

Something similar might have occurred if Joe Biden or Al Gore had stayed in the race. Like Hart, both had legislative experience on international issues from their service in the Senate. Both would, in all likelihood, have emphasized those issues in a general election if they had secured the nomination. Like Hart's, Biden's campaign was overwhelmed by scandal. In his case, the questions raised involved plagiarism of a speech delivered by a prominent British politician and plagiarism as a student earlier in his life. Biden dropped out of the race. Gore remained a candidate in the early primaries but failed to win the headline-grabbing victories that would give his campaign sustained national attention.

After the departure of Hart and Biden, Dick Gephardt, a congressman from Missouri, briefly made international trade a talked-about issue. In the run-up to the Iowa caucuses, which Gephardt won, his campaign ran ads saying that American jobs and wealth were being shipped overseas. The message was simplistic, but it tapped into real voter frustrations about the changing global economy and the degree to which foreign trade and unfair competition from Asian nations were weakening the prospects for American prosperity. That issue might have become a subject for more sustained political debate, as occurred in the Canadian election of 1988, but Gephardt's campaign ran out of money and steam in the cluster of primaries scheduled for March and commonly called Super Tuesday.

On the Republican side, Bob Dole, the Senate minority leader, was Bush's principal opponent for the nomination in the early caucus and primary competitions. The two Republicans were both World War II veterans who held similar positions on foreign policy issues. But they did have very different personalities and political reputations. No one ever accused Bob Dole of being a wimp. He had a sharp wit and was capable of showing anger in public political exchanges. He would have presented voters with a more vibrant and volatile personality than either Dukakis or Bush. That might have led to some discussion about how well Dole would negotiate with Gorbachev or make important decisions about the use of force. His personality would have provided both assets and liabilities in any consideration of his future actions as America's primary diplomat and commander in chief.

Dole won the Iowa caucuses, and Bush came in third behind both the Senate leader and the rogue candidacy of the television evangelist Pat Robertson. In New Hampshire, the Bush team began their practice of negative campaigning by running ads accusing Dole of straddling on important issues and voting for higher taxes. No senator, and certainly no Senate leader, can maintain a consistent voting record, and it is easy to accuse anyone in that kind of political career of straddling. Minority leaders often fight for changes in pending legislation and, if a suitable compromise is reached, vote for the final version of a bill they earlier opposed. This can falsely give the impression that they were against a particular proposition at the beginning of the legislative process and for it in the end, or the other way around. On the morning after Bush won the New Hampshire primary, Dole showed one of his flashes of anger and in a live NBC interview told his opponent to "stop lying about my record."[16] Dole won a few more primaries in the Midwest but lost in South Carolina and then in all the contests on Super Tuesday. He was effectively removed from the race.

Once the presidential election became a competition between Dukakis and Bush, public and media attention were focused on the usual landmarks in a trip to the White House: the party conventions, the nomination acceptance speeches, the personal appearances, the media interviews, the stump speeches, the advertising, and the debates. In each of these conventional campaign activities, foreign policy had a place. In 1988, that place was surprisingly small.

The Conventions

Both parties ran effective conventions. The Democrats met in Atlanta and showed an unusual degree of unity. There had been some tensions between the Dukakis campaign and Jesse Jackson, the civil rights activist and Chicago community leader who won a significant number of votes in the primary season, prior to the convention. But, in Atlanta, Jackson supported the Dukakis nomination and gave an effective convention speech. Bill Clinton gave a long one. Edward Kennedy gave a speech about Iran-Contra and other issues on which Bush claimed not to be involved, using the effective refrain, "Where was George?" Ann Richardson, a rising star in Texas politics, won wide praise for a humorous and hard-hitting attack on her fellow Texan who was soon to be the Republican nominee. Reflecting on Bush's family background and his penchant for misstatement, Richardson famously observed: "Poor George, he can't help it. He was born with a silver foot in his mouth."[17]

When it came time for Dukakis to speak, he was ready with a heartwarming account of his Greek heritage and stories about family members who came to the United States and lived the American Dream. His speech was primarily about the domestic policy initiatives that would be necessary to make that dream come true for more American families. He had only a few comments about international affairs and national security. He promised a strong military, praised Reagan's success on nuclear arms reduction, and expressed his hopes to go further on various initiatives in arms control. His primary attack on the Reagan administration was a statement that the greatest threat facing the nation from Latin America was not the Sandinistas in Nicaragua but the avalanche of drugs flooding our shores from that part of the world. He promised to make the war on drugs a real war for a change.

When the Republicans met in New Orleans for their nominating convention, the bulk of the news coverage involved the candidate's selection of a young and little-known senator from Indiana as his running mate. Dan Quayle had unseated Senator Birch Bayh in a convincing election victory but was clearly not ready for the spotlight and the media attention that suddenly surrounded him in New Orleans. Questions quickly arose about his service in the Indiana National Guard during the Vietnam era. That was a time when the sons of wealthy and well-connected families often got preference for admission into national guard units in order to avoid a draft into the army or the marines. Beyond questions about his past, Quayle faced commentators who challenged his qualifications to serve in the oval office in the event of a presidential death or disability. Quayle made most of the news at the convention until Bush gave his acceptance speech.

Carefully crafted by Peggy Noonan, one of Reagan's accomplished speechwriters, Bush's acceptance speech was very effective. It began with some self-deprecating humor when the candidate promised to "keep his charisma in check," then moved on to a litany of the issues—school prayer, the pledge of allegiance, the death penalty, gun control—that the campaign would use to define Dukakis as unacceptably liberal. When the list of differences between Democrats and Republicans reached its crescendo, the candidate made his famous commitment to approve no new taxes and did it in language that was memorable and absolute: "Read my lips: no new taxes." That decisive declaration was loudly cheered in the convention hall and quietly lamented by students of public policy, who understood that responding to the Reagan-era deficits would almost certainly involve both reductions in government spending and upward adjustments in taxation.

Both acceptance speeches were well written, well received, and nicely delivered by candidates who did not always score points for rhetorical flare.

According to David Gergen and E. J. Dionne: "The acceptance speeches by George Bush and Michael Dukakis were the finest performances of their careers."[18] Both championed traditional American values and promised a less divisive political climate. Where Dukakis pledged to pay more attention to competence than to ideology, Bush promised to soften the edges of political conflict and work toward creating "a kinder and gentler" nation. Neither candidate said much about world affairs. The word *international* appears in neither speech. Dukakis used the phrase *foreign policy* once, while Bush made one specific reference to *foreign affairs*. Bush did use the word *peace* multiple times and, like Dukakis, promised to continue the Reagan-era policies that were leading to substantive arms control agreements with the Soviet Union and a spread of democracy across the globe.

Each candidate mentioned drugs three times. Dukakis, as already noted, promised a real war on the drug problem. Polling in 1988 clearly indicated that the American people were more concerned about drug trafficking than they were about any traditional national security issue. Exit polling after the 1988 election asked voters about the most important problem facing the nation. There were only three answers to that question that scored in double digits. Twelve percent of voters said that the budget deficit was the most important problem; another 12 percent said the economy; 11 percent said drugs.[19] The campaign managers in both political parties knew this and tailored their messages accordingly. If Manuel Noriega paid any attention to American presidential politics, he might have noticed that he was the only world leader mentioned by name in either of the convention acceptance speeches. Both candidates were hostile to his line of work. This was not good news for the Panamanian dictator. Earlier in the campaign, Bush publicly criticized the Reagan administration for its efforts to negotiate a deal with Noriega. The normally loyal vice president who was reluctant to ever say anything that was out of line with Reagan programs or policies publicly objected to the attempts to kill federal indictments against Noriega in exchange for his promise to step down from power.[20]

As serious campaigning began following the two political conventions, the basic layout of the public policy landscape in the presidential contest was already clear. Both candidates acknowledged that something would have to be done to address the budget deficits that grew throughout the Reagan years, but neither was willing to say very much about what that something might be. Bush famously, and perhaps foolishly, took new taxes off the table in his acceptance speech and made vague statements about a flexible freeze in government spending. Dukakis reminded voters that as a governor he had actually balanced budgets, without saying that for most governors there was a legal obligation to do so. And at the same time that Dukakis was talking about balanced budgets he was simultaneously talking about expanding the American Dream with more efforts in education, job training, and economic assistance for the poor and the middle class. Neither candidate had budget proposals that could stand up to simple arithmetic, and both were constrained by what they could say on this subject without getting in trouble. That debate was going nowhere.

In foreign policy, both candidates liked the INF agreement. Both approved of the diminished tensions that accompanied the series of meetings between Gorbachev and Reagan. But neither was prepared to embrace the radical ideas about a zero option for nuclear weapons or for the missiles that carry them that the two leaders discussed at Reykjavik. Neither was saying that the Cold War was over. Both promised a strong defense and support for the military, though the nagging budget realities clearly dictated that defense spending had to move in a downward direction.

It would not be fair to say that the two candidates were without significant differences to debate and discuss. They had plenty of differences, but many of them were on small-scale issues, and Bush would run his campaign by highlighting some of the smallest. In an era of relative peace and prosperity, neither candidate could find much traction for new projects or programs that had no feasible source of funding amid acknowledged budget restraints and deficit dangers. There was general public satisfaction with the direction of the economy and with recent developments on the world stage. The sitting president, Ronald Reagan, had a steadily rising approval rating throughout the campaign cycle. It was not a time when the public cried out for change or demanded new or big ideas; neither candidate left his respective political convention as the champion of any.

The Speeches

It is customary for presidential candidates to deliver two kinds of speeches during an election cycle. The standard stump speech is refined and revised throughout the campaign season and delivered on multiple occasions to audiences across the country. That speech sticks to established themes and often uses phrases from the convention rhetoric. In addition, candidates from time to time give substantive policy speeches to friendly forums in which they lay out in more detail what they would do in particular policy areas. Every serious candidate gives one or more major campaign speech about foreign policy.

The Dukakis stump speech had almost no foreign policy content.[21] It began with autobiography and the immigrant family saga he used at the convention before listing a litany of woes at the end of the Reagan years: a low minimum wage, suspended health care for workers who lose their jobs, declining access to higher education, Republican opposition to civil rights, children living in poverty, Bush's support for a capital gains tax cut benefiting the wealthiest Americans, and the possibility that future judicial appointments to the Supreme Court would be nominees like Robert Bork. The speech did have a hint of the Gephardt message on trade when Dukakis said: "George Bush sat on the sidelines for eight years while America got beaten in world markets, while they mortgaged our children's future to a mountain of debt; and a piece of America was being sold off at bargain-basement prices every day." But there was very little said about what Dukakis would do to reduce the debt or make America more competitive.

The other foreign policy paragraph in the stump speech was an attack on Bush that challenged his international credentials by pointing out the implausibility of his claims to having been unaware of what was happening in the Iran-Contra affair and unaware that Manuel Noriega was involved in the drug trade. "When they sold arms to the Ayatollah, he went to 17 meetings where the matter was discussed—and then he said he wasn't in the loop. When they put Noriega on the payroll, *The New York Times* knew he was selling drugs, NBC knew, the C.I.A. knew, the National Security Council knew—but George Bush said he didn't know." Again, there was no detailed account of what Dukakis would do to prevent mistakes like those on Iran and Nicaragua or what he would do about Noriega. The stump speech did not have much in the way of domestic or foreign policy initiatives; it had criticisms of where the country was after eight years of Republican rule and criticisms of Bush as a weak leader who would not be able to get the country on the right track.

Dukakis did give substantive national security speeches in mid-September. After a well-publicized meeting with members of Congress who played a significant role in these matters, including Senator Sam Nunn and Representative Les Aspin, he spoke to the Chicago Council on Foreign Relations. Later in the same week, he spoke to a gathering at Georgetown University. The governor did not have extensive foreign policy experience, but he spoke four languages and had served in the army. When he was an instructor at Harvard's Kennedy School of Government, he met some of the nation's leading foreign policy experts, who later endorsed his candidacy and provided assistance to his campaign staff.

In his two September speeches, Dukakis outlined his positions on a variety of weapons systems, arms control initiatives, and dealing with the Soviet Union.[22] He was opposed to any precipitous deployment of hardware related to the Strategic Defense Initiative (SDI) but in favor of well-funded research into future missile defenses. He was in favor of cutting redundant weapons-development programs but also wanted enhancements for conventional forces that might well cost as much as or more than the weapons-system savings he proposed. He was hopeful about better dealings with the Soviet Union but cautious about how much we could expect from the Gorbachev era.

In an earlier speech, one given in the summer of 1988, Dukakis proposed asymmetrical cuts in conventional forces in Europe that would bring NATO and the Warsaw Pact to a rough parity in troops and conventional arms deployed on the continent. Significantly, Bush did not criticize this speech and actually called it an interesting idea.[23] In the summer of 1989, he would make the idea, or something similar to it, his own and get the NATO allies to endorse it. Dukakis cannot be faulted for failing to discuss serious national security issues, but he did so ineffectively. The week in September 1988 that he devoted to major addresses on these subjects was also the week he was photographed riding in a tank.

The Bush stump speech, unlike the one used by Dukakis, had several paragraphs devoted to foreign affairs.[24] He reminded his listeners about the Reagan military buildup and the successful negotiation of the INF treaty, saying further, in traditional Cold War phrasing: "The Soviets understand one thing: and that is strength on the part of the United States and the free world." He reminded his audience about the bombing of Libya and the intervention in Grenada and suggested that Dukakis was in favor of turning American sovereignty over to the United Nations and carrying out unilateral defense cuts. He promised to work for new arms control agreements, including one that would restrict chemical and bio-logical weapons.

The rest of the stump speech was the standard Bush attack on Duka-kis. He was a liberal who was against school prayer and the pledge of allegiance. The Massachusetts governor admits to being a "card-carrying member of the A.C.L.U. [American Civil Liberties Union]." Bush told his audience that he would hate to be his opponent "going around the country telling everybody how bad things are": "Things are not bad in the United States and I want to keep this expansion going." His plan to do so involved reducing the deficit while holding the line on taxes and defense spending. This was the common, and arithmetically challenged, message of 1988, but it was delivered with enthusiasm. The vice president's only specific deficit-reduction ideas were a call for a presidential line-item veto and a sarcastic rejection of Dukakis's proposal for better tax law enforce-ment. "It used to be a chicken in every pot; now it is an I.R.S. [Inter-nal Revenue Service] agent in every kitchen." The Bush stump speech was more disjointed than the Dukakis speech, but it was also more hard-hitting, with frequent reminders about peace and prosperity together with the description of a Democrat who was unacceptably liberal.

Bush gave a major foreign policy speech in August just before the Republican national convention. Speaking to Chicago business execu-tives, he called for a "new American internationalism."[25] That internation-alism would involve a continuation of Reagan-era initiatives, but with, it was hoped, more bipartisan support. Bush reiterated his support for SDI but emphasized that missile defenses might not be needed to address a Soviet threat alone. He pledged, if elected, to appoint a senior official to monitor developments in missile proliferation in rogue states. On Gor-bachev and changes in the Soviet Union, he warned against responses from the United States that fluctuated between "unjustified euphoria and exaggerated pessimism," saying that we would have to measure the Sovi-ets' reform by their actions, not by words.

Though it was not given much media attention at the time, Bush's August statement about Gorbachev was significant. Vice President Bush had had a brief conversation with Gorbachev in December 1987. He told the Soviet leader that he might have to criticize him in the forthcoming presidential campaign and that it would be wise to ignore the "empty canons of rhetoric" that often accompany electoral politics.[26] But, in his major speech on foreign policy, he did not criticize Gorbachev. Instead, he criticized the Reagan administration for its excesses, both the excesses in the first term, when the Soviets were demonized, and the excesses in the second term, when Gorbachev was embraced. He promised to avoid both extremes and begin his presidency with a long recalibration of superpower relations before initiating his own high-level meetings with Soviet leaders. While advising caution in dealings with the Soviets, he simultaneously pledged to use military force if it was needed "to help douse regional flashpoints" and warned that this was no "time for timidity, hesitancy or on-the-job training."[27] The August speech provided important indicators of what Bush would actually do during his first year in the White House when Panama became a flashpoint and the object of a large-scale American intervention.

The Bush foreign policy agenda differed from the one articulated by Dukakis in terms of its enthusiasm for missile defense and its willingness to consider the possible use of military force in regional conflicts. But there were also points of agreement. Both candidates were cautious about what might be happening in the Soviet Union and anxious to build on the success of the INF agreement. Both were worried about drugs entering the United States. Both called for a strong defense while acknowledging that some Pentagon budget cuts would have to be made. Bush talked often about Dukakis's lack of national security experience, while Dukakis kept asking how Bush could have been intimately involved in the Reagan-era foreign policy successes and simultaneously out of the loop during the controversial Iran-Contra decisions.

The Debates

There were two presidential debates in the 1988 election cycle and one between the vice presidential candidates.[28] The Dukakis campaign wanted more debates and wanted at least one of them focused exclusively on foreign affairs. The Bush camp refused. They did not want a debate in which Dukakis could go toe-to-toe against the vice president on international issues for fear that a good performance on his part would diminish their campaign rhetoric about the governor's lack of foreign policy experience.

The two presidential debates that the campaigns settled on used a common format with a moderator and a panel of journalists posing questions. Short answers were followed by even shorter rebuttals.

The most widely discussed question-and-answer exchange was the one that opened the second debate when the CNN moderator, Bernie Shaw, asked Dukakis what he would do if his wife were raped and murdered.[29] Most of the other questions and answers were quickly and easily forgotten. In all, there were forty-five questions posed during the two debates. Only fourteen of those dealt with issues related to national security and international affairs, and five of those fourteen were focused on the defense budget and where the two candidates would make the cuts that everyone understood would have to be made. Two questions dealt with the qualifications of the prospective vice presidents who might be called on to assume the duties of the presidency. Of the remaining seven questions, one dealt with Latin American loans, one with a hypothetical hostage crisis in the Middle East, one with the actual hostage taking that was part of the Iran-Contra affair, one with SDI, and two with nuclear weapons policy.

One—and only one—question dealt with the fundamental changes that were taking place in the Soviet Union under Gorbachev's leadership. The question was initially addressed to Vice President Bush. "Mr. Vice President, you said you've met with Secretary General Gorbachev, you've met with Mr. Shevardnadze, but for the last forty years Americans have been taught to regard the Soviet Union as the enemy. Yet, President Reagan has signed two arms control treaties and he's promised to share Star Wars technology with the very country he once called the evil empire. So, perhaps you can tell us this evening, should we be doing a lot to help the economics and the social development of a country that we have so long regarded as an adversary?"[30]

Bush responded with his conventional caution, welcoming glasnost and perestroika, but wondering whether the new Soviet leaders "can pull it off." He did not repeat the observation he had made in August that the Reagan foreign policy team might have been too severe in their initial criticisms of the Soviet Union and too enthusiastic about the prevailing optimism regarding Gorbachev. Instead, he mentioned that there were positive developments in China and interesting prospects in Eastern Europe before slipping into gratuitous criticisms of Carter's grain embargo against the Soviet Union and Democratic proposals for unilateral disarmament.

The Democratic candidate's rebuttal was not any better. Dukakis largely avoided the question. He rejected the idea that he was an advocate of unilateral disarmament, reminded the audience that the Soviet Union still had major problems with human rights and democratic practice, and reverted to the observation that any competition with the Soviet Union would be difficult unless we had a plan for dealing with our own domestic economy: "Let's not forget that our national security and our economic security go hand in hand. We cannot be strong militarily when we're teeter-tottering on top of a mountain of debt which has been created in the past eight years."

Critics of American presidential debates have long lamented the way we design and deliver televised opportunities for voters to hear directly from candidates. The question-and-answer format with multiple journalists skipping from topic to topic is not really a debate in any traditional sense. It is two simultaneous press conferences in which the candidates get to comment on each other's answers. That format guarantees short responses and the likely repetition of prepackaged campaign rhetoric and prepared sound bites. Thoughtful comments are rarely heard and little rewarded, while gaffs and mistakes are mercilessly repeated and excessively punished. This makes all candidates cautious and unlikely to say anything new or interesting if it carries the risk of being classified as an error. Neither candidate made significant mistakes or misstatements in the two 1988 presidential debates, and it is hard to say how their performances in either encounter might have significantly affected the election's outcome.

Dan Quayle may have made a mistake when he pointed out that he and Jack Kennedy were nearly the same age when each ran for national office. It was not a mistake of fact; the two were nearly the same age. The mistake was the opportunity it created for Lloyd Bentsen to respond with the sharpest barb of the three 1988 debates: "I served with Jack Kennedy. I knew Jack Kennedy. Jack Kennedy was a friend of mine. Senator, you're no Jack Kennedy."[31]

Dukakis's reputed mistake while responding to the question about a violent crime against his wife was similar. It did not involve any factual errors. Dukakis repeated his opposition to the death penalty, talked about crime, things he had done in Massachusetts to reduce it, and the national drug problem that contributes to criminal activity. His was a failure of style, not substance. He did not show the genuine emotion that most viewers would have expected. His excessively calm and low-key response may be related to the fact that he was tired and ill on the day of the second debate, as his campaign manager has reported, or it may have been an unusually honest moment in the 1988 presidential campaign.[32] It may have shown voters something about who the Democratic candidate was and how he would act in the White House. Dukakis was, in fact, a calm and rational individual unlikely to show flashes of emotion in his public pronouncements. That is not necessarily a bad trait for a prospective president. Dukakis's demeanor throughout the campaign, and particularly in the second presidential debate, may have given voters' a relevant and reasonable basis for judging his character and evaluating his fitness for holding the highest office in the land. Conversely, the political advertising in 1988 rarely gave voters any information that was either rational or relevant to making such evaluations.

The Advertising

There were plenty of negative ads, nasty accusations, and distracting issues throughout the 1988 presidential election. Gary Hart's problems with infidelity were partially self-inflicted. Hart resented questions about his personal life and challenged the press to follow him and to stake out his home in Washington if they wanted to know whether he was keeping company with attractive young women. They did, and he was. The accusation that Biden had plagiarized from a British politician is reported to have come from the Dukakis camp. The first references to Willie Horton and furlough programs in Massachusetts came from Al Gore in one of the Democratic candidate primary debates. On the Republican side, there were harsh ads and hard feelings in the race between Dole and Bush.

By the time the regular campaign began, the Bush team was in full gear with a carefully orchestrated negative campaign against Dukakis. "We can't elect George Bush," one Republican strategist allegedly said, but "we can defeat Michael Dukakis."[33] The strategy was worked out at a meeting in Kennebunkport in the summer of 1988.[34] Hot-button issues had been tested with focus groups, and Lee Atwater, Bush's chief political strategist, was ready to exploit all the weaknesses that were found. These included prayer in schools, the pledge and flag issues, the pollution in Boston Harbor that Dukakis claimed to have cleaned up, and especially the furlough issue and the crimes committed by Willie Horton.

The Horton attacks were unfair. Governor Dukakis had nothing to do with the approval of individual prison furloughs and inherited the legislation permitting them. Similar programs existed in California while Reagan was governor and in the federal prison system during his presidency. After Horton's crimes, the prisoner-leave program in Massachusetts was reviewed and modified. Though he did not play a leading role in the efforts to revise the program, Dukakis did sign a new law that restricted inmate furloughs. Nevertheless, because a heinous crime occurred while Dukakis was governor, the Bush campaign considered it a legitimate issue. They knew it played into voter fears about public safety and into the campaign's antiliberal narrative. Lee Atwater boasted early in the campaign: "If I can make Willie Horton a household name, we'll win the election."[35] Criminal justice reforms and Supreme Court decisions protecting the rights of the accused were unpopular and could be blamed on liberal justices and liberal policies. Dukakis could be tied to all of it. Moreover, and most importantly, the Horton furlough crime involved a black perpetrator and white victims, the kind of crime that added a racial dimension to the existing public fears related to violent crime.

The negative advertising worked. A CBS/*New York Times* poll in 1988 asked voters which ads made the biggest impression on them during the campaign. The largest group answered that it was the one depicting a revolving door in front of a prison.[36] That ad was prepared and funded by the Bush campaign. It talked about the prison furlough program in general and did not mention Willie Horton by name. The actors in prison garb walking through a turnstile made of prison bars were mostly white. All of them were looking down as they made their circle, except the black actor who looked up and directly into the camera after passing through the turnstile.

There was another ad covering the same material. This one was funded by outside groups not directly affiliated with the Bush campaign and able to spend money outside the limitations imposed by post-Watergate campaign finance reform. The unaffiliated campaign ad was thirty seconds long and had straightforward and sharp language comparing Bush and Dukakis on the death penalty and crime. Bush favored a death penalty for serious criminal offenses; Dukakis supported "weekend passes" for first-degree murderers. The ad then described the two crimes committed by Horton, the one that landed him jail (a multiple stabbing during a robbery) and the one that he committed while on furlough (assaulting a young man and raping his fiancée). Throughout the descriptions, pictures of Horton were shown. He is black and tall and in one photograph has a blank expression that, when juxtaposed to the grim description of his crimes, makes him seem all the more menacing. The message was clear. And, in case anyone missed it, the victims of Horton's furlough crimes made appearances on television programs and attended Republican political rallies across the country. Leaflets with Dukakis's picture next to Horton's were widely distributed with inflammatory language about Dukakis's weakness in responding to crime.

Because the ads and the associated activities were controversial, they were the subject of stories on many news programs. The commentary concerning the advertisements was often critical, but the repetition of the advertising images in the news coverage amplified their impact.

Conclusion

A presidential campaign that was almost immediately followed by one of the most revolutionary periods in international history is most often remembered for the negative advertising about a heinous crime committed by a Massachusetts inmate on leave from a prison cell. The foreign policy dog may not have barked during the 1988 presidential campaign, but there were plenty of loud and obnoxious noises.

Twenty years after the campaign, Michael Dukakis recalled his biggest mistake. He never responded effectively to the Bush attacks.[37] In fact, he did the opposite. He tried to run a decent campaign focused on his economic accomplishments as governor of Massachusetts. When his staff was implicated in the distribution of materials about Joe Biden's plagiarism, he fired his campaign manager, John Sasso.[38] When another senior staff member made a public statement concerning rumors that George Bush had had a long-term affair with a government employee, that staff member resigned from the campaign.[39] Dukakis did his best to run a race for the White House that was not also a race to the bottom of what was permissible in the conduct of a presidential campaign. He lost.

The best book written about the 1988 presidential race, and one of the best ever written about any campaign, is called *What it Takes*.[40] Though the title is primarily about the personal sacrifices that candidates for the presidency are required to make, it is also an apt description of how the Bush campaign team approached the contest in 1988. They were well organized, disciplined about keeping on message, and fully committed to the negative attacks that gave them traction against their Democratic opponent. They were willing to do whatever it took. Bush won.

Not without some remorse. Just before his death from cancer in 1991, Lee Atwater, Bush's campaign adviser and an outspoken advocate of the Willie Horton advertising, published an article in *Life* magazine in which he reflected on what he had learned in the course of his illness. He apologized for the "naked cruelty" of some of the things he said and did in the 1988 presidential election. He regretted that some of his words and actions were deemed to be racist.[41]

Students of American foreign affairs have a different regret. They lament the absence of serious discussion in 1988 about the future of American foreign policy and the enormous global transformations that were on the horizon. But they would have to admit that, in most presidential contests, international issues are less important than domestic debates and that most voters never acquire sophisticated or detailed knowledge about the policy positions, foreign or domestic, taken by opposing candidates. Instead, elections are often about the impressions that candidates give of themselves and broad public judgments on whether the country and the economy are headed in the right direction. The small role given to foreign policy in the 1988 election may have been a more extreme version of what typically occurs in American presidential politics.

Moreover, it is possible to read the broad political judgments rendered in the 1988 presidential election as serious and sensible. Both candidates welcomed the shift in American foreign policy that took place in Ronald Reagan's second term, and neither proposed any dramatic changes in the way the United States should deal with the Soviet Union. Both agreed that we should welcome reforms in Communist regimes and pursue additional arms limitation agreements. Both were also cautious about what might be happening in Gorbachev's Soviet Union. Neither candidate was willing to talk about an end to the Cold War. Both wanted a strong American military posture even though budget realities would almost certainly require cuts in Pentagon spending. On the core questions regarding national security and East-West relations, there were no big differences between the candidates. One wanted prompt deployment of missile defenses; the other was more wary of their immediate value but unwilling to rule them out should they ever become technologically and economically feasible. There were disagreements about some specific weapon systems and about how willing the United States should be to use force overseas, but they were not fundamental or demonstrably important to many voters. Both candidates said that drug trafficking was a new and major threat to the United States that would require additional American actions.

Voters in 1988 may reasonably have concluded that there were no major foreign policy differences between the two candidates. There were, however, significant differences and distinctions between them with regard to background and demeanor.

Bush unquestionably had more experience in international affairs. The Dukakis campaign tried to raise questions about that experience, particularly with regard to the vice president's role in the Iran-Contra affair, but never succeeded in doing serious damage to public perceptions of Bush's foreign policy credentials or reputation. In a feisty live interview with Dan Rather of CBS News early in the campaign, Bush pushed back against repeated questioning on his actions in connection with Iran-Contra and made a favorable impression on the many voters who were suspicious of national media anchors and news organizations.[42] After the Rather interview, it was harder to raise the Iran-Contra connections in attacks on Bush. If voters, in general, were satisfied with America's position in the world at the end of Reagan's second term and wanted continuity in the conduct of foreign affairs, Bush was, and remained throughout the campaign, a logical and legitimate choice.

Dukakis came across as articulate and capable, but his competence and conscientiousness may actually have hurt him. Roger Ailes, Bush's media adviser, once observed that Dukakis reminded people of "the kid who puts up his hand in school on a Friday afternoon and says, 'You forgot to give us our homework.'"[43] Moreover, though Bush often exhibited an "awkward amiability" and frequently misspoke at campaign events, he was a candidate that voters could relate to and understand.[44] Dukakis had a harder time making personal connections to potential voters.

He seemed aloof and mechanical. His famously dispassionate response to the debate question about his wife as a victim of violent crime may have solidified that image. The pictures of him riding in a tank did not help give voters a favorable impression. More broadly, his slow and ineffective responses to the political attacks launched by the Bush campaign camp made those attacks more effective and could easily have created a public perception of weakness for some of the voters making their final decisions.

In the end, Dukakis did reasonably well. He got more votes in 1988 than either Carter in 1980 or Mondale in 1984. Despite the progress Dukakis made over his immediate party predecessors, however, Bush won a clear victory, with nearly 54 percent of the popular vote and a solid Electoral College majority.

Bush became the first sitting vice president to win a presidential election since Martin Van Buren followed Andrew Jackson into the White House in 1838. George H. W. Bush became president at a unique time that involved extraordinary and potentially explosive international events. He and his experienced team of foreign policy advisers would make the most of the East European revolutions, manage the collapse of the Soviet Union, and organize an impressive multilateral response to Iraqi aggression in Kuwait. They would do all this and more without an electoral mandate that was in any significant way related to their international actions and accomplishments.

Four years later, following those significant international successes, Bush and his foreign policy team would be removed from office in another election in which foreign policy played a surprisingly minor role.

Notes

1. Bruce Russett, *Hegemony and Democracy* (London: Routledge, 2011), 129–30.

2. "When I left office, the cold war was over." George P. Shultz, *Turmoil and Triumph* (New York: Scribner's, 1993), xi.

3. Reagan quoted in *Guide to U.S. Foreign Policy: A Diplomatic History*, ed. Robert J. McMahon and Thomas V. Zeiler (Thousand Oaks, CA: Congressional Quarterly Press, 2012), 433.

4. At the outset of the campaign season, George McGovern observed: "So clearly is communism neither the wave of the future nor the major challenge to American security that our anticommunist orientation has become irrelevant and

obsolete." George McGovern, "The 1988 Election: U.S. Foreign Policy at a Watershed," *Foreign Affairs* 66, no. 3 (1988): 614–29, 614.

5. The 1988 election is most often connected to the following words: *issueless, personal, trivial,* and *negative.* See Norman Ornstein and Mark Schmitt, "The 1988 Election," *Foreign Affairs* 68, no. 1 (1989): 39–52, 39.

6. Voter Turnout in Presidential Elections: 1828–2012, *The American Presidency Project,* http://www.presidency.ucsb.edu/data/turnout.php.

7. "George Bush: Fighting the 'Wimp Factor,'" *Newsweek,* October 19, 1987.

8. See *West Virginia State Board of Education v. Barnette,* 319 U.S. 624 (1943).

9. Robin Toner, "Kitty Dukakis Stings G.O.P. with Her Attack," *New York Times,* September 25, 1988.

10. Ornstein and Schmitt, "The 1988 Election," 40.

11. As he left the stage, Dukakis told his campaign manager: "I blew it." Jack Germond and Jules Witcover, *Whose Broad Stripes and Bright Stars: The Trivial Pursuit of the Presidency, 1988* (New York: Warner, 1989), 447.

12. See Kathleen Hall Jamieson, *Dirty Politics: Deception, Distraction and Democracy* (New York: Oxford University Press, 1993); and Jeremy D. Mayer, *Running on Race: Racial Politics in Presidential Campaigns, 1960–2000* (New York: Random House, 2002).

13. *New York Times* editorial quoted in David S. Myers, "The Editorial Pages of Leading Newspapers in 1988," in *The Media in the 1984 and 1988 Presidential Campaigns,* ed. Guido H. Stempel III and John W. Windhauser (Westport, CT: Greenwood, 1991), 155–186, 178–79.

14. Elizabeth Drew, *Richard M. Nixon: The American Presidency Series* (New York: Times Books, 2007), 144.

15. For the best account of Hart's implosion during the buildup to the 1988 presidential campaign, see Matt Bai, *All the Truth Is Out: The Fall of Gary Hart and the Rise of Tabloid Politics* (New York: Knopf, 2014).

16. Anthony Bennett, *The Race for the White House from Reagan to Clinton* (New York: Palgrave Macmillan, 2013), 95.

17. Bennett, *The Race for the White House,* 106.

18. David Gergen and E. J. Dionne, "Election Campaign Strategy: Conventions, VP Choices, and Debates," in *Campaign for President: The Managers Look at '88,* ed. David R. Runkel (Dover, MA: Auburn House, 1989), 197–262, 197.

19. For this question and other exit-polling results, see 1988 Presidential Election, Roper Center, http://www.ropercenter.uconn.edu/polls/us-elections/presidential-elections/1988-presidential-election.

20. David Hoffman, "Bush Splits with Reagan on Handling of Noriega," *Washington Post,* May 19, 1988.

21. A version of the speech was published in the *New York Times* on October 25, 1988. The quotes in this paragraph and the next are taken from this version.

22. For coverage of the Chicago speech, see Ben Bradlee Jr., "Dukakis Spells Out Soviet Policy," *Boston Globe,* September 14, 1988. For the Georgetown speech,

see Michael McQueen and Tim Carrington, "Dukakis, with Tougher Tone on Defense, Pledges Support for Weapons Systems," *Wall Street Journal,* September 15, 1988. For commentary on the September speeches, see William Safire, "Rat-Tat-Tatting," *New York Times,* September 15, 1988.

23. Gerald Boyd, "Restrained Bush Taking New Tack," *New York Times,* June 17, 1989.

24. A version of the speech was published in the *New York Times* on October 24, 1988. The quotes in the following two paragraphs come from this version of the speech.

25. "Bush Pledges to Forge Ahead on 'Star Wars,'" *Chicago Tribune,* August 3, 1988.

26. George H. W. Bush and Brent Scowcroft, *A World Transformed* (New York: Knopf, 1998), 5.

27. "Bush Pledges to Forge Ahead on 'Star Wars.'"

28. The Bush campaign dominated the negotiations over terms for the debates. See Interview with James A. Baker III, January 29, 2000, Miller Center, University of Virginia, http://millercenter.org/president/bush/oralhistory/james-baker-2000.

29. Full transcripts of the 1988 presidential debates can be found at the Web site maintained by the Commission on Presidential Debates, http://www.debates.org/index.php?page=debate-transcripts.

30. The Second Bush-Dukakis Presidential Debate, October 13, 1988, Commission on Presidential Debates, http://www.debates.org/index.php?page=october-13-1988-debate-transcript.

31. The Bentsen-Quayle Vice Presidential Debate, Commission on Presidential Debates, http://www.debates.org/index.php?page=october-5-1988-debate-transcripts.

32. Susan Estrich commenting on the second debate in Runkel, ed., *Campaign for President,* 253.

33. Robert Shogan, *The Double-Edged Sword: How Character Makes and Ruins Presidents, from Washington to Clinton* (Boulder, CO: Westview, 2000), 171–72.

34. Paul Taylor, *See How They Run: Electing the President in an Age of Mediaocracy* (New York: Knopf, 1990), 203.

35. Atwater quoted in Taylor, *See How They Run,* 190.

36. See www.insidepolitics.org/ps111/candidateads.html.

37. Charles E. Pierce, "President Duke," *Boston Globe,* August 3, 2008.

38. "The Road to the White House Paved with Dirty Tricks," *Guardian,* November 8, 1988. Dukakis later rehired Sasso.

39. "Donna Brazile: Born for Politics," *USA Today,* May 23, 2000.

40. Richard Ben Cramer, *What It Takes* (New York: Random House, 1992).

41. "Gravely Ill, Atwater Offers Apology," *New York Times,* January 13, 1991.

42. Peter Goldman and Tom Mathews, *The Quest for the Presidency, 1988* (New York: Simon & Schuster, 1989), 198–201.

43. Goldman and Mathews, *Quest for the Presidency,* 366.

44. Goldman and Mathews, *Quest for the Presidency,* 366–67.

14

Internationalism Challenged

Foreign Policy Issues in the
1992 Presidential Election

John Dumbrell

Debates about foreign policy did affect the 1992 presidential election, the first such post–Cold War contest, but only to a very limited extent. At the general election, only 8 percent of voters responded that foreign policy "mattered most" in determining their vote. Of that 8 percent, 7 percent voted for the incumbent president, George H. W. Bush, rather than the Democratic candidate, Bill Clinton, or the independent candidate, Ross Perot. According to Leon Sigal, this was the election that "pushed the wider world to the periphery of American politics."[1]

Quite apart from the limited saliency of foreign policy in the campaign, 1992 had some strikingly unusual features. This was the election where Bush's over 90 percent approval ratings immediately following the 1991 Gulf War developed into the lowest popular vote for an incumbent presidential candidate since Herbert Hoover in 1932. To some commentators, it seemed as if Prime Minister Winston Churchill's defeat in the 1945 British general election had been replayed. The 1992 election was the first US presidential election since 1912 where a third candidate was able to command significant numbers of votes—Perot won just under 19 percent, without any success in the Electoral College—on a national scale. Bush's defeat is usually linked to an array of contingent, short-term factors, such as the impact of recession, the backfiring of negative campaigning, Clinton's success in prioritizing domestic issues, a generalized anti-incumbent mood, and the impact of Perot. The 1992 recession is plausibly portrayed as affecting (whether directly or through fear of unemployment) millions of middle-income Americans in an era of corporate downsizing. Republican negative campaigning in 1988 against the Democrat Michael Dukakis, and particularly Bush's attempts to blame Dukakis for the release of the Massachusetts criminal Willie Horton, undermined GOP efforts to "go negative" in 1992. The post–Cold War environment seemed to herald a new looseness in the electorate as old certainties, particularly those linked to traditional perceptions of how the two main parties related to issues of national security, dissolved. The sense of older political moorings being dislodged linked into a slightly random but often remarked sense of public hostility to incumbents. Although Perot's precise impact on the election result is disputed, there is no question that the insurgent Texan trained his general election guns more on Bush than on Clinton.[2]

This chapter will consider the ways in which debates on foreign policy did emerge during the 1992 nomination and the general election races—always bearing in mind that domestic issues dominated and that international themes tended to center on questions of foreign economic policy rather than the national security agenda of earlier presidential contests. Trade policy certainly influenced the campaigns. However, the 1992 contests also saw candidates clashing over contrasting interpretations of how the Cold War had ended, over issues of trust and competence in foreign policy, and over the resurgence of neoisolationism, protectionism, and nationalist populism. Following a review of the campaigns, this chapter will consider the degree to which his 1992 foreign policy stances provided guidance to the kind of foreign policy that Bill Clinton followed after he assumed office.

The Nomination Races

Bush was faced with a significant nomination challenge from Pat Buchanan, the rightist political commentator and former speechwriter for President Nixon. He was also challenged briefly from the far Right by David Duke from Louisiana. Buchanan polled 37 percent in the New Hampshire primary and 36 and 32 percent in Georgia and Florida, respectively. The Democratic primary race was extremely open, affected by the general assumption that Bush was very likely going to be reelected in November and by the decision of New York governor Mario Cuomo not to run. Several other potential Democratic candidates, including Al Gore, Jesse Jackson, Bill Bradley, and Richard Gephardt, decided against mounting campaigns. The Democratic field included Senators Tom Harkin of Iowa and Bob Kerrey of Nebraska, former senator Paul Tsongas from Massachusetts, and two candidates (Clinton from Arkansas and Jerry Brown from California) with a gubernatorial background. Of these, Tsongas won in eight states; Brown won in five but failed to beat Clinton in California on June 2, by which time the future president had an unassailable delegate lead. Harkin won three states, while Kerrey managed just one primary victory in South Dakota.[3] A poll taken on June 4, before Perot's temporary withdrawal from the race in July, saw Clinton polling at 25 percent, Bush at 31 percent, and Perot at 39 percent. The extreme volatility of 1992 electoral politics was evidenced in significant swings in Bush's approval ratings in the early part of the year and with Clinton taking clear poll leads from the Democratic convention on.[4]

The Buchanan campaign was a maverick affair, sounding "America First," right-wing populist and neoisolationist themes. At times, it seemed as if Robert Taft, the heartland Republican senator from Ohio and internationalist skeptic of the post-1945 era, had been reborn. At one level, Buchanan offered a conservative version of the Cincinnatus myth, which was also to become one of Perot's themes. The Cold War had, in this particular narrative, seen the temporary (and necessary) abandonment of authentic conservative values of nonentanglement and stout American independence. With the Cold War won, American conservatism could now return home to a true "conservatism of the heart." In promoting protectionism and immigration restrictions, Buchanan also signaled his fear that this opportunity for conservatism to refind itself was in danger of being lost in a breakneck rush toward post–Cold War globalization. Buchanan's America Firstism accepted that American industrial enterprise was not invincible. It needed to be protected, not least because foreigners often did not respect the rules of international free trade. Buchanan also explicitly rejected the view that protectionism either caused or contributed to the Great Depression of the 1930s.[5] As Buchanan's 1992 campaign developed, it acquired distinctly unpleasant racist and anti-Semitic accretions. Buchanan had opposed the 1991 Gulf War on the grounds that it did not involve core American interests and that it reflected Bush's deference to "two groups beating the drums for war in the Middle East—the Israeli defense ministry and its amen corner in the United States." Announcing his candidacy prior to the New Hampshire primary, he declared: "When we say we will put America first, we mean also that our Judeo-Christian values are going to be preserved and our Western heritage is going to be handed down to future generations and not dumped into some landfill called multiculturalism." A key Buchanan theme in the New Hampshire primary (which he went on to win in 1996) was that Bush's foreign economic policy was leading to American jobs being exported. As the ideological cement from the Cold War disintegrated within the Republican Party, there appeared evidence from New Hampshire both in 1992 and in 1996 that Buchanan was attracting self-identified moderate as well as conservative Republicans. The Bush campaign effectively acknowledged a significant threat from the Right by issuing a televised attack on Buchanan's foreign policy stances during the Georgia primary race in early March. Fronting the advertisement for Bush, retired general P. X. Kelley discussed Buchanan's opposition to the Gulf War: "The last thing we need in the White House is an isolationist like Pat Buchanan. If he doesn't think America should lead the world, how can we trust him to lead America?"[6]

Some of the Democratic hopefuls in 1992 had particular foreign policy records that affected the way in which they were perceived by primary voters. Tom Harkin had been involved in leftist human rights initiatives in the Senate since the later years of the Vietnam War. Bob Kerrey was a decorated Vietnam veteran who had opposed the Gulf War. Paul Tsongas was a strong advocate of free trade and of the North American Free Trade Agreement (NAFTA). These stances put him at odds with Democrats who leaned toward positions favored by organized labor. Jerry Brown ran a leftist populist campaign that in certain respects, such as opposition to NAFTA and skepticism toward foreign aid, echoed some of Buchanan's stances. Similar themes were already being sounded by Ross Perot, who tentatively announced his independent campaign on February 20. Jerry Brown argued that America should not have fought the Gulf War and declared that he would not "give a penny" to foreign aid "until every small farmer, businessman and family" in the United States was relieved of debt.[7] Both parties' nomination races thus reflected what commentators were widely seeing as a "come home America" mood in wider US public opinion.[8] The Democratic nomination race turned into a contest primarily between Tsongas and Clinton, with both Kerrey and Brown achieving occasionally credible surges.

Bill Clinton managed to win the nomination without making too many specific promises on foreign policy. At least in foreign policy, he thus managed to avoid the structural Democratic dilemma of tacking too far to the Left in the nomination race to appeal to core Democrats, only to store up problems for the general election. In this, he was helped by the sheer variety of the Democratic field. Clinton seemed broadly but still somewhat ambivalently to support NAFTA. On one issue relevant to recent foreign policy, however, the nomination race did potentially go straight to issues of trust, patriotism, and the still uncomfortable divisions within the Democratic Party. This was the question of Clinton's record (or nonrecord) in the Vietnam War.

Clinton's nonservice in Vietnam had been a concern for his campaign team since the days of running for gubernatorial office in Arkansas. Frank Geer, Clinton's media adviser, recalled discussing the Vietnam issue with him in August 1991 and concluding that mere nonservice— as distinct from actual draft dodging—"isn't going to be a problem" for 1992.[9] James Carville, who joined the Clinton campaign in December 1991, later described the way in which Bill Clinton intended to handle the Vietnam War issue. Clinton "would not have gotten elected governor of Arkansas in 1978 on a platform of 'It was a stupid war. I didn't want to go and get my ass shot off.'" Essentially, according to Carville, Clinton's line was to be as circumspect as possible, "saying just enough to satisfy reporters but not enough to inflame voters."[10] However, the circumspection strategy threatened to unravel in the primary campaign, following the publication in early February of a *Wall Street Journal* story alleging that Clinton had signed up for a Reserve Officers Training Corps program in order to avoid the draft. Potentially highly damaging to the Clinton campaign was the surfacing of a letter written by Bill Clinton from Oxford, England, in December 1969 to Colonel Eugene Holmes, head of the Arkansas Reserve Officer Training Corps (ROTC) program. The letter described the young Clinton's opposition to the war and his involvement in antiwar activities while in England. The letter thanked Holmes for "saving me from the draft."[11] The Vietnam War issue combined with a sex scandal and pushed the Clinton campaign into crisis. However, in relation to Vietnam, Clinton was able to present himself as an authentic opponent of the war while also plausibly arguing that he was "saved" not so much by the ROTC enrollment as by the issuing of a high draft lottery number when he was no longer shielded by his involvement in an ROTC program many miles from Oxford. Both Paul Tsongas and Bob Kerrey publicly accepted Clinton's explanation of his conduct with regard to the draft. The draft issue arose again in early April, during the New York primary campaign, when another letter surfaced—this time indicating that Clinton's joining of the ROTC program had taken place *after* he actually received a draft induction notice. Clinton's victory in the New York primary (41 percent of the vote compared to 29 percent for Paul Tsongas and 26 percent for Jerry Brown) seemed to indicate that the issue, at least for Democrats, had run its course.[12]

The General Election: Bush and Clinton Foreign Policy Themes

The Bush campaign tried to keep the Vietnam draft issue alive as the country moved toward the November election. The most direct exchange between the two leading candidates occurred during the first television debate between Bush, Clinton, and Perot, held on October 11. Bush directly raised the character issue, saying it was "wrong to demonstrate against your own country or organize demonstrations against your own country in [*sic*] foreign soil." Clinton responded: "You were wrong to attack my patriotism. I was opposed to the war but I love my country and we need a president who will bring this country together, not divide it."[13] Bush made some vague accusations relating to a visit made by Clinton to Moscow while studying at Oxford University. Plausible evidence that the White House was implicated at least to some degree in the searching of Clinton's passport files backfired as the Democratic candidate accused the Bush team of "not only rifling through my files but actually investigating my mother, a well-known subversive."[14]

Draft-dodging accusations were undermined by examination of the war record of the vice presidential candidate Dan Quayle, who had served in the Indiana National Guard rather than in Vietnam. Quayle complained that the media treatment of Clinton's Vietnam record contrasted sharply with press criticism of his own war record during the 1988 campaign.[15] Clinton's Vietnam vulnerability was also lessened to some extent by lingering doubts about the degree to which Bush, as vice president under Reagan, had been cognizant of the illegalities associated with the Iran-Contra scandal. Al Gore, Bill Clinton's running mate, referred to the Bush defense that he had not been in the Iran-Contra "loop" as opening up a "credibility canyon."[16] James Carville recalled: "My view was that the American people didn't want an election about Iran-Contra or about the draft: they were interested in paying their bills. Iran-Contra was a godsend only because every time the Republicans would bring up the draft they would get Iran-Contra right back in their face."[17] In the final days of the campaign, the Iran-Contra special prosecutor, Lawrence Walsh, issued an indictment against former defense secretary Caspar Weinberger in a form that did seem to call into question Bush's claim of being out the Iran-Contra loop.[18]

The character issue was potentially a strong card for the Bush team to play. It extended beyond Clinton's sexual indiscretions to include his Vietnam record, his lack of more than academic foreign policy or military experience, and his "slick Willie" reputation. Bush's own stature as a World War II veteran and commander in chief in the Gulf conflict stood at the center of several Bush television advertisements. The underlying difficulty for Bush, however, related to the decreased saliency of national security agendas in a time of peace. Bush's pursuit of character and personal issues stimulated memories of counterproductive negative campaigning in 1988. The character agenda was also damaged by the sheer awkwardness and oddity with which George Bush expressed it. The president took to referring to Al Gore as "Ozone," a clumsy reference to the future vice president's identification with environmental issues. At a Michigan rally, Bush attacked Gore: "This guy is so far off in the environmental extreme, we'll be up to our neck in owls and out of work for every American. This guy's crazy." Bush declared that he would rather consult Millie, his dog, "before I'd go to Ozone and Governor Clinton." Referring to Clinton's "waffling," Bush inexplicably continued: "You cannot have a lot of butts sitting there in the Oval Office."[19] Bush's frequent inarticulateness and tin ear unquestionably contributed to the sense of indirection that haunted what Dan Quayle called "the most poorly planned and executed incumbent presidential campaign in this century."[20]

Despite the low visibility of foreign policy themes, the two main campaigns had, by November, sketched out distinct foreign policy stances. To some extent, this clarification reflected the cut and thrust of the election, as Democrats responded to particular arguments advanced by the White House. Thus, Gore tried to deflect the crazy/Ozone charge by arguing that global environmental activism was not a recipe for losing American jobs. Bush's ignoring of environmental agendas was, according to Gore, "costing the United States millions of jobs by pretending that our strategy should be to protect the old, polluting, inefficient ways of the past."[21] Clinton responded to Republican claims that Reagan and Bush had won the Cold War by ridiculing such claims as examples of "the rooster taking credit for the dawn."[22] Further examination of, in particular, the St. Louis presidential debate—the only televised debate that dealt with foreign policy in any depth—indicates that serious and substantive foreign policy exchanges did take place between Bush and Clinton.

Aside from trade issues (to be considered below), the main foreign policy themes discussed at St. Louis were defense-spending priorities after the Cold War, democracy promotion, and the conflict in Bosnia. In each of these areas, Clinton and Bush offered competing approaches. According to Clinton, the deployment of 150,000 troops in post-Soviet Europe was excessive. Bush emphasized the gains made during his administration in terms of nuclear deals, notably the elimination of the intercontinental Russian SS-18 missile. Bush's tactic in the St. Louis debate was to cast both Clinton and Ross Perot as leaning toward isolationism, while Clinton sought to disassociate himself from the more obviously contractionist and unilateralist stance of Perot. For Clinton, President Bush was too timid in his promotion of democracy. The White House had failed, in his opinion, to respond robustly to the Tiananmen Square massacre of 1989. The United States should not shrink from promoting democracy and human rights in China: "So I would be firm. I would say if you want to continue Most-Favored-Nation status for your government-owned industries as well as your private ones, observe human rights in the future." In regard to Bosnia, Clinton fell well short of recommending any ground troop commitment but supported the hardening of the trade embargo on Belgrade and even a tougher military posture: "We can't get involved in the quagmire but we must do what we can." Bush promised "moral persuasion" in promoting human rights in the Balkans and elsewhere but clearly favored engagement over the "isolation" of human rights abusers. At St. Louis, Clinton outlined a version of neo-Kantian democratic peace theory: "We ought to be promoting democratic impulses around the world. Democracies are our partners. They don't go to war with each other."[23]

The positions developed at St. Louis were extended in other debates and, in Clinton's case, drew on a series of foreign policy addresses mainly written by Tony Lake (who would become President Clinton's national security adviser) and beginning with an event at Georgetown University in December 1991. Where Bush invoked his record of success, Clinton questioned the "coddling" of Saddam Hussein prior to the Gulf conflict of 1991.[24] In Milwaukee in September 1991, Clinton declared: "I believe our nation has a higher purpose than to coddle dictators and stand aside from the global movement towards democracy."[25] On defense spending, an extended dialogue between the two leading candidates emerged over the extent to which cuts could or should be made in the new environment and over differing interpretations of a post–Cold War domestic "peace dividend." Clinton emphasized the need for smaller, more mobile forces. At one stage, Bush, countering Democratic calls for defense cuts being made to fund domestic investment, seemed to defend high troop levels in Europe as a kind of public works scheme: "If you throw another 50,000 kids on the street because of cutting recklessly in troop levels, you're going to put a lot more out of work." Clinton spoke of cutting an additional $60 billion from the Bush defense budget over five years but continued to defend controversial weapons such as the Seawolf submarine and the V-22 Osprey tilt-rotor helicopter.[26]

Clinton seized the initiative in the 1992 foreign policy position taking, leaving Bush as a president who seemed to be resting on his laurels, devoid of vision, and offering only periodic support for his main foreign policy concept, the New World Order. During the second presidential debate, held in Richmond, Virginia, Bush described his New World Order as simply "freedom and democracy." He reminded the audience: "Since I became President, 43, 44 countries have gone democratic."[27] Conspicuously, however, he failed to develop a compelling defense of his New World Order. His apparent preference for prioritizing the character issue allowed Clinton to make the running. Thomas Friedman wrote in the *New York Times* in October 1992 that Clinton had developed a coherent "sober internationalist" foreign policy stance.[28] The election certainly was not won by Clinton's statements on foreign policy, nor was foreign policy remotely the main concern of the Clinton team. As Tony Lake later wrote: "Those of us doing foreign policy were always aware that we were a wholly owned subsidiary of the campaign."[29] However, Clinton did manage to subvert the character attacks on his foreign policy competence and integrity. By implying that, for all his foreign policy successes, Bush essentially belonged to a disappearing era, Clinton put the president on the defensive.

Perot and Foreign Economic Policy

Foreign affairs arose as an important presidential election issue primarily in the context of trade and foreign economic policy. Relative neglect of the traditional national security/foreign policy agenda—something that particularly damaged Bush—was, of course, primarily a function of the termination of the Cold War.[30] The shift to a trade/foreign economics agenda was greatly accelerated by the extraordinary, on-off candidacy of Ross Perot. Perot's amateur status would have undermined his appeal in times of greater international danger. In 1992, however, America seemed ready to take seriously a candidate who embraced the theme of "come home, America." As Perot himself put it in the second presidential debate: "[For] 45 years we were preoccupied with the Red Army. I suggest now our number one preoccupation is red ink and our country and we've got to put our people back to work."[31] Perot was, as Jack Germond and Jules Witcover put it, "for all his wealth a walking man-in-the-street."[32] Even he, however, had occasionally to put his economic populism within a wider foreign policy framework. I begin this section with a brief account of Perot's wider foreign policy compass.

Almost inevitably, the foreign policy section of Ross Perot's 1992 campaign book was entitled "Start at Home."[33] His wider view of foreign policy amounted to a mixture of international political neoisolationism, unilateralism, and the promotion of global capitalism. In the St. Louis presidential debate, Perot attacked free-riding American allies: "If I'm poor and you're rich, and I can get you to defend me, that's good. But when the tables get turned, I ought to do my share. Right now we spend about $300 billion a year on defense; the Japanese spend about $30 billion in Asia, the Germans spend about $30 billion in Europe. For example, Germany'll spend a trillion dollars building infrastructure over the next 10 years. It's kind of easy to do if you only have to pick up a $30 billion tab to defend your country." Bosnia "is basically a problem that is a primary concern to the European Community." Surprisingly, Perot nonetheless supported the extension of aid to the former Soviet Union to facilitate its route to peaceful, democratic capitalism: "We need to help and support Russia and the republics in every possible way to become democratic capitalistic societies and not just sit back and let those countries continue in turmoil because they could go back worse than things used to be. And believe me there are a lot of old boys in the K.G.B. and the military that liked it better the way it used to be." On China, Perot referred to a "delicate tightwire walk that we must go through at the present time to make sure that we do not cozy up to tyrants, to make sure that they don't get the impression that they can suppress their people."[34]

Perot was prepared to criticize the prewar Bush policy toward Iraq in terms stronger than those advanced by Bill Clinton: "If you create Saddam Hussein, over a 10-year period, using billions of dollars of US taxpayer money, step up to the plate and say it was a mistake." He accused the Bush administration of telling Saddam prior to the 1990 invasion, via US ambassador April Glaspie, that "he could take the northern part of Kuwait."[35] For Perot, the Gulf War should have been preceded by "a war tax . . . so that all of us had skin in the game." He contrasted World War II, which saw the two sons of President Franklin Roosevelt flying air missions, with the Gulf War, where only two "members of Congress had sons on the battlefield in the Persian Gulf."[36] He also pointed out that the Bush administration had supported General Noriega in Panama prior to the 1989 invasion of that country.[37] During the presidential debates, as in the remarks on China quoted above, Perot tended to be more sympathetic to Clinton's than to Bush's foreign policy positions. In the St. Louis debate, he also criticized the raising of the character issue in a way that could be judged only as leaning toward Clinton; although his stance on the character issue conflicted with remarks made by his running mate, Admiral James D. Stockdale, in the latter's disastrous television debate with Al Gore and Dan Quayle. (On being asked by the moderator at one stage to start the discussion, Admiral Stockdale pleaded that he was "out of ammunition on this.")[38]

Perot never really established much in the way of credibility when it came to any aspect of foreign policy. Perot volunteer activists interviewed in 1992 gave him a relatively low rating on foreign policy, compared to very high ratings for his stance on the economy (including the global economy).[39] He did, however, come across as a man of action—a man who could respond swiftly, as when he managed to rescue two of his employees from an Iranian jail in 1979.[40] Above all, he was seen by significant numbers of voters as a man who was talking sense about trade, outsourcing, and the foreign penetration of US markets. He was a businessman who had direct experience of the temptations of outsourcing and (at least in the view of his supporters) knew how much outsourcing damaged American workers: "I could make so much money [by manufacturing outside the United States] in the next five years it would be obscene. You know why I won't do it? It would cost American jobs."[41]

Perot's early policy statements were initially extremely vague. He did little more than link trade and patriotism, arguing, for example, that too many US trade negotiators eventually entered the employ of the country with which they were supposed to be negotiating.[42] Only after he reentered the race in early October did some of his positions become a little firmer. During the television debates, he focused especially on the federal deficit rather than on trade and NAFTA per se. His widely quoted statement on NAFTA came in the final debate: "You implement the NAFTA, the Mexican trade agreement, where they pay people at a dollar an hour, have no health care, no retirement, et cetera . . . and you're going to hear a giant sucking sound of jobs being pulled out of this country right at a time when we need the tax base to pay the debt and pay down interest on the debt and get our house back in order." Perot rather unpersuasively declared himself "for free trade philosophically" but indicated: "I have studied these trade agreements till the world has gone flat, and we don't have good trade agreements across the world." The "Japanese couldn't unload the cars in this country if they had the same restrictions we had."[43]

Ross Perot's simple rejection of the logic of bilateral (and, in the case of NAFTA, trilateral) free trade deals enabled Bush and Clinton to assume the mantle of economic liberalism. For Bush, whose team had negotiated the new deal between the United States, Mexico, and Canada, free trade was a good in and of itself: "It's free trade, fair trade that needs to be our hallmark, and we need more free trade agreements, not fewer." Clinton's equivocations over NAFTA were examples of his familiar waffling. Clinton, however, was able to offer qualified support for NAFTA within a plausibly pro–free trade framework. After all, it was Perot, not the candidate from Arkansas, who was in effect supporting trade protection. As Clinton put it: "I am the one who's in the middle on this. Mr. Perot says it's a bad deal. Mr. Bush says it's a hunky-dory deal. I say on balance it does more good than harm if, if we can get some protection for the environment so that the Mexicans have to follow their own environmental standards, their own labor law standards, and if we have a genuine commitment to re-educate and retrain the American workers who lose their jobs and reinvest in this economy."[44]

The 1992 Election and the Foreign Policy of the Bill Clinton Administration

A few specific promises from the election campaign did translate into actual policy after 1992. One example was Clinton's taking up of Northern Irish issues during the New York primary, when the future president promised to appoint a "special representative to push for an end to the violence in Northern Ireland."[45] There was to be a long journey before the achievement of the 1998 Belfast Agreement, but—at least in terms of Washington's close involvement with the peace process—it arguably began with Clinton's involvement with the constitutional nationalist group Americans for a New Irish Agenda in April 1992.[46] The NAFTA side deals on labor and the environment, mentioned by Clinton during the 1992 television debates, also did materialize in 1993. The notion of the democratic peace—the idea, introduced by Clinton into the St. Louis television debate, that democracies do not go to war with one another, especially if such democracies are interlinked economically—became central to the worldview of the Clinton administration.

Some themes from the campaign, notably to be tough on the Chinese human rights record—even to the extent of linking China's most-favored-nation trade status to human rights improvement—were forgotten fairly early on in the new presidency. Activism around Bosnia was more or less postponed until after the Srebrenica massacre of 1995. Yet, at least in terms of the general sense of direction, the three major foreign policy addresses of the Clinton campaign (at Georgetown University in late 1991, in Los

Angeles in August 1992, and in Milwaukee in October 1992) can be seen as developing important themes for the future. In these addresses, Clinton emphasized the interpenetration of domestic and foreign policy in post–Cold War conditions, along with an enhanced emphasis on economic foreign policy. In the speeches, and in the early days of the new administration, "managed trade" vied with free trade as a possible guide to the future. In general terms, President Bill Clinton became much more of an unabashed free trader and embracer of globalization than he appeared to be in 1992. The 1991–1992 speeches linked human rights and Wilsonian notes of democracy promotion to a strong commitment to economic agendas supplanting traditional security concerns. Tony Lake seems consciously to have seen the Clinton campaign of 1992 as a way to resume the efforts made during the Carter presidency to reunite the Democratic Party in the wake of its Vietnam War–related splits.[47] The foreign policy of Bill Clinton was indeed to emerge out of a debate between the often-conflicting claims of post–Cold War "sober internationalism," a strong (and increasingly free trade–oriented) commitment to economics first, multilateralism, and the ideals of human rights and democracy promotion. In October 1992, Thomas Friedman linked the tensions in the Clinton campaign to various distinct internationalist Democratic Party factions: human rights activists (often "veterans of the dovish, Cyrus Vance wing of the Carter Administration"); defense policy heavyweights like Senator Sam Nunn of Georgia; and neoconservative figures such as Joshua Muravchik, who actually supported Clinton in 1992.[48] The Clinton-Gore campaign book, *Putting People First,* did reflect the views of assertive internationalists such as those identified by Friedman as important influences on the Clinton campaign. It argued that the inhibitory "lessons of Vietnam" should be interpreted with caution, essentially summarizing the case that Clinton had made during his campaign against President Bush's cautious approach to the chaos in Bosnia.[49] Again, the actual policy of President Bill Clinton was to retain a strong imprint of both pragmatic caution and memories of the Vietnam War.[50]

There is a strong case for seeing the era of both the George H. W. Bush and the Bill Clinton presidencies as exhibiting more in the way of foreign and national security policy continuity than change. Despite the disagreements over defense spending in the 1992 campaign, the Clinton administration broadly followed the defense policy trajectory of the Bush administration, developing Bush's "base force" concept into the "bottom-up review" launched by the new secretary of defense, Les Aspin.[51] In terms of assessing Bush-Clinton continuity, it should be emphasized that the Bush presidency itself contained contradictory foreign policy strands. The assertive neoconservative approach embodied in the 1992 Defense Policy Guidance conflicted with the pragmatic realist conservatism associated with Bush himself and with figures such as Secretary of State Lawrence Eagleburger. It is by no means clear which of these strands would have emerged the stronger had Bush been reelected in 1992.[52] Nevertheless, and especially if we take pragmatic realist conservatism as the hallmark of the Bush approach to foreign policy, there was a considerable degree of continuity between Bush's New World Order policies and the outlook of the first Clinton administration. Clinton's version of the New World Order was much more oriented toward economics than Bush's and also more festooned with the rhetoric of human rights and democracy promotion. In essence, however, the Clinton approach—the approach of "enlargement and engagement"—built on the New World Order rather than challenging it in any fundamental way. Both Bush and Clinton were committed to continuing US global hegemony within a context of multilateralism, with the United States acting as an international "chairman of the board." Both presidents acutely appreciated the claims of simple pragmatism and an awareness of limits. There was not a huge distance between the New World Order and the concept, most famously advanced by Madeleine Albright (Bill Clinton's second secretary of state), of the United States as an "indispensable nation."[53] This apparent viability of the concept of the New World Order in post–Cold War conditions makes Bush's apparent inability effectively to defend the concept in the 1992 campaign doubly inexplicable.

Conclusion

Few voters made their choice in 1992 on the basis of conventionally understood foreign policy agendas of the various candidates, though character issues arguably had clear national security implications and foreign economic issues were very prominent.[54] This is not, however, to imply that in 1992 American voters were denied access to candidates who presented some genuinely important foreign policy alternatives. On one side stood the "new populists" and neoisolationists of the Left and the Right: Jerry Brown, Pat Buchanan, and Ross Perot. Any voter really wanting what Clinton described in the first television debate as "real hope for change" (at least in foreign policy) should have supported the new isolationism.[55] Against the new populists stood both Bush and Clinton, each one advancing his own brand of internationalism—in the Bush case, more obviously rooted in cautious pragmatism and less centrally committed to the primacy of economics. Bill Clinton went on to develop his own version of the New World Order, in the process ditching the kind of introverted populism with which his own candidacy had occasionally flirted.

Despite the degree to which (sometimes displaced and oblique) foreign policy themes found their way into the campaign, 1992 can be regarded as something of an anomaly among presidential elections. Cold War themes were either absent or transposed into images of candidate toughness or indeed into historical debates about exactly how the Cold War had been won for America. President George H. W. Bush's failure to convert the Gulf War victory into an election triumph was due to a combination of his own campaigning ineptness, the skill of the Clintonites, the Perot effect (on balance, harming Bush more than Clinton), and the post–Cold War (and pre-9/11) context. The succeeding presidential election saw signs of a return to international themes coming more directly into the campaign, as President Clinton cited his various foreign policy successes, at least as they appeared from a 1996 vantage point. These included Haiti, Bosnia, and North Korea policy, along with free trade initiatives and the rescue of the Mexican peso. The protectionist and neo-isolationist noises of 1992 resurfaced in the 1996 and Perot campaigns. By the time of the November 1996 election, the two main candidates (Clinton and the Republican challenger, Bob Dole) essentially offered competing versions of internationalism. Even in comparison with 1996—much less with Cold War and with other post–Cold War elections—1992 was an election in which foreign affairs played a muted, if far from completely insignificant, role.

Notes

1. See James Ceaser and Andrew Busch, *Upside Down and Inside Out: The 1992 Election and American Politics* (Lanham, MD: Littlefield Adams, 1993), 167; Leon

V. Sigal, "The Last Cold War Election," *Foreign Affairs* 71, no. 5 (1992/1993): 1–15, 1. On the changing saliency of national security issues in voting patterns in changing international conditions, see Clem Brooks, Kyle Dodson, and Nikole Hotchkiss, "National Security Issues and US Presidential Elections, 1992–2008," *Social Science Research* 39, no. 4 (2010): 518–26.

2. See Jack W. Germond and Jules Witcover, *Mad as Hell: Revolt at the Ballot Box* (New York: Times Warner, 1993); William Crotty, *America's Choice: The Election of 1992* (Guildford, CT: Dushkin, 1993); Michael Nelson, ed., *The Elections of 1992* (Washington, DC: Congressional Quarterly Press, 1993); Gerald M. Pomper et al., eds., *The Election of 1992* (Chatham, NJ: Chatham House, 1992); Emmett H. Buell, "The 1992 Elections," *Journal of Politics* 56, no. 4 (1994): 1133–44; and Tim Hames, "Foreign Policy and the American Elections of 1992," *International Relations* 11, no. 3 (1993): 315–30.

3. See Crotty, *America's Choice,* chap. 1; and Ross Baker, "Sorting Out and Suiting Up," in Pomper et al., eds., *The Election of 1992,* 59–71.

4. See Ceaser and Busch, *Upside Down and Inside Out,* 90.

5. See Patrick J. Buchanan, *Right from the Beginning* (Washington, DC: Regnery Gateway, 1990), and *The Great Betrayal: How American Sovereignty and Social Justice Are Being Sacrificed to the Gods of the Global Economy* (Boston: Little, Brown, 1998).

6. Quotations from Germond and Witcover, *Mad as Hell,* 135–36, 235. On Buchanan's moderate/conservative Republican support, see Ronald B. Rapoport and Walter J. Stone, *Three's a Crowd: The Dynamics of Third Parties, Ross Perot, and Republican Resurgence* (Ann Arbor: University of Michigan Press, 2005), 52.

7. Quoted in William Schneider, "The New Isolationism," in *Eagle Adrift: American Foreign Policy at the End of the Century,* ed. Robert J. Lieber (New York: Longman, 1997), 26–38, 29. See also Paul Tsongas, *Journey of Purpose: Reflections on the Presidency, Multiculturalism, and Third Parties* (New Haven, CT: Yale University Press, 1996).

8. See J. D. Rosner, "The Know-Nothings Know Something," *Foreign Policy* 101 (1995–1996): 116–29; and J. Citrin, E. B. Haas, C. Muste, and B. Reingold, "Is American Nationalism Changing? Implications for Foreign Policy," *International Studies Quarterly* 38, no. 1 (1994): 1–31.

9. Germond and Witcover, *Mad as Hell,* 169.

10. Mary Matalin and James Carville, *All's Fair: Love, War, and Running for President* (London: Hutchinson, 1996), 134–35.

11. Germond and Witcover, *Mad as Hell,* 196. See also Bill Clinton, *My Life* (London: Arrow, 2005), 388–90.

12. Germond and Witcover, *Mad as Hell,* 207, 278–79.

13. Presidential Debate in St. Louis, October 11, 1992, *The American Presidency Project,* http://www.presidency.ucsb.edu/ws/index.php?pid=21605.

14. Germond and Witcover, *Mad as Hell,* 481.

15. Clinton, *My Life,* 430.

16. Cited in Paul Kengor, *Wreath Layer or Policy Player? The Vice-President's Role in Foreign Policy* (Lanham, MD: Lexington, 2000), 228–29.

17. Matalin and Carville, *All's Fair,* 359.

18. Germond and Witcover, *Mad as Hell,* 497.

19. Ibid., 495–96.

20. Dan Quayle, *Standing Firm: A Vice-Presidential Memoir* (New York: Harper Paperbacks, 1994), 392.

21. Keith Schneiders, "Book by Gore Could Become a Campaign Issue," *New York Times,* July 27, 1992.

22. Quoted in Nancy Soderberg, *The Superpower Myth: The Use and Misuse of American Might* (Hoboken, NJ: Wiley, 2005), 14.

23. Presidential Debate in St. Louis, October 11, 1992.

24. Presidential Debate in East Lansing, Michigan, October 19, 1992, *The American Presidency Project,* http://www.presidency.ucsb.edu/ws/index.php?pid=21625.

25. Quoted in Thomas Friedman, "The 1992 Campaign: Issues: Foreign Policy," *New York Times,* October 4, 1992.

26. Sigal, "The Last Cold War Election," 13–14.

27. Presidential Debate at the University of Richmond, October 15, 1992, *The American Presidency Project,* http://www.presidency.ucsb.edu/ws/index.php?pid=21617.

28. Quoted in Friedman, "The 1992 Campaign."

29. Quoted in David Halberstam, *War in a Time of Peace* (London: Bloomsbury, 1994), 22.

30. See W. C. McWilliams, "The Meaning of the Election," in Pomper et al., eds., *The Election of 1992,* 192–210.

31. Presidential Debate at the University of Richmond, October 15, 1992.

32. Germond and Witcover, *Mad as Hell,* 7.

33. H. Ross Perot, *United We Stand: How We Can Take Back Our Country* (New York: Hyperion, 1992), 65.

34. Presidential Debate in St. Louis, October 11, 1992.

35. Presidential Debate in East Lansing, Michigan, October 19, 1992.

36. Perot Speech to the Symposium for Better Government, November 1991, quoted in Ken Gross, *Ross Perot: The Man behind the Myth* (New York: Random House, 1992), 212, 214.

37. Presidential Debate in East Lansing, Michigan, October 19, 1992.

38. Vice-Presidential Debate in Atlanta, October 13, 1992, *The American Presidency Project,* http://www.presidency.ucsb.edu/ws/index.php?pid=29423.

39. See Rapoport and Stone, *Three's a Crowd,* 104.

40. See Ceaser and Busch, *Upside Down and Inside Out,* 90–91.

41. Quoted in Solon Simmonds and James Simmonds, "The Politics of a Bittersweet Economy," in *Ross for Boss: The Perot Phenomenon and Beyond,* ed. Ted G. Jelen (Albany, NY: State University of New York Press, 2001), 87–115, 94.

42. Ibid., 94. See also Jacqueline S. Salit, *Independents Rising: Outsider Move-*

ments, Third Parties, and the Struggle for a Post-Partisan America (New York: Palgrave Macmillan, 2012), 5.

43. Presidential Debate in East Lansing, Michigan, October 19, 1992.

44. Ibid.

45. See Clinton, *My Life,* 401.

46. See Michael Cox, Adrian Guelke, and Fiona Stephen, eds., *A Farewell to Arms? Beyond the Good Friday Agreement* (Manchester: Manchester University Press, 2006).

47. See Derek Chollet and James M. Goldgeier, *America between the Wars: From 11/9 to 9/11* (New York: PublicAffairs, 2008), 3–32.

48. Friedman, "The 1992 Campaign."

49. Bill Clinton and Al Gore, *Putting People First: How We Can All Change America* (New York: Times Books, 1992), 110–12.

50. These arguments are developed further in John Dumbrell, *Clinton's Foreign Policy: Between the Bushes* (Abingdon: Routledge, 2009).

51. Ibid., 62–67.

52. See Steven Hurst, *The Foreign Policy of the Bush Administration: In Search of a New World Order* (London: Cassell, 2000).

53. See John Dumbrell, "President Clinton's Secretaries of State: Warren Christopher and Madeleine Albright," *Journal of Transatlantic Studies* 6, no. 3 (2008): 217–27.

54. On patterns of linkage between ostensibly domestic and foreign policy voter preferences, see Brooks, Dodson, and Hotchkiss, "National Security Issues and US Presidential Elections," 519; and Alastair Smith, "Diversionary Foreign Policy and Democratic Systems," *International Studies Quarterly* 40, no. 2 (1996): 133–53.

55. Presidential Debate in St. Louis, October 11, 1992.

Conclusion

Robert David Johnson

"Before this country declared independence," Justice Antonin Scalia wrote shortly before he died, "the law of England entrusted the King with the exclusive care of his kingdom's foreign affairs." Quoting Blackstone's *Commentaries,* he reminded his colleagues that the "royal prerogative included the 'sole power of sending ambassadors to foreign states, and receiving them at home,' the sole authority to 'make treaties, leagues, and alliances with foreign states and princes,' 'the sole prerogative of making war and peace,' and the 'sole power of raising and regulating fleets and armies.' The People of the United States had other ideas when they organized our Government. They considered a sound structure of balanced powers essential to the preservation of just government, and international relations formed no exception to that principle."[1]

Scalia's reasoning failed to persuade the Court in *Zivotovsky v. Kerry.* But his historical analysis was on point. In terms of foreign affairs, the most striking element of the Constitution was its departure not merely from British tradition but from that of the entire Western world. The Constitution's deliberate division of authority between the branches all but ensured that questions of international affairs would be the subject of political debate.

But the Framers never anticipated the development of political parties—whose existence would dramatically intensify the debate over foreign policy matters within the US political system. The First Party System, formed in the 1790s, both resulted from and exacerbated divisions over international affairs. In the wars of the French Revolution, Thomas Jefferson's followers sympathized with the French, while Alexander Hamilton's Federalists sided with the British. Debates of the 1790s were so ferocious in large part because partisans viewed members of the other party as stalking horses for a foreign rival.

Somewhat fittingly, the final presidential election associated with the First Party System produced perhaps the finest monograph on the general subject of this book: the linkage between foreign policy and a specific presidential election. Ernest R. May's *Making of the Monroe Doctrine* posited presidential politics as the likeliest explanation for John Quincy Adams's rejection of the British proposal to jointly protect the freedom of the newly independent Latin American states. Accepting the offer, as May noted, would have triggered criticism for subordinating the US national interest to the British—a particularly damaging line of attack for a former Federalist still distrusted among some Jeffersonians. Policy makers of the era, May understood, were driven "less by conviction than personal ambition."[2]

Foreign policy played a less prominent role in the creation of the Second (between the Democrats and the Whigs) and Third (between the Democrats and the Republicans) Party Systems. But the intersection between foreign policy and party politics remained in place, as the 1844 election demonstrated. The peculiar nature of the Democratic convention rules—which required the nominee to secure two-thirds of the delegates—denied Martin Van Buren the nomination, allowing James K. Polk and the expansionist agenda to become the party's standard-bearer. The peculiarities of the Electoral College, meanwhile, played a key role in the final outcome: In a mid-nineteenth-century version of Ralph Nader's role in the 2000 election, the Liberty Party candidate, James Birney, running on an abolitionist platform, siphoned enough votes from the Whig nominee, Henry Clay, a moderate on questions of imperialism, to throw the election to Polk. The 15,812 votes that Birney received in New York were more than triple Polk's margin of victory, and, if Clay had carried New York, he would have prevailed in the Electoral College.[3]

The first presidential election of the Third Party System, in 1856, likewise had critical foreign policy implications. Desperate for a candidate who could appeal in the arc of states from Pennsylvania through Illinois, Democrats turned to former secretary of state and minister to the United Kingdom James Buchanan. The choice paid political benefits, but Buchanan's foreign policy agenda, which envisioned an aggressive imperialism toward Latin America directed exclusively by the executive branch, produced a showdown between Congress and the executive for control over foreign policy. The battle lasted into the spring of 1859, before the legislature prevailed. Yet again, a presidential election had profoundly influenced the course the United States would take in world affairs.[4]

The initial contest of the Fourth Party System, which began in 1896 and ended with FDR's triumph in 1932, provided yet another reminder of the connection between presidential elections and the nature of US foreign policy. Though the two parties' platforms did not exhibit a significant difference on foreign policy and the election was fought primarily over economic issues, William McKinley's triumph paved the way for the war in Cuba, the annexation of Puerto Rico, and the brutal conquest of the Philippines. And William Jennings Bryan's defeat in 1900 in a campaign focused much more on foreign policy questions ensured that the imperialist agenda would persist.

Ironically, international affairs played a smaller role than any other twentieth-century presidential election in the two contests (1932 and 1936) that provide the run-up to the chapters in this volume. Roosevelt's triumph in 1932 ushered in the New Deal coalition, but, apart from foreign economic policy directly related to the Depression's effects, Roosevelt largely ignored international affairs or trimmed his foreign policy beliefs—as in his promise not to join the League of Nations as a way of securing the endorsement of William Randolph Hearst—to advance his political interests. (The effects of the Depression did undermine the political position of the peace progressives, Senate anti-imperialists who had played a major role in 1920s foreign policy debates.) And, even as the international situation deteriorated, Roosevelt's 1936 landslide was almost entirely inward focused.

That condition soon changed, and over the next half century foreign policy almost always played a key role—sometimes a decisive one—in US presidential elections. The chapters in this volume, of course, stand on their own. But they also illustrate four themes to help us better understand the connection between electoral politics and foreign policy between 1940 and 1992.

In two elections, chapters in this volume suggest, foreign policy was decisive to the outcome. Andrew Johnstone reconsiders our understanding of the 1940 presidential election, portraying the foreign policy differences between FDR and Wendell Willkie as more substantial than is conceded by either scholars or in political culture. He cites polls indicating that the country's formerly strong isolationist mood had dissipated and notes that a Democratic challenge against a noninterventionist GOP nominee would have been the easier course. Even Secretary of State Cordell Hull, a quite weak candidate, was running ahead of the then noninterventionist Thomas E. Dewey.

The chapter's narrative also provides a reminder of how significant the foreign policy events during campaign season were—the election took place amid the fall of France, the destroyers-for-bases deal, and the conscription debate. The European war, Johnstone argues, accounts for Willkie's nomination but ultimately proved his undoing; FDR's late-campaign promise not to send American boys off to fight a European war undercut a late Willkie surge and ensured the president's reelection.

Thomas Alan Schwartz's chapter dramatically reinterprets the role of foreign policy in the 1972 campaign, arguing that Nixon deliberately campaigned as the peace candidate—and sought to exploit Henry Kissinger's appeal in the elite media in the process. Schwartz argues that historians need to better appreciate the political motivations of Nixon's international gambit; for instance, the selection of Kissinger (and not, say, Secretary of State William Rogers) as the envoy for the opening to China ensured that the final policy would reflect best on the president. Nixon's emphasis on arms control, meanwhile, gave him a leg up on an issue that he correctly identified as important to the people in the early 1970s. But Schwartz also cautions that the perception of progress can be just that: perception. Even if a gambit serves short-term political goals, the reality of international relations will reintrude, as occurred with Nixon's inability to achieve peace with North Vietnam before the election and the resumption of bombing in the Christmas 1972 campaign.

In several elections, foreign policy played a critical, if somewhat indirect, role, framing the campaign and enhancing (or diminishing) the chances of particular candidates. The most obvious example came in the election of 1952. Steven Casey's chapter, which notes that the year's contest confirmed the Cold War consensus, also asks readers to consider a counterfactual of a Truman-Taft battle. This matchup might have provided a culmination of the "Great Debate" (which, in reality, was neither great nor much of a debate) between Congress and the executive over the structure of the US commitment to Europe.

Absent the combination of Taft's neoisolationism and his strength among party regulars, Dwight Eisenhower never would have entered the race. Eisenhower also believed—not entirely without reason—that Taft was playing politics with vital foreign policy issues. That said, in the fall, Eisenhower himself was willing to make compromises to win the election. He met with Taft and agreed to consider nationalist Republican appointments. He selected the hard-liner Richard Nixon as his running mate. Most infamously, he appeared with Joseph McCarthy during a campaign swing in Wisconsin—just after McCarthy had implied that George Marshall had committed treasonous behavior and in the midst of McCarthy's closer-than-expected reelection race with the Democrat Thomas Fairchild.

Eisenhower also engaged in some of the political games for which he had criticized Taft. Despite his general agreement with containment's principles, he articulated a much sharper critique of Truman's foreign policy—which he portrayed as too erratic and too taxing on American resources—than he likely believed. More controversially, he flirted with liberationist rhetoric that he would repudiate once elected president. And, in his highest-profile move, he promised to personally travel to Korea to end the war. As Casey points out, Eisenhower read the mood of the country correctly. By the end of the campaign, one poll showed that 52 percent of Americans considered Korea an important issue.

The role of international issues in framing the campaign also emerged in 1968, as Sandra Scanlon's chapter observes. Vietnam hovered over the campaign. It prompted Minnesota senator Eugene McCarthy to launch his long-shot campaign and score a near upset victory over President Johnson in the New Hampshire primary (even though many McCarthy voters wanted a *more* aggressive policy in Southeast Asia). Robert Kennedy, who already had distinguished himself for his criticism of the war in the Senate, then jumped into the race, ultimately leading Johnson to withdraw on the eve of the Wisconsin primary, which he was sure to lose. And Vietnam both bedeviled the Humphrey campaign by linking the Democratic nominee to an unpopular war and provided an opening for his late rally after his Salt Lake City speech urging a bombing pause.

Foreign policy also dictated—and restrained—the challengers. With hundreds of thousands of American troops fighting an overseas conflict, voters shied away from candidates, such as Ronald Reagan, who seemed too extreme. And the inflammatory statements of his running mate, retired Air Force general Curtis LeMay, blunted the momentum of George Wallace and his third-party bid. In this environment, Richard

Nixon seemed like the obvious choice, especially given his reinvention as a foreign policy statesman during the 1960s. A late August 1968 conversation reflected Nixon's new image; the GOP nominee told the president: "I don't give a goddamn what the politics is, and I hope, I'm sure Hubert [Humphrey] will feel the same way. But. . . . And I know how you feel about the whole peace issue. But we've got to stand very firm. And I won't say a damn word that's going to embarrass you. You can be sure of that."[5]

But, as Humphrey surged, Nixon's mask slipped. Fearful that a last-second peace deal would give the Democrat the election, Nixon agents—chiefly Anna Chennault—reached out to the South Vietnamese government of Nguyen van Thieu. The message was that a peace settlement under a Nixon presidency would be more favorable to the South Vietnamese. Johnson soon discovered that "our friend, the Republican nominee—our California friend—has been playing on the outskirts with our enemies and our friends."[6] In a conversation with Minority Leader Everett Dirksen, the president even accused the Nixon operatives of "treason" (Dirksen agreed) and threatened to go public with his information unless the GOP representatives ceased contact with the South Vietnamese.[7] Johnson's ultimate decision to keep quiet helped sway the election to Nixon.

The final election in which foreign policy set the mood came in 1980, as profiled in the chapter by Robert Mason. A sense of decline characterized the year's contest, with 1970s foreign policy reverses stimulating grassroots conservativism. The first sign came in 1978, when a long-shot Republican candidate, Gordon Humphrey, ousted the veteran Democrat Thomas McIntyre in the New Hampshire Senate race; Humphrey focused on McIntyre's positions on military spending and the Panama Canal Treaty. Two years later, in North Carolina, the Republican John East, a first-time candidate with a profile similar to Humphrey's, scored an upset victory over the incumbent Robert Morgan, aided by energized conservatives.

At the same time, foreign policy *aided* Carter, at least in the nomination process; Mason notes that the timing of the Iran hostage crisis revived the president's moribund primary campaign. Even into the fall election, foreign policy concerns seemed to bolster his chances, largely owing to fears of Reagan's bellicosity. Exemplifying these concerns, a woman in the Detroit suburbs commented: "Reagan might end the recession real fast, but we'd be in World War III quickly."[8] Mason convincingly argues that

Reagan overcame these fears by stressing his potential as a peacemaker, much as Richard Nixon had done in 1972.

If 1952, 1968, and 1980 were years in which foreign policy framed the campaign, in four other elections, it played a less important (but not unsubstantial) role.

Michael F. Hopkins accurately notes that most scholarly analysis of the 1948 election has focused either on horse-race aspects or the political impact of various domestic initiatives, such as farm unrest or Truman's relationship with the Eightieth Congress—and probably for good reason since domestic matters (and Truman's strategy) seemed to have been the decisive issues in the campaign. Yet, as Hopkins points out, foreign policy was not absent from the contest, particularly in the role played by former vice president Henry Wallace, whose Progressive Party bid challenged Truman's actions from the Left (and increasingly, as the campaign drew near its conclusion, from the fellow-traveler Left).[9] Recognition of Israel was a question on which widespread unity existed across the political spectrum; policy toward China generated more partisan divisions. Finally, the question of civil liberties and the Cold War also played a significant role in the outcome, especially in the GOP primary; the famous radio debate between Thomas Dewey and Harold Stassen over whether the Communist Party should be illegal set the stage for Stassen's defeat in the Oregon primary.

Hopkins offers a final, tantalizing point: Dewey's large lead in the polls might have diminished his incentive to attack Truman aggressively on international affairs. Perhaps a closer contest would have seen foreign policy playing a larger role.

Sylvia Ellis complicates the conventional wisdom about foreign policy and the 1960 campaign. Political journalists and historians alike recall the debates as a clear winner for John Kennedy. But they do so largely by focusing only on the first of the four debates between Kennedy and Richard Nixon. The final three debates, as Ellis points out, featured the emergence of two issues (Quemoy/Matsu and Cuba) that did not work to the Democrat's advantage. "Kennedy," according to Ellis, "learned a harsh lesson: The complexities of foreign policy are not easy to explain to the electorate, especially if your opponent reduces the debate to slogans; a sophisticated analysis of international issues can often be exploited ruthlessly in a presidential campaign."

Lyndon Johnson almost certainly would have defeated any Republican challenger in the 1964 election. But, as Thomas Tunstall Allcock points out, international issues consistently made appearances in the campaign. His chapter contains a fascinating discussion of an early 1964 crisis in Panama in which the president responded firmly to local unrest, lest he be attacked as weak at home. UN ambassador Adlai Stevenson promised a warm welcome from the *New York Times* if Johnson took a more diplomatic approach to the crisis. The president responded, as Tunstall Allcock notes, that he likely would get such a reaction "in the *New York Times*": "Then I think the *people* would run me out of the country." The Panamanian policy succeeded (politically at least) but provided a model of Johnson's tendency to approach foreign policy matters through a domestic political prism, which would serve him poorly in Vietnam later in his administration.

Tunstall Allcock also recalls the complicated role that Vietnam played in the campaign. The contest began with an extraordinary situation of a sitting ambassador in a war zone (former senator Henry Cabot Lodge) surreptitiously competing for the opposing party's nomination, a situation that complicated Johnson's handling of Vietnam throughout the spring, until Lodge's bid collapsed following a defeat in the Oregon primary. In the summer, Johnson secured passage of the Tonkin Gulf Resolution, but he worried about Senate opposition from Wayne Morse (D-OR) and Ernest Gruening (D-AK). And, in the fall, Barry Goldwater's militaristic rhetoric allowed the president to campaign as the candidate of peace.

Finally, Andrew Priest's chapter on the 1976 election notes the indirect effect of foreign policy on the outcome: foreign policy weakened the incumbent, Gerald Ford, in the primary. Without the right-wing challenge from Ronald Reagan, Ford might well have prevailed in the fall. Priest adds that, once the nomination process dragged out, "with hindsight, it is difficult to imagine a Gerald Ford victory in the 1976 presidential election." Perhaps so, though Jimmy Carter's faltering campaign did everything it could to rehabilitate Ford's chances. In a close election, any specific event can be decisive, but the president's disastrous debate performance—in which he denied that Poland and Romania could be considered Soviet satellites—obviously did little to improve his chances.

Of course, in some elections, foreign policy ultimately played only a minor role. As J. Simon Rofe observes, since 1940, the 1944 presidential campaign is the only one that occurred while the United States was facing a war for survival. The Roosevelt administration effectively neutralized the political debate over responsibility for Pearl Harbor; the GOP nominee, Thomas Dewey, heeded George Marshall's advice not to discuss Pearl Harbor, lest doing so compromise national security interests regarding the United States having cracked Japanese codes. Scott Lucas notes the anomaly twelve years later, in 1956, of foreign policy not being shaped by public opinion despite two crises (Hungary and the Suez) coinciding with the run-up to the election. Events of the year reflected Eisenhower's confidence that he would proceed with what he considered the best option, regardless of how the public thought about the issue. In an irony of history, Eisenhower's measured approach gave Adlai Stevenson an opening to suggest the president was too soft on communism.

Foreign policy also was not critical to the outcome of the final three elections profiled in the volume, perhaps reflecting the increasingly desultory debate over international affairs seen in both American politics and Congress since the mid-1980s. David Ryan points out that Reagan's "morning in America" theme symbolized more general content than a specific foreign policy agenda. The president campaigned as the candidate of peace in 1984 but had to avoid the possibility of another Vietnam in Nicaragua and Lebanon. In both instances, Reagan's policy failed to enjoy popular support. Robert A. Strong argues that, in 1988, foreign policy ultimately played little role in a battle between two weak candidates—although things might have been different if the Democrats had nominated Gary Hart or perhaps Albert Gore or Joe Biden, candidates with strong foreign policy credentials. And John Dumbrell suggests that foreign policy affected the 1992 campaign only to a limited extent, chiefly through the interventions of Ross Perot on foreign economic policy.

In the past generation, US diplomatic history has experienced a significant pedagogical evolution. The field always has been bifurcated between an international approach, involving rigorous analysis of foreign archives, and one that more explored the interaction between domestic forces and the making of US foreign policy. Recent years, however, have featured a dramatic shift in this second category, with greater emphasis on themes of race, gender, ethnicity, and other such questions. As interesting as these matters might be, much of US foreign policy, particularly concerning the intersection of domestic politics and foreign policy, does not comfortably fit into such cultural categories. The result has been—and, surely, this must be unintentional—a restriction of the sort of topics that fit into mainstream diplomatic history.[10]

In his 2008 Society for Historians of Foreign Relations presidential address, Thomas Alan Schwartz (as we have seen above, a contributor to this volume) made a "plea for recognizing the ongoing importance of politics in our work and perhaps acknowledging that more traditional political explanations may explain more about American foreign relations than some of the more recent and trendier undertakings in our field."[11] This book represents one response to Schwartz's call. The field desperately needs more such efforts.

Notes

1. *Zivotovsky v. Kerry,* 576 U.S. —— (2015), Scalia, J., dissenting (slip op., at 1).

2. Ernest R. May, *The Making of the Monroe Doctrine* (Cambridge, MA: Harvard University Press, 1975), x.

3. The conventional narrative of this topic remains Thomas Hietala, *Manifest Design: American Exceptionalism and Empire* (1985), rev. ed. (Ithaca, NY: Cornell University Press, 2002). For Birney, see D. Laurence Rogers, *Apostles of Equality: The Birneys, the Republicans, and the Civil War* (Lansing: Michigan State University Press, 2011).

4. Robert David Johnson, "Congress and U.S. Foreign Policy Before 9/11," in *Congress and the Politics of National Security, ed.* David Auersweld and Colton Campbell (New York: Cambridge University Press, 2011), 18–44.

5. Lyndon Johnson and Richard Nixon, August 20, 1968, WH6808.01, Citation no. 13309, Lyndon Johnson Presidential Recordings, Lyndon Johnson Presidential Library (hereafter LBJ Tapes).

6. President Johnson and Richard Russell, October 30, 1968, WH6810.10, Citation no. 13612, LBJ Tapes.

7. President Johnson and Everett Dirksen, October 31, 1968, WH6810.11, Citation no. 13614, LBJ Tapes

8. Rowland Evans and Robert Novak, "'Meanness' Backlash," *Washington Post,* October 13, 1980.

9. For an excellent recent summary of the role that foreign policy played in the Wallace effort, see Thomas Devine, *Henry Wallace's 1948 Presidential Campaign and the Future of Postwar Liberalism* (Chapel Hill: University of North Carolina Press, 2013).

10. I have argued this point in greater detail in "Intellectual Diversity and the

Teaching of U.S. History," US Senate, Education and Labor Committee, 108th Cong., 1st sess., *Hearings, Is Intellectual Diversity an Endangered Species on Today's College Campuses?* (Washington, DC: US Government Printing Office, 2003).

11. Thomas Alan Schwartz, "'Henry, . . . Winning an Election Is Terribly Important': Partisan Politics in the History of U.S. Foreign Relations," *Diplomatic History* 33, no. 2 (2009): 173–190, 173.

Acknowledgments

This book is the result of a workshop held in April 2013 at the Institute for the Study of the Americas (the Institute for Latin American Studies) in the School of Advanced Study, University of London. We are grateful to all the participants, most of whom are contributors to this volume, as well as those who have joined the project since then. We would like to thank the organizations that provided generous funding for that event: the Institute for the Study of the Americas; the Embassy of the United States of America in London; the University of Leicester; and Aberystwyth University. Since we held that symposium, the editorial team at the University Press of Kentucky has been extremely generous in helping us develop this collection of essays into a coherent volume. In particular we thank Allison Webster, Stephen M. Wrinn, and Jonathan Allison. We also thank series editor Andy Johns for encouraging us to be part of UPK's Studies in Conflict, Diplomacy, and Peace series. On a personal level, our partners, Zoe and Megan, deserve special thanks for supporting us through this process. Finally, we remember our dear friend Shannon Martin Watts (1974–2016), who generously welcomed us into her home when we were conducting research in the United States and also when were not. We feel privileged to have known her.

Contributors

Steven Casey is professor of international history at the London School of Economics. His books include *Cautious Crusade: Franklin D. Roosevelt, American Public Opinion, and the War against Nazi Germany, 1941–1945* (Oxford University Press, 2001), *Selling the Korean War: Propaganda, Politics, and Public Opinion, 1950–1953* (Oxford University Press, 2008), *When Soldiers Fall: How Americans Have Debated Combat Casualties, from World War I to the War on Terror* (Oxford University Press, 2014), and *The War Beat, Europe: The American Media at War against Nazi Germany* (Oxford University Press, 2017). *Selling the Korean War* won both the Truman Book Award and the Neustadt Prize for best book in American politics. Casey's articles have appeared in journals such as the *Journal of Strategic Studies, Presidential Studies Quarterly,* and *Diplomatic History.*

John Dumbrell is recently retired professor of government at Durham University. He is a former chair of the American Politics Group of the Political Studies Association and coeditor of the Routledge book series Studies in US Foreign Policy. He is the author of *Rethinking the Vietnam War* (Palgrave, 2012), *Clinton's Foreign Policy: Between the Bushes, 1992–2000* (Routledge, 2009), *A Special Relationship: Anglo-American Relations from the Cold War to Iraq* (Palgrave, 2006), and *President Lyndon Johnson and Soviet Communism* (Manchester University Press, 2004). His journal articles have appeared in the *Journal of Transatlantic Studies,* the *Journal of American Studies, Diplomatic History,* and *Diplomacy and Statecraft.*

Sylvia Ellis is professor of international history at Northumbria University. Her research interests lie in post-1945 British and American political and diplomatic history. She has recently published *Freedom's Pragmatist: Lyndon Johnson and the Civil Right Movement* (University Press of Florida, 2013) and is currently working on a critical edition on Harold Wilson and the Vietnam War and a study of female activism on US campuses. Her first book was *Britain, America and the Vietnam War* (Praeger, 2004), and she has published articles in the *Journal of Transatlantic Studies* and *Diplomatic History.*

Michael F. Hopkins is a senior lecturer in American foreign policy at the University of Liverpool. His interests include American foreign policy, British foreign policy, and Anglo-American relations since 1945. His books include *Oliver Franks and the Truman Administration: Anglo-American Relations, 1948–1952* (Frank Cass, 2003), *The Cold War* (Thames & Hudson, 2011), and (with Michael Dockrill) *The Cold War* (Macmillan, 2006). He is also the editor (with Saul Kelly and John W. Young) of *The Washington Embassy: British Ambassadors to Washington, 1939–77* (Palgrave Macmillan, 2009). His articles have appeared in the *Journal of Transatlantic Studies* and *Cold War History,* and he has just completed a book on Dean Acheson.

Robert David Johnson is a professor of history at Brooklyn College and the City University of New York Graduate Center. He has written seven books and edited or coedited six others on US diplomatic history, the presidency, and US legal affairs, including *All the Way with LBJ: The 1964 Presidential Election* (Cambridge University Press, 2009), *Congress and the Cold War* (Cambridge University Press, 2005), *Ernest Gruening and the American Dissenting Tradition* (Harvard University Press, 1998), and *The Peace Progressives and American Foreign Relations* (Harvard University Press, 1995).

Andrew Johnstone is an associate professor in American history at the University of Leicester. He is the author of two books: *Against Immediate Evil: American Internationalists and the Four Freedoms on the Eve of World War II* (Cornell University Press, 2014) and *Dilemmas of Internationalism: The American Association for the United Nations and US Foreign Policy, 1941–1948* (Ashgate, 2009). He is also the coeditor (with Helen Laville) of *The US Public and American Foreign Policy* (Routledge, 2010), and his articles have appeared in *Diplomatic History, Global Society,* the *Journal of American Studies,* and the *Journal of Transatlantic Studies.*

Scott Lucas is professor of international politics at the University of Birmingham. He began his career as a specialist in US and British foreign policy, but his research interests now also cover current international affairs, new media, and intelligence services. His books include *Divided We Stand: Britain, the US and the Suez Crisis* (Hodder & Stoughton, 1991) and *Freedom's War: The US Crusade against the Soviet Union, 1945–56* (Manchester University Press, 1999). And he has edited *Trials of Engagement: The Future of Public Diplomacy* (with Ali Fisher; Brill, 2011) and *Challenging US Foreign Policy: America and the World in the Long Twentieth Century* (with Bevan Sewell; Palgrave Macmillan, 2011). He has also published more than fifty major articles. And he is the founder and editor of *EA WorldView*, a leading Web site for news and analysis of international affairs.

Robert Mason is professor of twentieth-century US history at the University of Edinburgh. His research focuses in particular on American political history during the post–World War II years. He is the author of *Richard Nixon and the Quest for a New Majority* (University of North Carolina Press, 2004) and *The Republican Party and American Politics from Hoover to Reagan* (Cambridge University Press, 2012). He is also the editor (with Iwan Morgan) of *Seeking a New Majority: The Republican Party and American Politics, 1960–1980* (Vanderbilt University Press, 2013) and *The Liberal Consensus Reconsidered: American Politics and Society in the Postwar Era* (University Press of Florida, 2017), and he has published articles in the *Journal of American Studies, Media History,* and the *Historical Journal.*

Andrew Priest is a senior lecturer in modern US history at the University of Essex, and he was previously a lecturer at Aberystwyth University. His first book, *Kennedy, Johnson and NATO: Britain, America and the Dynamics of Alliance, 1962–68* (Routledge, 2006), examined US-UK relations in NATO during the 1960s. His articles have appeared in the *Journal of Military History,* the *Journal of American Studies,* and *Intelligence and National Security.* His current project is a study of ideas in US foreign policy in the late nineteenth century, focusing in particular on elite opinion of European empires and imperial practices, and he is in the process of writing a monograph on this topic.

J. Simon Rofe is a senior lecturer in diplomacy and international studies in the Centre for International Studies and Diplomacy at SOAS, University of London. His research interests lie in the field of US diplomacy and foreign relations in the twentieth century, with a focus on the era of Franklin D. Roosevelt and on international organization and postwar planning. He is the author of *Franklin Roosevelt's Foreign Policy and the Welles Mission* (Palgrave, 2007), the editor of books including *The Embassy in Grosvenor Square: American Ambassadors to the United Kingdom 1938–2008* (with Alison Holmes; Palgrave, 2012), and the author of numerous chapters in books including in *Nexus Years in the Cold War, Crucial Periods and Turning Points* (ed. Lorenz Luthi; Woodrow Wilson Centre/Stanford University Press, 2015) and *Wartime Origins and the Future United Nations* (ed. Dan Plesch and Thomas G. Weiss; Routledge, 2015).

David Ryan is professor and chair of modern history at University College Cork. He has published extensively on contemporary history and US foreign policy, concentrating on interventions in the post-Vietnam era. His books include *Obama, US Foreign Policy and the Dilemmas of Intervention* (with David Fitzgerald; Palgrave 2014), *US Foreign Policy and the Other* (ed. with Michael Cullinane; Berghahn, 2015), *Frustrated Empire: US Foreign Policy from 9/11 to Iraq* (Pluto/University of Michigan Press, 2007), *Vietnam in Iraq: Tactics, Lessons, Legacies and Ghosts* (ed. with John Dumbrell; Routledge, 2007), *The United States and Europe in the Twentieth Century* (Longman, 2003), *US Foreign Policy in World History* (Routledge, 2000), and *US-Sandinista Diplomatic Relations: Voice of Intolerance* (Macmillan, 1995). He is also the author of numerous articles and chapters.

Sandra Scanlon is lecturer in American history at University College Dublin, where she has taught since 2010. She received her Ph.D. from the University of Cambridge. Her research focuses on American political culture and its relationship with US foreign policy during the Cold War, and her first book, *The Pro-War Movement: Domestic Support for the Vietnam War and the Making of Modern American Conservatism,* was published in 2013 by the University of Massachusetts Press. During 2013, she was a Fulbright Scholar at the Department of History at Emory University.

Thomas Alan Schwartz is professor of history, political science, and European studies at Vanderbilt University. He is the author of *America's Germany: John J. McCloy and the Federal Republic of Germany* (Harvard University Press, 1991), which received the Stuart Bernath Book Prize of the Society of American Foreign Relations and the Harry S. Truman Book Award, given by the Truman Presidential Library. He is also the author of *Lyndon Johnson and Europe: In the Shadow of Vietnam* (Harvard University Press, 2003). He is the coeditor with Matthias Schulz of *The Strained Alliance: U.S.-European Relations from Nixon to Carter* (Cambridge University Press, 2009). He is currently working on a book about former secretary of state Henry Kissinger.

Robert A. Strong is the William Lyne Wilson Professor of Politics at Washington and Lee University and was a Fulbright Scholar at University College Dublin for the 2013–2014 academic year. He earned his Ph.D. at the University of Virginia and has been at Washington and Lee since 1989. His research involves national security issues and presidential foreign policy decisions in the modern era. In 2005, he was a visiting scholar at the Rothermere American Institute at Oxford University. His recent publications include *Working in the World: Jimmy Carter and the Making of American Foreign Policy* and a second edition of *Decisions and Dilemmas: Case Studies in Presidential Foreign Policy Making since 1945*. He has published essays in a variety of journals and national newspapers. Some of his recent writing can be found on the *Huffington Post* at http://www.huffingtonpost.com/robert-strong.

Thomas Tunstall Allcock is a lecturer in American history at the University of Manchester and specializes in foreign policy and presidential history. His work has been published in *Diplomatic History* and the *Journal of Cold War Studies,* and he is currently completing a book on US–Latin American relations tentatively titled "Problems Everywhere: Lyndon Johnson, Thomas Mann, and Latin America in the 1960s." He received his Ph.D. in history from the University of Cambridge, during which time he was Fox International Fellow at Yale University. He was subsequently a teaching associate at the University of Nottingham.

Index

McMahon, Robert, 3
McNamara, Robert, 166, 168
McNary, Charles, 24
Meese, Edwin, 283
Melanson, Richard, 8
Miller, Nathan, 161
Miller, Warren E., 184
Mindszenty, József, 118
Mitchell, John, 191
Moe, Richard, 20
Mohr, Charles, 137
Mondale, Walter, 186, 314; and the
    election of 1984, 285–86
Moore, Dick, 204
Moore, Jonathan, 252
Morgan, Edward, 140
Morgan, Robert B., 256, 341
Morgenstern, George, 49
Morse, Wayne, 343
Morton, Rogers, 235, 237
Motley, Tony, 282
Muravchik, Joshua, 330
Murphy, George, 203
Murphy, Robert, 120
Muskie, Edmund, 187, 189, 203, 210,
    213
Mussolini, Benito, 30, 32

Nader, Ralph, 337
Nagy, Imre, 114, 118
Nasser, Gamal Abdel, 108, 111, 116,
    120
Neal, Steve, 20
Nelson, Michael, 183, 186, 188, 197,
    253
Ness, Elliot, 42
Nicaragua, 271–77, 281–87, 300, 303,
    344
Niebuhr, Reinhold, 67
Nincic, Miroslav, 14, 263
Nixon, Pat, 215
Nixon, Richard M., 7, 9–10, 11–12, 55,
    90, 114, 117, 122, 165, 229, 233,

241, 242, 243, 253, 255, 256, 257,
260, 273, 297, 318, 339, 340–41,
342; and China, 207–9, 211–13,
214–16; and Cuba, 144–46; and
the election of 1960, 128–30, 146;
and the election of 1968, 177–82,
188–98; and the election of 1972,
203–5, 222–23; election strategy
(1960), 130–39; and Quemoy-
Matsu, 139–44; and the Soviet
Union, 209–11, 217–19; and
Vietnam, 206–7, 213–14, 216–17,
219–22
Nixon Doctrine, 189, 279, 281
Nofziger, Lyn, 261
Noonan, Peggy, 300
Noriega, Manuel, 301, 303, 327
North American Free Trade Agreement
    (NAFTA), 320, 321, 328–29
North Atlantic Treaty Organization
    (NATO), 83, 84, 86, 93, 157, 160,
    304
North Korea, 332
Novak, Peter, 184
Nunn, Sam, 304, 330
Nye, Gerald, 25, 47

Obama, Barack, 1
O'Brien, Lawrence, 134, 159
O'Donnell, Kenneth, 134
Orwell, George, 271
Ōshima, Baron Hiroshi, 52
Ostbyu, Sandra, 255

Page, Bruce, 179
Pahlavi, Mohammad Reza, 258
Pakistan, 207, 211, 239
Panama, 25, 156, 161–65, 168, 172,
    234, 235, 255, 301, 306, 327, 341,
    343
Patterson, James T., 74
Perot, Ross, 317–20, 322, 324, 326–29,
    332, 344

Studies in Conflict, Diplomacy, and Peace

Series Editors: George C. Herring, Andrew L. Johns, and Kathryn C. Statler

This series focuses on key moments of conflict, diplomacy, and peace from the eighteenth century to the present to explore their wider significance in the development of U.S. foreign relations. The series editors welcome new research in the form of original monographs, interpretive studies, biographies, and anthologies from historians, political scientists, journalists, and policymakers. A primary goal of the series is to examine the United States' engagement with the world, its evolving role in the international arena, and the ways in which the state, nonstate actors, individuals, and ideas have shaped and continue to influence history, both at home and abroad.

Books in the Series

CPSIA information can be obtained
at www.ICGtesting.com
Printed in the USA
BVOW11*1922150317

478184BV00003B/5/P

9 780813 169057